MINORITIES IN IRAN

Minorities in Iran

Nationalism and Ethnicity after Khomeini

Rasmus Christian Elling

First published in 2013 by
PALGRAVE MACMILLAN®
in the United States—a division of St. Martin's Press LLC,
175 Fifth Avenue, New York, NY 10010.

Where this book is distributed in the UK, Europe and the rest of the World,
this is by Palgrave Macmillan, a division of Macmillan Publishers Limited,
registered in England, company number 785998, of Houndmills,
Basingstoke, Hampshire RG21 6XS.

Palgrave Macmillan is the global academic imprint of the above
companies and has companies and representatives throughout the world.

Palgrave® and Macmillan® are registered trademarks in the United
States, the United Kingdom, Europe and other countries.

ISBN: 978–0–230–11584–2

Library of Congress Cataloging-in-Publication Data is available from the
Library of Congress.

A catalogue record of the book is available from the British Library.

Design by Integra Software Services

First edition: February 2013

10 9 8 7 6 5 4 3 2 1

CONTENTS

ACKNOWLEDGMENTS

I am deeply grateful to numerous people who have supported me, challenged me and believed in me during the six years of research that preceded this book. In particular, I must thank my parents and Dr. Don Watts for unwavering support and help. Among those encouraging me in the early stages of this research, I thank Drs. Claus V. Pedersen, Jørgen Bæk-Simonsen and Nikki Keddie, and for help and understanding in the later stage, I thank Dr. Nelida Fuccaro and the School of Oriental and African Studies, London. For hosting me at New York University, I thank Drs. Michael Gilsenan and Zachary Lockman. For valuable critique, comments and support, I would like to thank Drs. Touraj Atabaki, Rogers Brubaker, Kaveh Ehsani, Kevan Harris, Sune Haugbølle, Sinisa Malesevic, Rouzbeh Parsi, Khodadad Rezakhani, Richard Tapper, Bjørn Olav Utvik and Reza Zia-Ebrahimi. Finally, I would like to acknowledge *Studies in Ethnicity and Nationalism* (published by Wiley-Blackwell) and *Iran: From Theocracy to Green Movement* (edited by Negin Nabavi), two publications in which I first developed some of the ideas presented in this book.

INTRODUCTION

In 2003, during a dinner with friends in Tehran, I listened to a discussion that would motivate the research presented in this book.

The host family consisted of a father, who was a native of Tabriz and grew up speaking Azeri Turkic as his mother tongue; a Persian-speaking mother; and their children, who spoke Persian but knew very little Azeri. Relatives from both sides of the family were also present. The discussion soon turned to Iranian history, perhaps provoked by my presence as an "Iranologist" (*irānshenās*). While the discussants at the table appreciated my fascination with Iran, what they presented was mostly a very sad, depressing history: the destruction of ancient glory and civilization through repeated attacks by Macedonians, Arabs, Mongols and Europeans.

From their emotional responses to these tales of bloody invasions and foreign occupation, I got a clear idea that the people involved in the discussion identified themselves as *Iranians* vis-à-vis a foreign *Other*. This kind of identification was obviously not new to me. However, when it came to the question of the Safavids—the dynasty that ruled in the sixteenth to eighteenth century and consolidated the country that was to become the modern Iranian nation-state—the atmosphere around the table suddenly changed. "The Safavids, of course, were Turks: *tork budand*," the Azeri-speaking father declared with a sly smile, eliciting an angry response by the Persian-speaking maternal side of the family: "No, they were Persians, everybody knows that! *Fārs budand!*"

The ensuing debate seemed half-serious, half-joking. Someone tried to calm down the debaters, settling the issue with a simple slogan: "the Safavids were Iranians, nothing more, nothing less." The debate ended as abruptly as it had started. To lighten the somewhat serious atmosphere that had descended upon the table, someone told a couple of jokes about "Turks" that everybody could laugh at—perhaps particularly the Persian-speaking side.

During this discussion, it dawned on me that in studying Iran, I had not appreciated the importance of minority ethnicity to some segments of society: those for whom Persian is not their mother tongue or those who hail from outside core areas such as Tehran and Isfahan, where I had lived and studied. I also realized that this was actually the first time I had ever heard, in Persian, the word "Persian" used as an ethnonym: *fārs*. Since Iran is almost universally described, in non-Iranian sources, as a country in which an ethnic group called "the Persians" constitutes the majority, this was quite an astounding realization. Interestingly, the Persian-speaking side of the family had clearly used the somewhat awkward-sounding word *fārs* in reaction to the use of the word *tork* about the Safavids.

I soon came to understand that discussions such as the one around this particular dinner table reflected a much broader issue. After two decades of silence, "the
minority issue"—the question, posed in most societies with a culturally diverse population, of the place and rights of minorities—re-emerged with a vengeance in Iran
in the late 1990s. The issue is tied up with an emerging re-evaluation, among non-
Persian-speaking minorities, among certain progressive intellectuals and among some
scholars of Iranian Studies, of what "national identity" and "Iranian-ness" means, or
should mean. This re-evaluation breaks with an understanding of Iran that has dominated history writing for a hundred years: as being somehow multi-ethnic but at the
same time essentially "Persian."

Several signs of this re-evaluation and its ethnic framing can be detected in Iranian
society. First, there is a revival of interest in minority cultures and languages. This is
testified by an explosion in the number of magazines, books, websites and blogs in
the minority languages, and by ethnically framed local movements. Second, there is
a flourishing discourse that I term *ethnicism* among limited yet very active circles in
Iran and in exile. This discourse challenges the underpinnings of traditional Iranian
nationalism and the dominant narratives on Iranian history and society by questioning the prominence of the Persian language and the political, socioeconomic and
cultural hegemony of the mostly Persian-speaking Shiite majority.

Third, there are increasingly vocal minority demands for cultural rights and
political influence, as well as calls for administrative autonomy or even outright
independence. Apart from organizations and spokespeople that adhere to nonviolent
tactics, some of these demands have also been expressed forcefully, such as during the
ethnically framed protests and violence in the period 2005–7. Finally, there is acute
anxiety among policy-makers, intellectuals and the broad public about ethnicism and
minority mobilization as a threat to Iran's national identity and territorial integrity.
This anxiety has in turn motivated some politicians to directly address the minority
issue, particularly during election campaigns, where ethnicity is no longer a tabooed
topic.

Today, the minority issue constitutes a vast, complex field of discussion driven
by divisive notions of "identity." Iranian nationalists fear that minority discontent
and ethnicism pose an existential threat to a country otherwise known historically
for its ethnic or national stability; ethnicists fear that they are facing cultural annihilation. Nationalists see this potential or imminent "identity crisis" as a result of
foreign meddling, of elite mobilization or of faulty state policies; ethnicists see it as
a result of deep-running chauvinism and historical injustice. No matter what their
point of view, intellectuals, scholars, political activists, state ideologues and government officials have been forced to take a stand on an issue long distorted, forgotten
or tabooed.

The political scientist Mehrzad Boroujerdi stated in 1998 that "many
(ultra)nationalists worry that discussing the plight of ethnic minorities may open
a Pandora's box, and lead, even if indirectly, to Iran's eventual breakup." Today, the
proverbial ethnic genie is out of its bottle, and this merits attention not just for
reasons pertaining to Iran itself: the minority issue has several transnational dimensions, posing a challenge in an already volatile region. It is an issue that pertains
to millions of people, some of whom are now openly asking immensely important

questions: What is the place of minorities in modern Iran? What role should the state play vis-à-vis cultural diversity? How does the center relate to the periphery? Is the dominant notion of Iranian national identity inclusive? These questions, in turn, are directly related to the discussion about democracy and the future of Iran.

In this book, I will also argue that the Iranian minority issue merits attention for academic reasons: it provides a highly informative arena for studying social action, cultural difference and ideology, and thus for testing and challenging certain key ideas in social science as a discipline and in Iranian Studies as a field.

SCOPE AND STRUCTURE

This book examines how cultural diversity is dealt with in discourses on identity in Iran. Despite a strong tradition of tribal ethnography, the study of ethnicity in Iran has been severely neglected, both in Iranian Studies and in social sciences within Iran. Only since the late 1990s, when the minority issue resurfaced in public debates, has the full range of ethnic diversity received scholarly attention.

In Chapter 1, I probe issues of conceptual disarray, paucity of data and ambiguous truth claims in academic and putatively "authoritative" works dealing with the contested issue of ethnicity in Iran. I will argue that Persian-centrist views in Iranian Studies are only part of the problem and that the minority issue cannot be studied separately from the question of "the elusive majority." The dominant notion of Iranian-ness can be seen, as it is among ethnicists, to legitimize Persian-centrism; however, it can also be seen, as it is seen by nationalists, as an ideal identity that exists above and beyond ethnic divides. This will help us understand the various viewpoints on the minority issue that I explore in the rest of the book. Furthermore, I argue, it can add valuably to a broader discussion about how to understand the dynamics of ethnicity in the Middle East and, indeed, in human societies everywhere.

In Iran, four ethnic groups figure prominently in discussions about the minority issue: Azeris, Kurds, Arabs and Baluch. There are several reasons why I have limited the scope of this book to these four groups: as non-Persian-speakers, they are the four largest groups in terms of linguistic demography; two of them belong to the biggest religious minority, the Sunni Muslims; they have long histories of ethnically framed mobilization; and together, they occupy a large swath of Iran's western and southeastern peripheries. Chapter 1 contains a brief background of these four minorities, and in the subsequent chapters, they remain in focus. This focus has forced me to leave out many other minorities. I have not, for example, dealt with the important question of non-Muslim minorities, which is, at any rate, the topic of other studies.[1]

Chapter 2 contains a concise history of three decades of ethnic politics from the Islamic Revolution in 1978-9 to just before the so-called Green Movement in the aftermath of the presidential elections in 2009. The first half of the chapter outlines key aspects of Ayatollah Ruhollah Khomeini's rule with respect to minorities, the most important events in the minority regions during and after the revolution, the constitutional and legal framework of state-minority relations, the general socio-economic conditions in minority regions and the disparity of center–periphery relations, and finally, a general historical overview of major relevant political developments in and around Iran since the death of Khomeini.

This overview situates the minority issue in the contexts of domestic, factional struggles within the Islamic Republic and of growing geopolitical rivalry and international pressure on Iran. It should be stressed that this book cannot provide a full account of all the factors and events that play into the minority issue. The first part of Chapter 2 should, however, provide enough background to understand the topic of the second half: ethnically framed mobilization in post-Khomeini Iran.

With the death of Khomeini and the end of both the Iran–Iraq War and the Cold War, the political and socio-cultural arena in Iran changed dramatically. Spearheaded by reformists and pro-democracy movements, the arena was broadened for discussion and debate, artistic and intellectual expression, resurgent nationalism and political mobilization of marginalized and suppressed social forces—including the minorities. Post-9/11 developments brought the US-led "War on Terror" to Iran's doorsteps and again turned the minority issue into an acute security concern of the Iranian state. The failure of reformists to actually reform the system and then their gradual ousting by conservative forces, the repression of all kinds of opposition and the militarization of Iranian politics pushed minority discontent into new avenues. For the first time since the revolution, Iran witnessed major ethnic unrest in 2005–7.

When accused of repressing minorities, the ruling elite in Iran counters that Islamic and revolutionary ideals institutionalized in the political system has brought about a multi-ethnic equilibrium. They argue that Islam contains the answer to all societal problems and the key to Iran's self-defense against neo-imperialist schemes of creating discord along ethnic and sectarian lines in the Muslim world. While analyzing this idealist rhetoric, Chapter 3 presents the two central arguments: (1) the state ideology is in essence not pan-Islamic or even Islamist, but indeed nationalist, and (2) the ruling elite is struggling to forge a path between, on one hand, the traditionally Persian-centric Iranian nationalism and, on the other, the necessity of an ethnically inclusive discourse of solidarity and public participation.

To dissect this ideology, I present in Chapter 3 a series of analyses of (a) state-sanctioned literature and speeches by prominent figures on ethnic diversity and (b) the official state response to ethnically framed unrest in the period 2005-7. These analyses reveal how the ruling elite seeks to tackle the emerging challenge of minority discontent and how, through the depictions of *Self* and *Other* embedded in the official rhetoric, it presents visions of "Iranian-ness."

When confronted with increasingly loud assertions of ethnic identity and demands for minority rights, the dominant academic and intellectual elite in Iran often reacts with fear and alarm. Despite many internal ideological differences, the actors that I collectively term *nationalists* in this book share the key concern that Iranian national identity must be strengthened to prepare for a looming ethnic crisis. For this purpose, they invoke various nationalist themes through research, historical narratives and polemical diatribes. This book explores, for the first time in a comprehensive manner, post-Khomeini Iranian nationalist discourses as they are formulated within the minority issue debate.

This is the topic of Chapter 4: how the hegemony of Persian-centric Iranian nationalism that originated in the late nineteenth century is still defended and extolled in both subtle and explicit ways through research and public debate. In the first half of the chapter, I explain the emergence of key nationalist narratives on modernity in the late nineteenth and early twentieth centuries, and how these narratives created an *Internal Other* out of the minorities. I also trace the development of social sciences in Iran as they pertain to the minority issue, which is the background for understanding how nationalist-minded intellectuals and scholars deal with the issue today—the topic of the second half of the chapter.

In Chapter 5, I turn the focus to the broad and diverse wave of criticism directed at these dominant nationalist discourses. At one end of this spectrum we find a new breed of scholars who are challenging nationalist biases within Iranian Studies and social sciences; on the other end, we find ethnicists—including minority rights activists, independent intellectuals and ethno-political organizations—who claim that minorities are suppressed, marginalized or even threatened with cultural extinction. The ethnicists wish to settle the score with what they perceive as over a century of ethnic oppression in the name of a Persian-centric definition of national identity. Chapter 5 shows how these ethnicists frame their opposition, some rooted in leftist ideology or in ethno-nationalisms, and others taking a cue from human rights discourses and post-9/11 geopolitical changes. The chapter also provides an epilogue detailing important events in the three years following the 2009 Green Movement.

This book thus investigates certain basic, shared and contradictory aspects of Iranian nationalism and ethnicism that seem to propel contention over the minority issue. Ethnicists and nationalists are entangled in complex debates about history, identity and ideology that may warn us of an impending conflict. However, the two are rooted in the same socio-cultural, political and historical circumstances and should not, I will argue, be understood as essentially irreconcilable or even mutually exclusive discourses. Thus, Chapter 5 presents numerous examples of research, opinions and narratives that seem to be pointing toward an emerging reciprocal understanding in the name of moderation, tolerance, democracy and progress— and even pre-emptive solutions that could deflate the perhaps misplaced fear of "Balkanization."

With this focus on narratives and discourse, "language" naturally appears as a key concern throughout the text: topically, as a core site of contention between proponents of various ideologies of identity, and theoretically, as a study of how to read nationalism and ethnicity as languages of power and dissent. As such, this book treats the minority issue primarily from a discursive-ideological vantage point, and not from an ethnographic, demographic or anthropological approach. It is not a comprehensive history of minorities, a detailed survey of discriminative policies or a guidebook to conflict prevention; it is about how Iranians speak "about" and "to" the minority issue.

THEORY

The study of ethnicity and nationalism has since the 1950s taken up a central place in social sciences, history and cultural studies, flourishing into a large literature and yielding a plethora of theories. For this book, I am heavily indebted to the works of many brilliant scholars, but two stand out: Rogers Brubaker and Sinisa Malesevic. The power of their works lies in the fact that they both synthesize and develop upon existing ideas (in particular those of Max Weber, Pierre Bourdieu and Ernest Gellner), while they challenge contradictions and flaws both in existing works of social science and in taken-for-granted claims in the broader public debate.

Instead of claiming to have at hand a total frame of explanation, Brubaker and Malesevic question the existing frames. Malesevic proposes that ethnicity, rather than being an answer, is actually a question: "to invoke cultural similarity as a source of explanation," he argues, "is to reverse the order of things"—in the language of epistemology, ethnicity is not "an *explanans,* that is an outcome of the explanatory process," but rather "an *explanandum,* a phenomenon that requires explanation."[2]

It is in this spirit that Brubaker argues that many scholars, even the anti-essentialists, deconstructionists and post-structuralists, deliberately or inadvertently tend to reify ethnic groups as entities that are "discrete, concrete, tangible, bounded, and enduring."[3] Such reification reflects *groupism:* the propensity to treat any given large collectivity of individuals as a single actor, sometimes even anthropomorphizing a nation as a monolithic entity with a distinct will, soul or destiny. Instead, Brubaker calls on scholars to understand the concept of ethnicity (and nation and race) "in terms of practical categories, situated actions, cultural idioms, cognitive schemas, discursive frames, organizational routines, institutional forms, political projects, and contingent events."[4] Indeed, ethnicity should be treated not as "a thing *in* the world, but a perspective *on* the world," Brubaker argues.

While Malesevic's arguments are highly congruent with those of Brubaker, they differ on this latter point. Malesevic argues that we should rather understand ethnicity as *politicized social action:* "a process whereby elements of real, actual, lived cultural differences are politicised in the context of intensive group interaction."[5] Thus, Malesevic stresses that while ethnicity *can* be a perspective (or a discourse or a way of understanding), it is always linked to a "strong material underpinning" in the shape of geopolitics, socio-economics, state policies and institutions, social movements, and so on.[6] This book employs a middle ground: ethnicity is politicized social action based on aspects of cultural difference and "material underpinnings" within a context that is at once global and local; on the discursive level, this social action is partly expressed through ways of seeing and ignoring, talking and silencing, construing and misconstruing, remembering and forgetting.

As an expression of power relations, ethnicity plays into another concept that is of obvious importance: *minority.* Despite its apparent mathematic or statistic connotations, "minority" as a sociological category and a social phenomenon, is no less nebulous than "ethnicity." It should therefore be understood in the same situational, relational and processual sense: it is a term applied by social actors (and social scientists, including me) to distinguish particular collectivities in relation to each other based on cultural differences that appear static and clear-cut, but seldom are.

I will show in Chapter 1 how "minority" is a problematic concept and why there is a widespread tendency among Iranian scholars and political actors to reject the concept altogether (which I will discuss further in chapters 4 and 5). I have nonetheless chosen to use it in the title of this book since as a relational concept, "minority" can indicate some very concrete unequal practices, policies of disparity and institutionalized discriminative norms that express, generate and fuel complex dynamics of socio-economic and political competition.

The actual target of Brubaker and Malesevic's projects of deconstruction, and also of this book, is another formidable concept: *identity*. As a concept in academic writing, it has, especially in the past three decades, been asked to do too many things: social sciences have, in a sense, succumbed to "identity" as a paramount conceptual tool. Opaque and obscure, yet omnipresent and powerful, it "tends to mean too much (when understood in a strong sense), too little (when understood in a weak sense) or nothing at all (because of its sheer ambiguity),"[7] as Brubaker has demonstrated. While "strong" conceptions of identity tend toward essentialism, reification and truth claims, "soft" conceptions are too elastic and malleable to be able to perform any "serious analytical work."[8]

Malesevic explains that identity, a concept borrowed from mathematics, logics and psychoanalysis, is no less dubious and problematic than the disgraced terms it has replaced: "race," "national character" and "social consciousness"—terms that fell out of use in academic language following Second World War and the Cold War. Malesevic notes that there is "no empirical evidence that it is 'identity' that motivates individuals to form groups"—be the motivation rational, instrumental, traditional, habitual or emotional.[9] Malesevic clearly demonstrates this in the case of the break-up of Yugoslavia.

This leads us to the concepts of nationalism, nation and nationhood. There is no single catchall framework for understanding nationalism since it is a heterogeneous object of study: actually, the study of *nationalisms*. Modernists such as Ernest Gellner, Eric Hobsbawm and Benedict Anderson have taught us that nationalism, as a modern phenomenon, has *made* nations[10]—not, as other scholars (to whom we will turn attention in Chapter 4) have argued, the other way around. Scholars such as Michael Billig have shown that nationalism is more pervasive and ubiquitous than most people think and that it matters not only in overt political crises and conflicts, but also in everyday cultural practices—what Billig has termed "banal nationalism."[11] This omnipresent, multifaceted nature of nationalism has prompted Craig Calhoun to propose that we see nationalism as a *discursive formation*: "a rhetoric for speaking about too many things for a single theory to explain it."[12]

Nationalism is thus not merely a political principle: it is deeply embedded in our way of seeing the post-Westphalian world as "naturally" divided into sovereign nation-states that give order to chaos and define social relations (including in terms of "national identity"). Calhoun thus argues that the nation is a "particular way of thinking about what it means to be a people,"[13] which frames a nationalist belief in nation-state congruence: that the political, territorial state unit should mirror the national, cultural unit.

When collectivities that perceive of themselves as marginalized in a given political order (such as minorities) are mobilized through ethnically framed ideologies (becoming "ethnic minorities"), they sometimes develop nationalist agendas ("ethnonationalism") that appear to challenge the nation-state congruence. Even though it is not necessarily the aim of such movements to establish an independent nation-state, the ruling elite of the existing nation-state (often "the majority") automatically becomes suspicious and defensive. Indeed, to them, even a demand for respect for cultural difference can appear alarmingly like separatism—especially if the collectivity in question relates ethnically to other collectivities outside the borders of the existing nation-state.

While scholars such as Brubaker and Malesevic have criticized the use of the terms "ethnic" and "national identity" in academic language, they do not nurture any hopes of eradicating these concepts. They do, however, ask academics to consistently think about how they use them.[14] The fact that identity is a truly pervasive and powerful idiom in everyday politics does not mean that social scientists should "conceptualize 'identities' as something that all people have, seek, construct, or negotiate."[15] Just as one does not have to believe in the existence of races in order to discuss racism, analysts do not need to adopt "identity" as an *analytical, sociological* category in the academic study of the *practical, social* categories in native, folk and lay language.[16]

Hence, Brubaker argues that instead of identity, analysts should focus on identification and categorization (to understand how individuals identify themselves vis-à-vis others, and how they are categorized from "outside" or "above"); self-understanding and social location (to understand the situational and contextual processes behind identity claims); and commonality, connectedness and groupness (to understand what makes individuals feel connected to each other—the *Zusammengehörigkeitsgefühl*). In short, instead of treating *identity as a condition,* scholars should rather focus on *identification as processes.*[17]

Malesevic argues that instead of defaulting to identity, scholars should apply a term that has otherwise gone out of academic fashion recently: ideology. Malesevic shows that if it is understood as "a relatively universal and complex social process through which human actors articulate their actions and beliefs," and if it is liberated from the stigma of its historical connotations, ideology can do much of the work that "identity" as a sociological concept was supposed to do—without the negative side effects. Indeed, as a social phenomenon, the meta-ideology of *identitarianism* or "identity talk" has become a "leading ideological paradigm of our age."[18] This book is partly a reply to the "identity talk" that has until recently dominated Iranian Studies; however, it is also a broader questioning of the truth claims that identitarianism as a universal phenomenon brings about.

All of this comes with one overriding caveat. Critical approaches to rethinking ethnicity, nationalism and identity are not, as Brubaker and Malesevic cautiously stress, to be understood as a dismissal of the "reality" or power of these emotions, beliefs and ideologies. On the contrary, they are an attempt to take them seriously. While Brubaker questions the existence of groups in the reified sense, he does not question the lived reality of self-defined collectivities of individuals that feel closely connected. The reality of ethnicity does not, however, "depend on the existence of ethnic groups or nations as substantial groups or entities."[19] Malesevic similarly states that there is nothing inherently "wrong" with feeling an attachment to a collectivity. His criticism, rather, is aimed at social scientists who "have a certain responsibility towards the concepts [they] use, concepts that very often enter public policy discourses and find their application in the everyday practice and institutions of the modern nation-state."[20]

Hence, the purpose of this book is not to dismiss the salience of cultural values or the importance of emotional sentiments expressed in ethnic and national frameworks ("identities"), nor to dismiss the fact that in the lived experience of many people, "ethnic groups" are real and tangible entities. The purpose is rather to ask why and how ethnicity and nationalism "happens," and how we talk about it.

TERMINOLOGY AND SOURCES

That ethnicity and nationalism are universal phenomena does not make particular studies of them redundant. An analysis of the form and content of identitarian ideologies can yield much information about specific socio-cultural, historical and geopolitical contexts. In Iran, the minority issue is just as complex and nebulous as in any other multi-cultural society, so for the sake of clarity, I employ two labels that are at once similar and contradictory to describe the actors involved in the minority issue: nationalist and ethnicist. However, first we need to define "actor" in the context of this book.

A broad and diverse array of individuals are engaged in the debate, knowledge production, activism and policymaking connected to the minority issue—as part of either their professional career, a political agenda or a hobby. They have in common that their works and statements can be seen as commentaries on a broader discussion of modern Iranian culture and politics. Since such discussions do not take place in insular space, I have not limited the scope of actors to those residing within Iran. Although the focus is squarely on political developments within Iran, voices coming from the diaspora and, in extension, from Western-based academia will also be represented insofar as they relate to domestic issues.

The actors roughly fall into three categories: the first category includes government officials and scholars working in state-affiliated entities inside Iran; the second includes professional scholars generally, "freelance" or unaffiliated scholars, intellectuals and journalists, as well as political activists inside Iran; and the third includes scholars working with Iranian Studies seen from academic settings outside of Iran. This categorization is by no means clear-cut. Internet and communication technology, regular exchanges between diaspora and homeland, as well as family ties and political alignments facilitate significant overlaps and exchange.

Furthermore, the fact that most academic institutions in Iran are connected to, and under all circumstances tightly controlled by, the state makes a simplistic division between "regime" and "non-regime" or even "anti-regime" scholars near impossible. Nonetheless, as it will become apparent throughout the book, there are significant differences in the type of and aim with the knowledge produced in different research bodies. Indeed, the minority issue has, I will argue, become an ideological battleground within Iranian academia.

The two labels of "nationalists" and "ethnicists" are admittedly generalizing and simplistic, but nonetheless indispensable. Both sides champion nationalist and even ethno-nationalist ideas: the nationalists because they claim to represent a reified Iranian nation (*mellat-e irān*), which the ethnicists argue is based on one ethnic group ("the Persians"); the ethnicists because they sometimes present their ethnic groups as stateless nations (e.g., "the Kurdish nation," *mellat-e kord*). Indeed, most political actors anywhere are, as already argued, in a sense all nationalist: they all operate under the meta-ideology of nationalism. The fundamental difference here is that while ethnicists present their cause as an ethnic advocacy,

Iranian nationalists do *not* expressly claim to represent or defend a particular ethnic group.

Furthermore, as a catchall label, "nationalist" obviously does no justice to the broad range of opinions and agendas among the individuals I have chosen to label as such. One important aspect here is religion: there are considerable differences between, for example, an independent scholar affiliated with the secularist National Front and a cleric in the bureaucracy of the Islamic Republic—even if they share a common view on minority mobilization. Sometimes, I will indicate such differences as I just did above: by adding "secular" and "cleric," "independent" and "bureaucrat." At other times, I will explain more elaborately the differences between competing kinds of nationalisms.

However, the most problematic aspect of the labeling is that only very few of the actors I term "nationalist" would identify themselves explicitly as such. In the early days of the Islamic Revolution, the Islamist faction's animosity toward liberal and secular strands of nationalism in rival factions such as the National Front meant that the term *melli-garā*, or "nationalist," was thoroughly stigmatized. Khomeini's regime employed the term pejoratively to signify a materialist, colonialist, capitalist and apostate foe of the Muslim community. As a political self-designation, the term all but disappeared, only to partially resurface in the late 1990s. Despite this, today there are few actors, especially among the scholars, who publicly introduce themselves as nationalists. This is, of course, also true of academia elsewhere.

"Ethnicist" is also a label used to cover a broad range of actors who are not easily labeled. Their adversaries (the nationalists) tend to call them *qowm-garā*, which could be translated as ethno-nationalist or, as I have termed them, ethnicist.[21] Ethnicists can *also* perceive of themselves as Iranian nationalists: most of them, while advocating ethnicist demands, still declare their allegiance to Iran as a homeland. Some ethnicists do not see the collectivities they claim to represent in terms of a "nation," and even if they do, they only rarely have explicit agendas for creating a separate nation-*state* (for those nurturing such wishes, I use the term ethno-nationalist). Indeed, such is the complexity of ethnic politics that among the same ethnicists who are labeled separatists by the state, one may encounter actors who openly confess to being Iranian patriots.

We will return to all these nuances later, and it suffices here to state that the choice of descriptive labels is based on compromises. The labels reflect the ambiguities of ethnic politics in Iran. The battle over how to label others, and over the right to chose one's own label, is at the heart of the minority issue. This is inevitably reflected in my own research framework.

In both pre-revolutionary Iran and during Khomeini's rule in the 1980s, there was a profound paucity of research on and debate about the minority issue. Since the 1990s, however, a veritable wave of academic and political writing on identity, history and minority rights has gushed out in Iran. In an overview survey, two Iranian scholars of ethnicity, Hushmand and Kuhshekaf, singled out more than 550 research projects on the minority issue in "recent years" (approximately from the mid-1990s until 2007, when their article was published)—compared to only "5% of that number before the revolution."[22]

For this book, I have analyzed more than a hundred research-based articles from Iranian academic journals and two dozens of research monographs and dissertations, over 400 articles from Iranian newspapers, numerous official statements and declarations from state bodies, as well as scores of polemical texts, political analyses, official reports and organization communiqués. All of this material is in Persian, and all translations are mine unless otherwise specified. I follow a simplified system for transliteration of Persian that only uses one diacritical enhancement to replicate the long vowel *ā*. I have used italics for unfamiliar Persian words, and I have added a list of key concepts and abbreviations.

In addition, I have benefitted greatly from both English-language Iranian Studies and, as already indicated, from more general works of social sciences. These materials serve to contextualize and supplement my analysis of the primary material. I will introduce and discuss the specific sources in the relevant chapters. The distinction between Iranian Studies (understood here as the study of Iran from "the outside") and Iranian social sciences/humanities (the study of Iran from "the inside") will not appear clear-cut. Some scholars are fortunately now able to straddle the divide, and draw upon and contribute to both traditions and fields.

Since access to technology has spread at a rapid pace since the late 1990s, Iran is remarkably well represented in cyberspace, and many Iranian print media are available online. Despite restrictions and censorship, vast amounts of Persian-language web content are daily produced inside and outside Iran. Many Iranian academic journals are available for download, and regularly updated, accessible websites with search tools and archives have facilitated material sourcing for this book. The archives at *Bānk-e ettelā'āt-e nashriyāt-e keshvar* (MagIran.com) and *Pāyegāh-e majalāt-e takhasosi-ye nur* (NoorMags.com) proved indispensable. Persian-language books and ethnicist magazines were primarily located in bookshops in Iran, USA and Europe. In particular, the book series published by the state-affiliated Iranian Institute for National Research (*Mo'asase-ye motāle'āt-e melli*) provided valuable material. The Bobst Library of NYU and the library of the School of Oriental and African Studies, London, were very useful.

ETHICS

This book is the result of research carried out since 2005. Inspired by anthropology, I had originally hoped that I would be able to do extensive fieldwork research and to engage with government officials and minority activists. Even though I have been able to exchange with a broad variety of scholars, journalists, activists and ordinary people, the profound changes in Iranian politics after the election of president Mahmoud Ahmadinejad in 2005, and the constantly escalating international pressure on Iran, forced me to reconsider even before I started the research project.[23] I thus adjusted my research strategy to accommodate ethical concerns with the safety of my informants in an ever more sensitive and dangerous situation.

When I was accepted as a guest scholar at Tehran University, I was told in no uncertain terms that I would not be able to carry out research on this topic, and thus, I abandoned the idea. I met scholars in Iran who were friendly and appreciative of my project, but from behind the polite *ta'ārof* etiquette, I understood that they would have nothing to do with such a thorny topic. Friends and contacts dissuaded me from engaging with informants inside Iran or from visiting certain areas of Iran. Even though I have visited Iran several times since, I was nonetheless forced to abandon my original idea of extended on-site fieldwork, and turned instead toward studying the topic from "afar" and through texts.

My experience is just one example of a grave problem in Iranian Studies today: it is exceedingly difficult to obtain research permits, which means that many scholars are forced to do "hit-and-run" fieldwork on tourist visas with inadequately short time frames.[24] This is particularly true for those who are not willing to limit research to non-political issues. Many scholars are unable to go to Iran, even if it is their homeland, and many young students are simply discouraged from studying this fascinating country. Despite having visited Iran several times during my research, and even though I am in constant contact with Iranians inside and outside Iran, I cannot help feel that my research is perpetually incomplete—it is ethnography dispelled from its field.

Another more abstract ethical concern with this research project was its possible implications in a larger political picture. Anyone working with the topic is keenly aware of the interest that certain political, research and military establishments in the West have shown in the Iranian minority issue. These establishments had by the time I began my project already played key roles in launching two bloody wars in Iran's neighboring countries and seemed eager to start a new one in Iran—by, among other things, destabilizing Iran's periphery and inciting to ethnic and sectarian violence. Indeed, during my research, one story after another has popped up in Western and Iranian media, alleging US, European and Israeli support for various minority-based militant groups inside Iran.

All this has confirmed the suspicion that Western powers are blatantly pursuing an illegal, asymmetric and psychological war against Iran that is affecting not just its alleged target, the regime, but the broad population. At a couple of occasions, colleagues sought to dissuade me from publishing my research, mostly out of fear that it could somehow be used as yet another excuse in the hands of the war-eager faction in the West. Others seemed concerned that my research would help open the aforementioned ethnic Pandora's box by indirectly bolstering ethno-nationalism. While the latter concerns had no effect on me, the former certainly made me, on a couple of occasions, contemplate abandoning this book altogether.

It was in dialogue with common Iranians inside and outside Iran that I finally chose not to throw six years of original research away, and to finish this project with my initial goal in mind: to illuminate a perplexing question facing a country that is so much more diverse and colorful than the monochrome vision of menace that Western media daily perpetuate. While I am fully aware of the power of knowledge, I also acknowledge my responsibility as a critical researcher of culture. I thus present this book in an attempt to deepen the outsider's understanding of a country that appears so hard to decipher, and to add to the academic field in which I was trained.

We often hear in media and in scholarly works that Iranians are a highly nationalistic people. One scholar writes that "most Iranians evince nationalist sentiments"; another refers to an official survey that indicates that the majority of Iranians are "proud" to be Iranians.[25] Nationalism becomes a "fact" without any questioning of what "being Iranian," "nationalist" or "proud" actually means. We are led to believe that nationalism is intrinsic to Iranian society and culture. I believe this is wrong. Nationalism can be found anywhere and anytime, and given the situation and context, it will appear subtle or explicit, implicitly hinted at or blatantly flagged.

My home country, Denmark, was once known around the world, correctly or not, for values such as democracy, welfare, egalitarianism and internationalism—suddenly, it became associated in the global public opinion with a shift to the right, tough anti-immigration laws and an increasingly nationalist public opinion. Out of nowhere, it seemed, my generation has started thinking about our "identity" as Danes, to relate to debates about Danish-ness and to face a nationalistic, exclusivist and racist aspect of our own culture.

By opening up such broad issues in a largely unexplored field, this book will hopefully facilitate and provoke new studies about Iran's cultural diversity. During my first of many visits to Iran, as an undergraduate visiting student in 1999, I lived for a wonderful half year in Isfahan, surrounded by Persian-speaking Shiite friends and experiencing what was essentially my own romantic idea of "Persia." Apart from the Armenians in whose neighborhood I lived, I experienced little of Iran's ethnic diversity. Unfortunately, this has been the experience of many students of this richly layered, enchanting and perplexing country that defies stereotypical generalizations. I hope that this book can help establish new points of departure for studying the many ways in which culture is understood, lived and experienced in Iran.

I am grateful to the Iranians who talked with me, wrote to me and discussed with me over the years. It is with their support and encouragement, and with the inspiration that traveling and living in their beautiful and baffling country filled me with, that this book came about. I hope that it will provoke and facilitate new research and that Iran will once again become a country that is open to critical inquiry and free dialogue—not through any intervention by hypocritical forces and foreign powers, but through the free will of individual Iranians who see themselves as heirs to a struggle for democracy that stretches back more than a century.

CHAPTER 1

IDENTIFYING A PEOPLE

One man's Mede, another man's Persian.

—George S. Kaufman

IT SEEMS THAT SCHOLARS AND HISTORIANS OF MODERN IRAN have until recently dealt with ethnicity only when prompted to do so by minority claims, ethno-political agitation or historical revisionism. As a result, ethnicity as a sociological concept has rarely been discussed or theorized in established Iranian Studies. Today, scholars working with Iran still tend to casually mention "minorities" without providing any definition of what the term exactly means. Indeed, in much of the literature on Iran, in English and Persian languages alike, representations of ethnicity often reflect definitional ambiguity, conceptual inconsistency and simplistic generalizations. I will argue that there are two major reasons for this flaw in modern Iranian Studies: one has to do with ethnicity as a universal phenomenon, and the other with the study of Iran in particular.

As this chapter will show, arbitrary classificatory schemes for describing cultural difference, when presented as statistical or objective facts, are highly problematic. These schemes reflect what can be called "ethnic commonsense":[1] the idea that everyone can be divided into neat boxes of categorization and that each box constitutes a clearly bordered "group." In worst cases, such schemes give rise to taken-for-granted, totalizing and essentialist truth claims about the "identity" of a huge and diverse population.

The second layer of critique revolves around the prevalence of Persian-centric identitarianism in Iranian Studies. A very telling example is the routine conflation, in English-language literature, of "Iranian" with "Persian." This conflation is, I will argue, more than an issue of translation or proper language use: it is rooted in pervasive nationalist assumptions, and can no longer be excused by lacking consensus, ingrained habits or academic sloppiness. As this book will show, there are now several challenges to the Persian-centric paradigm, including new, critical directions in Iranian social sciences and Iranian Studies.

In an eloquent, early example of the latter, Mehrzad Boroujerdi in 1998 argued that with Persian-centric, nationalist and ahistorical accounts of Iranian identity, Iranologists have, in fact, contributed to the marginalization of minorities.[2] The

same year, Richard Tapper, an eminent anthropologist known for his life-long work
with Iran and Afghanistan, criticized the magisterial *Encyclopædia Iranica* for giving only "vague and very partial" coverage to non-Persian-speaking and non-Iranian
communities and factors in both Iran and Afghanistan.[3]

Taking these groundbreaking critiques a step further, I argue that the Persian-
centrism of what we should arguably by now call "classical Iranian Studies" is actually
just the tip of an academic and ideological iceberg. It is just one of several questions
with which we should problematize our understanding of Iranian society and, in
extension, the very concepts of ethnicity and identity. The conceptual disarray is,
in other words, not only or merely a matter of petty chauvinism. The concomitant
assertions and denials of particular self-understandings require us to take ethnicity
seriously, and not to default to vague clichés about "identity."

In order to question the "ethnic commonsense" about Iran, I draw in this chapter
on Rogers Brubaker's central argument about the study of ethnicity, as outlined in
the Introduction: that ethnicity should be treated as a processual, situational, relational and contextual dynamic of identification, and not as a marker signifying
essential traits or indicating membership of static, internally homogeneous, externally
bounded groups "out there."[4]

A broad range of situations exist, in which an individual is expected or demanded
to identify himself or herself in terms of belonging to a certain collectivity, and
depending on the context, he or she may answer differently. Conversely, there is a
range of instances in which individuals will be categorized from "above" or "outside,"
often by formal institutions or organizations vested with power by a state or political entrepreneurs. Each and every categorization must be scrutinized with sensitivity
toward the power relations at play. Taking such politics of representation into consideration, scholars can ask questions, in the words of Brubaker, about "the degree of
groupness associated with a particular category in a particular setting, and about the
political, social, cultural, and psychological processes through which categories get
invested with groupness."[5]

A productive analytical tool for this purpose distinguishes between autonyms
(the labels people put on themselves) and exonyms (the labels attributed to some
by others).[6] Richard Tapper has used this distinction in his seminal writings on
Iran and Afghanistan, in which he demonstrated how "ethnicity" can only be fruitfully employed as an *approximation of concepts* that are studied empirically.[7] In his
discussion about the Kuchis in Afghanistan, Tapper argued that as "definitional,
labelling, and typological exercises," ethnic studies tend not to take into account "the
autonymic self-identities or classifications of the people so labelled."[8] As Tapper's
valuable contributions show, such academic neglect produces simplistic or distorted
depictions of complex societies.

The lack of research, field-based qualitative surveys and critical approaches to how
Iranians understand and define themselves today is highly problematic. It means that
scholars tend to base their research on "ethnic commonsense" presumptions. That,
however, does *not* mean that "proper" research would simply enable us to correctly
"map" ethnic diversity, since the underlying presumption on which such maps are
drawn—that they can somehow reveal "reality" or real "identity"—is fundamentally
flawed. As Tapper argues:

Unfortunately, the expectation (desire? [sic]) of academics and administrators that every human being has a single, fixed, unchanging, objectively determinable—and mappable—"ethnic identity" will always be frustrated by those cussed creatures, human beings themselves... Beneath such expectations and assumptions seems to be the conviction that we, the scholars, know better than our subjects who they "really" are, and that we can establish a superior "truth" by our documentary ("scientific") research.[9]

While throughout history people have felt it "natural" to identify in relational terms (family or kinship ties, friendship and alliances, occupational relations), categorical identifications such as ethnicity and nationality have only in recent times assumed their cardinal importance. Such self- and other-identifications have become powerful tools of political agency, but no matter how ubiquitous they may appear, they are never uncontested or static. By recognizing significant discrepancies between representations, we can dissect power relations and problematize an "ethnic commonsense" that even if codified, formalized and ostensibly "proven" statistically, may in fact not make much sense to those represented.

ETHNICITY IN IRAN

THE ETHNIC COMMONSENSE

Just as "ethnic group" in English, *qowm* in Persian is a highly ambiguous term. In the magisterial *Dehkhoda's Dictionary*, *qowm* is defined as "a group of men and women," and in *Mo'in's Dictionary* as "a group of people" or "relatives." As such, *qowm* (pl. *aqvām*) has historically signified both "family"/"clan" and "community." *Qowm* still serves traditional functions: in religious language, old Koranic terms (such as *qowm-e yahud*, "the Jewish people") persist, and *qowm* is still used in the sense of "relatives," notably in obituaries and interment announcements, or in the sense of "kin" or "extended family" (*qowm-o-khish*).

As late as 1988, Tapper wrote that *qowm* "may be used for a major linguistic group, but more often in a strict family/descent-group sense" and that Iranians would rather identify each other "from manner of speaking, appearance, and answers to the standard question, *ahl-e koja'i?* ('Where are you from?')."[10] With time, however, *qowm* has also come to describe "a people," and minority communities specifically. Today, many scholars and lay Iranians alike use *qowm* in senses similar to that of "ethnic group" in Western societies, and the more recently coined *qowmiyat* in senses similar to that of "ethnicity" in English. The uses of such words, however, entail the same amount of confusion and ambiguity as elsewhere.

The general problem with ethnic "overviews" that aim to reduce the confusion is compounded by the fact that the Iranian state has never executed a nation-wide census with ethnic parameters. This is not to say that such a census would "clarify," and once and for all settle, questions about ethnicity in Iran. However, the lack of censuses has two interrelated consequences for the study of and debate on the minority issue. The first is that ethno-political entrepreneurs tend to refer to completely fictive numbers and statistics about various communities in order to either boost or deflate the political importance or cultural significance these communities supposedly have or should have in the overall picture. This has a tangible impact on the debate to which we return in chapters 4 and 5.

The second result is important for the present discussion: the lack of censuses and research means that scholars inside and outside Iran tend to refer to generalized overviews, tables and maps—even when they are aware that these do not reflect anything but contested figures based on vague approximations of fluid concepts. These dubious sources sometimes include political actors such as nationalist-minded scholars or ethno-political entrepreneurs, but mostly they are general works of reference in English. I will here use two examples of the latter to illustrate the problem: the *CIA Factbook* and a report from the US Library of Congress.

The latest estimate available from the *CIA Factbook* at the time of writing puts Iran's total population at 77,891,220.[11] In its 2007 estimate, the *Factbook* broke down Iran's ethnic composition as follows:

> Persian 51%, Azeri 24%, Gilaki and Mazandarani 8%, Kurd 7%, Arab 3%, Lur 2%, Baloch 2%, Turkmen 2%, other 1%[12]

To highlight the significant variations in this genre of estimates, we can compare with a 2008 report from another US state institution, the Library of Congress:

> The main ethnic groups in Iran are Persians (65 percent), Azerbaijani Turks (16 percent), Kurds (7 percent), Lurs (6 percent), Arabs (2 percent), Baluchis (2 percent), Turkmens (1 percent), Turkish tribal groups such as the Qashqai (1 percent), and non-Persian, non-Turkic groups such as Armenians, Assyrians, and Georgians (less than 1 percent).[13]

Note the very large difference in the number of "Persians" in the two estimates—in the Library of Congress report, potentially up to 11 million people more than in the *Factbook*; note also the difference in the number of the second biggest category, the Azeris—in the Library of Congress report, 6 million less than in the *Factbook*. It is also noteworthy that the third and fourth largest categories of the *Factbook* do not even figure in the Library of Congress overview. Such significant discrepancies underscore the problem with having only "qualified guesses" at hand. However, they also raise the question about what criteria should be employed to define the categories. Since identification processes are situational and contextual, scholars cannot rely on one simplified criterion ("ethnicity") in order to grasp the diversity in Iranian society. One will have to simultaneously look at a broad range of social, cultural, economic and political factors that all play into ethnicity. One is religion.

The above-mentioned type of sources normally estimate that 90 percent of Iranians are Shiite Muslims, 8 percent Sunni and 2 percent non-Muslim. The latter include Christians, Baha'is, Zoroastrians, Jews, Mandaeans and Hindus. Apart from recent Christian converts, the largest historic Christian communities are the Armenians and the Assyrians.[14] Both of these are also often considered ethnic groups, as are the Jews.[15] However, other religious communities such as the Baha'i, Zoroastrians and Mandaeans[16] are not normally categorized as "ethnic groups"—which is why they tend to appear in "religious" overviews, but not in ethnic overviews.

In other words, while some ethnic groups are primarily characterized as such on the basis of their religious beliefs, the variable of religion is not always seen as "enough" of a criterion to define an ethnic category.

The Sunni/Shia divide, however, does point to a clear majority-minority factor in more than mere demographic terms. Shiite beliefs and culture are articulated key elements in the dominant notion of national identity and at the heart of the current political system. Sunni activists claim that this primacy of Shiism marginalizes them as a religious minority of some six million members,[17] including most Turkmen and Baluch as well as disputed numbers of Kurds, Arabs and Taleshis. Since each of these collectivities is generally also identified as an ethnic group, they constitute a sort of "double" minority: ethnic *and* religious. A sub-sectarian dimension could possibly also be added: the various schools of Islamic law that different communities adhere to and the numerous sects, Sufi *tariqat*s and particular interpretations of Islam that divide and unify Iranians. Some of these factors play an important role *together with* or as *part of* ethnic self-identifications.

Another criterion used for categorization is linguistic. Languages with certain defined similarities in grammar and elementary vocabulary are related, which means they descend from one or more related languages; they are part of a linguistic continuum. Related Iranian languages of the Indo-European family include Persian, Kurdish, Lori, Gilaki, Mazi (Mazandarani) and Baluchi. The fact that these languages are, linguistically speaking, "Iranian" should not, however, be confused with the modern, political and territorial understanding of the term "Iranian." Related Turkic languages of the Altaic family in Iran include Azeri, Turkmen and a number of smaller languages. Arabic is a Semitic language. Unrelated languages from different language families can incorporate vocabulary from one another; there are, for example, many Arabic words in Persian.

It is considered conventional wisdom within Iranian Studies that a majority of Iran's population can communicate in Persian, which a significant segment also sees as its mother tongue. Persian is Iran's official language, the medium of education and lingua franca. When we see statistics that between 77 percent and 84 percent of the adult Iranian population is literate,[18] an implicit conclusion could thus be that they speak, read and write Persian. Yet even if this is true, Persian fluency in and by itself does not necessarily entail self-identification as "Persian." In the two earlier mentioned reports, figures for Persian speakers differ but are lower than the total figure for literacy. The *Factbook* puts "Persian and Persian dialects" at 58 percent, but 51 percent of the population as ethnic Persians, while the Library of Congress states that Persian "is spoken as a mother tongue by at least 65 percent of the population and as a second language by a large proportion of the remaining 35 percent."[19]

The "Persian" mentioned in the latter report must thus also include Gilaki and Mazi. However, Gilaki and Mazi are actually from a different branch of the Iranian language subfamily than Persian, and could as such be seen not as dialects, but as distinct languages. We will return to the importance attached to this distinction. Suffice it here to say that while some scholars see categories such as Gilakis and Mazandaranis as referring to separate ethnic groups due to their linguistic traits, others count them as "Persians" on exactly the same basis.[20] Again, this complicates the use of Persian literacy or fluency as a criterion of ethnic categorization.

As for the non-Persian languages, the *CIA Factbook* provides the following estimates:

Turkic and Turkic dialects 26%, Kurdish 9%, Luri 2%, Balochi 1%, Arabic 1%, Turkish 1%, other 2%[21]

Again, these numbers differ significantly from those in the Library of Congress report, where it is claimed that only 35 percent of the population have a mother tongue other than Persian.

A key problem, it appears, is the language categories themselves. The "Turkic and Turkic dialects" mentioned in the *Factbook* must include, to be more precise, Azeri, Turkmen, the Afsharoid languages (such as Qashqa'i) and Khorasan Turkic.[22] Whether these are treated as separate and independent languages, or as dialects of one language ("Iranian Turkic"), will impact on the depiction produced. Similarly, Lori is related to Persian and Kurdish, but the conflation of Lori with either of the two is problematic.[23] Conversely, while Kurdish is normally treated as one independent language, it in fact includes several languages and dialects of one continuum. More importantly, many, if not most, communities in Iran are bi- or multilingual, and many of the "ethnic groups" mentioned earlier in this chapter contain within them more than one religion.[24]

In short, this considerable obfuscation shows that ethnic categorization based solely on a religious or linguistic criterion is highly problematic.

OPAQUE DIVERSITY

At least three other criteria are sometimes employed in descriptions of Iran's diversity. Despite being somewhat outdated, the tribal criterion is one of them.

Certain communities in Iran still identify with tribal traditions, including some Kurds, Baluch, Lors, Turkmen and Qashqa'is[25]—yet there is no consensus on whether to define, say, the Bakhtiyaris as a tribal *and/or* an ethnic group. For example, while some depictions (e.g., that of the *Factbook*, we must surmise) group Bakhtiyaris (and possibly also Mamasanis and Boyer-Ahmadis) together with Lors, perhaps due to shared language, others simply place them together with "Persians" (e.g., the Library report, we must surmise). Another tribal confederacy, the Khamse, includes tribes consisting of mixed Turkic, Arabic and Persian speakers, which leaves us with the question whether "Khamse" can be considered an ethnonym.[26] All this notwithstanding, since tribalism today plays a limited role in Iran, the tribal criterion is obviously of limited use.

A second additional criterion stresses geographic location. At some instances, the names of linguistic communities correspond to the names of larger historical-geographical regions. Inhabitants of Azerbaijan, Baluchistan, Kurdistan, Luristan and Arabistan (today Khuzestan), notes Tapper, "speak the languages to which these names refer,"[27] even though these areas also contain significant communities speaking other languages. Most importantly, the issue of "center" and "periphery"—that is, the correlations between geographical location and socioeconomic and political disparity—plays into ethnicity and minority-ness on several levels.

However, this "regional" approach is sometimes abused politically to negate ethnic self-identifications that tend to flourish across handy, simplified geographic boundaries. Accordingly, we are talking about "regional identities," which appears to be perceived by nationalist-minded scholars as less dangerous than "ethnic identities" with their transnational dimensions. Additionally, it is very rare that the borders of linguistic communities are congruent with the borders of the administrative framework: more Kurdish speakers live outside the province of Kurdistan than inside, for example. This, ethnicists argue, is a deliberate outcome of discriminative state policies. Moreover, it is often unclear whether geographical location is "enough," so to speak, for a community to be deemed "ethnic."

Labels such as Semnani or Khorasani, for example, are regional self-identifications; however, Semnanis and Khorasanis are rarely treated in the literature as "ethnic groups." In Khuzestan, "Dezfuli," "Shushtari" and "Behbahani" are regional identifications pertaining to three specific cities, the populations of which tend to see themselves as distinct from other Iranians in more than "just" geographical terms: apart from Persian, Lori is Behbahan's native language, and one could thus argue that Behbahanis are Lors; "Dezfuli" and "Shushtari" also refer to two dialects of Persian that contain remnants of the extinct Khuzi language, and Dezfulis and Shushtaris generally see themselves as heirs to ancient local empires and Greek immigrants (and therefore not necessarily as "Persians"). In other words, although these distinct local cultures and histories are arguably expressions of ethnicity, those who identify with them are rarely treated in the literature as "ethnic groups."

Similarly, we could also add to the discussion the significant communities of refugees from Iraq and Afghanistan: should these be categorized according to nationality and diaspora status (as they tend to be in Iran), or by the ethnic, sectarian, tribal, geographic and socioeconomic affiliations they have or have had with their original homelands? The complex and dynamic nature of exonymic and autonymic identification processes is thus tied up with issues of location and citizenship, globalization and transnational developments, regional geopolitics and local micro-politics. Nevertheless, apart from the above-mentioned four criteria—religion, language, tribe and geography—there are still three additional factors that must be taken into consideration. The first is class.

Even though social scientists are not always clear on the extent to which class difference should be distinguished from cultural difference and ethnicity,[28] there can be no doubt about the importance of socioeconomic conditions to ethnic self-identifications. Certain labels used as "ethnic" labels today were in medieval times more or less synonymous with particular classes in a highly stratified society with very little mobility. In some cases, the labels implied a particular profession.[29] Despite significant progress, cultural prejudices and socioeconomic disparity still play into ethnicity. As Farhad Kazemi, for example, points out, low-income rural migrants tend to coalesce in ethnically defined enclaves within cities, whereas high-income migrants do not. Exogamy is also more prevalent in the high-income bracket of society.[30]

This leads us to the second factor, which threatens more than anything to spoil all the "neat" approaches to categorization discussed earlier in the text: ethnic mixing. Iran has a long history of intermarriage between various communities.

The medieval ruling classes practiced prolific exogamy, especially between Persian- and Turkic-speaking elites, but also through marriages with Lors, Kurds, Arabs, Georgians, Armenians, Jews and so on. Iranians, scholars and non-scholars alike, often state that apart from "Aryan" ancestral blood, the Iranian "stock" has been mixed, often involuntarily after invasions, with that of Greeks, Huns, Arabs, Turks, Tatars, Mongols and even black Africans. In Khuzestan and in northern Iran, some locals claim that British and Russian blood has entered the local "blend." Historical examples abound of how certain communities have shifted between exonymic categories. Put differently, self-identifications have only recently become understood as more or less inflexible labels.

The historical tendency of intermingling has arguably been augmented and accelerated in recent times by modernization, urbanization, nation-state-building and globalization. This is a hugely important but understudied topic with several implications for the case of Iran. With the possible partial exceptions of Turkmen, Hazara, "gypsies" (Dom) and the black African community in southern Iran, it can be very hard or impossible to distinguish communities that identify in different ethnic terms by their physical appearances.[31] The reason is of course interbreeding, which is normal elsewhere and does not preclude differentiated ethnic identifications. This observation, however, inevitably leads us to the third and final factor, which is sometimes held to have importance in the minority issue: race.

As elsewhere, "race" (*nezhād*) as a framework for social categorization has recently been scrutinized and to some extent stigmatized in Iranian Studies and in Iranian social sciences. However, it has not been universally abandoned, and the idea that most or all Iranians are from a so-called Aryan race (and therefore different from Semites and Turks) is still prevalent in some academic writing. The concept of race thus seems to creep into even writings aimed at presenting a nondiscriminative, full scope of diversity in Iran.[32]

In short, the most prevalent criteria employed in "ethnic mapping" are not merely "wrong choices," which implies that there could be "right choices"; the problem lies in the "ethnic commonsense" on which the mapping draws. This is not to say that we should never attempt to produce a depiction of diversity in complex societies such as Iran. However, we should never endow such depictions with academic legitimacy without reflecting critically on the analytical apparatus. Indeed, that would make the given depiction prone to abuse and exploitation for political ends.

All these criteria and factors aside, there is a more fundamental problem with the question of ethnicity in Iran: any approach that does not take into consideration the majority will create a distorted and incomplete picture of ethnic diversity.

ELUSIVE MAJORITY

Just as defining an ethnic minority is no small feat, neither is pinning down a majority: this cannot be reduced to a statistical task of demography or even to a problem of conceptual disarray. Majority ethnicity in Iran constitutes the arguably most pressing question that the "ethnic commonsense" in Iranian Studies never seems to directly answer: if non-Persian speakers are Iran's "ethnic minorities," then what is the "ethnic majority"?

Throughout its academic history, ethnicity as a concept has been related disproportionately to the question of "minorities," and it is only fairly recently that "majority ethnicity" has received research attention.[33] Scholars tend to "look for ethnicity," so to speak, among minorities only, as if the phenomenon, being somehow exotic or exceptional, was limited to communities that are different from the majority. In the case of the English-language literature on Iran, I will argue, the fact that scholars often claim or take for granted that "Persians" constitute the majority ethnic group is closely related to the problem with conflating "Persian" with "Iranian."[34] This argument calls for examples, the first of which is from a highly prominent and proliferate scholar of Iranian Studies, Ehsan Yar-Shater:

> The Iranian identity has been exposed to the peril of extinction many times throughout history; all its constituent elements have been threatened at one time or another. Persian territory has been repeatedly conquered, and foreign populations, primarily Greeks, Arabs, and Turks, have settled there. The national religion has been forced out and even the language threatened. Study of past responses to such threats should prove enlightening and help us to understand better the formidable challenges to Iranian identity today.[35]

The name of the paper quoted here is "Persian identity in historical perspective." From the outset, however, Yar-Shater talks not of Persian but of "Iranian identity"; conversely, he refers to something called "Persian territory," not "Iranian." Yar-Shater also mentions that "even the language" was "threatened," leaving us to surmise that Persian must be *the* language and that the threatening element must be non-Persian languages. Yar-Shater warns us that the only defense against the identity crisis that Iranians are allegedly facing is to nourish and cherish Persian language, Persian culture and a Persian worldview. In short, "Persian" and "Iranian" are completely conflated, and all things non-Persian are equated with foreignness and danger.

This conflation has for years been ubiquitous in works of English-language Iranian Studies, whether the scholar in question is Iranian-born or not. It is also present in writings that explicitly recognize Iran's cultural diversity, such as when another prominent scholar, William Hanaway, writes:

> The Persian past is not monolithic. Whose past, and therefore whose identity, are we talking about? There were social, economic, ethnic, regional, and linguistic differences among the population at all times in the medieval period. The greater part of the medieval Iranian past that has come to us, and which is the basis of Iranians' sense of identity today, was supplied by a small fraction of the population.[36]

Even a nuanced exposition such as this is based on a simplistic conception of modern Iranian-ness that conflates a "Persian past" with an Iranian identity, leaving an ambiguous place for the heterogeneity mentioned. Again, this is not due to mere confusion over the correct English term. Eminent scholars such as Yar-Shater and Hanaway were, of course, perfectly aware of the possible differences implied in the two terms at their time of writing (1993). The conflation is rooted in a particular view on Iran that privileges what is termed "Persian" above any other linguistic, cultural and historical elements—elements that can all, within particular contexts, become "ethnic."

However, the conflation is not limited to academic language. Many Iranians outside Iran tend to use "Persian" to identify themselves in English and other languages. For some, this has the effect of disassociation from the stigma attached in many Western societies to the label "Iranian." It may also be an attempt at association with Iran's pre-Islamic glory, which still is known to most Westerners in terms of a "Persian empire."[37] In Iran itself, however, "Persian" is rarely used as an autonym. Apart from in descriptions of an ancient people (*qowm-e pārs*), the very term "Persians" (*fārs-hā*) appears somewhat awkward; it *sounds* peculiar, and when used by Iranian scholars, it often appears only within quotation marks.[38]

Some scholars instead prefer the term "Persian speakers" (*fārsi-zabānān*), which indicates that we are talking about a *linguistic* category. In other words, depending on the theory framework to which the given scholar adheres, Persian speakers (alternatively Persophones or Persianates) certainly are a *linguistic* majority in Iran, but not necessarily an *ethnic* majority. Indeed, many scholars never use the ethnonym "Persian" (*fārs*) when writing in Persian (*fārsi*) about Iran. The question, then, is much more profound than "what sounds right?"—many scholars inside Iran simply do not believe in the existence of a Persian ethnic group. To them, there *is* no such thing as "the Persians." This argument has several dimensions. First, there is the issue of territorial belonging. The historian Babak Amirkhosravi[39] argues:

> If, from an ethnological point of view, the existence of a Persian ethnic group [*qowm-e fārs*] were to be proved, [this group] would not be in numerical majority at all: because everyone who speaks Persian are not ethnically Persian. Historically, *qowm-e fārs* lived in the contemporary province of Fars and its surrounding areas. It is not clear if the current inhabitants of that area have any ethnic characteristics or feel [that they have] any ethnic identity.[40]

In other words, Amirkhosravi sees "Persian" as primarily a regional and historical identification, and only *hypothetically* as a contemporary "ethnic identity." However, as Amirkhosravi himself indicates, even the inhabitants of Fars do not necessarily use *fārs* as an autonym. Indeed, it is telling that in the *Encyclopaedia Iranica* entry for the province of Fars, there is no mention of "Persians" in the section "Ethnography," which surveys the province population, including Lors, Kurds, Turks and Arabs.[41]

Ehsan Hushmand is one of several prominent scholars in Iran who have criticized the tendency among intellectuals to take for granted the existence of a Persian ethnic group. As illustrative examples, he uses Semnan, a province of Iran in which, he argues, the Persian-speaking population generally does not express any ethnic affiliation, or the cities of Shiraz, Bushehr and Hormozgan, which are, Hushmand claims, not as "Persian" as they are often portrayed. Rather, "Persian language," Hushmand argues, "is a symbol of the Iranian people's historical interaction and exchange, and it is the language of all Iranian ethnic groups—not of an ethnic group called the Persians."[42]

Hushmand explains that the modern idea of a Persian ethnic group stems from ancient Greece, where it was used as a convenient rubric for identifying a particular

Iranian tribe from others (such as the Medes and the Parthians). Later, Europeans named Iran "Persia" even though this was in no way a reflection of reality in Iran.[43] In this argument, Hushmand is supported by historians such as Khodadad Rezakhani, who has shown how the Greek word for an ancient people that had disappeared from Iranian history annals even before the dissolution of the Achaemenid Empire in 330 B.C. was revived by European Orientalists in the nineteenth century, and then applied to all Iranians regardless of their possible self-identifications.[44]

Without venturing too far into distant etymological history, which is not the purpose of this book, there is indeed a puzzling lack of references to the ethnonym *fārs* in pre-modern historical sources in Persian. Not even in the *Shāhnāme*, considered one of the greatest works in the Persian language and Iran's national epos, is there any mention of a people called the Persians. As an exonym, the label surely has a history, but rarely in a clear-cut sense of denoting a particular community. In medieval times, Arab observers sometimes called the inhabitants of the Iranian Plateau *fors*. However, this term seems to have included a broad range of communities, among them speakers of now-extinct languages as well as Kurdish. In other words, *fors* did not signify a homogeneous Persian-speaking community.

Arabs also designate all non-Arabic speakers to the east of Arabia as *'ajam*, while Turks inside and outside modern-day Iran have historically used *tājik* (or *tāzig* and *tāt*) to designate all the Iranian speakers in the realms they conquered in medieval times.[45] Tapper's studies among the Shahsevan show that these Turkic-speaking communities used *tāt* to denote "all non-Shahsevan villagers and townspeople collectively" and *fārs* to specifically denote Persian speakers within the broader category of *tāt*.[46] More research is needed to ascertain if these Persian-speaking inhabitants of northwestern Iran also used *fārs* as an autonym, and if so, when and why.

Even though the skeptical scholars mentioned in this chapter rarely venture into detailed historical argumentation, they are nonetheless unanimous in problematizing the historical "reality" of a Persian ethnic group. In his survey of the Pahlavi regime's ethnic policies, political scientist Mojtaba Maqsudi claims that the definitions of "Persian" presented in the literature are so broad and vague that they can encompass all Iranians. Ethnic interbreeding, Maqsudi maintains, has made it "impossible to separate and identify a 'Persian' ethnic group."[47] Maqsudi insists that this notion did not appear before Reza Shah's power consolidation and the modern era of state-building and European-inspired nationalism.[48] However, Maqsudi also seems somewhat irresolute on this moot point. For example, he argues that in times of "national identity crisis," Iranians *did* evoke the notion of "being Persian" (*fārs budan*), such as, he claims, during the invasions by Alexander the Great, the Arabs and the Turks. This indicates that his rejection of a Persian ethnic group, or perhaps "Persian-ness," is not total.

The argument that "Persian" is a label of self-identification *provoked* into use by external threats is somewhat similar to the claim that modern minority ethno-nationalists themselves have in fact *devised* the term *fārs* in order to denote an enemy.[49] In a more refined line of argumentation, Rezakhani points out the possibility that ethno-political entrepreneurs, working with a Western-inspired framework for minority rights and therefore in need of a "scapegoat" majority, have resorted to using a Persian equivalent of the Western-coined term "Persian."[50] If so, the adaptation of a "foreign" exonym as an "indigenous" autonym is a by-product of Western "ethnic commonsense."

SUPRA-ETHNICITY

This leads us to the argument that *fārs* should be replaced with "Iranian" (*irāni*), which is what can be deduced from the sociologist Sekander Amanolahi's assertion that "historically all ethnic groups in Iran, including the 'Persians', irrespective of their origin, language, or religion were always referred to, collectively, as Iranians (Irāni)."[51]

Conventionally—that is, in the "ethnic commonsense" of Western sources— "Iranian" does not denote a particular ethnic group. It can relate to the juridical categorization of citizens of the modern Iranian nation-state, to inhabitants of the Iranian Plateau, to the Iranian subfamily of Indo-Iranian languages or to historical, cultural or artistic phenomena such as Iranian carpets or Iranian mythology. Nonetheless, there *are* examples in the Iranian academic literature, and indeed in popular discourse, of the term *qowm-e irāni* employed in the singular, which indicates that all Iranians are to be seen as belonging to one *qowm*. Such a claim is often made in tandem with another: that there *is* no majority ethnic group in Iran. Amanolahi, for example, claims that

> [although] the Persian-speakers constitute nearly 85 percent of the population of Iran, they do not comprise a dominant majority, because they are not a unified and homogeneous entity. Moreover, they occupy only 20 to 30 percent of the total area of Iran. The "majority/minority" model simply does not work in the case of Iran.[52]

Hushmand and Kuhshekaf expand this argument to a broader one: that since existing theories on ethnicity are primarily based on Western scholars' experiences with Western societies, they are not universally applicable.[53] Indeed, they argue, comparing Iran's unique circumstances to those of any other country amounts to a flawed "grand narrative": it is positivism in its most unscientific form.[54]

As part of this nativist approach to the minority issue, Hushmand, Kuhshekaf and several other scholars claim to represent an insider point of view that challenges the view from "outside," that is, from Western academia with its Orientalist roots. The bottom-line is that Iranians, despite the diversity they exhibit and extol, are simply *Iranians*. It thus appears that to some, including prominent scholars, the Iranian community most universally recognized outside Iran ("the Persians") is somehow *sui generis* above the mundane categorization of "ethnic" and that the ethnonym "Persian" is based on a misunderstanding or that it is a political fiction.

Testing the idea of "hidden ethnicity" on the case of the white majority in the United States, the sociologist Ashley W. Doane shows that the "inability or unwillingness to identify oneself ethnically" is directly tied to "the nature of dominant group status": the dominant group has "appropriated the mainstream" and normalized its culture as the culture of "everybody" in the given state.[55] Thus, the dominant group equates the country's "national identity" with its own "ethnic identity." As we will see in this book, this may be somewhat similar to the case of Iran. However, there are also several factors that complicate such a wholesale allegation against "the Persians."

A key factor is what I term the "supra-ethnic notion of Iranian-ness." This notion is expressed as a reified Iranian national identity grounded in Persian culture. It is only rarely articulated explicitly in the sense of a *qowm-e irāni* mentioned earlier in text; however, it is often implicitly evoked in nationalist narratives of "Iranian-ness" (the topic of Chapter 4). An understanding of the interplay between the supra-ethnic notion of Iranian-ness, Persian-centrism and ethnicist counter-discourses can lead us toward a better understanding of the politics of cultural difference in Iran. The salience of the supra-ethnic notion on an everyday level, however, should be sought out in the lived experience of diverse communities in modern cities such as Tehran.

Here, people may not necessarily understand themselves as belonging to a particular ethnic group—unless, of course, we deem *tehrāni* to be an ethnic label. This points to a broader, general point: that while ethnically framed mobilization as understood today is a fairly recent phenomenon, the tendency toward ethnic intermingling and amalgamation is in fact as old as "the idea of Iran" itself.[56] Only in the past 100 years have there been overt state policies toward cultural homogenization, ethnically framed mobilization and academic discourses on ethnicity.

The notion of a supra-ethnic Iranian identity is thus tied up in contradictory ways with the dual dynamics in Iranian society of, on the one hand, a tendency toward increased ethnic demarcation and, on the other, a demographic and socio-cultural tendency toward homogenization. The question is that when prompted by "ethnically aware" minorities to identify in ethnic terms, what labels will the elusive or hidden majority (be forced to) choose? Unfortunately, the paucity of empirical data and the impossibility of conducting such broad-based surveys in Iran today prohibit this book from answering these questions. Instead, it will focus on the nationalistic appropriation of the supra-ethnic notion.

This appropriation takes shape through the nationalist conception of a *mellat* ("nation") that is culturally, linguistically and even, to some, racially more homogeneous *than it appears*. The nation has one common national language and culture (Persian-centrism), a national history that dates back to antiquity and beyond (perennialism or "ancientism"), and/or a common racial ancestry (Aryanism) and/or a Shiite religious identity (Shiite exceptionalism). The emphasis placed on each of these factors varies according to the particular form of Iranian nationalism the observer espouses.

However, seen from a minority perspective, these definitions of Iranian-ness are all exclusivist: they are primarily based on a particular culture, language, religion and set of symbols associated with Iran's Persian-speaking people. Thus, one could be tempted, in a simplistic manner, to argue that the majority is in fact "ethnic Persian." Yet there is one important caveat: many of those who identify with and promote the virtues of a supra-ethnic Iranian national identity, indeed some of its most fervently nationalist spokesmen, can trace their families to roots in non-Persian-speaking communities. They may even still speak the languages and dialects of their mothers or ancestors. Many are ethnically mixed or, more to the point, not aware of or interested in their "ethnic" background.

This is why it is wrong to talk of "Persian nationalism." The proponents of the dominant discourse of identity do not have to see themselves as an ethnic group, but rather as the Iranian people *par excellence*: the Iranian supra-ethnic nation.

Conceptual disarray and the dynamics, fluidity and malleability of ethnicity should not obscure the fact that ethnicity is lived as reality by many people. Ethnically framed mobilization and calls for minority rights are reminders of this. In this book, four particular ethnic groups figure more than others. To explain why, we now turn to a brief outline of the histories associated with these communities.

FOUR MINORITIES

AZERIS

Azeris make up the majority of the former Soviet Republic of Azerbaijan, as well as minorities in Turkey, Russia, Caucasian and Central Asian republics and other countries.[57] The largest Azeri community in the world, however, is located in the area of northwestern Iran historically known as Azerbaijan (*āzarbāyjān*).[58]

In Iran, Azeris are generally known as *tork* (Turks), and sometimes as *āzari* or *āzarbāyjāni*. However, the label "Azeri" does not carry in Persian the same clear-cut sense of an ethnic label as it does in English. This is reflected in the description of "*āzari*" in the Dehkhoda Dictionary: as something or someone connected to Azerbaijan or, alternatively, as a reference to a now extinct "dialect of Old Persian." We will return to this issue, and it suffices here to state that since the Azeris of Iran and Azerbaijan are closely related through a number of cultural similarities, I will here use "Azeri" for both.

Azeris are characterized by a common language and religion: they speak Azeri (also known as Azerbaijani, Azeri Turkic or simply *torki*), which belongs to the Oghuz or Western group of Turkic languages in the Altaic language family. Like the majority of Iranians, but unlike the majority of Turkic speakers outside Iran, Azeris are predominantly Twelver Shiite Muslims. Apart from language and religion, Azeris across the borders share a culture that includes musical, dance and theater traditions, folk tales and literature, as well as a distinct cuisine.

The number of Azeris in Iran is heavily disputed. In 2005, Amanolahi estimated all Turkic-speaking communities in Iran to number no more than 9 million.[59] CIA and Library of Congress estimates range from 16 percent to 24 percent—that is, 12–18 million people if we employ the latest total figure for Iran's population (77.8 million). Azeri ethnicists, on the other hand, argue that the overall number is much higher, even as much as 50 percent or more of the total population. Such inflated estimates may have influenced some Western scholars who suggest that up to 30 percent (that is, some 23 million today) Iranians are Azeris.[60] Iranian nationalists counter that these numbers are hugely exaggerated for political purposes or that Azeris should not even be considered a group distinct from the rest of the Iranians. Even though the denial of the existence of a distinct Azeri culture is obviously flawed, there are several concrete factors related to this claim that cannot be dismissed.

Azeris have played a very significant role in Iranian history, and they are considered by most scholars to be a seamlessly integrated part of Iranian society, economy and politics. Most Azeris are bilingual, and many families living in or originating from Azerbaijan practice exogamy and intermarriage with other communities, especially Persian speakers. In many of the families that have migrated from Azerbaijan to major cities such as Tehran over the past century, Azeri-specific cultural elements have to some extent lost importance. Today, some of these segments often identify with the supra-ethnic notion of an Iranian identity, and not in ethnic terms as Azeris—particularly since there is a certain stigma attached to the label *tork* in upper middle class urban Iran.

However, many signs of the opposite trend also exist: namely, a movement toward increased ethnically framed mobilization of culture among some Azeris, both in the provinces of Azerbaijan and in Tehran. The Azeri ethnicists claim to be part of an ethnic group of Turks who used to occupy a paramount role in Iranian politics and society, but were marginalized after the establishment of a modern, monolingual state by Reza Shah in 1925. They claim that the "assimilated" Azeris are victims of "Persianization" who have forgotten or lost their true cultural identity.

While *āzarbāyjān* in its Iranian context today normally indicates the four provinces of West Azerbaijan, East Azerbaijan, Ardabil and Zanjan, there are also Azeris in many other provinces, just as there are many non-Azeri communities in Azerbaijan. To some Azeris, *āzarbāyjān* encompasses all areas in which Azeris have historically resided, whether inside or outside Iran's current borders. However, the territory that is today the Republic of Azerbaijan was known as Arran and Shirvan (or Caucasian Albania in European sources) until medieval times, and only the area south of River Aras, in present-day Iran, was called Azerbaijan.[61] In 1828, Iranian military defeats led to the Treaty of Turkmanchay, which ceded the areas north of the Aras to Russia.

To Iranian nationalists, the 1918 naming of this area as the Republic of Azerbaijan was a political ploy to prepare the ground for further Russian annexations.[62] Stalin's 1923 decision to name a new Soviet Republic "Azerbaijan" only seemed to confirm this suspicion. To Iranian nationalists, the "true" Azerbaijan is that of Iran. Conversely, Soviet scholars have (erroneously) claimed that "Azerbaijan" was since ancient times used for both sides of the river, and this has in turn inspired the pan-Azeri ethnicist claim that Iranian Azerbaijan is actually just "South Azerbaijan."

Ancient Azerbaijan was since 6000 B.C. home to several peoples of which we have little information. Some of these early inhabitants spoke the Indo-Iranian language *āzari*, which was related to Middle Persian. As a name, Azerbaijan is probably derived from the same root as *Atropates*, which was the Greek name of a semi-independent state in Achaemenid times (ca. 550–336 B.C.). While scholars dispute the belief popular among Azeris that Zoroaster himself lived in Azerbaijan, the area was certainly a Zoroastrian stronghold at least by Sasanian times (224–651 A.D.). In the early ninth century, the local Babak Khorramdin led an uprising against the Muslim armies, an event later eulogized by both Iranian nationalists and Azeri ethnicists, albeit for different purposes.

Turkic-speaking peoples appeared in Azerbaijan from around the seventh century A.D., and large-scale migrations of Central Asian Turks took place from the eleventh

century. The first Turko-Iranian dynasty, the Ghaznavids, appeared in the tenth century in the eastern part of Greater Iran (today Afghanistan). Later, migration and
invasions brought a new influx of Turks and Mongols to Azerbaijan and beyond, and
Turko-Iranian dynasties such as Aq-Qoyunlu and Qara-Qoyunlu were founded in the
fourteenth century. Turkic-speaking tribes, returning from Anatolia to Azerbaijan,
founded the Safavid dynasty in 1501.

The first Safavid king, Shah Esma'il, wrote poetry in Turkic, and together with
poets such as Nesimi and Fuzuli, he was among the regional pioneers of Turkic
literature. Most importantly, he laid the foundation of the modern Iranian state
with Shiite Islam as part of its discourse of legitimacy. Fighting its Sunni neighbors, the Ottoman Empire and the Uzbeks, the Safavids ushered in a golden age,
extending their rule and consolidating Iranian lands while nurturing a cultural
blossoming. Iran was dominated by Turko-Iranian tribal dynasties all the way up
to 1925.

The sedentarization of Turkic tribes began with the partial closing of the Russian
border in 1886 and culminated with Reza Shah's policies of forced settlement in the
1930s. Only small groups of Shahsevan (in Azerbaijan) and Qashqa'is (in central
Iran) today continue a traditional way of semi-nomadic life.[63] Despite the limits on
commerce following the Russian annexation of the Caucasus, Azerbaijan has historically been a prosperous region of Iran. Azeris are generally considered progressive and
industrious people, boasting agricultural, industrial, educational and artistic centers
such as Tabriz, Orumiyeh (Urmia), Zanjan and Ardabil. Up until early modern times,
Tabriz functioned periodically as either capital or seat of the crown prince, and until
the 1960s, it was Iran's second biggest city.

Even though Persian was the lingua franca, Azeri Turkic had become the dominant
native language of Azerbaijan by the eighteenth century. Tabriz was home to Iran's
first primary school founded by Haji Mirza Hasan Roshdiyyeh, who authored the
first Azeri-language schoolbook. Despite Russian colonization, Azeris continued to
develop cross-border relations, in particular in the late nineteenth and early twentieth
centuries when large numbers of Iranian Azeris went to work in Baku's oil industry.
The many family ties across the border also facilitated literary, cultural and political
developments such as the spread of social satire and political theater. One of the
pioneers of this cultural blossoming was Mirza Fath-'Ali Akhundzadeh, who can be
considered among the early Iranian nationalists, but also wrote extensively in Azeri
Turkic.

On the crossroads between Iran, Turkey and Russia, Tabriz was a locus of polit-
ical movements, including the 1906–11 Constitutional Revolution and the 1978–9
Islamic Revolution. Azerbaijan also saw the first signs of the conflict between secularist and religious modernists that would characterize twentieth-century intellectual
Iran. During the tumultuous start of the twentieth century, Sheikh Khiyabani and
Abolqasem Lahuti led two different anti-state revolts. Khiyabani established the
first so-called Democrat Party (*Ferqe-ye demokrāt*), and in 1919 took control of
Tabriz under the banner *āzādestān* (Free-Land). Lahuti rebelled against the Shah
in 1922. Both of these short-lived uprisings were crushed with heavy force, and
even though they were not separatist movements, cultural factors were politicized
in this period. Khiyabani, for example, demanded that the provision for regional

autonomy enshrined in the first Iranian Constitution be implemented, and he instituted Azeri-language education policies.

The 1918 declaration of an Azerbaijan Democratic Republic to the north, and the 1922 establishment of a nationalist and sometimes pan-Turkist republic in Turkey, further fuelled ethnically framed mobilization among Iran's Azeris. Another trend brought Soviet-inspired socialism to both sides of the Aras, including the Leninist concept of minority self-rule that was applied in a way that portrayed Azeri dissent in Iran as a "national" struggle.[64] A third trend among the upper class Azeri intelligentsia strongly opposed the pan-Turkist and pro-Soviet trends and supported, in the name of modernization and progress, the Pahlavi state with its Persian-centric policies of homogenization. These competing ideas were exchanged in a fertile intellectual environment among Iran's educated Azeris, in Azerbaijan and in Tehran, throughout the twentieth century.

From the 1920s onward, Azerbaijan's prominence dwindled due to Pahlavi centralization, relocation of state resources and shifting patterns of economic development. Traditional *khān*-based power structures were replaced with a modernized bureaucracy in which key personnel, often with no links to Azerbaijan, were appointed from Tehran. Azerbaijan's status decline was concomitant with restrictions on Turkic aspects of Azeri culture and policies to strengthen Persian as Iran's sole language. New provinces were created so as to divide and rule Azeri strongholds, while important places were renamed in Persian, and Persian names were advocated for Azeri children.

During the World War II occupation of northern Iran, the Soviet Union made use of ethnic propaganda, but its call for the "unification" of "the two Azerbaijans" met with little support in Iran. Leftist and autonomist activism culminated in the 1945 establishment of a provincial government in Tabriz and a new Democrat Party under Ja'far Pishevari. The Democrat Party advocated linguistic rights for Iran's Azeris as well as increased self-rule from Tehran. Red Army backing, the declaration of autonomy and ethnically framed rhetoric aside, the Democrat Party did not intend on separation from Iran.[65] The provincial government instituted several cultural, social and economic reforms, the latter to the dismay of landowners. Crushed by the Iranian state already at the end of 1946, the movement and the subsequent violent clampdown in Tabriz nonetheless had a lasting impact on Azeri ethnicism.

Azerbaijan's decline did not affect the overall place of Azeris in Iran. Azeris, most notably in Tehran, dominate in many commercial activities today and are prominent in the upper echelons of political, military and religious institutions. Several major political figures in present-day Iran, including the Supreme Leader Ayatollah Khamene'i, have Azeri roots. Yet, at the same time, the restrictions on expressions of Azeri culture have accelerated post-revolutionary ethnically framed mobilization and cultural revival, to which we will return in the next chapter.

So far, this account has conformed to a generalized view, as opposed to the views of Azeri ethnicists and Iranian nationalists. However, the generalized view is itself problematic as it rests upon the ambiguity in the very word Azeri. On the one hand, there is the ancient *āzari* language, which was spoken in Azerbaijan until Turkic gradually replaced it from roughly the eleventh to seventeenth century. Even though some scholars claim that modern-day Tati is a direct remnant of this pre-Turkic *āzari*, it is clear that the language spoken by most of what we today call Azeris is Turkic (albeit with many Persian and some old *āzari* loanwords).

On the other hand, this Turkic language has come to be called Azeri today as part of two different but interrelated developments. In 1922, Stalin institutionalized the name Azeri for the Turkic language of Caucasus. Conversely, twentieth-century Iranian nationalists, in a bid to "prove" the inseparability of Azerbaijan to Iran, also promoted the word *Azeri* for what was formerly known as *torki*. The resulting confusion has quite important political implications.

From one perspective, Iranian nationalists glorify the pre-Turkic, Indo-Iranian *āzari* people, praising their extinct language as "Iranian" or even Persian (although *āzari* and Persian originate from two different branches of Iranian languages). The argument drawn from this glorification is that the existence of an "Aryan" culture before the advent of Turks in the area proves (a) the essentially *Iranian* identity of Azerbaijan, despite its current linguistic differences with the Persian-speaking core, and (b) that Turkicization has only been superficial.

From the opposite perspective, some Azeri ethnicists propose the radical counter-theory of a pre-Indo-European, *Turkic* culture in Azerbaijan. This hypothesis, although completely discredited by established Turcology and Iranian Studies, has given way to ethno-nationalist claims to primacy, including that early historical figures such as Zoroaster and Babak Khorramdin were actually Turks. Such claims are part of a broader challenge to nationalist history writing, to which we will return in Chapter 4.

KURDS

People identifying as Kurds are spread out over a region that is divided by several contemporary nation-states, most notably Turkey, Iraq, Iran and Syria. There are also Kurdish minorities in the Caucasus, Afghanistan, and Russia, and in a large diaspora in Europe and North America. The total number of Kurds is estimated at between 23 and 36 million. In Iran, estimates are disputed, varying from 7 to 9 percent of the total population (equaling 5–7 million people) to over 10 percent (7.7 million) to 12–15 percent (9–11 million).[66]

As articulated by ethnicists, Kurdish political identity was formulated in response to the arbitrary drawing of modern borders that have divided the Kurds and left them a stateless nation without a unified territorial entity. To these ethnicists, Kurdistan signifies a geographic homeland that covers a huge part of the Middle East. In its Iranian context, however, Kurdistan refers in its narrow, administrative sense to the province of Kurdistan (*Kordestān*), and in its broad, historical sense to the Kurdish-inhabited areas of western Iran that also includes communities living in what is now the provinces of West Azerbaijan, Kermanshah, Ilam and outlying areas.[67] There are also sizable Kurdish communities in the eastern province of Khorasan, estimated by one source to number around a million people.[68]

In its historical sense, Kurdistan in Iran stretches down along the Turkish and Iraqi borders from Maku in the north; over Lake Orumiyeh to the mountains around Mahabad, Saqqez and Marivan; and on to the hills and plains of Sanandaj and Kermanshah. In the north, Azeris, Kurds, Armenians and Assyrians live alongside each other, at times peacefully, at times not. Even though the area is underdeveloped, Kurdish agriculture is of some importance to the national economy. The main crops are tobacco, barley, wheat and rice, and livestock is primarily goats and sheep. In villages and urban centers, the population includes traders, shopkeepers and peddlers but few industrial workers.

Ethnicists tend to depict Kurds as a stateless nation with a discrete national identity (*Kordāyetî*) and as an externally bounded, internally unified and distinct ethnic group.[69] This view, however, obscures actual cultural heterogeneity. Many Kurds identify with particular beliefs in shared ancestry and belonging, and can be singled out from other communities by certain cultural and social features. Yet clear demarcation is very difficult. An example is whether and how to distinguish Kurds from other communities in Ilam and Kermanshah, which share many socio-cultural and linguistic traits with Kurds, but normally identify as Lors. *Kord* has not always been understood as an ethnonym: in Arab historical annals, for example, it was a socioeconomic designation.[70] In the course of history, several Arabic- and Turkic-speaking tribes *became*, so to speak, Kurds, while many Kurdish tribes became "Arabicized" or "Turkicized." Conversely, some Jews, Assyrians and Armenians became Kurdophone without abandoning their other "non-Kurdish" cultural traits.

Kurds are often divided into three generalized categories based on habitat: mountains, plains/villages and cities. While people in the first category are characterized by tribalism, pastoralism and, until recently, nomadism, the second and third are sedentary, relying on trade, agriculture, arboriculture and animal husbandry. Structural transitions within and between these categories and sedentarization were major factors in the rise of modern Kurdish nationalism.[71] Tribal Kurds are organized, stringently or loosely, in units based on kinship ideology and territorial identifications. These units traditionally comprised anything from small, tented encampments to huge confederacies.

Throughout pre-modern history, Kurdistan was incessantly marred by strife over pasturage and external political manipulation. Tribal chiefs held great power until their authority was gradually undermined in the nineteenth and twentieth centuries by the emerging modern states.[72] Even among sedentary and urban Kurds, tribal affiliation for protection has been, and continues to be, important. In the words of the prominent Kurdistan scholar David McDowell, "It is a commentary on the failure of states to meet all the individual's needs—employment, fair allocation of resources, arbitration, health and welfare and so forth—that this kind of tribalism persists."[73]

Diversity is also reflected in language and religion. Kurdish is not, scholars argue, one language:[74] in Iran, Kurds speak Sorani, Kurmanji or Laki, which belong to the group of "proper" Kurdish languages, or they speak Gorani (including Hawrami), Northern Zaza or Southern Zaza from the Zaza-Gorani language group. Both groups are from the Iranian language subfamily, but from two different sub-branches. Despite similarities and a high degree of mutual intelligibility, there are also deep differences between these languages. Importantly, many, if not most, Kurds are bi- or multilingual, and Persian is spoken by most. Nonetheless, Kurdish ethnicists promote an idealized notion of Kurdish linguistic unity.

The majority of Kurds are Muslims but adhere to different sects. While Sunnis are scattered all over Kurdistan, the Shiites are centered on Kermanshah. Because of lack of statistics and surveys, academic claims vary significantly: that Shiites are in slight majority, that Sunnis are in slight majority, that two-thirds of the Kurds are Sunnis or that Sunnis account for 75 percent.[75] It is not always clear whether scholars include, in the category of "Shiite Kurds," heterodox sects such as the Ahl-e Haqq (Yarsanis) that draw on elements of pre-Islamic religions and Shiite beliefs but are often considered heretics by Shiite clerics. While most other Iranian Sunnis adhere to the Hanafi law school, the Kurds mostly adhere to the Shafe'i, and a minority to the Hanbali. Interwoven into the fabric of Kurdish society are also many Sufi groups, which is a source of both division (between rival *tariqat*s such as the Qaderi and Naqshbandi) and unity (across tribal borders).

The Kurds' origins are contested. Their ancestors may have been among the Indo-Iranian-speaking peoples that migrated in the second millennium B.C. into what is today Iran. Kurdish ethnicists and some scholars argue for the contested claim that Kurds are direct descendants of the ancient Medes.[76] Ancestral myths relate Kurds either to King Solomon, to the Prophet Abraham or to an Iranian fable from the *Shāhnāme*. Kurds have been known since ancient times: particularly as a troublesome people on the borders of Sumerian, Urartian and Mannai kingdoms. The earliest surviving mention of Kurds as *Cyrtii* is in Greek sources from the second century B.C. From the tenth century A.D., Kurds established minor dynasties, and the first mentions of "Kurdistan" are from twelfth century Armenian and Saljuq annals. In early Islamic literature, "Kurd" was often synonymous with nomads or marauding villains, but many tribes were also incorporated into imperial armies.

The battle at Chaldiran in 1514 more or less settled the border between the Ottoman and Safavid empires, and turned Kurdistan into a buffer zone. To protect their interests and evade government control and taxes, chieftains were entangled in the intrigues of imperial geopolitics. The Safavids sought to subdue the unruly Kurds, forcibly relocating whole tribes but leaving the Kurdish Ardalan principality as a semi-independent emirate in western Iran. To keep Kurds disunited, the 1794–1925 Qajar dynasty sowed and managed feuds among the tribes. Animosities between Kurds, Azeris, Armenians and Assyrians were rampant as tensions with neighboring powers increased.

In the 1880s, Ottomans supported one Sheykh 'Obaydollah's incursions into Iran, and after signing a treaty with Britain, Russians occupied the region in 1912. Economic and political transitions gave rise to rebellions, the weakening of government galvanized inter-tribal hostilities and foreign forces used and were used by tribal leaders. In a context of widespread poverty and raging famines, socialist ideas spread in the early twentieth century, and in 1917–18, a Social Democratic Party took control of Sanandaj. The movement was quickly quashed but left a seed of class struggle in Kurdish soil.

An opportunistic chieftain fluctuating between Russian and Turkish support, Esma'il Aqa Shakak ("Simko"), led a series of raids and rebellions in 1919–26. Despite his self-centered ambitions and only vague allusions to a united Kurdistan, Kurdish ethnicists today revere Simko as a hero of independence.[77] His slaying in 1929 signaled the Iranian state's new approach toward the Kurds. In the following decade, Reza Shah used the modern army, shrewd policies and hostage-taking to subdue and coerce chieftains. Insurgents were severely punished, warriors disarmed, tribes forcibly resettled, local leaders exiled and animal flocks confiscated. Where tribes were no direct threat, Reza Shah left them alone. Later, the shahs also used certain armed, autonomist tribes in Iraq as proxies against Baghdad, a policy that often boomeranged into Iran.

In general, the establishment of a centralized, modern state under the Pahlavis disrupted traditional patterns of life, uprooted the feudal system and crushed local autonomy. Centralization brought about contentious issues of army conscription and land ownership, and new border demarcations that cut off many tribes from their historic migration routes, turning some Kurds toward smuggling. Modern development brought about a growing gap between the affluent and the extremely poor, and many Kurds moved to villages and cities, where they were exposed to new ideas of political agency through newly urbanized Kurdish elites looking for an opportunity to gain power.

During the unrest following the British and Soviet occupation of Iran in 1941, the Iranian government entered into a compromise with Kurdish leaders, letting them arm and wear traditional clothes again. The British did not answer Kurdish calls for support, so a delegation of Kurdish leaders instead visited Baku in 1941, where they gained lukewarm Soviet support. Among these leaders was Qazi Mohammad, who, despite Soviet instructions that the time for independence had not arrived, formed the Marxist-inspired *Komele* organization with support from Iraqi Kurds. These ethno-nationalists strove to replace traditional tribal authority with a modern, independent Kurdish state, fought for cultural rights and used Communist rhetoric to entice impoverished Kurds against reactionary chieftains.

On Soviet command, a Kurdish Democratic Party of Iran (KDPI) replaced the *Komele* in 1945. Not unlike its Azeri counterpart, KDPI at first demanded autonomy, but with the arrival in Iran of the powerful Iraq-based Barzani clan, the party went on to declare an independent Republic of Mahabad in December 1945. This was the first and only Kurdish nation-state in history. Tribal rivalries, lacking cohesion and a Soviet backer that was primarily interested in extorting an oil concession from Iran, made the state last barely a year. Sacking Mahabad, the Shah's forces burned Kurdish books, closed the press, banned the language and executed insurgents.[78] Kurdish ethnicists today eulogize Mahabad as a symbol of independence, and it inspired a wave of Kurdish cultural and literary activities.

Autonomy had failed and the Kurdish opposition went underground. Yet socioeconomic change, agrarian reform, enhanced communications, worker migration, population growth, peasant literacy and the uprooting of the landed class cemented the politicization of culture. In 1952, a KDPI-led peasant revolt in Bukan was violently suppressed by the Iranian army. In 1954, KDPI resurfaced and called for the liberation of all of Kurdistan, and in the 1960s it organized a series of peasant uprisings. In 1973, its slogan changed to "Democracy for Iran, autonomy for Kurdistan," and together with a new *Komele*, KDPI would regain prominence during the Islamic Revolution.

Despite historical, cultural and linguistic ties, the relationship between the Persian-speaking core and the Kurds in the western periphery has been complex and tension ridden. In comparison to Azeris, Kurds (particularly Sunni Kurds) are markedly marginalized in modern Iran. As a response to great power rivalries in the nineteenth and twentieth centuries in a hotly contested part of the Middle East, Kurds have nurtured a distinct cultural self-identification that has been shaped by their minority (and double-minority) status. In formulating this self-identification, ethnicists certainly gloss over the many inter-Kurdish differences and diversity. Yet the modern Iranian state's apprehensive and militaristic attitude toward the Kurds has spawned feelings of injustice and discrimination in the local population, and further cemented notions of a separate Kurdish "identity."

ARABS

"Arab" is an umbrella term that includes a broad range of peoples from Africa and Asia. Estimates of the size of the Arab community in Iran fluctuate from 1.3 to over 2 million to 2.7 and even 5 million.[79] These estimates are problematic since they are rarely accompanied with a specification of exactly whom they include. There are notable Arab communities in Semnan and Khorasan, along the Persian Gulf in Hormozgan and Bushehr, as well as in Fars and in Tehran. Yet the biggest community, the Arabs treated in this book, live primarily in the southern half of the southwestern province of Khuzestan (or Khuzistan), with small pockets in outlying provinces.

These Khuzestani Arabs share the region with Lors, Bakhtiyaris and Kowlis (or gypsies) as well as with large numbers of mostly Persian-speaking Iranians who emigrated from other parts of Khuzestan and from all over Iran in the twentieth century. There has been a degree of intermingling in Khuzestan's urban centers, and there were important fluctuations in population patterns during and after the Iran-Iraq War. While all these factors obviously complicate the question of whom to include in the category, there are a number of more or less discrete cultural factors with which 'arab is generally defined in Iran.

The Arab-populated part of Khuzestan is estimated by one source to cover around 65 percent of the province, and includes major cities such as Ahvaz (Ahwaz), Khorramshahr (Mohammerah), Abadan, Shadegan (Fallahiyah), Hoveyze and Susangard (Khafajiyyah), where Arabs reportedly make up between 65 and 95 percent of the population.[80] The majority of Khuzestani Arabs is Shiite, but there are also a few Sunnis, Jews, Christians and Mandaeans in Khuzestan. Khuzestani Arabs are closely related with southern Iraqi Arabs with whom they share a distinct dialect of Arabic, while bandari Arabs of Iran's Persian Gulf shores are mostly Sunnis who speak Gulf dialect.[81] The Arab culture of Khuzestan includes traditional clothing and tattooing, folklore, poetry and proverbs, food, music as well as unique religious ceremonies and rituals.[82]

Although Khuzestan is home to Iran's single most important source of income, the oil industry, and although it is a relatively important agricultural center, Arab ethnicists routinely complain that the place is severely underdeveloped, plagued by environmental problems and suffering from rampant unemployment and poverty, especially among rural Arabs. Ethnicists claim these problems stem from the central state's racist bias in social policies and allocation of funds for economic development;[83] some Iranian scholars, on the contrary, point out "cultural factors" that hinder progress among Arabs.[84] Illiteracy, in particular among women, is comparatively high, and discrimination against women, forced marriages and "honor killings" are reportedly widespread.[85]

Although significantly weakened in the twentieth century, tribalism is still important. Societal units range from *beyts* (household or group of families) over *hamule*
(clan) and *'ashire* (tribe) to *tāyefe* and *qabile* (tribal confederacies). Tribal leaders
(*sheykhs*) traditionally wield power of arbitration (*fasl*) in inter- and intra-clan matters. The reasons for the persistence of tribalism are many and include the historically
bad relations between ruling center and periphery, which made chieftains rather than
local bureaucracy a mediator between state authorities and individuals. In the more
recent history, the local population's unfamiliarity with the judicial system or with
the Persian language, the lack of Arabs in local governance and conservatism has
been mentioned.[86]

Long before Arab settlement, Khuzestan was home to the ancient Elamite civilization stretching back as far as 3200 B.C. Assyrians defeated the Elamites in 640
B.C., after which Indo-European-speaking tribes gradually settled in the region. The
Achaemenid and Sasanian empires ruled Khuzestan all the way up to the Islamic conquest. With these historical facts at hand, and for more recent ideological reasons,
some Iranian scholars do not treat Arabs as indigenous to Khuzestan.[87] However, the
fact that most Khuzestani Arabs are Shiites is often used as an argument for their
close connection with and loyalty toward Iran.[88]

The seventh century A.D. Muslim conquest of Iran was preceded by a long history of Iranian-Arab relations, including extensive trade, pre-Islamic Iranian political
involvement in Arabia and Arab migrations to the Iranian plateau.[89] Indeed, there
were several Arab tribes present in Iran before the conquest, including the Wa'el and
Tamim in Khuzestan. Some Iranian scholars today claim that these tribes were split
over the issue of the Muslim invasion, with some supporting the Iranian Sasanians.[90]
At any rate, Arabs settled in significant numbers throughout the conquered areas,
and there was further Arab settlement in Khuzestan in the tenth century.

Medieval Iranian rulers often left the Arab sheikhs of Khuzestan to their own
devices, including ongoing feuds with neighboring Bakhtiyaris. The Mosha'sha'iyya,
an extremist Shiite sect, spread throughout Khuzestan from the fifteenth century,
spearheading revolts as well as a stint at autonomy in Hoveyze that was subdued
by the Safavids in 1508. From the fifteenth century, the Bani Ka'ab tribe, including immigrants from present-day Kuwait, gained considerable power in Khuzestan.
In this period, southern Khuzestan was thoroughly Arabized and became known
as Arabistan (*'arabestān*).[91] During the nineteenth century, British infiltration of the
region gradually increased, while the wealthy and powerful Jaber Al-Ka'abi became
sheikh of Khorramshahr. Jaber's son Sheikh Khaz'al consolidated his power from
1897 by taking advantage of British imperialist objectives and chaotic Qajar domestic
politics.[92]

With the discovery of oil in Khuzestan, British involvement increased drastically.
After the 1909 establishment of the Anglo-Persian Oil Company, Britain signed a
treaty with Sheikh Khaz'al, lending the sheikh support and money in return for access
to the oil. The rapid expansion of the oil industry facilitated a quasi-colonial British
rule over parts of Khuzestan. Khaz'al led a revolt against Iranian authorities in 1916.
With some inspiration from Arab nationalism, and certainly motivated by personal
economic prospects, Khaz'al formed an Arab army and even proposed to separate
Khuzestan from Iran. This event has since inspired Arab ethnicists who see it as
evidence of a historic wish for independence. In the end, the British rejected the

idea of Arab independence, and in 1924 Reza Khan lured Khaz'al into a trap and abolished the sheikhdom.

The Pahlavi state consolidated its power by including Arabistan in the new provincial unit of Khuzestan, by renaming cities and uprooting traditional power structures and by implementing policies and practices that discriminated against the local Arabs. In this period of detribalization, parts of Khuzestan were thoroughly industrialized to satisfy a constantly increasing global appetite for oil. Yet while small pockets of urbanization and modern education grew, and large groups of outsiders moved into the province, most Arabs gained little or no political influence over local affairs. As the gap between poor and rich rapidly widened, Arab ethno-nationalism found an increasingly receptive audience among people left without traditional leadership.

Even though many accounts of Khuzestan's modern history focus on the claim that Arab ethnicism was the product of British manipulation and propaganda, new research shows that a genuine movement for Arab autonomy blossomed in the 1940s.[93] Yet the British government undeniably sought to exploit ethnic sentiments, and the oil industry has a long history of manipulating the various communities of Khuzestan.[94] One example was during the 1946 oil worker strike in Abadan when the oil company and its British backers fanned ethnic tensions, sparking violent clashes between Arabs and Persian-speaking Tudeh Party supporters.

Later, the Iraqi state sought to exploit Arab discontent against its rivals in Tehran, both before and after the Islamic Revolution, among other things by insisting on calling Khuzestan "occupied Arabistan." Exile-based organizations were instrumental in spreading pan-Arabist and separatist ideas among some Iranian Arabs from the 1960s onward. On the eve of the revolution, Khuzestan was teeming with political dissent.

In short, there are several reasons why the Arabs tend to identify and be identified as a distinct community in Iran. Their historical ties with co-ethnics across the present border and their language, which as a Semitic language is unrelated to the languages spoken by most inhabitants of Iran, are among the key reasons. The degree of Iranian Arabs' attachment to Iran as a political entity and the view of Iranian intellectuals on Arabs in general, however, is the topic of many discussions, to which we will return in chapters 4 and 5.

BALUCH

The Baluch (Baluchis, Baloch or Balooch) inhabit the area historically known as Baluchistan, located between the Iranian plateau and the Indian lowland, north of the Gulf of Oman, south of River Helmand. This area is today divided between Pakistan, Afghanistan and Iran, but until recently, the Baluch regularly moved unhindered across the borders. There are also Baluch exile communities in Oman, UAE and other countries. The total number of Baluch worldwide may be around 10 million. Estimates for the Baluch in Iran hover around 1–2 percent of the total population, that is, somewhere between 750,000 and 1.5 million people.[95]

Iranian Baluch are primarily concentrated in Iran's largest but most sparsely populated province, Sistan-Baluchistan. There are also scattered Baluch communities in Kerman, Hormozgan and Khorasan all the way up to and beyond the border with

Turkmenistan.[96] In the key cities of Zahedan and Zabol, Baluch make up about half of the population. However, the majority of Baluch is rural, scattered across the central and southern parts of the province in villages or small, fortified settlements, or living as semi-nomads.[97] Baluchistan is the driest part of Iran, dominated by deserts, arid mountains and soil that is hard to cultivate. Stable water sources are very scarce, and the climate is harsh, with extremely hot summers, erratic precipitation, frequent droughts and torrential floods.

Iran's Baluch express a particular territorial self-identification based on a distinct culture. They speak two different dialects of Baluchi (or Balochi), which is part of the Western group of Indo-Iranian languages, with affinities to ancient Middle Persian and Parthian. Most Baluch are Sunni Muslim of the Hanafi school with a small minority of Shiites. There are also an unknown number of Zikris, members of an Islamic sect, and allegedly a rising number of Sunnis adhering to the Wahhabi and Salafi movements.[98] The Brahui, who speak a distinct language that may be of Dravidian origin, are sometimes considered Baluch due to cultural similarities. There are also small pockets of Hindus and Sikhs in Baluchistan. Many inhabitants identify in terms of tribal affiliation, and sometimes these affiliations cut across ethnic boundaries. Baluchistan is paired administratively with Sistan, which has been populated since ancient times by Persian-speaking peoples and dynasties that have not always had amenable relations with the Baluch—especially since the Sistanis became Shiites from the sixteenth century.

Baluchistan's history is understudied. There is archaeological evidence of settlements as old as the fourth millennium B.C., as well as of trade between the Indus and Mesopotamia. Baluchistan corresponds roughly to the Achaemenid regions of Gedrosia, Maka and parts of Drangia in ancient Greek sources. The Indo-Iranian Saka Scythians inhabited these areas, and later principalities paid tribute to the Sasanians. Muslim armies invaded the Makran, the southern part of Baluchistan, in 644 A.D., but the region remained more or less autonomous for centuries.

Linguistic evidence indicate that the Baluch, or an original core of Baluch, once lived southeast of the Caspian Sea from where they gradually migrated southeast to Kerman some one thousand years ago, and then on to Baluchistan. The epic ballad *Daptar Sha'ir* contains Baluch myths of ancestry. One myth is that the Baluch descend from Mir Hamza, the Prophet Mohammad's paternal uncle, and from Arabs who migrated from Aleppo after the battle at Karbala in 680 A.D.[99] Conversely, Iranian scholars often claim that the Baluch are an "Aryan" people of pure Iranian stock (see Chapter 5). Iranian nationalists often also allude to the *baluch* mentioned in the *Shāhnāme* as a foe of the Sasanians, but some scholars have dismissed this as Ferdowsi's anachronism.[100] Nevertheless, *kuch va baluch* certainly signified marauding bandits in Ferdowsi's time.

The earliest existing written mentions of the Baluch are from an eighth-century Pahlavi text and from tenth-century Arabic geographies. The word *baluchestān*, however, may not be older than the eighteenth century, and the word *baluch* may originally have been a settled people's general designation for nomad tribes. Conversely, the genesis of a Baluch self-identification may have been, in the words of anthropologist Brian Spooner, "a product of the insecurity of a vast desert area which the governments of the period did not care to control despite their need for secure communications across it."[101] Thus, the Baluch often envision themselves as constantly threatened by outside powers, and they are presented in most accounts as a people that take great pride in self-defense.[102] Modern Baluch ethnicists have used these sentiments to present their current struggle as part of a historical drive toward an independent Greater Baluchistan.

Medieval Baluchistan was, on the one hand, a buffer zone between Iranian and Indian empires that often conducted campaigns in the area to subdue unruly tribes. On the other hand, Baluchistan also boasted several ports crucial to Indian Ocean trade. The Portuguese, Dutch and British navies visited, traded with and occupied parts of the coast from 1515 onward, and Baluchistan became an important piece in the geopolitical game between Safavids, Mughals and Europeans.

Baluch ethnicists today draw on a historical repertoire of heroes such as Mir Chakar Rind, who in the fifteenth century moved Baluch armies into the Punjab, and of the khanate of Qalat, which was established in the late seventeenth century in present-day Pakistan. In the late eighteenth century, Nasir Khan united rival Baluch and Brahui clans, and with Nader Shah's endorsement, built a rudimentary state apparatus around this khanate. Qalat remained nominally independent until British rule in the early nineteenth century. Seen as a golden age, this period is a source of inspiration for Baluch poets and writers, and has become an ethnicist symbol of pride.

With the growing importance of the region during the Great Game, Qajar shahs moved in to subdue the unruly Baluch, while Britain kept eastern Baluchistan as a strategic piece of the "forward policy" of securing Afghanistan against Tsarist Russia. The local tribal structure was kept intact. In the agricultural south, hereditary feudal lords (*hakom*) would collect a tithe of the crops *in lieu* of tax and, in return, maintain law, order and irrigation systems in villages. In the pastoral nomadic north, pasture was a collective tribal property, but each tribesman had to pay the chieftains (*sardār*), selected from the ruling clans, one-tenth of his animals. Trade, politics and social interaction linked the tribes and the fiefdoms, and at times they united militarily under a khan.

British colonial rule led to Baluchistan's division in 1896 and to a gradual weakening of traditional authority. Revolts against the Qajars and the British were frequent, and in 1896–7, Baluch insurgents ousted the Qajar army and killed Britain's representative. Retaliation was harsh, and one Baluch author claims that to this day, locals still call Persian speakers *gajar*, evoking the dreaded image of occupiers.[103] Conversely, frequent Baluch raids on Persian-speaking Shiite villages have left the image of a barbaric people among some Iranians.

After World War I, the famous leader Amir Dust-Mohammad Khan centralized Baluch power and confronted British forces, but was subsequently defeated during Reza Shah's campaigns in 1928. Revolts continued until 1935, but western Baluchistan was irreversibly incorporated into Iran. After a stint at independence from British rule, eastern Baluchistan was annexed by Pakistan in 1948.

With direct Iranian rule came attempts to forcibly Persianize Baluchistan. Reza Shah renamed Baluch towns and landmarks with Persian names, and grouped Baluchistan together first with Kerman and then with Sistan, making Baluchistan easier to administer for the shah's appointed Persian-speaking Shiite military elites. Local

Baluch history was censored away and the use of Baluchi language restricted. Cultural and political organizations were banned, insurgents punished and the region severely neglected in development policies. Forced settlement, nationalization of pastures, restrictions on cross-border movement and campaigns against local tribes uprooted traditional livelihoods, exacerbated poverty and brought about a situation that often resembled military occupation.

However, the gradual disintegration of feudalism also gave rise to a small urban middle class of Baluch with modern educations and ethno-nationalist aspirations. Inspired by events in India, Baluch elites began in the 1930s to form underground nationalist groups. In the 1950s, the tribal leader Dad Shah started an uprising in Iranian Baluchistan, allegedly in protest against the aggressive Pahlavi gendarmerie and its disrespect for Baluch codes of honor.[104] A 1957 attack on an American convoy traveling through Baluchistan brought Dad Shah brief international attention. While the Iranian state fought and killed Dad Shah as a bandit, Baluch ethnicists today revere him as a national hero.

Since the Baluch are a religious minority, the local Sunni clerics or *mowlavis* have since the early twentieth century played an important role in the political mobilization of intertwined religious, tribal and ethnic sentiments. Sunni theology seminars spread in Baluchistan under the Pahlavis, and bonds with Sunnis outside Iran, in particular in the Gulf, Saudi-Arabia and Pakistan, were strengthened. In the 1950s, the *mowlavis* led a violent uprising against the remaining traditional feudal elites, further galvanizing their role as political leaders. Conversely, Iraqi Ba'athists sought to exploit Baluch mythology to advance the pan-Arabist idea that the Baluch are in fact Arabs. While this strategy of creating an Iraqi proxy against Tehran seemed to fail, the Sunni factor is still central to Baluch ethnicist entrepreneurship.

In the 1960s, nationalist organizations such as the Baluchistan Liberation Front (BLF) emerged around underground and exiled supporters of Dad Shah. Their goal was an independent Baluchistan that should stretch to the Soviet Union, which, together with BLF's Marxist rhetoric, revealed Soviet leanings and backing. BLF also attracted support from PLO and Saddam Hussein. From the 1960s, BLF and other Baluch organizations waged a low-scale guerilla war against Iran, and from the 1970s, the Shah answered with a combination of violent clampdown and infrastructural development. A policy of amnesty and the termination of Iraqi support had by 1975 all but destroyed the Baluch insurgency, yet ethnic and sectarian tensions continued to mar the region.

The Baluch, in short, coalesce around a particular culture and historical tradition that they share with co-ethnics in Pakistan and Afghanistan, and which is recognized as distinct due to the particular socioeconomic and historical conditions of the region, the indigenous language and the fact that most Baluch are Sunnis—and as such, a "double minority" in Iran today.

DISCUSSION

It is clear that, on the one hand, the lack of distinction between categories and groups and, on the other hand, the myriad ways in which one can understand ethnicity, are two sides of the same academic problem: "the ethnic commonsense." The various statements about Iran's diversity outlined in the first half of this chapter, when presented as objective facts, are highly problematic. "Ethnicity" cannot be boiled down to self-identification with a particular *qowm*, or "ethnic group," but relates to a multitude of overlapping, intertwined and sometimes apparently contradictory factors. The only thing one can conclude "for sure" is that there is diversity—whether we view this diversity in religious, sectarian, linguistic, dialectal, tribal, regional, class or even racialized terms, or, most fruitfully, in all of the above terms simultaneously.

The outline of the four minorities shows that the linguistic criterion is rarely the sole basis of an ethnic self-understanding. Even though Azeris speak a Turkic language that is closely related to those of the Qashqais, Shahsevan and Turkmen, these four communities are divided by very different socioeconomic, historical and geographic trajectories. While Azeris are sedentary, partially urban and have played a key role in modern political history, the Turkmen, Qashqais and Shahsevan are or were until recently nomads; while the Azeris are Shiite, the Turkmen are Sunnis; while Azeris and Turkmen have co-ethnics across the borders, Qashqais do not. As such, the idea of "an Iranian Turk," distinguished by a linguistic commonality, is more a theoretic ethnonym than a reflection of lived experience.

In the case of the Kurds, language is certainly hailed by ethnicists as a main marker of "identity" that cuts across not only sectarian and tribal boundaries within Iran, but also across the territorial borders of Turkey, Iraq and Iran. However, the definition of the category "Kurd" is by no means uncontested: it is an umbrella term covering different peoples with certain shared cultural characteristics. The Arabs are perhaps the most "visible" of the communities in terms of language; in other words, the fact that they speak a Semitic language is arguably a key reason why their status as an "ethnic group" different from the majority is rarely disputed among Iranian scholars. Yet even if the Arabs spoke an Indo-European language, they would not necessarily have been better integrated with the Persian-speaking center: this can be concluded from the case of the Baluch, who are Indo-European speakers but among the least integrated of all communities.

There is no doubt that religion can play a pivotal role in ethnicity and that Sunnis are marginalized in the power structure of society in Iran. In the case of the Baluch and the Sunni Kurds, the situation is worse in the sense that they are discriminated against on two different but intertwined levels. This combination has arguably enhanced Baluch and Kurdish perceptions of marginalization. However, contrary to the Iranian nationalist argument, being a Shiite does not necessarily mean that one is well integrated. This is the lived experience of most of Iran's Arabs, who are Shiites, but in many ways deprived from economic development and barred from gaining political power. Choosing one criterion to the exclusion of others often results in downplaying either the commonalities or the differences between communities.

The four minorities have in their histories a number of similarities: a tribal past and/or present, which has intertwined the political trajectories of their communities with the centrifugal and centripetal fluctuations of Iranian state-building; historical periods of autonomy, secessionist activity, insurgency or banditry that are today hailed by ethnicists as symbols of a drive toward self-rule; and a geographical location in areas that are at once on the peripheries of the central authority in Tehran *and* within the spheres of interest of Iran's various historical foreign rivals and colonial powers. The similarities between the four collectivities, it can be argued, form a unique background on which modern ethnicist entrepreneurs were able to articulate narratives on identity and mobilize collective action, particularly in the chaotic aftermath of the Constitutional Revolution of 1908–11, in the 1940s after Reza Shah's forced abdication and again during the Islamic Revolution of 1978–9.

There are nonetheless significant differences among the four minorities and their role in Iranian history and contemporary society and politics. Seen in terms of a center/periphery question, the odd one out among the four is arguably the Azeris, who are generally well integrated and well placed in the socioeconomic and political hierarchy. However, as we shall see in the following chapter, Azeris have been no less active in ethnicist mobilization than, say, the Baluch. In other words, the socioeconomic or class factor is not a defining factor in ethnically framed self-identification and political activism. Nonetheless, it is important to appreciate that the three other minorities are among the poorest of all Iranians and that they live in areas that have been neglected in development policies and modernization schemes. In short, while socioeconomic standing may not always play a role in dynamics of ethnicity, when it does, it plays an important role.

In short, *āzari, kord, 'arab* and *baluch* were originally socioeconomic, geographic and linguistic categories used situationally according to changing contexts throughout history; these categories were invested with groupness through particular politicized social actions vis-à-vis modern state formation in the twentieth century. Yet even with this political mobilization, the categories still do not correspond neatly with clearly defined groups "out there"—not even when it comes to communities that appear culturally distinct, homogeneous and separated from other communities.

Proponents of minority rights today argue that the dominant position of Persian language and culture in state and society is a key source of marginalization. However, Persian-centrism is not a straightforward matter. On the one hand, if we accept that there is no specific ethnic group called the Persians, then Persian culture and language "belongs" to everybody, so to speak. This is the crux of the nationalist argument. On the other hand, it is impossible to fail to notice the pervasive Persian-centric notion in dominant narratives on "Iranian-ness." Persian language is fetishized to the extent that other languages in Iran are presented as secondary, if not outright antithetical to Iranian-ness. In public discourse, Persian language is sometimes simply called "the Iranian language" (*zabān-e irāni*), which creates a sense that non-Persian languages are *not* Iranian; indeed, as we saw in this chapter, some scholars have argued that Persian language is "the soul of Iran." While the proponents of Iranian nationalism do not understand the Persian-centrism as *ethnic* chauvinism, its critics perceive it exactly as such.

Similarly, we could argue that ethnic intermingling and the lack of distinguishable physical characteristics explain why Iranian nationalists can argue convincingly that cultural difference is unimportant, or that Iranians in fact constitute one homogeneous (supra-)ethnic collectivity. It facilitates a claim to racial unity, which is often rooted in the Aryan myth. If, for example, one scholar argues that around 85 percent of the current population is made up of "groups of Iranian origin,"[105] what role does that leave the rest? There is an implied notion of racial ancestry and historic precedence in such truth claims, one that leaves some parts of the population less "significant," or even alien, in the dominant discourse.

There is no easy or "correct" way to define the majority, yet posing the question in itself constitutes a challenge to long-held perceptions about Iran as seen from "outside"—and perhaps also from the "inside." As I have outlined in this chapter, the elusive majority can be explained either in terms of a "hidden ethnicity" or in terms of Iran being a special case for which Eurocentric, positivist frameworks of understanding ethnicity do not work. Both views, I will argue, are both right and wrong.

The problem with the first view, despite containing some cogent observations with interesting similarities to the Iranian case, is that it rests uncritically on the assumption that there are "groups" and "identities" *out there*. As we have seen, "Persians" are not simply a "group" that refuses to recognize itself as such. Thus, we may encounter a Persian-speaking Iranian from Tehran who would never identify as *fārs* in Iran, but would introduce himself as "Persian" when visiting Europe. When visiting a Turkic-speaking city in Iran, locals might identify him as *fārs*; probably, it would only occur to him to introduce himself as *tehrāni*. Even if we blame the hiddenness or elusiveness of the majority on a nationalist agenda, there is still no reason to insist on the actual existence of a Persian ethnic group or identity. What matters is how people identify themselves, when their identification labels change and why.

The second view is problematic for other reasons. While the supra-ethnic notion is presented by its nationalist proponents as an egalitarian idea of civic inclusivity, it is not non-ethnic. Even if we claim that Persians do not "exist" as a particular ethnic group, there still is a dominant majority: one that contains influential politicians, scholars, artists and intellectuals who are in one way or another shaping the dominant narrative of what it means to be Iranian.

While the supra-ethnic notion is thus not necessarily a convenient excuse for "Persians" to rule in the name of all Iranians, it certainly *is* utilized by a majority to legitimize Persian-centric views, policies and discourses. In representations of Iranian-ness, these views tend to neglect or belittle, by omission or over-glossing, ethnic diversity and the existence and importance of minorities. This politicization of culture is what Brubaker terms "ethnicity without groups."

Thus, even if we move away from reifying groups and essentializing identities, and even if we take into consideration the tendency toward exogamy, intermingling and lessened demarcation in some parts of Iran, we still have to take into account ethnicity. In the case of the supra-ethnic notion, we are dealing with ethnicity in the shape of a discourse on national identity. In the case of communities such as the Azeris, Kurds, Arabs and Baluch, we are dealing with ethnicity in the shape of discourses on local cultures. Neither of the two cases should be understood as "identities" *out there*; both are examples of politicized social action among certain, and by no means all of, the people who the politicizers (the ethno-political entrepreneurs, nationalist and ethnicist alike) claim to be representing.

CHAPTER 2

THE MINORITY ISSUE

THE DOWNFALL OF THE PAHLAVI MONARCHY DURING THE 1978–9 IRANIAN REVOLU-
TION brought about a short, intense period of activity in Iran's minority regions.
The movement against the shah was a broad coalition that spanned Persian speakers
and non-Persian speakers alike, and its leaders presented the revolution as an Islamic
road to social justice for women, minorities, industrial workers, students, farmers and
shantytown-dwellers.

Tapping into the stored-up discontent among Kurds, Arabs, Baluch, Turkmen and
Azeris, a range of political organizations rushed to champion demands for minority
cultural rights and socialist-inspired models of regional autonomy. Proponents of
ethnic rights among the minorities embraced these prospects of change, and many
pledged their allegiance to Ayatollah Khomeini in the belief that a state under him
would abolish the discrimination they had experienced under the Pahlavis. However, before long, these very same individuals and organizations turned into enemies
of the state. By the time of the Islamist power coup against moderates and leftists
in late 1979, many hopes of freedom and equality among the minorities had been
dashed.

The country was engulfed in violence, unrest and repression, while numerous
institutional and ideological barriers obstructed those minority activists who sought
to integrate themselves into the post-revolutionary political system. This system
showed little patience and tolerance for particularistic, local issues and demands.
Even though peripheral provinces were obviously far less developed than the center,
officials maintained that all regions had been equally oppressed under the Pahlavis:
no areas should receive special attention. Furthermore, the eight-year war with Iraq
made political leaders insist on national unity to the extent that demands from
minorities were tabooed, censored away and outlawed. An apprehensive, militant
and centralistic attitude came to dominate the state approach to the minority
issue.

Khomeini and his allies sought to merge ideals of theocracy and public participation into a coherent whole, relying on both Iranian nationalism and Shiite
fervor as sources of legitimacy. The system they instituted, however, was in effect
discriminative; to Sunni Muslim and non-Muslim communities, its Shiite nature
could be perceived as a fundamental, political challenge or even an existential threat.

Minority proponents soon questioned whether they would fare better under an Islamic Republic than they had under Pahlavi dictatorship.

In the first part of this chapter, I will outline major events, developments and changes in state-minority relations during and immediately after the revolution. The Azeris, Kurds, Arabs and Baluch will remain in focus to the near-exclusion of other minorities. Following this more or less chronological narrative, the chapter moves on to examine the legal-political implications of the new regime for the minorities and the socioeconomic conditions under which minorities have fared in post-revolutionary Iran. We then return to the chronology with an outline of key developments after Khomeini's death.

While the chapter refers to the results of a range of recent studies on the social, economic, infrastructural and developmental aspects of the center-periphery relation, it does not present new quantitative data or comprehensive statistical surveys. There seems to be plenty of indicators showing that the socioeconomic situation, rising expectations and a sense of relative deprivation all play into the minority issue—yet there is simply not enough research available to empirically establish any particular and clear correlation. Nonetheless, the socioeconomic overviews should allow us to understand ethnicity as variable and contingent processes shaped within particular social and political contexts.

The second half of this chapter explores moments in post-Khomeini Iranian history during which particular communities, with various motivations, have been mobilized, especially during what is termed here as ethnic unrest in the period 2005–7. The aim of detailing this unrest is to shift focus from ethnic groups to *groupness as event*. As Rogers Brubaker argues, such a shift of focus can enable us to take account of, and potentially account for, "phases of extraordinary cohesion and moments of intensely felt collective solidarity, without implicitly treating high levels of groupness as constant, enduring, or definitionally present."[1] It can also make us understand ethnicity as social action: events in which political entrepreneurs and organizations turn social, economic and political grievances into displays of antagonism. These events are situated—before, during and after the fact—in narratives on culture and history that reify groups.

"Organization" is here understood in its broadest sociological sense, spanning from social movements over political opposition groups and guerilla armies to the intellectual and ruling elites. This focus on entrepreneurship and organization does not imply a generalizing reduction of ethnicity to a cold calculation of rational instrumentalism. As social action, a range of often overlapping and sometimes contradictory motivations can drive ethnic framing, from spontaneous emotional outburst of anger to more abstract feelings of historical injustice.

As I will show in this chapter, Iran's minorities have since the revolution faced war, uneven development, regional disparity, political inequality, constitutionally embedded discrimination and a range of coercive measures. These are very real problems that feed into everyday micro-politics, which in turn can be framed ethnically at certain times and places—also by individuals we would not otherwise categorize with the somewhat dismissive terms "political entrepreneur." Since the official reaction to this ethnic unrest is the topic of a detailed case study in Chapter 3, I will here only outline the key events.

The sources used in this chapter range from generalized works of historical reference over important contributions to Iranian Studies to more recent social science and political literature from inside Iran and journalistic accounts. Despite drawing on this broad range of sources, this chapter cannot aspire to do more than scrape the surface of a huge complex of interrelated issues about which we have little accessible information. While the chapter is partly informed by documents recently made available in public archives in Britain, and by a growing literature from Iran, this is not a complete history of post-revolutionary ethnic politics. A proper, comprehensive historical account is still needed.

STATE AND MINORITIES FROM KHOMEINI TO KHAMENE'I

UPRISING TO SILENCE

During the transition from monarchy to Islamic Republic, Khomeini and the revolutionary leaders were naturally concerned that Iran's rivals would take advantage of the chaos. There was in particular a pervasive fear in the new ruling elite that foreign powers would exploit the volatile combination in the periphery of porous borders, fractured central authority and restive minorities. The outbreak of unrest and guerilla war in several minority regions already in the first months of the Islamic Republic's life seemed to confirm these fears.

With the Kurdish history of resistance to the Pahlavis in mind, it was to be expected that many Kurds participated in the overthrow of the monarchy. When the imperial army evacuated its mountain bases in 1978–9, Kurds seized the opportunity and took control of Kurdistan. However, it only took three weeks from Khomeini's arrival in Tehran on February 1, 1979, before clashes between Islamist revolutionaries and Kurds broke out. The ensuing guerilla war pitted the Revolutionary Guard and certain Shiite Kurds against leftist Kurdish parties (notably the Kurdish Democratic Party, KDPI, and the *Komele*), militias under local religious leaders (Mahabad-based Sheikh 'Ezz-od-Din Hosseini and Sanandaj-based Ahmad Moftizade) and various non-Kurdish guerilla groups that had split with Khomeini and now vied for Kurdish support (including the *Mojāhedin-e khalq*, or MEK, and the *Fadā'iyān-e khalq*).[2] Not before 1984 could the government again claim total control with Kurdistan.

The leaders of the Kurdish uprising were initially willing to negotiate with Tehran, and Khomeini originally suggested that the Kurds could obtain self-rule. Yet the gap in demands proved too wide for compromise. The Kurds demanded decentralization and autonomy; Tehran, however, was concerned with territorial disintegration and focused on combating a host of domestic rivals. Kurdish leaders presented their demands thrice in 1979, but these were rejected for being too broad—including the idea of a Kurdistan that would incorporate areas also inhabited by non-Kurds. The interim government instead prepared a solution guaranteeing Kurdish cultural and political rights, but Khomeini vetoed it before it was even presented. Indeed, Khomeini prevented the key Kurdish representative, the KDPI leader Abdolrahman Qasemlu, from attending the assembly that drafted Iran's new constitution.

According to some observers, the Islamic Republic leaders never genuinely wanted a peaceful solution,[3] and by 1980, dialogue had broken down. Disillusion turned the

Kurdish movement toward armed insurrection. While the KDPI demanded complete political autonomy from the central government, it never championed separation from Iran. Nonetheless, Khomeini maintained throughout the crisis that he was fighting "counter-revolutionaries" and "separatists."

The Kurds were split internally—primarily over land ownership, class issues and local bases of support, but also along communalist lines (Shiites against Sunnis, Sorani speakers against Kurmanji speakers, etc.). Sunni Kurds also clashed with Shiite Azeris in mixed cities such as Naqde. These fissures weakened the Kurdish resistance, and combined with Khomeini's intransigent opposition, all prospects of autonomy were thwarted. While the revolutionary leaders promised to pay attention to the plight of the Kurds, the Revolutionary Guard engaged brutally with insurgents (*peshmerga*) and the Hanging Judge, Hojjatoleslam Khalkhali, reportedly condemned hundreds of Kurds to death.[4]

By the end of 1983, practically all of Kurdistan was in Tehran's control although skirmishes continued. The KDPI, *Komele* and other Kurdish groups were outlawed and went underground or moved their headquarters to Iraq, Turkey and Europe. With this tenuous victory, the Islamic Republic had reached its main objective: to set an example in Kurdistan for the rest of the country's minorities. An estimated 50,000 Kurds lost their lives in 1978–88, which includes the Iran-Iraq War,[5] and the Kurdish movement never reached its objective of autonomy.

It did, however, successfully popularize narratives of a distinct national identity or *Kordāyetî*, as ethno-nationalism became the dominant discourse among some Kurdish communities. This discourse was fuelled in the early days of revolution by a renewed interest in the Kurdish language and literature, a flourishing Kurdish press, a revival of customs such as traditional dance and clothing and, for a short time, public schooling in Kurdish. The movement thus fostered a sense of solidarity despite and against internecine sectarianism, tribal rivalries and factional frictions with a profound impact on Iran's Kurds.

No part of Iran went untouched by the maelstrom of events that led to the consolidation of Islamist power. In Azerbaijan, the majority supported the Shah's overthrow, and many of the revolutionary leaders were of Azeri backgrounds. Yet there was also a marked fissure over leadership between the center and Azerbaijan, as many Azeris pledged allegiance to the local Ayatollah Shari'atmadari rather than to Khomeini. Combined with dissent over the drafting of the new constitution, tensions led to a short-lived uprising in Tabriz in December 1979. The Azeris expulsed pro-Khomeini forces from Tabriz, removed the governor and seized the radio station. The uprising was crushed, some Shari'atmadari supporters executed and the Ayatollah himself demoted and forced to silence.

Although Shari'atmadari did not promote any ethnic demands, and while he explicitly condemned any sign of separatism, he did hold open an option for future local autonomy. The movement thus had a regionalist aspect, and it has since been hailed by some Azeris as a symbol of blossoming ethnic awareness.[6] The revolution also prompted a sudden growth in the number of Azeri-language newspapers and journals, as well as the establishment of organizations, some of which fought for local autonomy, cultural rights and public education in the Azeri language.

In Baluchistan, the majority of the Sunnis reportedly did not participate in the revolution, arguably out of concern with the movement's overt Shiite radicalism.[7] Support for the revolution was limited to a small urban intelligentsia, and when Baluch militants took control of Baluchistan in 1979, the conservative Sunni clerics gained power. There were a few promising signs of change during the revolution. A Baluchi press came into being, as did various leftist groups and ethnicist organizations such as the Muslim Unity Party (MUP).[8] Most of these organizations called for autonomy but not, as the Baluchistan Liberation Front (BLF), for separation from Iran. For the first time in Iran's modern history, a Baluch was appointed Governor-General; he was, however, replaced with a Persian after just six months when Tehran sought to regain control of the province.

Khomeini allegedly promised MUP's leader Mowlavi Abdolaziz equal treatment of Sunnis and Shiites in return for his endorsement of an Islamic Republic at the March 1979 referendum.[9] Some Baluch groups, however, boycotted the referendum, attacked polling stations, took the new governor hostage and fought with Islamists. In the Experts Assembly, MUP representatives protested that the constitution did not mention local autonomy, or Sunni or ethnic minority rights, and Abdolaziz demanded that no particular school of Islam should be enshrined as national religion.[10] After a boycott of the second referendum in December 1979, clashes between Baluch and the Revolutionary Guard intensified. There were arguably also ethnic-sectarian dimensions to Baluch attacks on Shiite Sistanis, and vice versa.

As the Islamists consolidated their power, thousands of Baluch fled to Pakistan, the Gulf States and Europe, and some were imprisoned as separatists in Iran. While most ethnicists moved their activities abroad, a handful continued low-scale guerilla warfare against the Islamic Republic into the 1980s. Among these were some with Iraqi support, and others allegedly with monarchist support (such as the Baluch Unity Front).[11] Certain Sunni *mowlavis* gained power as the regime's intermediaries while others were prosecuted, executed or "vanished." Dissent was stifled through intimidation and a heavy military presence.

Khuzestan too was a hotbed of political activism.[12] In March 1979, a prominent local leader with tribal support who had participated in the revolution, Ayatollah Sheikh Shabir Khaqani, took control of Khorramshahr. Following internal disputes in early 1979, Shabir broke away from the local pro-Khomeini revolutionary committee, and formed an Arab ethnicist organization. Tensions spilled over into the streets as Shabir's Arab supporters clashed with pro-Khomeinists in Khorramshahr, with unrest spreading to nearby Abadan. While Shabir was firmly against secession, he did demand local autonomy; recognition of an Arab nationality in Iran's constitution; greater Arab representation in parliament; Arabic language in local administration, education and judicial system; as well as an allocation of the oil wealth for local development.

More militant ethnicists,[13] however, joined forces with leftist groups in the so-called Cultural Association for Arab People,[14] which allegedly received weapons and training from Iraq. When a demand for disarmament was rejected in the end of May 1979, armed clashes broke out, claiming many casualties. Negotiations were fruitless, and the new government deployed the Revolutionary Guard. Hanging

Judge Khalkhali's threats of executing Arab "traitors and separatists" provoked further protests. The final showdown came in July, when pro-regime militants captured Shabir, placed him under house arrest in Qom and executed several insurgents, but sabotage against oil installations continued.

Even though not all Arabs supported the rebellion,[15] the alleged ties of ethnicist groups with pan-Arabists abroad raised a fear in the ruling elite that persists to this day. Officials emphasize the important role played by Arabs in defending Iran against the Iraqi aggressors, thus implying that Khuzestan rejected Saddam's ethnic overtures. Indeed, apart from a 1986 demonstration against a newspaper article that allegedly contained insults against Arabs, there was apparently no ethnic unrest during the war. However, from exile, various groups continued to agitate for independence. In April-May 1980, one of these groups stormed and occupied the Iranian Embassy in London, demanding the release of their comrades from Iranian prisons.

Minorities outside of this book's focus were also affected directly by the revolution. In March 1979, clashes broke out between Turkmen and Islamist forces in the northeastern region of Turkmensahra (*torkamansahrā*). Here, leftists had established an organization to radically reorganize the agriculture by distributing former crown lands to local landless peasants. They denied paying taxes and together with various non-Turkmen, leftist guerillas, they formed 300 armed rural councils that clashed with the Revolutionary Guard throughout 1979, resulting in many casualties.[16] Even though some argue the rebellion did not receive broad local support,[17] it has nonetheless become a symbol of Iranian repression to Turkmen and leftist organizations. Sporadic guerilla warfare continued into the 1980s, and some Sunni Turkmen organizations are still fighting for their minority rights.

All in all, the downfall of the shah and the ensuing turmoil and war ushered in serious short- and long-term changes and challenges for Iran's minorities. As fighting grew bitter between leftists and ethnicists, on the one hand, and pro-Khomeini forces, on the other, minority activists realized that they would not achieve the promised autonomy. With violent clampdown, the advent of a new form of authoritarianism and the onset of war, they were forced into underground activism, exile, submission or silence.

A NEW ORDER

While the revolutionary leaders took a harsh stand on minority activism as a result of insurgencies and fears of foreign power manipulation, they also disseminated propaganda of ethnic equality. This equality, the leaders argued, was secured by the religious values of the Islamic Revolution. To implement these values in the new Islamic Republic, the state ushered in a far-reaching campaign of Islamization that changed all of Iranian society. The revolutionary leadership envisioned society as one Muslim body politic, where everyone was equal under God. The issue of minorities thus came across in Khomeini's speeches mostly as reactions to specific insurgencies or oppositional groups, or as part of a broader idealist narrative of breaking with the monarchic past and presenting a new vision of freedom and equality.

This vision of a new order in Iran was enshrined in the new constitution. Indeed, Article 19 of the constitution ensures equal rights for all citizens, while Articles 2 and

3 promise to eradicate all kinds of oppression and discrimination, and ensure that all people can participate in determining their own political, economic, social and cultural destiny. Article 14 claims to secure the rights of religious minorities. Yet, at the same time, the constitution is permeated with Shiite-Islamist exceptionalism, and as such, it can be read as a testimony to a new system of discrimination against large parts of the Iranian population.

It is, for example, demanded that the president not only be of "Iranian origins" and of "Iranian nationality," but also that he adhere to the Islamic Republic's fundamental principles and the official religion (Article 115). Since the official religion (*mazhab*) is specified as Twelver Shiism (Article 12), non-Shiites (and non-Twelver Shiites) were and are naturally barred from office. It is furthermore automatically demanded as a prerequisite, of any candidate for any political post, that he or she be completely loyal to the concept of *velāyat-e faqih* (Rule of the Jurisprudent), which is the Islamic Republic's foundational principle derived from Shiism. Together with the constitution's strict compliance to Islamic principles and law as interpreted by Shiite jurisprudents (Article 4), this creates a legal-political order that fundamentally discriminates against all non-Muslims and all non-Shiites—not to mention all women, no matter religious denomination.

Thus, while Islamist leaders maintained that they had endowed particular non-Muslim minorities (Zoroastrians, Jews and Armenian Christians) with a protected status under the new constitution, the same constitution actually imposed severe limitations on the rights of these and all other minorities. There are in effect numerous barriers to the advancement of non-Muslims and non-Shiites in administration.[18] Furthermore, the constitution recognizes the existence of only the three religions mentioned earlier in text, thus neglecting what is arguably one of Iran's biggest religions apart from Islam, namely Bahaism, and several other religions. Even mention of the diversity within Shiism itself is missing: while it refers briefly to other law schools of Islam, the constitution does not deal with the rights of heterodox Islamic sects, Ismailis, Sufi orders or alternative theological schools.

The constitution thus has had profound impacts on Iran's largest religious minority. Sunni Muslims are barred on the basis of their religious beliefs from supreme leadership, presidency and most of the key positions within the system. Even though Article 12 also mentions other law schools of Islam, Sunni Islam itself is not mentioned—and either way, those who practice these alternative schools of law are only free to do so within limited spheres, namely religious education, personal status affairs and litigations in courts of law. Unlike Jews, Christians and Zoroastrians, Sunnis do not have a set number of reserved seats in Parliament.

Furthermore, the administrative infrastructure is arranged in a way so that Sunnis arguably do not constitute a majority in any province,[19] which therefore makes the provision of Article 12—that regions with a majority of non-Shiites can have local regulations based on the alternative (Sunni) schools of law—a symbolic gesture rather than an actual possibility. In effect, the constitution makes second-class citizens of non-Shiite Muslims to the same extent as it does non-Muslims.

This was the key contention of Sunnis who criticized the constitution draft process in 1979. Yet the protests of the few Sunni spokesmen who were allowed into the proceedings were drowned by the votes of powerful Shiite clerics. Numerous official meetings with Sunni clerics proved to be little more than symbolic shows. Sunni mosques were closed down while new Shiite mosques sprang up everywhere, including in Sunni-majority areas. State media does not broadcast Sunni calls to prayer, and many Sunni theological schools are unable to function. Faced with no alternative, Tehran's Sunnis still have to pray at the Pakistani embassy mosque or in private homes.

There is also a high degree of tacit discrimination in administrative routines and culture. Non-Shiites are normally barred from heading ministries, state media, governorships and municipalities. Non-Shiites rarely advance within the military establishment, and they are naturally barred from the numerous clerical institutions that hold real political power. Non-Shiite minorities are severely underrepresented in the political system, and with the exception of Azeris (and to a much lesser extent, Shiite Kurds and Arabs), non-Persian speaking ethnic minorities in general are underrepresented in the upper echelons of official Iran.

However, a key issue is arguably not the constitution itself but the failure to implement it as law and policy. Article 15 of the constitution stipulates that Persian is "the official and common language and script"—yet it also allows for "the use of local and ethnic languages in their press and mass media" and for "teaching of their literature in school, along with Persian language instruction." Indeed, during the constitutional drafting process, minority representatives were promised minority language instruction in future state-run schools.[20]

Yet there was no obligation specified in the final draft, and the state has never acted on the promise. The literature of the "local and ethnic languages" was and is not taught in public schools, and only a few are subject to sporadic research, under the wary eyes of authorities, in a handful of academic institutes. Despite a short blossoming during the revolution, non-Persian languages and their speakers are in effect severely curtailed by a consistent state opposition.[21] Those involved with non-governmental minority-language media have suffered from repression, censorship and intimidation, and only at intervals and under tight control have minority journalists and authors been permitted to publish in their own languages. Ethnic, religious and linguistic diversity were until recently seldom treated in school textbooks,[22] and children are generally not allowed to speak other languages than Persian in school.

In the Supreme Council for Cultural Revolution's doctrinal resolution, "The Principles of Cultural Policy in the Islamic Republic of Iran," Paragraph 5 of Section C states as key objectives "the strengthening of national and religious unity." It also declares that these objectives should be pursued with "attention to ethnic and religious aspects" (vizhegi-hā-ye qowmi va mazhabi).[23] It is, however, noticeable that while the constitution mentions minority languages, the Supreme Council only stresses the importance of promoting and disseminating Persian. In post-Khomeini Iran, such examples of omissions and emphases, indicative of institutionalized ethnolinguistic preferences and discrimination, have become key issues for a new wave of ethnically framed protests.

Like its predecessor, the Islamic Republic is a centralized state. Revolutionary leaders initially promised that the new state would endow all local communities with their own representative bodies. "All the affairs of the country should be managed through councils," the high-ranking revolutionary leader Ayatollah Taleqani announced during the constitutional drafting process. In contrast to the Pahlavi period, when the state apparatus forced an "Aryan identity" upon all ethnic groups, there would be no such "fascist demands" in the Islamic Republic: "it is not necessary for a Sunni Baluch to become a Persian-speaking Shiite," as Taleqani put it:

> If all the people who lived in Iran believed in Shiism, spoke Persian and hailed from one nationality [*melliyyat*], then a [normal] parliamentary system could solve all problems. We all know that this is not the case. There is only one solution: for the self-rule of peoples [*khod-mokhtāri-ye khalq-hā*] to be recognized officially.[24]

Yet in the same discussions, other politicians stated that it was too early to institute a federal model for Iran, and the suggestion of a "Council of Peoples" (*majles-e khalq-hā*) or a "Council of Provinces" (*majles-e iyālāt*) to represent minorities and regions alongside the national parliament was eventually rejected.[25] The upheavals in minority regions and, subsequently, the war were used as excuses for not decentralizing power.

Local governance in the shape of "City and Village Islamic Councils" (*showrā-ye eslāmi-ye shahr va rustā*) was nonetheless enshrined as a principle in the constitution (Article 7). Article 101 explicitly states that the purpose of such councils is to "prevent discrimination in the preparation of programs for development and welfare of the provinces." Yet council elections were not instituted before 1999, and today, the power of these councils is severely curtailed by parliamentary, clerical and military institutions. The state has furthermore not lived up to Article 103, which stipulates that centrally appointed officials must abide to local council decisions.

Crucially, provincial governorships in minority regions were and to some extent still are in the hands of Shiites recruited from outside the areas they govern. Even though parliamentarians nominally represent specific areas and in theory are supposed to address home region concerns, minorities were and are generally not allowed to form their own political organizations. Such organizations are, almost automatically, suspected of disloyalty, treason and separatism. Furthermore, one observer has interpreted Article 9 of the constitution as being implicitly addressed to minority autonomists:[26] "no individual, group or authority has the right to harm even slightly the political, cultural, economic, military or territorial independence of Iran by exploiting the name of freedom."

Minority proponents were and are thus forced to work within "cultural" or religious organizations created or approved by the state, and then only if they can provide evidence of their loyalty toward the *velāyat-e faqih*. To all this, it should be added that Iran's Islamic Penal Code is formulated in sufficiently vague language to encompass a wide range of cultural, political and civil activities that can be deemed as attempts to "disturb" public order and security.

In short, while the revolutionary leaders announced the abolition of Pahlavi discrimination and promulgated an image of ethnic equality, and while they did formulate the basic tenets and shape the institutional framework in a way that could ostensibly safeguard at least some minority rights, the reality of the post-revolutionary order was nonetheless one of legal and institutional discrimination.

CENTER AND PERIPHERY

At the time of the revolution, many of Iran's ethnic minorities lived in villages, often isolated and scattered over rugged, inaccessible terrains. Even though broad programs for modernization, commercialization and land reforms had changed Iran under the Pahlavis, traditional agrarian structures were largely intact in minority regions. Education and hygiene campaigns notwithstanding, many of these peripheral regions still suffered under illiteracy and a lack of health services and access to basic utilities.[27] With the partial exception of Khuzestan's oil industry, the Pahlavi state had concentrated investment and infrastructural development in the Persian-speaking center, neglecting the minority periphery.[28] Even the once prominent provinces of Azerbaijan fell behind in the rapid economic progress of the late Pahlavi years.

The Islamic Republic inherited these problems of severe regional disparity. In addition, the revolutionary chaos, the regional uprisings and then the onset of the 1980–8 Iran-Iraq War had a severe impact on the periphery. Kurdistan and Khuzestan were heavily militarized while the civilian population suffered under indiscriminate bombings, claiming huge casualties and causing rapid depopulation. Some 65 percent of all Kurdish villages were damaged, abandoned or totally destroyed during the war,[29] thousands of Iraqi Kurds fled from Saddam's chemical warfare into Iran and long stretches of border were mined while farmland was expropriated for military use. In Khuzestan, major cities were bombed and some almost entirely evacuated, and while infrastructure suffered greatly, it was often rebuilt only to meet military purposes. Some 16,000 Khuzestanis lost their lives during the war, and many towns are still in disrepair. Large military bases were erected on Iran's borders, and nearly a decade after the war, there were still 200,000 troops stationed in Kurdistan.[30]

The fear of minorities becoming a fifth column in the geopolitical game fostered a political culture of suspicion toward minority demands. Minority organizations, media and public personalities were treated as hostiles and potential spies. Research on the minority issue was limited to security aspects of military importance. After the war, western Kurdistan and eastern Baluchistan remained militarized, ostensibly to combat smuggling and fight insurgents. At times, these areas have been administered from military bases and through martial law, and economic investment has often focused on military infrastructure. Since locals' relations with central authorities were thus often conducted through military representatives, these circumstances further cemented a feeling of being under occupation among some minority members.

During and immediately after the revolution, agriculture and industry in many areas suffered from sudden structural changes, spontaneous confiscations and redistributions of land. Revolutionary land reforms were often met with local resistance.[31] The state announced as a goal that by 1992, Iran should be self-sufficient in agricultural production. Though it has failed to reach this goal, the state increased its financial assistance to agriculture from the late 1980s onward. In a bid to win back hearts and minds in the rebellious peripheries, the Islamic Republic announced in 1982 a plan to develop "marginalized regions" (*manāteq-e mahrum*). During the war, this plan was partially set into motion through the so-called Construction Effort (*jahād-e sāzandegi*) scheme. Iranians from across the country were sent to the war-ravaged regions to build and rebuild roads, bridges, ports, railways and irrigation systems; to install electricity grids and dig wells; to distribute seed and fertilizers and to construct parks and recreational facilities.

With a renewed attention to the economic situation after the war, President Hashemi Rafsanjani also launched a broad reconstruction drive to rebuild war-torn areas. As a result of these and subsequent efforts, the general infrastructure has improved greatly across Iran since the revolution. While there were 26,000 km of paved roads in Iran at the eve of the revolution, there are now over 160,000 km; in just ten years, roads in rural Iran were extended from 8,000 km to 64,000 km. Such improvements greatly assisted the integration of far-flung peripheries into a rapidly developing national grid of transport and commerce.

However, while these efforts somewhat improved conditions in Khuzestan and Kurdistan, eastern regions such as Baluchistan rarely benefitted from attention. Authorities found it difficult to persuade doctors, engineers and experts to station in such remote and dangerous regions.[32] At the same time, it seems that concerted state attempts to encourage migration to Baluchistan have also created considerable local resentment.[33] Coupled with rural-urban migration and its detrimental impacts on agriculture, Baluch society became embroiled in narcotics trafficking and the related crime that flourishes across the Afghan border. Westernmost regions such as Khuzestan and Kurdistan also saw a rise in smuggling throughout the 1990s, in part exacerbated by sanctions against Iran and by war in neighboring Iraq.

After the Iran-Iraq War, healthcare, educational and welfare systems expanded in the peripheries. In an effort to meet the explosive population growth, the state built numerous new universities in minority regions, some plagued by inefficiency but all badly needed. In particular, the foundation of the semi-private Islamic Azad Universities across Iran and the allocation of state-supported university enrollment for students from "deprived areas" constituted important improvements. Even though universities in minority regions often remained unattractive choices for students and academics alike, and although skilled students from minority regions often chose universities and jobs in bigger cities, the spread of higher education had a profound impact.

While the urban-rural migration tendency may in the long run speed up individual integration and ethnic intermingling, it rarely contributes to the progress of the minority regions themselves. Whereas literacy rates reached 88 percent in Tehran province in 1998, they were still at 68 percent in Kurdistan province.[34] Sistan-Baluchistan today remains the province with the fewest educational facilities, the largest number of illiterates and the least in terms of social amenities and cultural activities. Nonetheless, increased literacy arguably raised awareness in many areas, including minority regions where parts of the young population felt left behind in the rapid progress of the 1990s.

A recurring source of discontent among minorities is that the ruling elite did not proceed to decentralize power and economic development as promised during the revolution. Regional planning, in the words of Hooshang Amirahmadi, "became subordinated to sectoral planning, as in the past, and received little attention."[35] By the 1990s, the bulk of heavy industry was located around cities such as Tehran, Isfahan, Zanjan and Mashhad, and as much as 40 percent of the total industrial labor force was employed in Tehran Province. As only one-fifth of Iran's population is located in the eastern half of the country, regions such as Baluchistan and Khorasan saw little development.

Decades of inattention, mismanagement and neglect in development policies were reflected in various indicators of welfare and progress. In 1991, Kurdistan and Sistan-Baluchistan scored lowest in life expectancy of all the provinces. In 1996, Sistan-Baluchistan was singled out as the most "neglected" of all provinces. Together with Khuzestan, Sistan-Baluchistan was among the five provinces receiving the least state support for rural infrastructural development, and together with Kurdistan, among the five receiving the least support for urban development.[36] Even certain Azeri-inhabited areas, especially Ardabil, were far behind the economic progress seen in the central areas. Sistan-Baluchistan and Kurdistan today still have some of the highest rates of unemployment in Iran.

An official report concluded in 2006 that development of minority regions since the revolution has been insignificant.[37] However, while it is true that most of these regions have consistently lagged behind in indicators of post-revolutionary economic growth, it is important to appreciate the overall general growth—and in particular, the significant developments in welfare achieved under the Islamic Republic. In the words of sociologist Kevan Harris, the "welfare regime has registered success at reducing poverty, lessening rural-urban gaps, and stabilizing population growth," and in doing so, it has managed to target "some of the gaps in social policy that earlier corporatist welfare regimes across the Third World failed to address."[38] By expanding the national welfare, education, transport and commercial frameworks, the Islamic Republic has managed to incorporate large sections of the population in a developmentalist state-building project, even when some of these sections are opposed to the regime.

This is a crucial aspect in understanding the rise of ethnicism: seen on a national scale, the general socioeconomic progress has made those residing in the periphery aware of relative deprivation. While certain "big-push" projects such as the sugarcane industry in Khuzestan has benefitted minority regions on some levels, it has also underscored the unequal distribution of power and resources. In the words of Harris, it has become easy for political entrepreneurs to create a "social consensus" that while protecting the networks supporting the ruling elite from downward mobility, the state is excluding others from the middle class.[39] This sense of exclusion limits the horizon of possibility within a context of raised expectations and civil empowerment. When combined with a sense of exclusion based on cultural parameters, it creates a perfect breeding ground for ethnicist activity.

INTEGRATION AND SEGMENTATION

Post-revolutionary Iran has been characterized by the reciprocal dynamics of integration and segmentation, ethnic intermingling and ethnic demarcation. The Iran-Iraq war seems to have simultaneously accelerated these processes. Some scholars argue that since ethnic sentiments were put aside to defend the nation-state, Iranian nation-building reached its apex during the war;[40] indeed, the participation of minorities in the war effort is routinely praised in state-sponsored literature.

Azeris, for example, played a highly important military role, and as such, the importance of national defense combined with the mobilization of religiously framed sentiments seemed to outweigh any other sentiment, including that of ethnicity. However, in the post-war era, a new generation of Azeri ethnicists has used the eulogized image of the Azeri war effort as an asset in promoting specific local concerns. Similarly, wartime displacements played a mixed role: among the thousands of Khuzestani war refugees, for example, more Arabs than non-Arabs returned to the southern cities of the province,[41] even when there were no economic prospects. On the other hand, significant numbers of Kurds, Azeris and Arabs who had fled their home regions settled permanently in other, mostly-Persian-speaking, cities of the center, where they either integrated with their surroundings or coalesced in ethnic enclaves.

Several other dynamics seem to have enhanced post-revolutionary ethnic inter-mixing and exchange. Apart from rural-urban migration and trade, the practice of dispersing both military service and allocated university seats throughout the country have, for example, had the impact of introducing different communities to each other. The rapid spread of Persian literacy among minorities after the revolution has made millions of non-Persian speakers able to consume, and contribute to the production of, nationwide media. Domestic tourism is a large industry in Iran, and the state has actively promoted it as a way of cementing national unity. These signs of intermixing and integration notwithstanding, it seems that the sense of being situated in a neglected periphery has augmented feelings of ethnic discrimination among many minorities after the revolution.

Little research has been conducted on inter-ethnic relations in post-revolutionary Iran. In one of the few examples, an interesting study on marriage preferences, scholars showed that among eight ethnic groups, Azeris, Kurds and particularly Arabs were less likely to marry outside their communities than Persians (fārs)—and, surprisingly, the Baluch.[42] The study concluded that Arabs experienced the greatest "social distance" from other ethnic groups. Although mostly geared at "proving" the supposedly strong loyalty of minorities toward Iran, another study, derived from a national survey, showed that Persians and Azeris had the lowest levels of economic cooperation and cultural exchange with other ethnic groups. The Baluch were shown to be the recipients of the fewest attempts at outreach, exchange and cooperation from other ethnic groups.[43] The study also showed that Persians and Azeris had the greatest similarities in views on "national identity" and that Persians enjoyed complete cultural advantage and prestige over all other groups.

The dynamics of ethnic segmentation and integration, and its inherent contentious issues of equality on the societal micro-scale, began to be reflected on the political macro-scale in the 1990s. Despite the creation of a number of new units after the revolution, provincial borders were nowhere congruent with the borders of historical minority regions. Azeris are today spread out over five provinces, of which two carries the name Azerbaijan. In one of these two provinces, there are also significant numbers of Kurds and other minorities. The Sunni Baluch still share their province with the relatively more powerful Shiite Sistanis, while Arabs since 1925 have been paired administratively with the largely non-Arab areas north and east of what was previously known as Arabistan.

Revolutionary calls for minority self-rule did not, in other words, translate into significant post-revolutionary ethnic reshuffling of provincial borders. The post-Khomeini period, however, saw a marked tendency toward regionalism (*mahal-garā'i* or *nāhiye-garā'i*), that is, regionally framed demands for increased access to economic resources, political power and administrative independence. Prior to and after the revolution, rivalries between various regional elites spawned a number of new administrative units. In the few cases where the state gave into ethnically framed regional demands, it either masked the new province with non-ethnic terminology (such as in the case of Golestan or "Garden," which partly corresponds to Turkmensahra) or created a province that was nominally "ethnic" but only contained a slice of the total community (such as in the cases of Kurdistan and Lorestan).

Regionalism, however, does not always have explicit ethnic framing. In one of the few examples of research on this important topic, Houchang Chehabi has documented how the Azeri people of Ardabil fought for and gained status as a separate province in 1993—among other things, by evoking their collective war effort. The research shows that local concerns need not be tied up with explicitly "ethnic" concerns; that the Azeris are not a single, united and unified entity; and that there are, in the words of Chehabi, "peripheries within the periphery."[44] However, with the revolutionary father's death in 1989 and the gradual opening of space for public debate, Iran entered a new period of ethnically framed mobilization of discontent. As Chehabi has argued, the very populist discourse of the post-revolutionary regime had allowed for citizens in the peripheries to become more assertive in their demands from the center.[45]

As they slowly returned to the political and public arena in the late 1980s and early 1990s, ethnicists who had abandoned the leftist organizations and their particular idea of self-rule for "national minorities," or were too young to have been associated with the revolution and its warring factions, turned to more ethnically demarcated, locally based demands. It was, however, the reformist wave of the late 1990s that made it possible for them to express these demands more clearly and boldly. The nationalization of politics in post-revolutionary Iran had brought with it new forces.

A MOMENT OF RELEASE

The end of the Iran-Iraq War and the demise of the Islamic Republic's father brought about a relatively more open political atmosphere. Under President Rafsanjani (1989–97), Iran underwent economic reconstruction and international rehabilitation. With Khomeini's death, however, Iran also lost a strong-handed arbitrator, and factional rivalries behind the curtains soon spilled over into the public arena. Rafsanjani's attempts at cooling the regime's radical rhetoric and policy also paved the way for reformist currents, and eventually the presidency of Mohammad Khatami (1997–2005). The early years of Khatami's presidency was a period of rhetorical moderation, rapprochement with the West and relaxation of social and cultural policies. Mahmud Ahmadinejad's election as president in 2005, in contrast, marked a fundamental militarization of the political system, as well as increasing tensions within the ruling elites. All of these developments affected Iran's minorities.

The ideological and factional differences aside, the three presidencies had in common the dual rise of nationalist state rhetoric (the topic of Chapter 3) and new currents of ethnicist counter-state discourse among the minorities. These developments were molded by international changes challenging the Islamic Republic. The collapse of the Soviet Union in 1991 had a significant impact on Iran. To the north, numerous new states took shape, some of them with populations that identified in ethnic terms similar to those of Iran's minorities. In the east, the Soviets had left Afghanistan with a civil war that was eventually quelled by a new Sunni fundamentalist Taliban state hostile to Shiite Iran. To the west, Iraq suffered under the Second Gulf War while its Kurds became more self-assertive. With the gradual spread of satellite TV and, eventually, the Internet, all of these changes became topics of discussion and sources of inspiration among Iran's minorities.

Under Khomeini, the state had restricted the use of minority languages. Only a handful of minority language periodicals were allowed to operate, and then only if they adhered to state ideology. Apart from state propaganda, the literature permitted in minority languages was generally limited to religious topics. After Khomeini's death, however, the state allowed a handful of publishers and bookshops to cater to non-Persian speakers. The licensed literature was still limited to the non-critical kind, but with the gradual easing of restrictions, bookstores began to carry literature from neighboring countries. Under Rafsanjani, some minority language journals and newspapers were revived and a number of new ones came into being. The state launched several radio programs, and eventually radio stations and TV programs in the languages spoken by minorities, as well as by extra-territorial audiences in which the state had a propaganda interest: Arabic, Azeri and Turkish, Sorani Kurdish and Baluchi. Ethnic diversity was now also depicted in schoolbooks and state media propaganda, as were nationalistic symbolism and sporadic references to Iran's pre-Islamic past.

While the political and cultural arena thus somewhat expanded under Rafsanjani, it was a loose coalition of reformists, religious nationalists, intellectuals and students that spearheaded the boldest attempt at redefining the Islamic Republic in this post-Cold War world. In the 1997 presidential elections, the coalition mobilized voters enthusiastic for Khatami's promises of *mardomsālāri* (popular rule), increased participation of women in public affairs and respect for minority rights. The combination of suppressed discontent, the spread of higher education institutions in the periphery and the emergence of new media turned some minority regions into breeding grounds for student unions and grassroots organizations supportive of Khatami's discourse on civil rights and civil society.

Under Khatami, sensitive issues became common topics of discussion in the press, in political associations, on universities and in the public sphere in general. As intellectuals, artists, journalists and political activists ventured to address head-on the state of human rights, cultural freedom and social equality, stored-up concerns of ethnic minorities also surfaced. In 1997, Khatami's new cabinet announced that "strengthening national unity and harmony while respecting local cultures" was part of its strategy.[46] For the first time since the revolution, minority members were appointed to key positions in local and provincial administration, and reformist organizations sprang up across minority regions.

Even though censorship and self-censorship continued to prevail, the reformist government markedly broadened the limits for minority cultural activity and research. Following Khatami's election, the number of independent minority-language media rose exponentially and, despite occasional clampdown, had a huge impact in some areas. By 2000, Iran had 15 radio channels and 7 TV stations allocated for regional and provincial programming, including some in minority languages. Khatami had talked directly about the problems of communities such as the Arabs and Kurds—sometimes even speaking *in* Arabic and Kurdish—and subsequently won the majority of their votes. He had thus demonstrated the power of a largely neglected political potential.

This new trend of politicians addressing the minority issue intensified throughout the reformist period 1997–2005. Minority regions voted overwhelmingly for reformists who expressed concern with provincial disparity. Voter turnout rose drastically in Kurdistan and Baluchistan, the two provinces that previously had the country's lowest turnouts.[47] One survey claimed in 2005 that 93 percent of the Kurds interviewed believed they had experienced positive political developments under Khatami.[48] During the first ever elections for City and Village Councils, held in 1999, minorities embraced the opportunity to vote for local representatives. In 2003, voter turnout for the second City and Village Councils elections increased in minority regions, even when there was a nationwide decrease in participation.[49]

Yet as Iran experienced a freer atmosphere, a gap appeared between reformists and ethnicists. To some of the minority members who had supported Khatami in 1997, the reformists did too little, too late. In 2001, minority spokesmen complained about the president's lack of support for minority rights and about insufficient funding for minority cultural activities. At the same time, the resurgent secular-nationalist opposition and the religious-nationalist reformists grew increasingly worried with the ethnicists, and each side accused the other for willingly or unwillingly threatening national security and unity. Reformist politicians had given way to more radical demands and discourses: the minority issue was no longer a taboo in Iranian politics, spokesmen had become emboldened and discontent soon boiled over.

The 2005 presidential election campaigns took place as ethnic unrest shook Khuzestan and Kurdistan (see later in text), and most contenders engaged in some form of interaction with minority constituencies: the reformist candidates visited Luristan and Baluchistan and prayed with Sunni clergy; conservative candidates visited Azeri, Turkmen and Arab regions. Khatami's spokesman, Abdollah Ramezanzadeh, angered conservatives by threatening with an election boycott in his Kurdish constituency. Due to general discontent with the political system, this threat eventually materialized with a very low turnout in Kurdistan. While ethnicity had now become a key variable in Iranian election dynamics, it was nonetheless Ahmadinejad—arguably the only candidate who did *not* address the minority issue specifically, but rather social injustice generally—who won the elections.

THE STATUS QUO

As president, Ahmadinejad has so far taken a cautious line, and rarely addresses the minority issue in the same direct fashion as the reformists. Yet he has also proved to be keenly aware of discontent in the peripheries, and has spent significant time touring far-flung and impoverished border provinces. Ahmadinejad's populist tendencies eventually led him and his supporters to a flirt with nationalist rhetoric unheard of in the history of the Islamic Republic. Yet, so far, this has arguably not meant that his policies have been manifestly more Persian-centric than other presidents. Ahmadinejad ritually emphasizes that all Iranians are equal and that "Iranian" does not signify one ethnic group. Nonetheless, the general clampdown on reformist and oppositional activity under Ahmadinejad has had detrimental impact on minority politics, and combined with the nationalist rhetoric, his government has been perceived by ethnicists as discriminative and chauvinistic.

The increased attention to minority grievances during election times should not obscure the pervasive anxiety that the minority issue generates among Iran's ruling conservative elites under the Leader Ayatollah Khamene'i. When local and regional demands are framed ethnically, they are perceived almost automatically as dangerous stepping-stones to separatism. Minority activists are routinely branded as traitors to the nation and mercenaries of foreign powers. In 2000, the Leader warned an assembly of government officials that foreign enemies were seeking to undermine the Islamic Republic by exploiting minority discontent. Khamene'i also made a rare reference to his own Azeri roots to stress that "all Iranian ethnic groups care for Iran and the Islamic Republic, and they see Iran as their homeland."[50]

The same year, the Minister of Intelligence warned that enemies are seeking to manipulate the minority issue, and in 2004, he gloomily predicted that future domestic conflicts in Iran would be "social and ethnic" rather than "political."[51] Since then, military authorities have regularly warned of foreign enemy infiltration in minority regions, and of attempts to sow discord along ethnic and sectarian lines within Iran. Whereas the reformists opened the floodgates of minority mobilization, conservatives re-employed the hostile vocabulary of the Khomeini era. The minority issue thus also played into factional disputes in Iranian domestic politics.

During the 2005–7 ethnic unrest in Iran (see later in text), conservative politicians and media routinely blamed reformists with their lenient policies and "naivety" for having allowed ethnicist groups to operate and grow. The popularity of reformists in minority regions was seen by some conservatives as evidence that the reformists were in fact inciting unrest in order to discredit the conservative government that took over from Khatami in 2005.[52] In 2005, the high-ranking conservative Ayatollah Jennati attacked those who exploited ethnic sentiments for their presidential campaigning and warned that they were in fact doing the enemy's work by creating discord among Muslims. This concern was not limited to politicians. Professor Hamid Ahmadi (see Chapter 5) of Tehran University warned that the candidates' "instrumentalist" abuse of ethnicity was detrimental to national unity, potentially opening inroads for both foreign manipulation and domestic "anti-Iranian currents."[53]

These anxieties were and are closely connected to regional and global developments, and particularly with the so-called War on Terror. The US President George Bush's inclusion of Iran as part of an *Axis of Evil* in 2002 marked the end of all previous attempts at establishing a dialogue between the United States and Iran. The Americans ramped up pressure on Iran through sanctions, intimidation and psychological warfare. With the invasions of Afghanistan and Iraq in 2001 and 2003, Iran found itself surrounded by US military and allies. Tehran has since repeatedly claimed that the United States has employed militant organizations among Iran's minorities as proxies against the Islamic Republic. Washington, on its part, routinely accuses Iran of interfering in Afghanistan and Iraq, including manipulation of ethnic and sectarian divides. This belligerent relationship impacted directly and detrimentally on Iranian state-minority relations.

However, the belligerence also went beyond the tangible military threat. Biased Western "research" on the minority issue in Iran and conferences hosted by US neo-conservative think-tanks under banners such as "a federal solution" for Iran's ethnic groups seem to confirm Tehran's suspicions and have elicited negative Iranian responses across the board.[54] Former CIA directors and operatives have openly recommended that the US government strive to turn ethnic tensions into military advantages against the Islamic Republic.[55] Arrogant, delusional "well-wishing," such as "how a *better* Middle East would look" if maps were redrawn along ethnic lines,[56] has reinforced the feeling among many Iranians that they are a target for neo-imperialist divide-and-conquer strategies. Such statements and activities fuel a siege mentality that bears directly on ethnic politics inside Iran.

Iranian fears have been reinforced by numerous journalistic reports of covert Western infiltration. In 2006, the investigative journalist Seymour Hersh claimed, through unnamed high-level US officials, that the United States already had "units" working among Iran's Azeris, Kurds and Baluch. Hersh reported that apart from intelligence gathering, the aim with these units was to undermine the regime by encouraging "ethnic tensions."[57] Hersh and other journalists have also alleged that Israel is mobilizing Kurdish groups in Iraqi Kurdistan against Iran. Indeed, there have been numerous reports and information leaks about US and Israeli support for militants in Baluchistan and in Kurdistan (see later in text). Such allegations correspond with other Western media reports about how US Marines have conducted research on whether Iran could be prone to violent ethnic and sectarian fragmentation, and with reports that radical minority organizations and terrorist groups inside Iran have been funded by a $75 million allocation by the US Congress for promoting democracy in Iran or through CIA's classified budgets.[58]

Such reports appeared while US neo-conservatives were pushing for a removal of the armed wing of the *Mojāhedin-e Khalq* organization from official terrorist lists and while the United States pushed for harsher international measures against Iran. Reports alleging covert activities are almost always based on anonymous sources, but US (as well as British and Canadian) officials have also officially invited and met with representatives of various ethno-nationalist and separatist organizations.[59] These signs, indicating the existence of a program for indirect warfare against Iran, have made it easier for an increasingly militarized state apparatus in Tehran to brand discontented minority activists as foreign stooges. It has placed all human rights activists, the opposition and even the reformists in a precarious position, forced to balance between support for minority rights and resistance to foreign manipulation.

With the gradual elimination of reformists that began in 1999 and intensified in 2005, and with the far-reaching clampdown on all kinds of opposition activity following the post-election unrest in 2009, Iran's human rights activists and pro-democracy movements have seen many setbacks. These setbacks were directly related to the heightened anxiety concerning US aggression in the region, which was in turn enhanced by the actual military threat on Iran's borders. On the trajectory from post-Khomeini moderation and post-war reconstruction over post-Cold War diplomatic rapprochement to post-9/11 militarization, Iran's minorities experienced both an opening and a closing of avenues for expressing ethnically framed sentiments and releasing pent-up frustrations. Even though Khamene'i has managed by and large to maintain a conservative status quo and suppress major challenges, ethnicist activists have succeeded in placing the minority issue on any future Iranian government's agenda.

ETHNIC MOBILIZATION IN POST-KHOMEINI IRAN

AZERBAIJAN

The well-documented role of Azeris in the creation of the modern Iranian nation-state, their integration with the overall society and their long history of staunch patriotism invite prominent scholars to make sweeping statements such as the Azeris "do not suffer any discrimination due to their ethnic backgrounds."[60] While it is true that Azeris generally have good access to power in Iran, the same scholars, however, also recognize that there is among some of them a growing movement for ethnic rights, cultural awareness and local autonomy.[61] This is the paradox of Iran's largest minority—a community so large that most Iranian scholars never use the word *minority* to describe it.

The current Azeri ethnicist movement took shape during the revolution when relatively small but very vocal organizations such as the *Anjoman-e āzarbāyjān* (Azerbaijan Society) demanded, through pamphlets and seminars, an end to what they considered historical oppression against Azeris as an ethnic group. Scholars and political activists spearheaded this post-revolutionary mobilization.[62] Through journals such as *Vārliq* and *Yoldāsh*, these ethnic entrepreneurs propagated Azeri cultural links across the border while criticizing Iranian state policies. Despite the political ruptures in the region, many of them retained direct links with Marxists and ethnicists in the Republic of Azerbaijan (henceforth ROA).

In the Soviet era, Moscow first pursued a strategy of promoting autonomy for Iranian Azeris, but from 1981, it strategically shifted toward the idea of uniting what was now termed "North" and "South Azerbaijan" (Iran). In the glasnost years, new Azeri organizations in ROA, many headed by former Communist apparatchiks, benefitted from a more open political climate. They cultivated the so-called literature of yearning (*adabiyāt-e hasrat*), which conveyed a poetic nostalgia for an imagined time when all Azeris were one. The nationalist People's Front of Azerbaijan,[63] established in 1989, grew in importance after the ROA's independence declaration in 1991 and during the Nagorno-Karabakh conflict of 1991–4. Among the Baku-based ethno-nationalists were also a number of Iranian-born activists who "converted," after the disintegration of the USSR, from socialism to ethno-nationalism.

Cross-border ethnicist activity gradually increased in the years leading to the breakdown of the Soviet Union. In 1989, a crowd surged over the border post at Nakhjavan and into Iran, where family members greeted them. As this symbolic action was repeated along the border, the Iranian state reluctantly welcomed it in the name of Shiite brotherhood; ethnicists, however, used it to revive cultural bonds. Most important was the establishment of a pro-Western Azeri state to the north, which changed Iran's foreign policy calculus and, to some extent, influenced its internal dynamics.

The 1992 election of nationalist president Abulfazl Elchibey in Baku caused some concern in Tehran, even though Elchibey's pro-Turkey and "unification" rhetoric did not procure him much support among Iran's Azeris. The occasional Iranian support for Armenia during the Nagorno-Karabakh War further soured the relationship between the two countries. Elchibey's successor, Heydar Aliev, initially took a more pragmatic approach, but in 1995 he expelled Iran from an important oil deal due to US pressure. In 2001, there were heightened tensions between Iran and ROA (and in extension, Turkey and the United States), fuelled by disagreements over naval borders in the Caspian Sea, access to oil reserves and ROA's friendly relations with Israel. Despite significant improvement, there are still occasional tensions.

A variety of Azeri ethnicists are active in Iran today. Some, particularly university students, call themselves *hoviyat-talab*, "identity-seekers." One scholar has traced the first signs of this movement to 1993: that year, Azeri students protested against a survey, allegedly conducted by Iranian state media, on public attitudes toward Azeris, and at a meeting with MPs from Azerbaijan, students forcefully raised their concerns.[64] The demands of the Azeri student movement range from increased autonomy to federalism, but student activists, primarily concerned with human and civil rights agendas, generally advocate the protection of Iran's territorial integrity.

At the other end of the spectrum, there are pan-Turkists and ethno-nationalists inspired by chauvinist ideologies from Turkey and Caucasus. These radicals argue for federalism, separation of Azerbaijan from Iran, uniting with "Northern Azerbaijan" or even the idea of a "Greater Turan" that includes all Turkic speakers from Greece to China. Due to the complete lack of unbiased and comprehensive surveys, it is impossible to estimate how many Azeris feel that their culture is threatened by the current regime or by general Persian-centric nationalism. However, it seems clear that among ethnicists, moderates by far outnumber radicals, pan-Turkists and separatists.

Apart from the activities of these organizations, the more significant events of ethnic mobilization often appear to be more or less unorganized: young people who may not otherwise be politically articulated sometimes flag ethnic symbolism when regional issues are raised, such as during sports events, cultural events or demonstrations to save or protect local landmarks. Similarly, there may be many Azeris who privately support the cultural revival without being willing to risk direct political involvement.[65] Even estimating their numbers would be futile, and there are certainly also a great number of Azeris who disagree with ethnicist agendas. The latter includes numerous Azeri intellectuals with Iranian nationalist tendencies who deem the ethnicist agenda to be misguided and detrimental. It could also be said to include the masses of "Persianized" Azeris—that is, Iranians who hail from Azerbaijan, but do not speak Azeri or associate with Azeri culture.

One of the articulated Azeri grievances concerns their representation in Iranian popular culture as backward or ignorant. In this (Persian-language) culture, rural

Azeris are portrayed as old-fashioned "hillbillies," Azeri-accented Persian is ridiculed and the stereotypical *tork* is seen as synonymous with an exaggerated and misplaced sense of pride. For centuries, jokes about *tork-e khar* (Turk donkey) have flourished among Iranians, and there are numerous examples of negative stereotypes in modern movies and literature. Only very recently have progressive Iranians advocated against portrayals that link negative cultural aspects to particular minorities. Ethnicists nonetheless perceive of this ridicule as part of a historical pattern of discrimination and marginalization that persists today.

This pattern, ethnicists argue, is most evident in the denial of Azeri language rights. Although Azeri is by all accounts Iran's second largest language, Azeri ethnicists claim that for almost a century, the state has systematically prevented its use and growth. Language rights have become a key concern at this time despite, or perhaps because of, the fact that Azeri culture and language arguably fare better today than ever before in modern Iranian history. Many of the Azeri ethnicists today combine the demand for language rights with a drive to imbue the self-designation as *tork* with pride and respect. They deem the word *āzari* as an ethnonym to be a Persian-centric historical distortion.

Azeri media, literature and research flourished under Khatami, and access to media based abroad became much more widespread. US-funded media such as *Rādiyo Fardā* regularly focus broadcasts on the Azeri issue, and the Azeri-language division of *Radio Free Europe/Radio Liberty* allegedly has a broad following among Iranian Azeris.[66] In reaction to the broad popularity of satellite TV from Turkey, there is now a state-run, domestic TV station catering to the Azerbaijan provinces with many shows in Azeri—although some ethnicists complain that the Azeri spoken on these shows is deliberately diluted with Persian. Furthermore, the drastic spread of access to online social media has arguably facilitated new bonds between Iranian Azeris and Turkic speakers abroad.

There are signs of a surging interest in Turkic languages and literatures, which has increased the ability of Iranian Azeris to read and write Azeri. One study claims that 60 percent of Iranian Azeris are now able to read Azeri, despite lacking standardization in spelling.[67] Such developments are augmented by new research, mostly non-state and amateur endeavors, which have yielded new dictionaries, educational material and several new publishing houses. Azeri literary masters such as Mohammad-Hosein Shahriyar and Samad Behrangi have been rediscovered and reprinted, as have Turkic tales popular in neighboring countries such as *Dede Qorqud, Qāchāq Nabi* and *Kur Oghlu.*

From the early 1990s onward, Azeri scholars regularly delivered public lectures and organized cultural events in Tabriz and beyond. Private Azeri classes were established in the 1990s although Azeri was and still is not permitted as teaching language in public schools. For the first time, an academic program on Azeri opened in Tabriz University in 1999, and since, a few Turkic and Azerbaijan Studies departments have appeared in other universities. Azeri student organizations popped up across Azerbaijan and in Tehran, where they arranged Azeri poetry-reading sessions and lectures on Azeri linguistics.

Under Khatami, a number of local Azeri-language newspapers were given license to operate, including some with radical agendas such as support for Turkey's policies, anti-Armenian rhetoric and historical revisionism. However, several of these were closed in a clampdown in 2001–2. Student organizations and their newsletters have flourished since the 1990s, even though they too have been subject to occasional bans under the accusation of promoting pan-Turkism or separatism. A scholar stated that in 2006, 146 Azeri-language and 73 bilingual periodicals were published in Iran.[68] There is, additionally, a multitude of Azeri-language weblogs and websites, although some have been targeted by state censorship.

Azeri ethnicist organizations today range from officially recognized cultural centers and NGOs over student groups to outlawed parties of varying size.

Groups in the latter category have only once had a chance to be an official part of post-Khomeini politics. Mahmud-'Ali Chehregani (aka Chohraganli), a linguistics professor of Tabriz, ran for the 1996 parliamentary elections. As a self-professed supporter of the Islamic Republic with a background in the Revolutionary Guard, Chehregani was able get away with advocating Azeri cultural rights as a key part of his election program. Despite rumors of official manipulation in the first round, Chehregani won around 100,000 votes. Yet on the morning of the second round, the election committee suddenly removed him from the ballot. In the ensuing unrest, hundreds of supporters were allegedly detained and beaten by security forces.[69] Chehregani is now leading a radical ethno-nationalist organization from exile. The clampdown on him and his followers, however, arguably fed into an already existing trend of radicalization among some circles of Azeris.

Among other things, this radicalization expressed itself in anti-Armenian sentiments. Azeris vented their frustrations with Iranian support for Armenia during the Nagorno-Karabakh War in the early 1990s, and a number of ethnicists were arrested during demonstrations.[70] Iranian officials and nationalists have routinely accused both ROA and Turkey for exploiting Azeri sentiments in Iran (see Chapter 4), and in the late 1990s, scores of Azeris were arrested in Iran on accusation of being "Turkish spies." In 2001, an Iranian Azeri poet and ethnicist leader was subject to a failed assassination attempt by unknown perpetrators in Baku.[71] Grassroots cross-border solidarity aside, Iran's Azeris have rarely benefited from official foreign support.[72] Nonetheless, the American (and allegedly an Israeli) military and intelligence presence in ROA has provided the Iranian authorities with a handy standard explanation with which to dismiss ethnicist activities.

Due to its sheer size and economic importance, the Azeri community in Iran has been the most successful of the four minorities in gaining representation in the political system. During the reformist years, MPs have been increasingly vocal in pushing regional agendas, and when Khatami was putting together the cabinet for his second government in 2001, Azeri MPs successfully demanded at least two ministers with Azeri backgrounds. The MPs were also able to demand native Azeri governors for the provinces of East and West Azerbaijan.

However, despite these developments and despite the 1990s cultural revival, there were also signs of dissatisfaction with Khatami. In September 2000, Azeri intellectuals wrote an open letter to Khatami, protesting the government's disrespect for Azeri language and demanding a national television channel, the right to education in Azeri and the employment of more Azeris in local governance. There have also been numerous outbursts of collective, symbolic ethnicist activity to which we return in Chapter 6. It was, however, the 2006 Azerbaijan unrest that finally placed Azeri ethnic grievances on the political map of post-Khomeini Iran.

KURDISTAN

Simplistically speaking, three strains of ethnicism are active among Kurds in Iran today. One is found among activists who took advantage of the freer political climate under Khatami, when the government sought to tentatively reconcile with some of the Kurdish oppositional groups that had been branded enemies under Khomeini. These activists are sometimes organized in NGOs that operate with tenuous state acceptance, but most work as independent intellectuals, artists, scholars and human rights activists. They generally adhere to principles of non-violent resistance, and some believe that the Islamic Republic can be reformed to accommodate Kurdish aspirations. The second strain is represented by ethno-nationalist underground organizations and by guerilla armies, several of which operate across the border from bases in Iraq. The third and arguably largest strain is the internalized discontent among the mass of Kurds who have experienced revolutionary mobilization over civil war to violent post-revolutionary clampdown, as well as their children who grew up after the death of Khomeini.

Due to restrictions on freedom of speech in the sensitive border areas, it is impossible to estimate the numerical sizes of the three strains of ethnicism, between which there is, additionally, a significant overlap. While the major political changes in the region in the 1990s and 2000s had a great impact on Iran's Kurds, it is also evident that domestic socioeconomic conditions fuel much discontent today, some of which comes to the fore in ethnically framed outbursts of anger and protests. Furthermore, the avenues chosen for expressing discontent also seem to depend to some degree on sectarian, tribal and linguistic affiliations. There is ample evidence that ethnic unrest is more prevalent among Sunni than Shiite Kurds,[73] but there is practically no research available on current differences in loyalties and sympathies in relation to geographical location and tribal ties.

While Kurds did see some positive political improvements during Khatami's rule, their region remains underdeveloped in economic terms. Kurdish-inhabited provinces scored very low in the 1999 UNDP human development index,[74] and in an official 2006 report, they ranked as among the least developed provinces in the country.[75] In 2001, local MPs claimed that 80 percent of the Kurds lived under the poverty line,[76] and in 2005, the UN's Special Rapporteur claimed that Kurds "seem to suffer [a] disproportionate inadequacy of services such as water and electricity and unsatisfactory reconstruction efforts."[77] Generally, Kurdistan is today marred by weak infrastructure and few educational facilities and health services, and Kurdish society is characterized by poverty and high rates of unemployment. There have been numerous cases of unrest related to this underdevelopment, including riots caused by cuts in gas supplies during harsh winters. However, apart from these socioeconomic problems, the main grievance appears to be cultural repression.

Branded subversive, Kurdish cultural activities were repressed during Khomeini's rule.[78] In the late 1990s, however, there was a cultural blossoming, and the use of Kurdish languages in the public sphere, for example, is today more widespread than under Khomeini. In 1994, two state-sponsored Kurdish-language magazines appeared, and these were supplemented under Khatami by five new journals and a number of student newsletters. The Kurdish art scene also experienced a relatively more open period under Khatami, as exemplified in a handful of internationally acclaimed movies. For a brief period, Kurdish languages were taught at Sanandaj University. Yet Kurdish today suffers the same general discrimination as other minority languages. Students have regularly protested against this discrimination and the failure of the state to fulfill promises of establishing Kurdish university courses.

The spread of the Internet and satellite TV has enabled a new generation of activists, and outlawed Kurdish parties, to communicate across borders. Those with satellite dishes potentially have access to at least five party-affiliated TV stations catering to Iranian Kurds.[79] Cultural events and political manifestations became more organized, numerous, visible and outspoken under Khatami, and sometimes such manifestations led to clashes with security forces. The reformist years furthermore saw the reappearance of Sunni Islamic literature and publishing houses in Kurdistan, and the establishment of new Sunni religious associations. Khatami's Shiite Kurdish governor of Kurdistan Province, Abdollah Ramezanzadeh (see Chapter 3), appointed, for the first time since the revolution, a number of Sunni Kurds to important official positions.

However, following Ramezanzadeh's complaint against the Guardians Council's nullification of parliamentary elections results in two Kurdish cities in 2000, and following widespread protests and clashes, Ramezanzadeh was removed from the post and was succeeded by a non-Kurdish governor. Despite the Council's ruling, 18 Kurdish politicians were elected to parliament, raising hopes of increased influence. A Kurdish parliamentary coalition was formed, but already by 2001, its members threatened to resign en masse to protest continued discrimination against Kurds and Sunnis. Today, there are few Sunni Kurds in local administration, and there are many indications that Sunni Kurds feel alienated and marginalized from official institutions, particularly those with religious framing.[80]

The wars in Iraq and the establishment of a Kurdish Regional Government (KRG) in 1991 had profound impact on Iran. The lessened restrictions on cross-border exchange and the sense of pride espoused by Iraqi Kurds have bolstered Iranian Kurdish ethnicism. The late 1990s also saw visits of political and cultural delegations on both sides of the border. Iran's official relationship with KRG is, however, complex and tense. Kurds have claimed that Iran assassinated 200 activists on Iraqi soil in the early 1990s,[81] and Tehran has often hosted Iraqi opposition while fanning intra-Kurdish rivalries. Similarly, KRG hosts thousands of Iranian refugees, among them anti-Iranian guerillas and their supporters. The Kurdish issue constitutes a complex geopolitical problem.

Among the militant groups are the *Komele,* KDPI (the Democratic Party of Iranian Kurdistan) and PJAK (the Party for Kurdistan's Free Life). These organizations have been engaged in a protracted war with the Iranian state. In 1989, the KDPI leader Qasemlu was assassinated in Vienna; in 1992, his successor, Sharafkandi, was killed in Berlin. No one has accepted responsibility, but Kurds blame Iranian agents. KDPI and *Komele,* both very active during and after the revolution, have today either scaled back their military operations or laid down weapons, but persist as underground parties. It is hard to estimate their support within Iran, but they certainly have active members in the large Kurdish diaspora.

The third group, the elusive PJAK, was formed either in Iraq in 1991 or in Iran in 1997.[82] According to most observers, PJAK is, or used to be, the Iran wing of the PKK (Kurdistan Workers' Party), which was based in Turkey until 1999, after which many members fled to northern Iraq. Following PKK founder Abdullah Öcalan's ideological line, PJAK has shifted from a leftist to a liberal discourse on democracy and human rights. It is ambiguous on the issue of Kurdish independence. In 2006, PJAK had an estimated 3,000 fighters, and relied on financial support from the Kurdish diaspora.[83] From its base in Iraq's Qandil Mountain range, PJAK launched a series of attacks against Iranian police and military in 2004.[84]

The group has ambushed convoys and outposts; downed helicopters; bombed energy pipelines and assassinated judges, religious leaders and Kurdish civilians deemed to be regime collaborators. PJAK also runs a sophisticated information campaign through various websites, an affiliated TV station and, until 2010, offices in Germany. Iran announced that 120 of its soldiers were killed by PJAK in 2005, and that number was possibly exceeded the following year. Battles were particularly intense during 2006–7, with Iranian aerial bombings across the Iraqi border—attacks that may have killed civilians and certainly created a huge refugee problem.

Examples of popular discontent and unrest are abundant, and often they are intertwined with cross-border events. In February 1999, scores of Kurds in Sanandaj protesting against Turkey's arrest of Öcalan were detained and beaten and three were killed, prompting Kurdish activists to express outrage at Khatami's apparent indifference. In 2005, just before the summer unrest, there were three episodes of clashes: in March, during *Nowruz* celebrations, in April when Kurds celebrated Jalal Talabani's election as President of Iraq and in June when Mas'ud Barzani was elected President of KRG. According to local sources, at each event, Kurds had gone into the streets of several cities in Western Iran to celebrate, dance, sing, chant slogans, hand out sweets, light fires, honk car horns and display the Kurdish flag and pictures of PKK leader Abdullah Öcalan. In all cases, security forces reportedly intervened, resulting in violence.[85] Yet by far the most widespread and violent outburst of ethnic discontent since the early 1980s occurred in the summer of 2005.

KHUZESTAN

Although Khuzestan is somewhat more accessible to researchers and journalists than Baluchistan and Kurdistan, state control and restrictions still makes it difficult to gauge public opinion. Research indicates that the majority of Arabs in post-war Khuzestan retain a traditional way of life and a distinct Arab culture, and that it is in this segment that varying degrees of Arab ethnicism flourish.[86] While the revolution saw significant ethnically framed unrest, scholars agree that Saddam's overtures to the Arabs during the Iran-Iraq War were largely dismissed and that ethnicist currents only resurfaced after the death of Khomeini. Khuzestani civil society organizations were instrumental in bringing about a landslide victory for the reformists in this province, and this in turn emboldened ethnicist advocates. Radical ethno-nationalists, mainly based abroad, also used this window of opportunity to renew calls for autonomy or independence.

Khuzestan was severely damaged during the Iran-Iraq War, causing large-scale displacements. Despite post-war efforts, the province still suffers from socioeconomic and infrastructural problems related to the war, including lack of sufficient housing, health services and educational facilities. Key cities such as Khorramshahr and Abadan still suffer from power cuts, polluted water and incomplete gas distribution networks. Environmental issues such as pollution from the oil and sugarcane industries also plague Khuzestan. Unemployment is grave and poverty widespread, particularly among Arab Khuzestanis, who also report numerous health problems related to poverty.[87] As with other minority regions, drug addiction is rampant among Arabs in Khuzestan.

Discontent with life in what is one of Iran's richest provinces in terms of natural resources is not always expressed in ethnic terms. Indeed, industrial action has a long history in Khuzestan, and in 2006–7 and 2008, there were protests among workers in the oil and sugarcane industries. Ethnicists, however, tend to link the dire socioeconomic position of Arabs directly to what they perceive is Persian-centric discrimination, and deliberate attempts to deny Arabs a share of the region's progress and welfare.[88] Their claims have been somewhat corroborated by the UN's Special Rapporteur, who after a very rare permission to investigate the minority issue first hand in 2005 announced that Arabs suffer from a variety of discriminative practices.[89]

These practices include forced relocation from areas with planned industrial development to camps without water, electricity and gas, as well as state expropriation of land simultaneous with the import of labor from Persian-speaking areas of Iran. Indeed, a key source of ethnicist discontent is the alleged expropriation of huge tracts of land from Arabs who stand little chance of defending themselves without the required documentation and in Persian-speaking courts. At least one MP has criticized the state-owned sugarcane industries and the military complex, and alleged that there was an ethnic aspect to their business operations in Khuzestan.[90]

Ethnicists claim that a 1998 document revealed a state strategy to eliminate Arab culture and change the composition of Khuzestan in favor of non-Arabs. They also point to the continued practice of using newly coined Persian names for places, cities and villages instead of the local Arabic names; the ban on teaching modern Arabic in the local dialect on the excuse that classical, Koranic Arabic is already taught in elementary schools; and the repression of Arab intellectuals, artists and journalists. The latter type of repression includes refusing licenses for many Arabic-language publications and refusing permissions to establish NGOs. Ethnicists also point to figures that allegedly show discrimination against, or at least disadvantages for, Arabs in all levels of education. Ethnicist organizations, both peaceful and militant, claim that their members are subject to systematic repression, including harassment, imprisonment and heavy sentences on charges of separatism or espionage.

The Arabs enjoyed some progress under Khatami, including a slight increase in the number of Arabs assigned to key local administrative posts. Ahmadinejad's government may have halted or reversed this trend, since one source claimed in 2008 that out of "the top 25" administrative positions in Khuzestan, only "two or three are Arabs."[91] Political organizations representing Arabs inside Iran are few and subject to a host of limits. The so-called Arab Women of Khuzestan Association played a role in Khatami's 1997 victory while the Islamic Concord Party[92] was apparently refused permission to operate under Khatami's government. Members nonetheless ran for office under a similar name, the Islamic Concord Committee, and won a number of seats in the 1999 City and Village Councils elections. Yet these pro-reformist groups soon suffered setbacks, and its leader and the Concord appears to be defunct.[93]

Several questions about Arab ethnicism in Iran are difficult to answer due to censorship, restrictions and dearth of research. The state claims that radical activities are instigated by Iran's enemies and directed from abroad. Iranian media often accuses various Arab governments of agitating the Arabs and provoking unrest. Developments in post-Saddam Iraq have impacted on Khuzestan, but it is impossible to ascertain to what extent. There have been scattered Iranian accusations of Saudi-funded covert activities in Khuzestan, including clandestine campaigns for mass conversion from Shiite to Sunni Islam.[94] Additionally, there is the question of the influence of Arabic-language satellite TV that is now widespread among Khuzestan's Arabs. Finally, there is the impact of a very active diaspora, particularly in the UK, on locals in Khuzestan.

Illegal groups headquartered abroad include the Arab People of Ahwaz's Democratic Front (Al-Ahwaz) and the Ahwaz Liberation Organization (ALO). The former is based in England and led by Mahmoud al-Ahwazi, who is accused by Iran of sabotage, terrorism and treason in aiding Iraq during the war. In a pan-Arabist, socialist-inspired rhetoric, the group claims that "Al-Ahwaz" (Khuzestan) has been occupied by Persians since 1925 and must be liberated. The latter, ALO, is based in Holland and was established by Arabs who were involved in the short-lived occupation of the Iranian embassy in London in 1980. The ALO argues for the separation not only of Khuzestan, but also of the Iranian side of the Persian Gulf. The ALO leader al-Mansouri was arrested in Syria in May 2006, from where he was allegedly extradited to Iran and sentenced to 30 years in prison.[95]

More seemingly moderate groups include the Al-Ahwaz Democratic Solidarity Party and its affiliate, the British-Ahwazi Friendship Society, which are based in the United States and UK, respectively, and champion a non-violent resistance strategy and autonomy within a federal Iran. The latter is registered with the Unrepresented Nations and People's Organization (UNPO), and is lobbying the Arab cause abroad. These organizations seem highly active online, but there is little evidence of broad support from within Iran. There have been several unconfirmed reports about historical cooperation between the British government and exiled Iranian Arab separatists.[96] It is very likely that this history of cooperation with colonial powers and regional neighbors has discredited some of the exile organizations in the eyes of Arabs inside Iran. That does not, however, mean that ethnicism is not a strong current. This has been testified by numerous cases of post-Khomeini ethnic unrest—the most violent of which erupted in April 2005.

In short, while the peaceful pro-reformist organizations have been closed down and civil society activists repressed, militant groups continue their activities—some probably with the support of foreign governments, and others certainly financed by the exile community. Much more important, however, is the general discontent among Arabs with socioeconomic conditions in Khuzestan, which is often connected in ethnicist discourses with what is perceived as ethnic discrimination.

BALUCHISTAN

Baluchistan remains Iran's most backward and neglected region. Many factors play into the dire economic situation, including a notoriously harsh climate, rugged terrain and meager sources of subsistence, and a region marred by droughts, storms, floods and earthquakes. Locals complain that they are not receiving sufficient state assistance to alleviate the impact of such natural catastrophes.[97] Even though Baluchistan has seen significant rural-urban migration since the revolution, at least half of the Baluch still live in villages or as nomads. In the mid-1980s, over 90 percent of Baluch villages lacked health facilities,[98] and even though this has improved since, Sistan-Baluchistan was still estimated in 1999 to be three times poorer than the richest province in Iran.

Today, the province has the lowest indicators for life expectancy, adult literacy, primary school enrollment, access to water and sanitation, as well as the highest rates of infant and child mortality; it also scores lowest on all indicators of economic development in official statistics.[99] Baluch women, in particular, suffer from lack of access to education and health care, as well as from forced marriage and sex trafficking. The marriage age of Baluch women is significantly lower than that of other ethnic groups—one study suggested an average marriage age of 16 years, two years below the national average. The same study showed that over 70 percent of the Baluch respondents were married to relatives and that only 15 percent had been able to choose their own spouse.[100]

Not a single of the already very few industrial production centers survived the political chaos of the revolution, and many construction projects initiated before the revolution were simply abandoned.[101] By 1994, there were only three medium-sized factories in Baluchistan, and today there is still little in terms of industry. Abject poverty, rampant unemployment and decades of underdevelopment have forced many Baluch into crime—to the extent that as much as half of the population in Sistan-Baluchistan may be directly or indirectly connected to smuggling of oil, gasoline and narcotics.[102] Even though Iranian media's coverage of the region is scarce and arguably biased toward military establishment views, there are constant reports of violence related to the smuggling industry, including armed skirmishes that have claimed many lives on both sides.

Ethnicists allege that the state covers up actions against Baluch ethnicist groups with the excuse that they are fighting narcotics, and drug smuggling and insurgent activity are indeed routinely conflated in state rhetoric.[103] While it is possible that militants finance their activities through the region's sole lucrative business, the Iranian state has yet to produce concrete evidence. Each year, dozens of people are executed for drug-related crimes, and Baluch organizations claim that many of them are in fact political activists. The state denies any ethnic discrimination in its security measures, but state-funded research recognizes the direct links between poverty, underdevelopment, regionalism and militancy.[104]

As a result, Baluchistan has become heavily militarized. Iran has built walls and trenches along parts of its Afghan and Pakistani borders, new military bases with advanced surveillance equipment have sprung up and the state may be maintaining extensive land mine fields along the border.[105] Baluch activists claim that security forces use excessive force to harass the local population, while special courts have been set up to deal with "bandits." State-run provincial media reports are often written in a tone that seems to warn or threaten locals.[106] Instability in neighboring countries often spills over into Iranian Baluchistan, which has also become home to thousands of Afghan refugees.

While urban civil society activism in regional centers such as Zahedan and Chabahar is slowly growing, Baluch ethnicist groups often operate in an isolated, rural region outside the vigilant view of human rights monitors. It is impossible to ascertain whether the few militant groups enjoy support in the broad population or only in specific areas or tribes or whether, as the state claims, they are simply foreign mercenaries with no local base of support. What is certain is that authorities have adopted harsh measures against these militants. Amnesty claims that there has been "a pattern of extrajudicial executions" since the 1990s, including assassinations of Iranian Baluch insurgents in Pakistan.[107]

The violence in Baluchistan is not always of the organized kind. Numerous clashes between Baluch tribesmen and state forces took place in 1990–1. In 1992, locals outraged by the establishment of a new military base clashed with the Revolutionary Guard in Zahedan. Since, there have been regular reports about tribesmen, insurgents and drug smugglers engaging Iranian security forces in sporadic fighting across the province.

To stifle discontent, Khomeini shut down Baluchi newspapers in 1980, and the small number of periodicals that have been allowed since face constant harassment and frequent suspensions—especially during times of unrest.[108] Many locals view the few radio programs broadcasted in Baluchi by the state as propaganda channels, and there is reportedly only one bookshop that carries Baluchi literature in the whole province. Endeavors to preserve or promote Baluchi language are limited to unofficial initiatives. Dissatisfaction with this cultural repression arguably fed into mobilization in support for Khatami, which in 1997 led the province to the highest voter turnout in Iranian history (91 percent). Under Khatami, the Baluch saw some improvements, even though there were still only two Baluch employed in important positions of local administration. Civil society organizations, cultural associations and student unions have been subject to a host of obstacles.

Baluch ethnicists argue that the political, socioeconomic and cultural marginalization of their province is rooted in Persian-centric prejudice. They claim that the central government is seeking to restrain the Baluch by forcibly relocating Baluch to isolated areas while encouraging non-Baluch migration into the region through promises of land, jobs and subsidized housing, thus manipulating the ethnic composition of major cities.[109] Resettlements have led to confrontations between locals and security forces in 1995, 2005 and 2009.[110] In September 2000, Baluch MPs wrote an open letter to Khatami complaining about the socioeconomic conditions that had deteriorated further with the onset of a severe drought. The same year, there were numerous reports of violent clashes between locals and security forces.

Baluch ethnicists often frame their identity discourse from the vantage point of a religious minority oppressed by a Shiite theocracy. The post-revolutionary shift in the local power balance away from traditional tribal leaders toward Sunni clerics has endowed these *mowlavi*s with the role of mediators of Baluch grievances. The encroaching religious-political propaganda of the state has further alienated many Baluch who nurture little hope of social integration and personal progress in a Shiite-dominated society.[111] At the same time, the increased power of the *mowlavi*s has also reportedly paved the way for increased conservatism, receptiveness to Taliban-style ideologies and even opposition to pre- and non-Islamic traditions such as *Nowruz* and music.[112] There have been several cases of sectarian violence, including riots, abductions and assassinations of both Shiite and Sunni clerics.[113] These tensions express a strained Baluch relationship not only with the state, but also with local Shiite Sistanis who are sometimes viewed as state collaborators.

Most significant was the emergence, around 2002 or 2003, of the small but highly active militant group *Jondollāh*. This group, probably not numbering more than a hundred members, claims to fight for democracy and minority rights in Iran, and utilizes Sunni-flavored rhetoric and symbolism in its videotapes and websites. The group's leader, Abdolmalek Rigi (d. 2010), was, according to Iranian media, a former student of a Wahhabi theological school and had fought with the Taliban in Afghanistan.[114] In his few communiqués, Rigi alluded to unity with fellow Baluch outside of Iran, as well as with other non-Persian-speaking minorities. In interviews, Rigi stated that *Jondollāh* aims to "protect the national and religious rights of the Baluchis and Sunnis in Baluchistan province,"[115] and he claimed that *Jondollāh* is not fighting for independence but for a democratic, federal Iran.

Jondollāh is nonetheless accused by Iran of separatist terrorism, of being ideologically aligned with Taliban and Al-Qaeda, and of being supported financially and logistically by the United States, Pakistan, Saudi-Arabia and/or the MEK. *Jondollāh*'s first publicized operations were when it allegedly abducted Iranian military and intelligence personnel along the Pakistani border in June and December 2005. The group then unleashed a series of bloody ambushes, assassinations, bombings of civilian and military targets and hostage takings in 2006–7 that together constituted the worst unrest in the province since the revolution.

Some Baluch in Iran also seem receptive to ethno-nationalist calls from across the border in Pakistan, where their co-ethnics enjoy a somewhat broader public space for expressing ethnic sentiments. The Baluch diaspora, mainly based in Sweden, UK, UAE, Oman and Saudi-Arabia, also plays a key role in the ethnicist demand for federalism. Numerous organizations in exile, some with leftist leanings, are very active online and abroad, yet it is uncertain whether these groups enjoy a considerable measure of support inside Iran, and in particular, outside the limited urban elites with access to the Internet. Nonetheless, family and tribal bonds stretch well beyond Iran's borders, and there is no doubt that ethnicist agendas travel along the networks created by these bonds.

Transnational Baluch ethnicism is a sensitive issue for many powers in the region. Intelligence shows that Taliban and Al-Qaʿeda use Pakistani Baluchistan as a safe haven. Iranian sources also claim that Saudi and UAE-funded Sunni madrassas actively disseminate ideologies of Sunni militancy, anti-Shiism and Wahhabism among Iran's Baluch, in particular by offering lucrative education opportunities to theology students.[116] With the straining of Iran's relations with Sunni powers, and with war still raging in Afghanistan, Tehran is naturally wary of Sunni extremism spreading into Iran. Finally, larger economic prospects also play an important role: in a bid to win the race to present resource-rich Central Asia with a commercial port, Iranians have focused on Chabahar while Pakistanis have developed Gwadar, both in Baluch areas. The much-discussed Iran-Pakistan-India natural gas line will also have to pass through Baluchistan, raising concerns of militant activities in the area.

As with Khuzestan and Kurdistan, the Baluch thus suffer from a combination of socioeconomic despair, constraints on political organization and cultural activity, and a position in a sensitive area of geopolitical importance.

ETHNIC UNREST, 2005–7

The suppression of ethnicist and ethno-nationalist organizations after the Islamic Revolution obviously did not eradicate general dissatisfaction in the periphery. Suppressed frustrations with a state that did not live up to the revolutionary promises of freedom and equality were gradually released after Khomeini's death in 1989. Beginning with the election of Khatami in 1997, ethnic mobilization became a prominent feature of Iranian politics, and discontent finally boiled over into protests and violence in the period 2005–7 when ethnic unrest shook Iran.

The April 2005 unrest in Khuzestan was triggered by the distribution of an allegedly fake government letter attributed to Khatami's advisor and in content similar to that of 1998 (see earlier in text). Apparently fanned by exile ethnonationalist organizations and Arab satellite media, riots, demonstrations and clashes with security forces engulfed Ahvaz and several other cities in Khuzestan from April 16.[117] There was widespread damage to banks, administrative buildings and facilities belonging to the police. Ethnicist groups claimed that security forces sealed off Ahvaz and disconnected water supply, electricity and telephone lines to certain Arab-populated neighborhoods. In the city of Mahshahr, at least two died when special police forces and *Basij* units used tear gas and bullets fired into the air to disperse rioters, who threw stones and burned car tires. Although the government only officially admitted to a couple of deaths, Iranian media spoke of dozens wounded and killed throughout the province.

Exile Arab organizations alleged that during the "Bloody Weekend Massacre" in Ahvaz, authorities employed "helicopter gunship," "live ammunition" and "debilitating poison-filled bullets."[118] Allegedly, forces were brought in from non-Arab parts of Khuzestan, including the city of Dezful. Over 200 people were arrested according to official sources, while according to the British Ahwazi Friendship Society, "more than twenty" were killed, "500 injured and 250 arrested" during unrest.[119] Amnesty later claimed that "at least 31 people" had been killed through "excessive use of force" and "unlawful killing," "possibly including extrajudicial executions"; Human Rights Watch quoted local sources and unconfirmed reports that over 50 had been killed. Authorities also arrested groups of people accused of planning sabotage actions, presumably against oil industry installations.[120]

The Iranian state blamed the UK, the United States and "Ba'thist" groups connected to Iraq for stage-managing the unrest in order to weaken the Islamic Republic.[121] State-affiliated media reported that the riots had started when members of a "separatist, Pan-Arabist" group, named the Arab People's Democratic Front, had read out an Arabic translation of the fabricated letter during a small demonstration in Ahvaz. They also reported that slogans in Arabic, such as "This is Arabistan," had been painted on the walls of Ahvaz prior to the unrest, and that ethno-nationalist propaganda material had been distributed on CDs and DVDs. State-run media also claimed that Arab satellite TV stations, especially *Al-Jazeera*, had instigated the unrest by airing propaganda. *Al-Jazeera's* offices in Tehran were closed, its employees expelled and its activities in Iran suspended indefinitely.

While Khatami dispatched a parliamentary committee to investigate the unrest, conservatives in Iran used the occasion to criticize the reformist government for not acting in a timely and appropriate fashion, and indeed for bringing about the ethnicist currents active in the unrest. Reformist media in turn suggested that the distribution of the fake letter was a conservative plot to disgrace the government, on the eve of elections, in a heavily pro-reformist region.[122] Khuzestani MPs collected signatures to petition the release of innocent detainees and for the security forces to show restraint. The Minister of Defense, Admiral 'Ali Shamkhani (himself an ethnic Arab), was dispatched to open a dialogue with Arab tribal leaders.

Shamkhani was also among several leading politicians who pointed out the many problems that had exacerbated local discontent, such as lack of access to drinking water, unemployment, cross-border arms smuggling and, generally, "mental distress" among locals who were still traumatized by the war with Iraq.[123] Despite such official signals of sympathy and understanding, the state nonetheless launched a widespread clampdown in which, Amnesty reported, "scores of Arabs were arrested."[124]

The June-August 2005 unrest in Kurdistan took place at a time of both heightened democratic prospects among locals inspired by events in Iraq and increased tension between state and ethnicists. As already mentioned, security forces confronted Kurds in at least three incidents prior to the unrest. However, the event that finally triggered the unrest was the July 9 brutal killing at the hands of the security forces of a young, local man (Shwane Qadiri, accused of being a member of an unnamed opposition group). When the news of Shwane's death spread, it sparked the most widespread protests in Kurdistan since the revolution. In the following weeks and months, almost all of Kurdistan was engulfed in demonstrations, riots and guerilla warfare.

Kurdish youth reportedly ransacked state property and attacked people considered regime collaborators. The riots coincided with the anniversary of the assassination of the KDPI leader Qasemlu, which further incensed locals in key cities such as Mahabad, where the unrest lasted for at least three weeks.[125] As photocopied pictures of a mutilated body and stories of Shwane's gruesome death circulated, the bazaar was closed in protest while demonstrators shouting slogans against the Islamic Republic clashed with anti-riot forces and set government buildings on fire. At least one officer died, a large number of locals were arrested and civil society organizations reported excessive use of force against the protesters.

Militant organizations took advantage of this popular unrest to launch a series of strikes on the Revolutionary Guard and local police. As unrest, demonstrations, guerilla attacks and assassinations spread throughout the region, martial law was imposed on several cities and anti-riot police and Special Forces were deployed. The cities and towns of Oshnaviye, Marivan, Saqqez, Sanandaj, Bukan and Orumiye were particularly affected.[126] An official investigation committee was dispatched to the area, while Kurdish MPs used the occasion to raise longstanding issues in parliament.[127] Iranian media coverage was relatively sparse and focused on accusations against foreign powers and separatists. International media were prevented from covering the events and had to rely on possibly exaggerated opposition accounts. Nonetheless, various domestic and international sources spoke of many casualties and hundreds of arrests, and of a broad clampdown on Kurdish opposition and human rights activists in the aftermath of the unrest.

The Baluchistan unrest differs from the other cases mentioned here in several ways. Most importantly, rather than being a broad-based popular uprising of the kind seen in Kurdistan, Khuzestan and Azerbaijan (see later in text), the unrest in Baluchistan was caused by guerilla and terrorist operations carried out by a small group. It also differs in the sense that what is here termed the *Baluchistan unrest* was actually a series of incidents spanning several years, and arguably continuing at the time of writing. The focus here, however, is limited to the period 2006–7, starting with an ambush on a motorcade near Tasuki in Baluchistan in March 2006 in which the *Jondollāh* killed 21 or 22 people, including civilians, prominent local officials and members of the security forces.[128] According to Iranian media, film footage showed victims being shot down execution style, and officials stated that the brutal attack was part of a foreign plot by the United States, UK and/or Al-Qaʿeda against Iran, aimed at sowing discord between Sunnis and Shiites. Authorities claimed that the attackers had fled to Pakistan, where local authorities were either unwilling or unable to locate or confront them.

Jondollāh announced they had taken seven hostages, and demanded in return the release of activists from Iranian captivity. A video recording was aired on *Al-Jazeera*, which allegedly showed the hostages pleading for the Iranian government to comply with *Jondollāh*'s demands. Other videos allegedly showing the killing of some of the hostages sparked outrage in the Iranian population. Officials promised retaliation and increased security measures. In the following month, Iranian media spread rumors of the *Jondollāh* leader Abdolmalek Rigi's death during anti-terrorist operations, while foreign media reported continued unrest in Baluchistan—including the assassination attempt on one official's life and the abduction of another. There were also signs that the security forces tried to appease locals to stem the rising tide of discontent.[129]

Then, on May 13, the *Jondollāh* again attacked a convoy and killed 12 persons, this time in the province of Kerman, west of Baluchistan. Army helicopters chased the attackers to a mountainous area near Bam, and while security forces reportedly killed several *Jondollāh* insurgents, Rigi himself remained at large.[130] In the days following the attack, Iranian forces claimed they had found weapons and documents proving *Jondollāh*'s affiliation with foreign powers. Tehran also demanded more effort from Pakistan in hunting down Rigi and his men. Meanwhile, another Baluch organization in exile claimed that the Iranian government had ordered indiscriminate aerial bombings of Baluch villages and that it strove to create tensions between Shiite Sistanis and Sunni Baluch.[131]

Scattered bombings occurred in December 2006, but the third major incident took place on February 14, 2007, when a car filled with explosives was brought to detonation in front of a military bus in Zahedan, Sistan-Baluchistan's provincial capital. Eighteen Revolutionary Guards and Basij personnel were killed, and a number wounded. It appears the bombing was meant as retaliation for a confrontation the previous day, during which three persons had been arrested and one killed in clashes with police.[132] However, when taking responsibility, *Jondollāh* announced the attack was an act of revenge for the execution of Khuzestani Arab activists. Authorities reported that they had apprehended five perpetrators who would later confess to working for Western powers during a session to be aired on national TV.

However, the arrests did not put an end to the unrest. On February 16, state-run media announced that a bomb had detonated at a school, that security forces were storming militants' safe houses and that there were gunfights throughout Zahedan. On February 17, state media announced that "ordinary people" had foiled two additional plots, one to bomb a mosque and another to assassinate a local cleric. The security forces additionally claimed they had discovered plans to assassinate both Shiite and Sunni clergymen. *Fārs News,* connected to the Revolutionary Guards, published pictures on their website, allegedly documenting that the militants were in possession of US-made weaponry. *Kayhān,* the Leader's mouthpiece, stated that a videotape had been confiscated during raids, which would conclusively prove *Jondollāh*'s ties to the United States and Britain. By the end of February, unrest in Zahedan finished, but the region remained volatile.

In Azerbaijan, it was a caricature that finally made discontent boil over. On May 12, the state-run *Irān* daily printed a drawing of an Azeri-speaking cockroach,[133] which was deemed deeply offensive by many Azeris, and triggered weeklong demonstrations and riots throughout Azeri-inhabited areas, spearheaded by student activists in Tabriz, Orumiye and Zanjan.[134] Unrest soon spread to other cities such as Hamadan and Ardabil, to villages such as Naqdeh and Meshkinshahr, and to Tehran, where there were demonstrations in front of parliament. The unrest culminated with huge demonstrations in Tabriz on May 23–24, where police, anti-riot forces and *Basij* units shooting tear gas clashed with protestors throwing stones, chanting slogans in Azeri and attacking public and private property.

Several people were allegedly killed during these and other clashes with security forces, and there were mass arrests. Slogans apparently went well beyond criticizing the newspaper: they reportedly included *"Hey, hey, I'm Turk!," "Death to Chauvinism!," "Russian, Persian, Armenian—all enemies of the Turks!," "Self-Sacrificing Azerbaijan is not indebted to anyone!."*[135] State officials initially showed sympathy with the outraged Azeri public, and were generally careful not to further antagonize them. In order to appease the Azeris, the state-run daily was suspended for a period and the caricaturist imprisoned, while the Minister of Culture apologized on national TV.[136] Some MPs vociferously condemned the daily and expressed support for the Azeris.

Yet at the same time, officials suggested that foreign governments such as the United States and Israel had infiltrated the movement, and were taking advantage of the Azeri outrage.[137] Media affiliated with the Revolutionary Guard allegedly claimed that some of the protesters were "separatists," "pan-Turkists," "anti-Iranians" and "anti-Islamists" who should be executed.[138] The unrest was followed by a comprehensive clampdown on ethnicist groups, including numerous arrests and intimidation.

DISCUSSION

The suppression of ethnic uprisings and the armed conflict between minority and leftist militants, on the one side, and the Iranian state and its new security apparatus, on the other, created a deep rift between center and periphery already in the earliest days of the Islamic Republic. Just as under the shah, but now under increased foreign pressure, the periphery became a multilayered zone of concern to the ruling elite: challenges to Khomeini's leadership, bases for armed insurgencies and sensitive areas bordering countries that were increasingly worried with Khomeini's radicalism. In addition to these concerns, Iran also had to face the Iran-Iraq War, the violent centralization of power in the hands of Khomeini and the far-reaching Islamization of public life and politics.

After a few years of more or less successful resistance, leftist forces were defeated in their attempt to use minority regions as strongholds for the anti-Khomeinist struggle. At the same time, the minority communities themselves were fraught with fragmentation caused by differing stands on the Islamic Republic, intra-minority factionalism, sectarianism and tribalism. Voices of minority discontent drowned and did not resurface before the end of the war and the death of the Islamic Republic's towering figure. By then, the position of ethnic and religious minorities as second-class citizens had been institutionalized through both tacit and explicit discrimination. The revolution had placed Shiite exceptionalism at the core of the new state's constitutional-legal framework, and in regard to minorities, the few constitutional changes since the Pahlavi years were mostly rhetoric.

Since only very few minority elites, intellectuals and activists had access to the new political system, avenues for political opposition and social critique were few and narrow. A new generation of post-revolutionary activists instead turned toward revamped ethnicist discourses that sought to explain the relative deprivation, social inequality and regional disparity in terms of ethnic and cultural discrimination. The dissemination, development and elaboration of these discourses were facilitated by the spread of new information and communication technology, by the expanding education system and by the reformists and student movements in the late 1990s. In short, the ethnicist movement is both the product of and a reaction against the Islamic Republic.

The small window of opportunity opened by the reformists was used to its fullest extent, and by the time minority discontent and ethnicist discourses had re-entered the public arena, it was too late for the authorities to wholly censor them away again. Instead, the post-Khomeinist state today relies on a carrot-and-stick strategy toward minorities: suppressing the loudest voices and clamping down when discontent is expressed in an organized manner, while at the same time projecting an image of ethnic equality, permitting state-controlled media content in minority languages and allowing for symbolic shows of multi-culturalism during election periods. The strategy of the ruling conservative elite seems to be to rely on the quasi-democratic mechanisms of political representation and participation, populist figures such as

Ahmadinejad and the corporatist welfare state to incorporate the masses and legit-imize their rule. When these measures fail to curb discontent, the Islamic Republic has a wide range of coercive mechanisms at hand. To justify clampdown, the ruling elite has a perfect excuse in the international pressure to which Iran is subject.

The dashed hopes and broken promises of reform and progress that Khatami left behind in the minority regions have in many cases turned into general disillusion with the political system in its entirety. In was in this context that Iran was rocked by ethnic unrest in 2005–7. It should be stressed that not all participants in the unrest necessarily perceived the protests in ethnic terms. As already mentioned, there could have been a wide variety of motivations at play, and the four cases described above differed widely. Yet while there were significant differences in the specific structural sources of discontent, in the tactical modes of creating disorder and in the slogans and demands presented, the four cases did have a number of similarities.

The first was location. Despite differences, the four areas are all highly sensitive border areas. As parts of an underdeveloped periphery, they are plagued by socio-economic problems that appear to be a structural malaise when compared to the center. In Khuzestan, key issues of discontent include land ownership and rights, lack of economic and infrastructural reconstruction, unemployment and environmental pollution. In Kurdistan and Baluchistan too, local discontent is rooted in poverty, unemployment and disappointment with the dismal pace of economic progress and political reform. The odd one out is Azerbaijan. Even though some Azeri areas are relatively underdeveloped, the Azeris in general fare well. Nonetheless, Azerbaijan is a periphery in both a domestic political and geopolitical sense, which was evidently a concern in the official response to the 2006 unrest.

The second shared factor was the role of social actors and ethno-political entrepreneurs. In Azerbaijan, and possibly also in Kurdistan and Khuzestan, the unrest was spearheaded by university students and civil society activists drawing on a legacy that stretches back to before the revolution. Azeri student activists were the first to organize hunger strikes and demonstrations that then spilled over into the streets. In Kurdistan and Khuzestan, it seems that demonstrations started more or less spontaneously in particular areas of cities known for being strongholds of ethnicism (Mahabad and Ahwaz, respectively). Also here it seems that young local activists (or, in the words of officials, hoodlums) played a key role.

While in the case of Kurdistan, militants (PJAK), from their rural strongholds, took advantage of an already existing situation in the urban centers, the reverse was true in Baluchistan: here, the unrest was sparked by a series of highly coordinated and well-planned actions in remote rural areas by armed insurgents (*Jondollāh*). Due to the many limits imposed on media access to Baluchistan, the extent to which the broader population participated in disturbances is hard to gauge; yet even official Iranian media reports seemed to indicate that either *Jondollāh* had operatives inside cities such as Zahedan or sympathizers spontaneously took advantage of the situation.

In short, ethnicist activists and ethno-political entrepreneurs played a key role. We do not have sufficient information to judge how organized the early protesters were. However, in all cases, Iranian state media indicated a level of technical sophis-tication and tactical organization, even though accusations of premeditation often seemed exaggerated to fit conspiracy theories of complex foreign infiltration.

The third common aspect is of course the ethnic framing. In three cases, the protests were sparked by what was seen as particular evidence of the state's gross misconduct and of deep-seated Persian chauvinism in the ruling elite: a caricature in a state-run newspaper (Azerbaijan), the actions of security forces (Kurdistan) and a politician's letter (Khuzestan). In the fourth, the Baluchistan attacks were legitimized in both a sectarian discourse and with reference to the suffering of other minorities.

There were also numerous indications of ethnic or sectarian tensions preceding the unrest. In Khuzestan, there had been reports about ethno-political graffiti and circulating ethnicist materials. Iranian officials directly acknowledged the power of Arabic-language satellite media in fanning the discontent. In Kurdistan, the unrest happened after a series of violent confrontations with security forces that had all been triggered by the marking of days with local and ethno-political importance by Kurdish activists. During the unrest, there were reports that protesters waved Kurdish flags and pictures of Kurdish heroes. In Azerbaijan, businesses that had the words *Fārs* or *Pārs* in their names were reportedly targeted, and in response to having been the object of ridicule, protesters shouted slogans that emphasized their "Turk" identity. In Baluchistan, *Jondollāh* targeted Shiites and Sunni "collaborators," and there were clear signs of Shiite-Sunni tensions in cities such as Zahedan.

Finally, in all cases, there were sporadic reports of the state and the military establishment using ethnic and sectarian differences to its own advantage: employing non-Arabs against Arabs, non-Azeris against Azeris, Shiites against Sunnis, and so on. This is a topic on which more research is needed. While it seems unlikely that the Iranian state is interested in deliberately and blatantly playing particular ethnic communities against each other, there is a long history of deploying forces from particular communities to other parts of the country.

The timing, our fourth and final factor, is also important. The unrest happened during a period of Iranian history characterized by contradictory dynamics. On the one hand, Iran had undergone a reformist period in which stored-up discontent could to some extent be canalized into open critique and a cultural revival; it was also a period when some among Iran's minorities were optimistic about the changes in the region, including the establishment of Kurdish autonomy in Iraq. On the other hand, the conservative offensive against reformism culminated with Ahmadinejad's election as president in 2005. This was a time when foreign powers, spearheaded by the United States, seemed determined to force through regime change in Iran, which naturally affected Iranian politics and security concerns. It was against the background of these contradictory developments and dynamics that ethnic discontent boiled over into radical and violent protest.

CHAPTER 3

DIVERSITY AND ORDER

[When] Hellenes fight barbarians and barbarians with Hellenes . . . this kind of antag-
onism should be called war; but when Hellenes fight with one another we shall say that
Hellas is then in a state of disorder and discord . . .
—Plato, The Republic

WHILE NUMEROUS STUDIES HAVE BEEN DEVOTED to the relation between religion and
politics in Iranian history generally,[1] less has been written about the relation between
Islam, nationalism and minorities in post-revolutionary Iran specifically. Any such
study has to start with the founder of the Islamic Republic, Ayatollah Khomeini.

In a simultaneous attempt to counter the latent, divisive Persian-centrism of
Iranian nationalism and the threat of minority mobilization, Khomeini portrayed
Islam as a progressive, all-inclusive answer to regressive, racialized thinking. The
objective, of course, was to distance the Islamic Republic from the Pahlavi state,
which with its particular brand of Iranian nationalism had glorified Iran in terms
of a monarchic civilization, created by a superior, Aryan race. This Pahlavi historical narrative was castigated by Khomeini as secular, Western, anti-Islamic and
heretic. Instead, Khomeini presented his own ideology as an internationalist, universal and God-given solution to the suffering of humankind, no matter what
color or nationality. In this idealist narrative, nationalism, and in particular secular,
European-inspired, Persian-centric nationalism, became a symbol of moral, spiritual
and ideological decay and decadence.

In the following chapter, I will, however, argue that nationalism as a state ideology
was only nominally abandoned in the post-revolutionary political order in Iran. I will
argue that the authoritarian concept of this order, the *nezām*, is legitimized by an
ideology of Islamo-nationalism that can be understood properly only with an eye
to the geopolitical and historical context. Indeed, since Khomeini's death, there has
been a marked resurgence in more overtly articulated nationalism in state rhetoric,
despite the castigation of exactly such nationalism by Khomeini. In order to justify
this resurgence, various propaganda institutions of the Islamic Republic have engaged
in an attempt to endow nationalist virtues with theological justification.

Ethnic mobilization among minorities, I will argue, is an important motivation
for this concerted attempt at re-legitimization. While the Islamic Republic's stand

on the minority issue has mostly been ambiguous, opaque, hesitant or conveniently shrouded in the putative expediency of silence, ethnic mobilization in the immediate aftermath of the revolution and again since the late 1990s onward has forced the state to formulate an official position: what role do or should ethnic minorities play in Islamo-nationalist Iran? This question became evermore pressing with the 2005–7 ethnic unrest in Iran. Indeed, the issues of nationalism and identitarianism point toward a broader question of the role of ideology today.

Departing from the dominant paradigm of post-structuralism in studies of ethnicity and nationalism, Sinisa Malesevic has argued that the concept of ideology, if understood correctly, can stand in for more vague and problematic concepts such as "identity," "discourse" and "meta-narrative."[2] Drawing primarily on Weber, Malesevic proposes to move the theory of ideology from structure-centered toward agency-oriented approaches, and to shift the analytical focus from function to form and content. In order to dissect the ideology of the Islamic Republic as it relates to nationalism and ethnicity, I will here employ Malesevic's analytical distinction between *normative* and *operative* layers. The first layer contains the official narrative and the "central pillars of any particular value system," while the operative layer is the institutionalized narrative "that is encountered in the features and patterns of everyday life in any given society."[3]

In my analyses, I follow Malesevic's proposal to study ideology by focusing on the following: (1) statements relating to four categories vital to any society (*economy, politics, culture* and *the nation,* the latter of which is my central focus); (2) the individual and group actors as depicted in key narratives; (3) the language employed in these narratives and (4) the representation of counter-ideologies.[4] Such an analysis, Malesevic argues, can yield a better understanding of "the human condition" than the "unproductive fixation on the 'economics of untruth' and 'politics of truth'" found in structuralist, Marxist and poststructuralist analyses: "The point of a successful ideology analysis," Malesevic argues, "is not to demonstrate that somebody else's views are wrong or dishonest—this is often no more than simple daily politics—but rather to identify some relatively universal forms of collective thinking and acting."[5]

As Malesevic himself has shown in his work, Iran is an interesting case on which to test this revised approach to ideology. With it, we can dispel the myth of the Islamic Republic's exceptional or extraordinary nature by understanding that practically all political regimes are nationalist: they are permeated by what Michael Billig calls "banal nationalism" because nationalism itself is an overarching meta-ideology of the post-Enlightenment, post-Westphalian world of nation-states.

That, however, does not mean that it is worthless analyzing the Islamic Republic's ideology on both normative and operative levels. Indeed, a detailed analysis can, in the words of Malesevic, "bring us much closer to understanding the complexities of nationalist appeal."[6] Such an analysis, this chapter will show, can yield many important findings about Iran's specific socio-historical, geopolitical and cultural context, and about statecraft and popular mobilization.

In this chapter, I employ a broad range of sources to discuss how the minority issue is understood within the various Islamo-nationalist visions of Iran expressed through the state apparatus and the ruling elite. The sources can be divided into three types. The first is what I call "regime literature." This admittedly simplistic category contains works of a more or less academic framing produced by scholars, intellectuals and politicians who are expressly supportive of the regime (or at least of the idea of an Islamic Republic)—works that are, in most cases, published by state-run organs. In any society, "nationalist ideology is heavily dependent on the work of concrete social organisations," Malesevic argues, since there are no "all-embracing (Durkheimian) *conscience collective* able to galvanise automatic popular support."[7] As "state intellectuals," academics and politicians play a key role in institutionalizing ideology.

The second body of sources includes non-academic texts from state institutions such as the *nahād-e rahbari* (the Leadership Foundation, Khamene'i's representative body) and the government, as well as from political organizations working within the framework of the Islamic Republic. These sources include speeches, sermons, decla-rations and official documents. I will use the first and second body of sources in the first half of the chapter to explore the rebranding of Khomeini's image as a nationalist, the resurgence of state nationalism and the various ways in which state intellectuals and politicians have sought to tackle the tricky question of cultural difference and ethnic diversity within the nationalist project of state-making in modern Iran.

Finally, the third body of sources is drawn from a collection of more than 400 arti-cles from Iranian news media. These sources are used for a case study analysis, in the second half of this chapter, of the Islamo-nationalist rhetoric employed by the regime in reaction to the chain of ethnic unrest that shook Iran from 2005 to 2007. Within these official sources, there is, however, a diversity of views on fundamental issues. Most importantly, there are significant differences between, on the one hand, regime apparatchiks, expressing the official line of the Leader, and on the other, reformist politicians and intellectuals.

While the former tends to have a more practical, simplifying and instrumentalist approach, the latter is critical, placing the minority issue and nationalism within a broader reformist agenda. While such differences may seem, to ethnicists and minor-ity activists, largely irrelevant, perhaps even as parts of an elaborate attempt to feign pluralism, they are nonetheless important for the discussion about Iran's immediate future. Hence, anchored in an understanding of "identity" as a form of ideology, these analyses present the state narratives on the minority issue as part of a wider debate on "Iranian identity": an exchange between the state's ideological machinery, on the one side, and rival political and societal trends, values and developments, on the other.

A STATE OF BALANCING: ISLAMISM, NATIONALISM AND MINORITIES

THE NATIONAL CONSTANT

The discussion about the role of the state in Islam, and of Islam in the state, obvi-ously predates the advent of modern nation-states. Since Shah Isma'il (d. 1524), the founder of the Safavid dynasty, the historical relationship between Iranian monarchs and the Shiite clergy has been close and prone to fluctuation. When the clergy was weak, it was co-opted to endow monarchic rule with religious aura and endorse the king as a "Shadow of God on Earth"; when the clergy was strong, it would pressure the ruler to concede economic privileges and political power. It was from this influential position that the Shiite clergy came to play a crucial role in Iranian politics and state-formation from the seventeenth century onward.

All early modernist thinkers grappled in one way or another with the question of how to frame the state within, alongside or without religion. Examples of theologically justified defenses of the modern, European-inspired state include Jamal-od-Din "Al-Afghani" Asadabadi (1838–97) and Mohammad-Hosein Na'ini (1860–1936). Others cloaked the ideals of the French Revolution in Islamic language (such as Mirza Yusef Mostashar-od-Dowleh, 1813–94), but few were the intellectuals like Mirza Fath-'Ali Akhundzade (1812–78) and Mirza Agha Khan Kermani (1854–96), who advocated the complete separation of religion and state, if not the outright eradication of religion.[8] Early Iranian nationalists often criticized clerical conservatism and popular superstitions, but just as often, they relied on the language of religion to convey their ideas to the broader population. Religion was mirrored even in territorial integrity, that most material aspect of nationalism, and defense of the homeland was formulated simultaneously as a defense of the religion.[9]

This prominent role of religious tradition and novel Islamist ideas in modern nationalism had a profound impact on Iranian nation-state-building, which was mirrored in key moments of change. As anti-absolutist and proto-nationalist movements, the Tobacco Revolt in 1891 and the Constitutional Revolution in 1905–6 had unmistakable secular aspects, but were nonetheless mostly clergy-led;[10] despite its expressly secularist program of Westernization and marginalization of the clergy, the Pahlavi state was not alien to Shiite symbolism; the movement for oil nationalization under Prime Minister Mosaddeq in 1951–3 was not completely secular in origins and rhetoric; and the Left, recent studies argue, was not as free of its religious past as its outwardly secular and/or atheist programs would seem to suggest.[11]

Nor were the intellectual forefathers of the Islamic Republic, in practice, as squarely opposed to the tenets of nationalism as their critique of Pahlavi state nationalism seems to suggest. Influential Islamist intellectuals of the 1960s and 1970s such as 'Ali Shari'ati, Jalal Al-e Ahmad, Morteza Motahhari and Mehdi Bazargan have all argued that Iranian nationalism, as a product of a distinct Islamic-Iranian culture, can play a constructive role in society. They argued that instead of succumbing to the destructive and divisive nationalism that imperialist Western powers sought to disseminate in the Middle East, Iranians should look to their own history and religious traditions to formulate a new nationalism. In the words of Motahhari, "we have religious, Islamic beliefs just as we have patriotic beliefs in Iran."[12] Or, in the words of Bazargan,

> [To] oppose Islam to Iranian nationalism is tantamount to destroying ourselves. To deny Iranian identity and consider nationalism irreligious is the work of the anti-revolutionaries.[13]

Nonetheless, most scholarly works have focused on the religious aspect of Khomeinism to the point that the nationalist aspect has been largely overlooked. Challenging the supposed dichotomy of religion and state or Islam and nationalism is not to imply that Iran does not have a tradition of secular politics. It rather suggests that nationalism has played an important role even in the most theocratically inclined of political agendas, despite the philosophical association of nationalism with the West and secularism.

In fact, it was only with the promulgation of an explicitly internationalist pan-Islamism under Khomeini that the question of a potential opposition between *eslāmiyyat* (Islamic-ness) and *irāniyyat* (Iranian-ness) arose—and then mostly as a theoretical questioning of the normative layer of state ideology. The question of whether or not Khomeini was in fact anti-nationalist nonetheless continues to occupy an important space in the ideological battles within, for and against the Islamic Republic.

Despite the abolition of the monarchy, the Islamic Republic that Ayatollah Khomeini and his allies brought into existence after the revolution of 1978–9 naturally inherited the nation-state framework of the Pahlavi regime with its particular institutions and mechanisms. To conjure the illusion of paradigmatic revolutionary change, the Islamic Republic has sought vigorously to create an ideological image different from that of the Pahlavis. Khomeini drew upon Shiite mythology, Islamic notions of justice, support for anti-imperialist struggles and expressions of solidarity with Third World countries to formulate a radical departure from the discourse of the *ancien régime*.

Instead of glorifying pre-Islamic times and looking to the "Aryan" brethren in the West, the new regime would focus on the *Ummah,* the world community of Muslim believers. In the idealist vision of Khomeini and his followers, the Islamic Revolution would not only encompass Iran, but also extend to the entire Muslim world and, eventually, all of humanity. The new ruling elite rhetorically castigated nationalism as the product of a secular Western modernity antithetical to Iranian realities and detrimental to Muslim beliefs. Some regime ideologues today continue to reject nationalism, at least nominally and rhetorically.

Yet, at the same time, nationalism as an operative ideology automatically framed the Islamic Republic's policies and narratives. A key reason was that the notion of exporting the revolution (*sodur-e enqelāb*) met with obstacles already in the new regime's infancy. First, neighboring Iraq's 1980 attack on Iran reminded the ideologues and their audiences that the revolution was in fact a national rather than an international project. The war was initially presented in Iran as a defense of Islam against blasphemy, and not a war of nationalisms.[14] Yet many Iranians inevitably understood Iraq's attack in nationalistic terms, and as the war dragged on for eight years, the leaders of the Islamic Republic relied increasingly on appeals to the Iranian public duty to mobilize and defend the homeland.

Second, while the revolution had inspired many Muslims across the world and provided Iran with some allies, the cultural differences between Iran and its neighbors prevented the revolution, as an Iranian, Shiite phenomenon, from spreading into Arab, Sunni lands. The export of the revolution did not find many clients in Central Asia, Afghanistan, Caucasus or Turkey either. The lack of support from other Muslim countries, the traumatic experience of the war and the need for national unity during testing times of regional and minority upheavals thus forced the regime to slowly move focus from the internationalist agenda to one more focused on Iran itself.

Thus, while Khomeini continued all his life to advocate the pan-Islamist utopia of a de-territorialized *Umma* united in brotherly love, he also had to rely—as the national leader of a nation-state with a nationalistic-oriented population—on the cultural constant of often Persian-centric Iranian nationalism.[15] Even with his malleable re-interpretations of Islam that set in place a novel political system, Khomeini obviously did not have all the answers for running a modern state. The very novelty of the system created numerous self-contradictions and ambiguities, and problems were solved ad hoc. Khomeini and his followers thus supplemented the articulated pan-Islamic idealism with more subtle tones of nationalism, and with nation-oriented policies that have been described as "realist" by several scholars.[16] Politicians routinely flagged the banal symbols, aesthetics and rhetoric of nationhood, and Khomeini conceded that the interests of the state should take precedence over the religious traditions.

Khomeinist ideology was, in other words, neither inflexible nor antithetical to nationalism. As Haggai Ram has pointed out, the classic portrayal in Western scholarship of the Islamic Revolution as the "ultimate defeat of nationalism at the hands of radical Islam" is simply erroneous.[17] Simplistic dichotomies and the contraposition of "Islamic identity" and "national identity" (and, in some works, "radicalism"/"fanaticism" versus "pragmatism"/"rationalism") have served, in the words of Ram, to present nationalism in the Islamic Republic as a "deviation" rather than an "integral part" of official doctrine:

> [n]ationalism was transformed into a kind of false consciousness, an unnatural growth with which the Iranians had to come to terms, a pragmatic "compromise" they were compelled to strike in light of changing realities.[18]

It was exactly in its negation of Western nationalism that Khomeinism was a form of Iranian nationalism: a nativist response to essentialized Western culture and politics that ultimately is bound up with a particular nation-state and its particularistic concerns, and not, as the idealists had hoped, with the global Muslim community and the universalistic concerns of Islam. In this Islamo-nationalism, the lived experience of Iran's political isolation in the world fed into state policies of material and spiritual self-sufficiency, as well as into popular traditions and histories that explain Iranian identity in exceptionalist and defensive terms.

Islamo-nationalism became significant as a response to the profoundly changing geopolitical picture of the late 1980s and as part of the regime's attempts to muster popular support after the 1989 death of its charismatic leader. Overt nationalist language has gradually crept into state rhetoric under Ayatollah Khamene'i and presidents Rafsanjani, Khatami and Ahmadinejad. As an example of this re-emergence, Hooshang Amirahmadi observed of Ayatollah Akbar Hashemi Rafsanjani's 1988–97 presidency:

> In early 1995, no less august a figure than Rafsanjani ordered the Islamic Republic News Agency to establish a newspaper called *"Iran."* Not "Islamic Iran," just *"Iran."* Large advertisements for the newspaper—comprised of the three-color Iranian flag with no Islamic logos—adorned Tehran's walls and billboards. In keeping with its name, the newspaper itself displays a similar pattern. It is telling that the first issues of *Iran* reached

the stands at the same time [that] the government banned *Jahan-e-Islam* (the world of
Islam), a leading pan-Islamist newspaper.[19]

This move was one of many in Rafsanjani's effort to improve the state's image and
soften its rhetoric, both when addressed to a domestic audience exhausted by years of
revolutionary zealotry and when addressed to a surrounding world concerned with
the extra-territorial ambitions of the radical pariah state. Pan-Islamic romantics were
replaced with pragmatic technocrats who evoked nationalist symbols to marshal support for the post-war reconstruction drive. In tandem with powerful Shiite imagery,
such symbols were deployed to cement a regime that no longer had war exigencies as
a uniting factor of cohesion. The image of unity in diversity became the centerpiece
of the state discourse on national identity.

During Mohammad Khatami's presidency from 1997 to 2005, Iran witnessed a
blossoming of civil society movements, opposition activity and cultural-artistic life.
As referred to in Chapter 2, this period also saw re-emerging mobilization of ethnic
sentiments among minorities. At the same time, secular-nationalist (*melli-garā*) and
religious-nationalist (*melli-mazhabi*) trends resurfaced after decades of censorship and
repression. Even though most nationalist organizations (such the National Front and
the Freedom Movement) were officially or effectively outlawed, Khatami nonetheless sought to appeal to their sympathizers, and to voters with similar nationalistic
proclivities.

As scholars have shown, *irāniyyat* took place alongside *eslāmiyyat* in the reformist
government's discourse as a main pillar of national identity.[20] With this discourse,
the reformists sought to capitalize on the nationalist constant in Iranian political culture to strengthen a political order that was increasingly challenged by the combined
pressure of, on the one hand, a young population with little or no memory of the
revolution, rival political ideas and societal trends in a diverse population, and on the
other, the external agitation and pressure for regime change.

The most blatant employment of nationalist rhetoric in post-Khomeini Iran,
however, has so far come from Mahmud Ahmadinejad, whose presidency began in
2005 and continues at the time of writing. On numerous occasions, Ahmadinejad
and his allies have evoked nationalist symbolism bordering on that of the secular-
nationalist opposition, and sometimes even that of the pre-revolutionary monarchy.
Apart from the ritual flagging of the nation (*mellat*), this includes numerous references to Iran's pre-Islamic splendor and kings, to the national epos the *Shāhnāme* and
to pre-revolutionary Prime Minister Mosaddeq, a nationalist figure that has otherwise
been more or less censored away since the revolution.

Ahmadinejad's supporters have likened the president to the pre-Islamic King
Cyrus and to the *Shāhnāme*'s national savior Kaveh the Blacksmith, they have instituted an official day to celebrate King Cyrus and they routinely claim to defend the
Persian identity of the Persian Gulf. One of Ahmadinejad's key advisors has even
pronounced the end of Islamism, and declared that in order to promote "the truth of
Islam to the world, we should raise the Iranian flag," that "without Iran, Islam would
be lost," and that "from now on, we must present to the world the School of Iran
[*maktab-e irān*]."[21]

Even though expressed in a more subtle way, nationalism has also crept into the
Supreme Leader's rhetoric. While observers of the Islamic Revolution feared that

Islamist radicals would bulldoze the ruins of the Achaemenid palaces at Persepolis as symbols of monarchic decadence, the Leader today praises this World Heritage site as a symbol of Iranian identity, and while observers may have feared a thorough "Arabicization" of Iranian culture, Khamene'i has established a council to "purify" the national language, and expressed his commitment to "strengthening Persian and preserving its authenticity."[22] At the time of writing this book, Iranian flags, pre-Islamic symbolism and nationalistic themes adorned as much public space in cities such as Tehran and in state-run media as did strictly Islamist themes.

Today, under Khamene'i, the "Islamo-Nationalist synthesis" predicted by at least one scholar two decades ago[23] has come full circle. This allows a president such as Ahmadinejad to identify symbolically both with the heathen forefather of Iran, King Cyrus, and with the Islamic saint-leader Ayatollah Khomeini. However, as the clergy's outrage with Ahmadinejad and his advisors' statements have shown, these flirtations with secular-tinged nationalism do not occur without a measure of resistance from the old revolutionary elite and its pan-Islamic ideologues.[24] This resistance has to be understood with an eye to the role of secularism as part of a broader oppositional discourse.

Khomeini's rhetorical rejection of nationalism has long been upheld as a parameter in the state's division of Iran's political landscape into *khodi* ("of the Self," "those who are with us") and *gheyr-e khodi* ("those who are against us," "Other"). The old guard of Islamic revolutionaries fears that the public embrace of nationalism by political leaders such as Ahmadinejad has violated these parameters and upset the status quo—even to the extent that some fear that the clergy may, paradoxically, be losing its grip on the quasi-theocratic state.

Nonetheless, it seems that those with real power in Iran today—the Leader, the Revolutionary Guard and the second-generation lay politicians—have decided that nationalism constitutes a valuable reservoir of sentiments, mobilization and legitimacy indispensable to their future rule: the national constant. They have broken the boundaries that separated the normative and operative layers of Khomeini's ideological legacy.

REINVENTING A PATRIOT

The secular and liberal nationalist opposition has since the revolution continuously challenged the Islamic Republic's legitimacy by accusing its leaders of sacrificing Iran's national interests on the Islamist altar. Khomeini's detractors have presented the Ayatollah as someone utterly disinterested in or even outright opposed to not only nationalism as an ideology but even to the very idea of a nation. Such views are sometimes echoed in the general literature on Iran. In an example from an English-language biography of Khomeini published outside of Iran, we are told that the Ayatollah, on his way to exile, stated that he had defended Iran's honor, but on his return to Iran, Khomeini, when asked about his feelings about returning to the homeland, had replied "None!" The biographer interprets this as follows:

> For a man who felt himself permanently imbued with the love of God, a homeland did not mean much. For mystics and puritanical Muslims, it is the *Dar al-Islam,* the House of Islam, not the *patria,* which is all-important.[25]

Surely, some of Khomeini's speeches included vehement condemnations of nation-alism and nationalists as tools of colonial powers "planted" in the Middle East to destroy the unity of the *Ummah*. Khomeini regularly criticized exaggerated pride in the nation, rejected the use of pre-Islamic culture as a symbol of national identity and condemned any form of ethno-national chauvinism. Secular nationalists, mostly in exile but also in Iran's domestic opposition, use such statements to portray Khomeini, the clergy and the ruling elite as treacherous anti-nationalists. This critique is some-times augmented by anti-Islamic and anti-Arab sentiments, such as when, Khomeini is presented as someone who favored Arab over Iranian culture.

Together with the re-emergence of overt nationalist sentiments and symbolism in state discourse, among intellectuals and reformists, in public discourse and in youth subcultures, these challenges to Khomeini's image have forced the Islamic Republic's propaganda machine, including state-run research institutes, to rebrand Khomeini as an iconic patriot. The aim of such an image recasting is to strengthen, by association, the image of the Islamic Republic under Khamene'i as a political order expressing the national will and identity of the people. The need for such a recasting has been compounded by the changing geopolitical situation of Iran, surrounded from 2001 onward by the US military and its allies and under increasing international pressure over its nuclear program.

Such was the context in which a number of books were published by the state-run Center for Documents on the Islamic Revolution in the 2000s. As a research institution and publishing house under the direct control of the Supreme Leader, the Center is a key institution in the ideological machinery of the state. In the new books, the authors treat the issues of national identity and ethnic diversity in ways that differ from the previous regime literature, which was generally calibrated to demonize nationalism.[26] In what seems to be an attempt to bridge the gap between the regime and a middle class alienated from the Islamist rhetoric, two of the books in this new regime literature attempted to recast Khomeini as a patriot: *Ummah and the Nation in Imam Khomeini's Thought* by Ali-Mohammad Baba'i-Zarech (2004) and *Imam Khomeini and National Identity* by Yahya Fowzi Toyserkani (2006).[27]

Baba'i-Zarech and Toyserkani claim that not only did Khomeini accept the exis-tence of nation-states, but he actually viewed nationalism—or rather, "love for the homeland" (*hobb be vatan, mehr-varzi be vatan* or *mihandusti*)—as something natural and beneficial. Indeed, the authors claim, Khomeini did *not*, as the opposition fears, call for the merging of all Muslim nations into one but rather wished to preserve Iran as a national unit. This reading of Khomeini, which glosses over his utopian ideal of a borderless Muslim community, explicitly legitimizes nationalism—albeit only in a particular variant that is deemed historically authentic (*asil*), culturally homegrown and religiously justifiable. The authors stress that this authentic nationalism (*mihan-dusti* instead of *nāsiyonālism*) is not in any way opposed to Islam and that Iranian national identity is unthinkable within anything but an Islamic framework.

Nonetheless, a critical reading of the new regime literature suggests that in the Islamic Republic today, Khomeini's fundamental principle that only Islam is impor-tant to an individual's identity can basically be circumvented with the argument that Khomeini was a pragmatic who operated with a combination of idealism and real-ism in his policies—even when it came to "identity politics." Khomeini's view on national identity, accordingly, was instrumental or tactical: part of a shrewd balancing act between far-reaching idealist visions for humanity and the *Umma,* on the one hand (the normative layer), and "pragmatic" short-term goals, national interest and popular patriotic sentiments, on the other (the operative layer).

Yet the balancing act is portrayed in the official regime literature as a natural, indeed divine, equilibrium, and not the product of cold political calculations. The bottom-line is that Iran's national identity and territorial integrity must be protected under the aegis of a Leader such as Khomeini: a Supreme Jurisprudent (*vali-faqih*) that is simultaneously the worldly and spiritual father of his people, a Leader that embodies the Order. As Khomeini is reinvented as a patriot in the genealogies of Islamo-nationalism, Khamene'i's rule as his successor, as the Hidden Imam's representative on earth and as the national leader of Iran is legitimized.

THE ETHNIC VARIABLE

Ayatollah Khomeini rarely articulated his views on ethnicity and minorities clearly and directly. In his pre-revolutionary literature, such issues are barely mentioned. Scholars such as David Menashri have interpreted this to mean that Khomeini "vigorously denied the existence of ethnic or Muslim-religious minority groups within the Islamic community."[28] From one of the Ayatollah's few statements on minorities, one can indeed deduce that he saw the minority issue as a creation of imperialist powers:

> Sometimes the word minority is used to refer to people such as the Kurds, Lurs, Turks, Persian [sic], Baluchis, and such. These people should not be called minorities, because this term assumes that there is a difference between these brothers. In Islam, such a difference has no place at all. There is no difference between Muslims who speak different languages, for instance, the Arabs or the Persians. It is very probable that such problems have been created by those who do not wish the Muslim countries be united . . . They create the issues of nationalism, of pan-Iranism, pan-Turkism, and such isms, which are contrary to Islamic doctrines. Their plan is to destroy Islam and the Islamic philosophy.[29]

This and other statements clearly support the idea that Khomeini was opposed to, if not ethnicity, then at least, the labeling of certain communities as minorities. In this view, the very concept is foreign, implanted into the Muslim community by imperialist powers to sow disunity and strife. The minority issue—the political sentiments that enemies might try to manipulate into existence out of Iran's social fabric—was thus in the Khomeinist view linked directly to questions of colonialism and religion. The minority issue, ethno-nationalism and racism were seen as politically instrumentalized weapons against not just Iran, but Islam itself. Hence, minority insurgents were condemned not in ethnic terms, Menashri observes, but as "enemies of Islam."[30]

However, Menashri's argument that Khomeini and his followers denied the existence of ethnic minorities is too simplistic. A more nuanced picture emerges from a reading of Khomeini's Islamic Republican Party's pamphlet *Mavāze'-e mā* ("Our Viewpoints"). In it, the party declares that "the spiritual and emotional bond between members of an ethnic group or a tribe or a nation" is a "natural matter" that should be respected.[31] Accordingly, "any ethnic group is free to use, practice and develop its language, literature, culture, art and rituals." Yet all Muslims must be aware, the party stated, that their primary identity is Muslim and that Islam should come before any other attachment. Therefore, "ethnic, racial and nationalist extremism (*ta'asobāt*), and ethnic or racial chauvinism, are religiously forbidden (*harām*), and against Islam."

Khomeini repeatedly stated that "in Islam, race is fundamentally not an issue," and that in Muslim history, the co-existence of various ethnic groups "has never been an issue."[32] He argued that Islam would iron out the differences and inequalities between ethnic groups or "races" (*nezhād*). Khomeini ostensibly saw racism as a grave threat, and in his historically important 1979 "Speech to the People of Kurdistan," he attacked ethnically framed ideologies as racist and therefore harmful to Islamic unity:

> [T]o the inhabitants of Kurdistan[:] you . . . should not be fooled by these small groups. They have created an instrument against Islam! The instrument of racism[:] the project of separating Kurd, Lor, Persian and so on from each other, and of bestowing on each an independent entity for themselves. This is what Islam has come to destroy[:] these walls; Islam has come to . . . place all of you and all of us and all Muslims under the banner of "There is No God But God," and to be together in unity, breathing together, and bringing forth Islam.[33]

Surely, the underlying message in this speech was directed at Kurdish separatist guerillas (which are referred to as "small groups"). However, the statement also addressed the broader problem of racism, which Khomeini sometimes called *nezhād-bāzi* ("race game") and described as that which happens when a Turk wants to pray in a "Turkish" fashion, an Arab demands that "Arabism should govern" or an Iranian claims that "the Aryan race must rule instead of Islam."[34] Islam came to destroy this "race game," Khomeini proclaimed, and those who tried in modern times to revive ancient glory by looking 2,500 years back in time to Iran's pre-Islamic splendor were reactionaries.

As part of the recent recasting of Khomeini, the new regime literature also deals directly or indirectly with the minority issue. In one of the two books mentioned earlier in text, the author Toyserkani describes Iranians as a "heterogeneous conglomerate" that came into being through successive waves of migration, war and political-economic rivalries, and is characterized by "racial and ethnic diversity."[35] History, Toyserkani argues, has endowed Iran with a mixed population of "Aryans and non-Aryans, Greeks and Macedonians, and other groups such as Black Africans."[36] Furthermore, he emphasizes the fact that various ethnic groups such as Arabs and Turks have ruled Iran to argue that each of these groups have contributed to Iranian national identity and culture.[37] Toyserkani concludes:

> [E]ven though Iran today is made up of different ethnic groups, there is no specific ethnic group that defines [Iranian] identity and basically, this [ethnic] factor does not enjoy an important standing in the national identity of Iran.[38]

According to Khomeini, as distilled through this new regime literature, ethnicity should not be rejected or dismissed, but rather described as point of departure or intermediate level on human beings' road to perfection. In the end, Islamic identity will override the significance of other identities such as ethnicity. In short, Khomeini's Islamism, and therefore also ideal Iranian nationalism, is not opposed to ethnicity as a concept, but does not deem it important. All this notwithstanding, Toyserkani also accepts a potential contradiction between ethnic and national identity:

> If we acknowledge family, ethnicity, society, nation and the *Umma* as markers of collective identity, some will naturally be interpreted on the surface as homogeneous and others as heterogeneous... Since the emphasis on elements that make up an ethnic identity stands in opposition to national identity, these differences conclude in a natural heterogeneity [*nā-hamguni-ye tabi'i*] in identities. One of the markers of ethnicity is an emphasis on the racial or linguistic element, which is different from other ethnic groups; and on the other hand, in national identity, emphasis is on common, national features, and no attention is paid to ethnic elements."[39]

Toyserkani explains that Khomeini saw the existence of such heterogeneity as "necessary and essential," "natural facts" and part of "historical and social reality."[40] Indeed, ethnic identities are "acceptable to Islam" as long as they are not turned into "radical sentiments" (*ta'assobāt*).[41] With Islam, Khomeini minimized the risk of radicalism, the author assures us. Hence, Khomeini stated that "in Islam ... there is no separation between two Muslims who speak two [different] languages."[42] The anti-racist view on diversity was, according to Toyserkani, based on Khomeini's understanding of the Quran and the Islamic philosophical notion of "unity in diversity, diversity in unity" (*vahdat dar 'eyn-e kesrat, kesrat dar 'eyn-e vahdat*).[43]

As part of the drive to distance Khomeini as a patriot from the shahs, and Islamo-nationalism as an ideology from secular nationalism, two other books from the Center for Documents on the Islamic Revolution deal with pre-revolutionary Iran: *Ethnicities and Their Role in the Political Developments under Mohammad-Reza Pahlavi* by Mojtaba Maqsudi and *Critique and Evaluation of Modernist Nationalism in the Age of Reza Shah* by Esma'il Mo'azzampur.[44] The aim of these two works is to present Islam as a progressive answer to regressive ethno-centrism—whether that of the Pahlavis (Persian-centrism) or of radical minority groups (ethno-nationalism). In this way, the regime literature simultaneously challenges secular nationalism *and* contemporary minority activism by associating both with the morally corrupt shahs and their faulty policies toward the population.

Maqsudi's book is focused on the last shah's policies toward ethnic minorities on the premise that inter-ethnic relations prior to the Pahlavis were largely harmonious and peaceful. During Reza Shah's rule, however, a number of negative policies antagonized minorities and propelled them toward ethno-nationalism, including the state's "exaggerated emphasis on Persian language," its prohibition of other languages and cultural degradation of minorities, the state's drive toward homogenization and cultural uniformity, the economic marginalization of minorities, the forced settlement of nomads and anti-tribal policies, as well as the conscious efforts of privileging the center over the peripheries.[45]

Interestingly, the author presents the hypothesis that as an ethnonym, *fārs* ("Persian") was "invented" under the Pahlavis to drive a wedge through the population and legitimize a harsh policy vis-à-vis the minorities.[46] To underscore the argument that the last shah was in fact a racist, the author focuses on Aryanist aspects of Pahlavi state discourse. In one speech, the shah declared that in contrast to the Turkic-speaking Qajars, his Pahlavi dynasty's ancestors were "authentic Iranians," and in another that Iran is the "oldest homeland of the Aryan race."[47] The shah, Maqsudi adds, never mentioned any of Iran's non-Persian-speaking ethnic groups in his speeches, which is further testimony to his Persian-centrism. The current discontent among minorities, Maqsudi argues, does not stem from any systemic, inherent discrimination in Iranian society, but rather from Pahlavi authoritarianism. The Islamic Republic and the revolution are thus implicitly hailed as a progressive disavowal of previous ignorance and tyranny.

The second book by Mo'azzampur elaborates on the racist and Aryanist aspects of early Iranian nationalism, and in extension, challenges the secularist and anti-Islamic notions inherent in this nationalism. The author argues that "the footprint of fascism is clearly detectable" in the early Iranian nationalists' fondness for German theories on "the soul of a nation."[48] With their "ancientism" (bāstān-garā'i), these nationalists in turn influenced the authoritarian Pahlavi regime, which glorified pre-Islamic Iranian civilization as one "superior to contemporary civilizations," to the extent that Iranians were presented as "a chosen people, graced with God's particular favor."[49] As a consequence of the Persian-centrism inherent in such glorifications, the Pahlavi regime was encouraged by the secular nationalist intellectual elite to pursue a policy of radical homogenization: "aimed to impose among Iranians a uniformity in lifestyles, language and even in dress, without tolerating the existence of any subculture alongside the national culture."[50]

According to some in the contemporary minority movement, the ideology of the Islamic Republic aims to promote cultural or even racial and ethnic homogeneity, if not outright Aryan supremacy (see Chapter 5). However, the regime literature seems to suggest otherwise. It puts forward a distinctly non-racial and supra-ethnic definition of national identity. Islam is presented as the ultimate tool to combat discriminatory, reactionary ideologies that are by-products of Western modernity and imperialism, and the Islamic Republic is thus presented as the epitome of egalitarian unity.

Referring to the sparse (and admittedly vague) references in Khomeini's speeches, the literature depicts Khomeini's views on national identity as ethnically inclusive but ideologically exclusive. The enemy, so to speak, is not and has never been the non-Persian-speaking, the non-Shiite or the non-Muslim minorities, but rather those who seek to abuse these communities for political goals contrary to those of the Islamic Republic. By stating that the threat is ideology, not ethnicity, the ruling elite is seeking a way to deal with an unpredictable and potentially very dangerous ethnic variable in Iranian society and politics. This requires a balancing act in the representations in the regime literature of the ideal of unity.

UNITY IN DIVERSITY

President Khatami brought a new twist on the Islamist discourse into Iran's public sphere: an approach that stressed pluralism, diversity and a vibrant civil society to an extent and in a fashion hitherto unheard of among high-ranking politicians. In order to understand the effects of this new approach on public debate and political deliberations about the minority issue, two works are particularly enlightening: Abdollah Ramezanzadeh's doctoral dissertation *Internal and International Dynamics of Ethnic Conflict: The Case of Iran* (1996) and Seyyed Reza Salehi-Amiri's report *Ethnic Conflict Management in Iran: Critique and Analysis of Existing Models and Presentation of Ideal Model* (2006).

The two works were published on each side of the reformist decade: Ramezanzadeh completed his PhD in Belgium and his English-language dissertation was published in 1996, on the eve of the movement that led to Khatami's election, after which Ramezanzadeh himself became a reformist politician. Salehi-Amiri presented his report for the Expediency Council in 2006, after Ahmadinejad's election had brought an end to the reformist government, but at a time when this Council was still dominated by reformist-minded or moderate politicians such as Khatami, Mir-Hosein Musavi and Rafsanjani. As such, the two works can be considered "before" and "after" snapshots of the reformist-Islamist agenda as it relates to the minority issue.

Ramezanzadeh was already politically active before he started research for his PhD. His activist background allegedly brought him to Khomeini's inner circle during the revolution, and to the front during the Iran–Iraq War. After finishing his degree and returning to Iran, he served as governor of Kurdistan Province, as a member of Khatami's government and as an outspoken reformist. Apart from this political trajectory, Ramezanzadeh's work is influenced by the fact that he is himself a Kurd: this is reflected in his attention to the sense of alienation and discrimination among Iran's non-Persian-speaking communities. Indeed, Ramezanzadeh has been praised by reformists for his work as the first Kurdish governor of Kurdistan since the revolution, while conservatives have blamed him several times for fanning ethnic unrest in his home province.

Salehi-Amiri was the Head of Cultural and Social Studies at the Strategic Research Center of the Expediency Council, which Khomeini established after the constitutional revision in 1988 to arbitrate between the clerical Guardians Council and the parliament on matters of legislation.[51] Ramezanzadeh and Salehi-Amiri were, in other words, influential voices in the reformist circle, which is reflected in the fact that the former served as Khatami's spokesman and that the latter could include an appreciative foreword by Khatami in the final publication of his report.

Both works include a historical survey of state-minority relations in Iran that aims to show that the Islamic Republic is the hitherto best political system for addressing minority concerns. Ramezanzadeh argues that before Reza Shah, there were no ethnic conflicts in Iran, and that uprisings in places such as Khuzestan and Kurdistan should rather be understood as clashes between state and tribes. After the Second World War, and in the immediate aftermath of the Islamic Revolution, foreign intervention and manipulation created a number of ethnic crises and minority uprisings. Ramezanzadeh thus argues for a direct correlation between foreign power meddling in Iranian affairs and the occurrence of ethnic conflict: when Britain withdrew its support for regional movements in the 1920s, for example, center-periphery conflict all but disappeared.

Recently, Iran's relationship with immediate neighbors has played a decisive, largely negative role—such as when some Kurds were forced to side with Saddam during the Iran–Iraq War.[52] Ramezanzadeh also acknowledges the importance of the state's level of tolerance for minority cultural rights. Combined with economic marginalization, the Pahlavi restrictions on the minority language press and control with cultural manifestations of ethnicity reinforced a "sense of neglect" among minorities, Ramezanzadeh explains.[53] Indeed, "Persian chauvinism was the basis of [Reza Shah's] nationalism, rather than 'Iranian-ness'," and this further cemented a "sense of separateness."[54]

Ramezanzadeh thus emphasizes the correlation between the overall political climate and the minority issue: when political freedom was at its height—such as, Ramezanzadeh claims, during the first two years after the revolution—stored-up ethnic grievances boiled over. The reason why these grievances did not turn into full-scale wars or separatism, Ramezanzadeh argues, was that the Iranians' main concern at the time was for the *Ummah*, the Muslim society at large; that the revolution represented a departure from Pahlavi nationalism; and that the Islamic Republic discarded ethnic preferences.[55] Ramezanzadeh claims that post-revolutionary initiatives have greatly benefitted minorities, including the post-war reconstruction drive, "redistributive policies and affirmative actions [*sic*]," and the emphasis on developing agriculture and education in deprived areas.[56]

Some of these measures were sometimes rendered ineffective by logistical, geographical and socio-economic obstacles, but the revolution has been, Ramezanzadeh maintains, to minority advantage. The state has "continued to exercise and promote cultural autonomy," has lifted the "ban on ethnic languages and cultures," and has recognized the minorities' "separate identity from the Persians," he claims.[57] However, Ramezanzadeh acknowledges that the state has not yet reached its goal of absolute equality, since Persians and Azeris continue to dominate the political arena, and since there are in effect still certain bans on ethno-political activity. Ramezanzadeh even expresses his concern for the possibility of ethnic conflicts escalating in the near future.[58]

In short, Ramezanzadeh, writing on the eve of the reformist wave, fundamentally adheres to the basic Islamist tenets of the Islamic Republic. He argues that minority grievances stem from a combination of economic, political and cultural factors, but that the main culprits in creating ethnic tension were and are the *ancien régime* and foreign powers. In contrast to the Pahlavis' failed, Western-inspired nationalism, the Islamic Republic has revived the non-ethnic, non-discriminatory communalism of true Iranian-ness, which is tolerant of minorities.

With the benefit of hindsight and a decade of new research, Salehi-Amiri's work extends the historical outline to include the reformist period and Khatami's policies on the minority issue. It also contains in its title the promise of an *ideal model* for solving the issue, namely *vahdat dar kesrat*, Unity in Diversity. This principle, Salehi-Amiri maintains, is embedded in the legal and constitutional framework of the Islamic Republic, but is yet to be put into action. The revolution, he explains, happened in a turbulent period of "contending identity discourses," which did not bring about a single, overarching strategy toward the minority issue—a problem that the Islamic Republic shares with previous political systems in Iran.

Salehi-Amiri connects this problem to the issue of nationalism. The revolutionary leaders were unconvinced as to the usefulness of nationalism in securing national unity, and tended to discard some of the non-Islamic elements that Salehi-Amiri believes bind together Iranian national identity. However, in recent years, Iranian politicians have discovered that there is in fact no contradiction between Islamism and Iranian nationalism.[59] Indeed, the two concepts of *eslāmiyyat* (Islamicity) and *melliyyat* (nationality), Salehi-Amiri argues, have always been intertwined and inseparable, together constituting "the Iranian spirit."[60]

The minority issue in Iran today has many faces, reasons and outcomes: economic (such as lack of investments), cultural (such as the establishment of cultural associations with "anti-national goals"), social (such as social anomie) and political, including domestic (such as the attempts by domestic political forces to exploit the democratic system and ethnic sentiments) and international (the instrumental utilization of minority rights issues as excuses for intervening in Iran's domestic affairs).[61] To solve these problems, Salehi-Amiri revives the slogan of Unity in Diversity, which was originally among the slogans of Motahhari and Khomeini.

In this slogan, Salehi-Amiri sees a model that is based on a universal, Islamic ideal that is simultaneously compatible with the structure and laws of the Islamic Republic, and with the culture, social fabric and geographical specificities of Iran. With a brief comparative allusion to the case of India versus that of the Soviet Union, he argues that international experiences have shown that a polity accommodating ethnic diversity is more successful than one that stresses homogenization. Even Turkey, Salehi-Amiri mentions, has had to make changes, however small, in its policies toward the Kurds.[62]

It is Salehi-Amiri's central hypothesis that by "accepting the existing diversity," Unity in Diversity as a practical model for managing society respects and strengthens territorial integrity, national unity and societal coherency, and that with this model, "the historical and natural balance of the Iranian nation" can be protected into the future.[63] Salehi-Amiri argues that all the laws required for making Unity in Diversity the overarching state strategy are already present in Iran's constitution, including principles of power decentralization and respect for minority rights. Yet Salehi-Amiri also seems to suggest that the constitution should be slightly amended—namely the stipulation that presidential candidates must be Persian-speaking Shiites.[64]

Salehi-Amiri claims that due to domestic and international circumstances, Iranian political leaders have not been able to fully translate the theory of Unity in Diversity into actual practice. Only under the reformist government, he maintains, have ideals been close to actual policy. The real problem behind the minority issue, he argues, is not violent ethno-nationalist groups, but rather a deeper "national identity crisis" (*bohrān-e hoviyat-e melli*). This crisis arose from a society in which the political culture is particularistic and oriented toward family, clan and ethnic group interests rather than national interest.[65] Such a political culture, combined with a feeling of injustice, discrimination and economic deprivation has created a societal distance between ethnic groups and given rise to political forces that are solely geared toward local, regional and ethnic demands.

In order to deal with this national identity crisis, Salehi-Amiri argues, the state needs to focus its propaganda and outreach on the cultural elements that unite

Iranians (including collective history, Persian literature, Islam, common mythology and historical heroes); to promote "national pride and positive zealotry" (*ghorur-e melli va ta'assob-e mosbat*) and to stimulate "love and affection for the Persian language" while not attributing this language to one particular ethnic group or attempting to eradicate other languages.[66] Politicians need to address the economic situation in the periphery, create new avenues for political participation that can canalize minority discontent into a legal framework rather than toward illegal organizations and accept diversity as an asset rather than a threat.

This also entails that politicians must refrain from blowing the problem out of proportions, or belittle its importance; from ridiculing, deriding, demonizing or dismissing the existence of minorities; from using violence and repression to solve ethnically framed issues and from promoting "Persian-centrism and Persian chauvinism," "extremist nationalism" and "Aryanism."[67] Finally, Salehi-Amiri argues that globalization, with its embedded trend toward cultural revivals among minorities, is a fact that cannot be dismissed, and therefore, should be taken into serious consideration in the overall political strategy of the state.

Ramezanzadeh and Salehi-Amiri represent a reformist discourse that suddenly gained widespread popular support in the late 1990s and was then pushed aside by conservative forces in a slow-motion coup that began with the violent repression of the student movement in 1999 and culminated with Ahmadinejad's second presidential election victory in 2009. Today, reformism has lost its platform within the political system and much of its appeal to the broader population, yet the legacy of the reformist days is still clear in both. This includes the idea of unity within diversity, which continues to be upheld as an ideological principle, albeit, some would argue, in a hollowed out fashion.

While the 2009 uprising, to which we return in Chapter 5, shows that the ideals of the reformist period, popular participation and respect for civil rights, still live on, actual power, however, has been centralized in the hands of the Supreme Leader. Under him, a conservative status quo now defines the state and its approach to the minority issue.

STABILIZING AUTHORITY

In the theatrics of Iranian politics, the Supreme Leader is supposed to play the role of the nation's father, the spiritual guide of all Iranians (and, ideally, all Muslims) who is "above" the mundane world of day-to-day politics. In sermons, speeches and talks, he addresses general problems and fundamental discussions in broad strokes. Despite being the Leader of a multi-ethnic country, Khamene'i thus rarely addresses issues of minorities or ethnically framed politics head-on. When he does, it is mostly within the context of larger geopolitical and religious questions.

A key point in many of Khamene'i's speeches and sermons is unity in the *Ummah*, or global Islamic community, and how Muslims are religiously obligated to resist ethnic differences turning into tensions or conflicts. Indeed, Khamene'i has often stated that "ethnicity" is the "greatest agent of division" in the Islamic world.[68] During visits to minority regions, in speeches before crowds of government employees or when visited by non-Iranian allies from around the Muslim world, Khamene'i routinely stresses that bridging the Sunni-Shiite gap, resisting foreign plots to mobilize ethnic sentiments and creating a united front against Western imperialism and secularism are among the most important goals for Muslims and their political and religious leaders.[69]

Such general statements aside, there are only few examples of Khamene'i addressing Iran's domestic minority concerns directly. Indeed, such concerns are rather relegated to the Leader's representatives (under the aegis of the Leadership Foundation), to local administration and to the government and its president. The Leader simply needs not to address these issues, it appears. This is of course rooted in strategic considerations: the less said about a thorny issue, the fewer the questions. Whereas the reformists have opened the ethnic can of worms, the minority issue strategy that characterizes the conservative ruling elite is one of prudent silence, deliberately ambiguous abstraction or expediently brief mention.

In his 2005 inaugural speech as a president, Ahmadinejad swore that his government would spend all resources on promoting a spirit of brotherly love and unity among all units of society without any ethnic discrimination. In Ahmadinejad's subsequent speeches, mentions of minorities generally fall into three categories:[70] (1) when addressing crowds at events in minority regions, praises about particular ethnic groups, sometimes while wearing the traditional local attires or uttering short phrases in the local languages or dialects; (2) in abstract speeches about the equality of human beings before God, no matter what skin color, nationality or ethnicity; or (3) as passing references to foreign meddling in Iran's domestic affairs in order to weaken Iran as a regional power by sowing discord, destroying national unity and preventing Iran from making economic progress. Touring provinces and peripheral regions of Iran has figured as a key part of Ahmadinejad's public relations strategy since his election in 2005, and during these publicity events, it has sometimes been impossible for him and his entourage not to address the minority issue.

In Azerbaijan, the president answered a question about the government's attention to the local language by stating that Azeri is "an important part of the backbone of national identity" and that nothing could be gained from weakening local cultures and languages. In Baluchistan, Sunni-Shiite tensions have been brought up in passing, and then dismissed as the product of foreign powers' ultimately futile schemes of splitting the Muslim community. In Kurdistan, Ahmadinejad have dressed up in traditional Kurdish tribal attire and proclaimed Kurdistan the "homeland of heroism and pride." In Khuzestan, he hinted at inter-ethnic solidarity with vague references to "the Iranian nation's unshakeable unity." Press coverage of the tours is often accompanied with reports about how the local minorities welcome Ahmadinejad and how they express support for their president, even with slogans in their own local languages.[71]

When Ahmadinejad touches upon ethnicity in his speeches, it is sometimes as part of a response to his intra-regime detractors. In this respect, the word "ethnicity" is a negatively laden allusion to Persian-centric nationalism. Ahmadinejad has thus stated that his government's emphasis on the word "Iranian" should not be misunderstood as a kind of ethno-centrism or nationalism, but rather as an attempt to bring balance to the Iran-Islam equation on which the state should formulate and present itself internationally and domestically. He stresses that the Islamic Revolution was not a movement spurred by the interests of a "particular party, group, ethnic group or tribe"—not even by "pure national interests." On this abstract level, Ahmadinejad's oft-repeated slogan "Today, Iran is not an ethnic group or a tribe" is coupled with statements explaining that across the world, "Iran" is seen, or should be seen, as a symbol of justice, audacity, resistance against tyranny, purity, God-worship, monotheistic faith and so on—in other words, a symbol of global relevance and not that of a particular ethnic group.[72]

When Ahmadinejad and his team directly address diversity in Iran, it is with the flowery symbolism of a *golestān* or "garden."[73] The depiction of ethnic harmony and colorful diversity now feature regularly in state-run media and propaganda: portrayals of ethnic groups wearing local clothes or producing traditional handicrafts, or of idyllic scenes of village life and nomad migrations appear in numerous TV shows, on posters advertising domestic tourism and on banners and murals decorating cities across the country. In military parades, units are dressed up as pre-modern tribal warriors, and in state-organized exhibitions and fairs, the local cuisines, products and arts of ethnic minorities are put on display. *Nowruz,* the Iranian New Year, is utilized as a symbol not only of the unity of ethnic groups in Iran, but also of the impact of Iranian civilization and culture abroad. Often, propaganda contains clear references to pre-Islamic Iranian culture and imperial monuments such as Persepolis.

Thus, on the one hand, the reformist period not only broadened the scope for public debate but also legitimized a more flexible governmental use of symbolism that had been more or less tabooed under Khomeini. Khatami, one could argue, has thus made it near-impossible for his rivals and successors not to speak the overt language of nationalism and not to address cultural diversity. However, on the other hand, the gradual marginalization of moderates such as Rafsanjani and reformists such as Khatami since the late 1990s, the entry of second-generation military figures such as Ahmadinejad and the centralization of power in the hands of Khamene'i have meant that these changes in rhetoric, discourse and parameters of debate have so far not translated into systemic democratization or tolerance of political pluralism.

Combined with geopolitical rivalry and the West's constantly escalating war of words and sanctions, the regime has turned toward a two-pronged propaganda strategy of bolstering Iranian nationalist sentiments while seeking to de-ethnicize this nationalism by claiming a place within it for all ethnic groups. The proliferation of rosy depictions of ethnic unity aside, however, the minority issue is in effect still treated as a security problem by a regime that is increasingly militarized and intolerant toward dissent in its attempt to stabilize the power equation of the Islamic Republic.

ORDER AND DISORDER: OFFICIAL REACTIONS TO ETHNIC UNREST, 2005–7

DIRTY HANDS OF DISORDER

As detailed in Chapter 2, Iran was rocked in the period 2005–7 by a series of ethnic unrest in Khuzestan (April 2005), Kurdistan (July–August 2005), Baluchistan (March–May 2006, February 2007) and Azerbaijan (May 2006). This unrest took the shape of demonstrations, riots, sabotage, ambushes, kidnappings and terror-bombings. On the surface they did not appear directly interlinked: the triggers, tactics and outcomes differed widely, as did the state responses to each case. Yet together, the events represented the most widespread and violent ethnic minority unrest since the revolution, and at root, the discontent expressed similar grievances among the four minorities. Indeed, the state reacted, in its representation of the unrest as part of a foreign plot against Iran, as if toward one overriding threat.

However, simultaneously, it also reacted to this emerging threat with the rhetoric of unity. Violent protestors and minority organizations were branded as small handfuls of agent provocateurs, and contrasted with an imagined majority that supported not just Iran in general but the Islamic Republic specifically. In the representations of Self and Other generated by these threat/unity narratives, the state apparatus in effect conjured an image of the Holy Order of the Islamic Republic (*nezām-e moqaddas-e jomhuri-ye eslāmi*) not just as a political system per se, but rather as an all-encompassing societal order.

With narratives drawing on Islamic history and Islamism, nationalist symbolism, populist rhetoric and authoritarian notions of stability, regime officials portrayed this Order as the natural antidote to the unnatural state of disorder that the ethnic unrest represented. The regime spoke a language of power addressed not just to minority activists but also to the Iranian population in general.

An analysis of these narratives, I will argue in the following, presents us with a highly informative insight into the complex dynamics of domestic Iranian politics: the unrest and the state response together constitute a convoluted discursive battleground, which cannot be reduced to a simple question of "state versus minorities." Political history, inter-community relations, sectarianism, religion, socio-economics and geopolitics all played into the battleground. By contextualizing the political semantics of the state responses, this analysis will contribute to a broader and more nuanced understanding of Iranian society today.

The analysis is based on a close, contextualized and critical reading of more than 400 articles from Iranian print and online media. The articles were published during the 2005–7 unrest primarily by state-run and state-affiliated dailies, magazines, news agencies and news websites, which were in one way or another connected to "the regime" in its broadest sense. The prevalence in Iran of supposedly "private" dailies that are in fact owned or run by politicians, alliances or pseudo-non-governmental bodies makes it somewhat difficult to distinguish state from private media. Often, state-affiliated media express the views of high-ranking officials even when these officials are not directly quoted.[74]

For this analysis, I have concentrated primarily on media that was run, during the unrest, by managers appointed directly by the Leader or by the government (under Khatami until August 3, 2005, and then under Ahmadinejad), as well as those media that had the state as a primary source of funding. Secondarily, I concentrated on media that are widely believed by scholars[75] to be affiliated, through ownership, staff appointments and/or funding, with dominant regime factions.[76] Together, these media expressed the view of high-ranking officials from across the factional spectrum.[77] The different cases will be mentioned with broad geographical labels (Khuzestan, Kurdistan, Baluchistan, Azerbaijan). Each signifies the cultural-historical regions in which unrest occurred and not necessarily the specific, present-day provincial units.

A common characteristic throughout all the cases was that officials spent much time and space in the media to portray the unrest as the result of foreign meddling. During the Khuzestan unrest, a headline in the state-run daily *Kayhān* read: "The hands of foreigners exposed." The article claimed that the Ministry of Intelligence had identified "the dirty hands of disorder" (*dast-hā-ye nā-pāk-e fetne*).[78] This phrasing, I will argue, in many ways summarizes the state approach to ethnic unrest: it denotes a symbolic contamination, by the impure and corrupting "hands" of the foreigners, of the "purity" and "sanctity" of Iran as a territorial entity and as a religious community. Such a reading is based on a semantic deconstruction.

First, there is "hands": the verbal construction *dast dāshtan*, "to have a hand (in something)" is used in Persian to denote malicious schemes. Here, it conveys the notion of imperialist powers clandestinely involved in practically every major negative political event in modern Iranian history. The "hands" represent the omnipresent intrusion of foreign agents and culture into Iran. Second, *nā-pāk*, the negation of "pure," carries implications that can be read along the dichotomizing lines of *halāl* (permitted, clean) and *harām* or *najes* (forbidden, impure) in Islam; the separation of social space according to a person's relational status as either *mahram* (intimate, related, permitted to enter a private sphere) or *nā-mahram* (stranger, forbidden to enter), and the aforementioned division of the political landscape, by regime officials and intellectuals, into *khodi* ("Self") and *gheyr-e khodi* ("Other"). "Dirty" thus implies an intrusion and contamination of what was in essence "pure" prior to the unrest.

Third, "disorder" is here a translation of *fetne*. Other possible translations of this originally Arabic term with its religious connotations include "schism," "upheaval," and "anarchy." In classical Islamic thought, *fetne* is one of the signs of the coming apocalypse and the return of the Messiah. In Persian, the term has been used in poetry (in the sense of the tempting and alluring dangers of a beloved whose lover(s) will create turmoil not only in their own hearts but in all of society), or for political purposes (in the sense of "sedition," "revolt" and "riot"). In the latter sense, which is not unlike the unnatural state of internal discord described by Plato in the introductory quote, the regime has also applied the term to demonize protesters in the 2009 uprising. In the case of ethnic unrest, it carried particular connotations of the fragmentation of the Muslim community between extremism and moderation, between Sunni and Shiite and between true believers and hypocrites.

All together, the string of words sums up the notions of threats to the territorial integrity of the nation-state, to the religious solidarity of the Muslim community and to the spiritual and worldly power and authority of the Order. It represents the cross-fertilization of interlaced and interwoven myths, tropes and narratives, which endows the overall Islamo-Nationalist state discourse with impact strength.

CUNNING FOX AND GLOBAL ARROGANCE

Officials used media to ritualistically remind the national audience of the official line: that the ethnic unrest was the result of foreign plots against Iran. Indeed, this claim

104

was repeated to the extent that sometimes officials did not even deem it necessary to specify *which* of Iran's many enemies were in question. Accordingly, officials talked of an unspecified "conspiracy" (*towte'e*), of "foreign agents" (*'avāmel-e borun-marzi*) and "foreign elements" (*'anāser-e khāreji*), and of unnamed "enemies" (*doshmanān*) that had either provoked, fanned or indeed organized the unrest down to the minutest detail.[79]

These enemies, officials maintained, had convinced naïve Iranians to take to the streets, and/or hired professional mercenaries to attack public property, and/or simply transported agent provocateurs, from unspecified locations outside the country, and "planted" them inside Iran to sow discord. Words such as *bi-rishe* ("rootless" or "non-indigenous"), *khodbākhte* ("one who has lost himself/herself," "sell-out"), *khā'en* ("traitor") and *mozdur* ("mercenary") were all key adjectives used by officials to otherize protestors and violent activists. The notion underlying such statements was that those who had taken to the streets were either traitors to their own country or not even Iranians.

Thus, during the Khuzestan unrest, the Minister of Intelligence announced that "the enemies" had tried to "introduce rootless elements" into Iran, and that these elements strove "to get arrested in order to become famous" and attract attention to their cause.[80] The minister claimed that opposition abroad was facing such a severe crisis of incompetence and lack of leadership that it had been forced, in a desperate attempt to get heard, to provoke ethnic strife in Khuzestan. Indeed, the minister maintained, there simply *was* "no domestic opposition capable of creating unrest" inside Iran. In other words, the unrest was provoked and stage-managed by foreign powers employing a demoralized, cowardly and nation-betraying exile opposition as their agents. The contrast implicit in the portrayal was thus between a people rooted in its culture and history, and the "sell-outs" who had lost their identity.

However, apart from these vague allusions, officials often did put names to the enemies, as Table 3.1 shows.

The British and the United States were the two by far most prevalent enemies alluded to by officials. The prevalence of the former should be understood on the historical background of over 200 years of British meddling in Iranian politics, annexation of Iranian territory, coup d'états and military invasions, and a towering presence in the shape of the Anglo-Iranian Oil Company.

This history has fostered both healthy suspicion and political paranoia among Iranians, and has given rise to the political, popular-cultural and literary trope of the

Table 3.1 Enemy tropes invoked in official reactions to ethnic unrest, 2005–7.

Unrest	Enemies perceived
Khuzestan	UK, USA, Israel, 'Ba'thists' (Sunnis in Iraq), Arab states and media, oil companies, monarchists, Sunni extremist organizations
Kurdistan	Kurdish separatist organizations (including PKK), USA, Israel, Turkey, Sunni extremist organizations
Baluchistan	UK, USA, Pakistan, Saudi-Arabia, Sunni extremist organizations (including Taliban and Al-Qa'eda)
Azerbaijan	UK, USA, Republic of Azerbaijan, Israel, Turkey, Pan-Turkist organizations

conniving, omnipresent and almost miraculously powerful British.[81] Officials thus alluded to the longstanding British interests in and manipulation of ethnic politics in oil-rich Khuzestan to back up the accusation against Britain for pursuing "imperialist goals" and a policy of "malice" (*sheytanat*, related to *sheytān*, Satan) aimed at dividing and eventually conquering Iran.[82] In their reactions to the Khuzestan unrest, officials particularly focused on a supposed link between Arab forces and the British government.[83] Iranian media claimed that after the 2003 invasion of Iraq, exiled Arab ethno-nationalist organizations had promised that Britain would soon have Khuzestan in its possession. A fact that gave further weight to such accusations was that after the US-led invasion of Iraq in 2003, British forces took control with parts of southern Iraq bordering Khuzestan.

The Attorney General thus announced that Arab media had played a key role in fanning the Khuzestan unrest and were in fact "instruments of the British." Other officials alleged that the British Foreign Secretary had met, prior to the Khuzestan unrest, with a prominent leader of an outlawed separatist group in London, which is known to be a center for Khuzestani Arab ethno-nationalist lobbyism. On top of this, an official added that the separatist leader in question was in fact the son of a "torturer from SAVAK," the Shah's dreaded intelligence agency. In this manner, the conspiracy gained a triangular effect, linking up British imperialism, Arab nationalism and the despised monarchy of yore.

Such accusations take shape on the background of Britain's historical involvement in Iran generally, including its support for the Shah—and Khuzestan specifically, including its support for Sheikh Khaz'al, a semi-independent ruler of southern Khuzestan (then Arabistan) in 1881–1925. While some Arab ethnicists today view this period as evidence of an Arab will to self-rule or independence, official Iranian historiography see it as yet another testament to Britain's imperialism. In their reaction to the Khuzestan unrest, officials thus conjured the image of an elaborate conspiracy, ultimately aimed at gaining control with Iran's considerable oil resources.

At the bottom of these somewhat hazy allegations lay the fear that by nurturing and provoking ethnic sentiments, foreign powers wanted Khuzestan to secede from Iran, depriving the country of a cradle of civilization and robbing it of natural wealth. Indeed, accusations were often associated with Iranian speculation that international oil companies, including "the Zionist company Shell," had played a role in the unrest. According to officials, this company had nurtured extensive relations to social and political forces in Khuzestan, and, among other things, opened cultural centers that carried out "suspicious activities" among Khuzestani Arabs—just as the company had done, a reporter for a state-affiliated news agency added, in places such as Nigeria.[84]

Apart from the British, the United States of America is undisputedly the Islamic Republic's archenemy. Since the revolution, the United States and Iran have engaged in a wide-ranging exchange of actions of proxy warfare, sabotage, political and economic pressure, accusations and demonization.[85] Dubbed "The Great Satan" (*sheytān-e bozorg*) by Khomeini, the United States is known in Iranian state narratives and popular discourse for the CIA-orchestrated coup against Prime Minister Mosaddeq in 1953, for its support for the shah and then for Saddam Hussein in the Iran–Iraq War, for the bombing of a civil airliner in 1988 and for numerous other actions and sanctions against Iran. Iran, in turn, is remembered in the United States for the Embassy hostage crisis in 1979–81, for its alleged support for Islamist and anti-American terror groups, and from US president Bush's 2002 State of the Union Address onward, as part of the so-called Axis of Evil.

As already outlined, the Khuzestan unrest occurred at a time when reports surfaced in global media about US covert operations inside Iran, including among ethnic minorities. Whether or not the Iranian state had any evidence for such manipulation in the case of Khuzestan, officials nonetheless stated in no uncertain terms that the unrest was part of the US strategy of "soft subversion" (*bar-andāzi-ye narm*)[86]—a Persian neologism for regime change through a "velvet revolution" orchestrated by foreign powers and their local "native informant" operatives. Specifically, officials claimed that by encouraging "radicalization" and "extremism," both euphemisms for ethno-nationalism, the United States sought to "destroy the image of the Order [of the Islamic Republic]."

Iranian officials thus connected the wave of "velvet revolutions" from Georgia in 2003 over Ukraine in 2004 to Kyrgyzstan just before the Khuzestan unrest with broader US aims. By the time unrest broke out in Azerbaijan in May 2006, officials were openly arguing that all the cases were related to a US plot against Iran. The events in Khuzestan and Sistan-Baluchistan, a high-ranking officer in the police force declared, were proof that "American dollars have been spent on destabilizing Iran." Indeed, the Minister of Interior lamented, "certain governments" that "pretend to be democratic and to be fighting terrorism" were in fact "promoting sabotage, arson and destruction of public property" in Iran. An editorial in Khamene'i's mouthpiece *Kayhān* stated that since it had failed to drum up sufficient international support for its actions against Iran, the United States now focused on sowing discord inside the country. One phase of this campaign concentrated on exploiting ethnic sentiments.

An example that Iranian state media used to underscore US hypocrisy was the alleged US support for the militant organization PJAK during the Kurdistan unrest in 2005. PJAK is more or less the Iran wing of the PKK, which in turn was and is considered a terrorist group by many states, including the United States.[87] In the case of Baluchistan, *Jondollāh* provided the Islamic Republic with an even more blatant example: *Jondollāh*'s ambushes, kidnappings and terror-bombings were militant acts of violence by a small and suspiciously well-equipped, well-informed and well-organized unit operating across borders with a significant US military and intelligence presence. In the official rhetoric, *Jondollāh* was easily portrayed as a mercenary terrorist outfit in the pay of the United States, and thus as part of the US hypocrisy and neo-imperialist agenda that Iranian officials label *estekbār-e jahāni* or "Global Arrogance."[88] In the words of a high-ranking officer in the Revolutionary Guard:

> The root and source of terrorism is America, which, while dictating its so-called New Order to the world, has caused the spread of instability and mushroom-like growth of terrorist groups... Unfortunately, USA today points an accusing finger at Islamic countries and groups [labeling them as] terrorists... Terrorism, which knows no borders, is one of the biggest problems of the world today, and it seriously threatens the security of [all] countries."[89]

In this fashion, Iranian officials turned the US narrative on terrorism on its head, emphasized American double standards and alluded to the US history of supporting radical Sunni militants across the region. The officer quoted above even alleged that the United States was involved in the gigantic narcotics industry that had blossomed in Afghanistan after the US invasion. The extent to which Iranian officials managed to level accusations against the United States, it should be remembered, matched the extent to which Iranian audiences were familiar with the US track record of political meddling in the region.

This was particularly true in a case such as that of Baluchistan, which was and is marred by drug smuggling and crime, and is bordering a volatile area dominated by Sunni extremist forces often supported by the United States. When the UN Security Council issued a condemnation of *Jondollāh's* bombing of a bus in Zahedan in 2007, Iranian state media in turn asked how the United States dared sign condolences for victims of crimes committed by its own henchmen.[90]

In evoking the Global Arrogance trope, the United States—and by extension, international bodies such as the UN and countries such as Israel—were portrayed in the Iranian state rhetoric as the ultimate evil in the world, a hypocrite promoting fake democracy while exploiting Muslim societies.

ENEMY NEXT DOOR, ENEMY WITHIN

In their responses to ethnic unrest, Iranian officials were often walking a thin line: on the one hand, they accused troublemakers of being foreign agents, but on the other, they had to be careful not to frame this claim as a wholesale accusation against entire minorities. Hence, the enemy was often described in terms of "small groups" (*goruhak*), "opportunists" (*forsat-talab*) or "gangs" (*bānd*). However, since all cases of unrest had, at least potentially, a transnational ethnic dimension, and since two cases (Kurdistan and Baluchistan) had a potential sectarian dimension, officials sometimes had to downplay the larger context by being rather specific in naming the enemy. In this fashion, officials hoped to defuse the ethnic and sectarian dimensions of domestic grievances. The blame was placed on an external Other.

In the case of Khuzestan, officials dug out from Iran's recent history the enemy trope of Saddam Hussein.[91] Several high-ranking officials insinuated or directly named "the Ba'thists," Saddam's defunct party, which Iranian officials believed had been rehabilitated within post-Saddam Iraqi intelligence agencies. One Iranian media outlet alleged that Iraq's Minister of Defense had been personally involved in organizing the Khuzestan unrest, and another that Iraqi "Pan-Arabist" Saddam-supporters had stage-managed the riots. Officials then connected such accusations directly to the painful popular memory of the eight-year war with Iraq, such as when the Attorney General stated that troublemakers in Khuzestan were in fact the same "agents" who had "carried out bombings" during the war, "martyring many of our Arab compatriots."

The depiction of the evil "agents," contrasted with "*our* Arab compatriots," was a referential strategy aimed at distinguishing Other from Self. It is, however, impossible to know from the statement whether the Attorney General meant that the troublemakers had come from outside or within Iran. This vagueness reflected the underlying ambiguity in the Arab Friend/Foe schism: Iraqi Arabs were evoked in several ways to indirectly demonize Iranian Arab ethnicists while the incontestable enemy image of Saddam was utilized to link ethnic unrest to tormented memories of a war that was, by all accounts, the most traumatic event in modern Iranian history.

In this image of an Arab foe there were embedded nationalist narratives. The Qatar-based Arabic satellite TV network *Al-Jazeera* was blamed for fanning the Khuzestan unrest, acting as a "propaganda loudspeaker for a marginalized separatist group." Indeed, as an "anti-Iranian octopus of the Arab world," *Al-Jazeera* had "offended the territorial integrity of Iran."[92] A state-affiliated Iranian website placed *Al-Jazeera* within a long history of Arab animosity toward Iran. In it, the author claimed (wrongly) that Egypt's Nasser was the first to call the Persian Gulf "The Arabian Gulf" and Khuzestan "Arabistan," that Libya's Gaddafi allegedly supported militants in Khuzestan and that Iraq's Saddam had imagined that Khuzestanis would welcome him during the Iran–Iraq War, enabling him to separate Khuzestan from Iran in the name of pan-Arabism.[93]

State media also connected the unrest to wider nationalist issues. The issue of the Persian Gulf being co-named "the Arabian Gulf" on the 2004 National Geographic map had caused uproar among Iranians across the world. During the Khuzestan unrest, officials capitalized on this nationalist anger, claiming to defend the "Persian" identity of the Gulf against Western and Arab powers' ignorance of history. The primitive but effective equation conjured up by official rhetoric was thus that participating in ethnic dissidence equaled serving Arab and imperialist objectives, and thus betraying the country.

Another major concern, as already mentioned, were the effects of the US invasions of Iraq and Afghanistan on regional sectarianism—effects that could be felt deep into Iran and particularly among its Sunni minority. Iranian officials argued that the United States was exploiting sectarian differences to prevent Muslim unity in the face of Western hegemony. Hence, they routinely presented the bombings and ambushes in Baluchistan as part of a shared strategy of the United States, Sunni Arab states and Sunni extremist groups—sometimes even Israel. The "Western and Zionist enemies," the Attorney General stated after the 2006 Tasuki attack in Baluchistan, "are striving to sow sectarian and ethnic discord"—and therefore, he argued, there was a direct link between the bombing of Shiite mosques in US-occupied Iraq and the *Jondollāh* attacks in Baluchistan.[94]

Iranian officials focused on *Jondollāh*'s alleged affiliation with Sunni extremists in Pakistan and Afghanistan, particularly the Taliban.[95] Iranian hatred of Taliban has a long history. In August 1998, when Taliban killed eight Iranian diplomats and one journalist in Mazar-e Sharif, this nearly resulted in a war between Iran and Afghanistan. Throughout Taliban rule, Iran supported the opposition while reports of Taliban's atrocious crimes, in particular against Shiites, created the image of the Afghan regime as the quintessence of medieval barbarism in the Iranian public. Therefore, linking *Jondollāh* to "the Taliban" was a convenient way of demonizing it as an extremist force creeping across porous borders and into the comparatively moderate, modern and civilized Iran.

Conjuring the image of a Sunni extremist enemy also had the purpose of evoking Shiite solidarity. Iranian officials consider Wahhabism, an ultra-conservative and virulently anti-Shiite interpretation of Sunni Islam originating in Saudi-Arabia, as a major threat to Muslim unity. Even during the Khuzestan unrest, which took place in a majority *Shiite* area, officials hinted at Wahhabi infiltration.[96] In Baluchistan, the Sunni extremist nexus between *Jondollāh* and Wahhabism was further elaborated with the suggestion that the then head of Iraq's Al-Qa'eda, Abu Musab al-Zarqawi, was in fact in control of *Jondollāh.*

The Attorney General also placed the Baluchistan unrest within a history of sectarian animosities: the unrest, he argued, was rooted in the same *fetne,* or "calamity" of cosmic dimensions, which gave birth to "the *Khavārej* of Nahrawan."[97] The *Khavārej* (Kharejites) were a Muslim sect that split with and then fought the main body of Shiites at the Battle at Nahrawan in 657. In the end, *Khavārej* assassins killed Imam 'Ali. Hence, the *Khavārej* were evoked as a historical enemy tormenting the Shiite community with injustice and betrayal, now in the guise of *Jondollāh* assassins.

In the same vein, officials often branded troublemakers as *monharef,* derived from *enherāf,* which signifies "deviation" and "perversion," and is used to denote both extremist sects rejected by the clergy as well as deviant behavior in modern society. In some cases, the enemy was portrayed as not even being Muslim, such as when a high-ranking cleric declared that the Darzin attackers in Baluchistan had committed "treason against the country and the Koran by claiming to be either Sunni or Shiite" when in fact they were neither.[98] In the words of the Leader's representative in Baluchistan, the *Jondollāh* were simply *kāfar,* "unbelievers."[99]

In other cases, such as the Kurdistan unrest, Iranian officials and state media hinted more subtly at the sectarian dimension, arguably in order not to further provoke inter-communal tensions. An example was the claim that PJAK had set fire to a local *hosseiniye* in a Kurdish village.[100] A *hosseiniye* is a Shiite congregational place for lectures and ritual mourning. Hence, it is insinuated that in the hope of sparking sectarian violence, the (presumably Sunni) PJAK Kurds had deliberately insulted and provoked Shiite sentiments. The restrained language indicates a political concern with overtly demonizing Sunnis; yet the fact that the *hosseiniye* is mentioned at all points to either a concern with possible sectarian dimensions to the ethnic unrest, or perhaps an attempt to muster Shiite sentiments against PJAK.

A final "enemy within" trope of religious origin is "the Hypocrite" (*monāfeq*), which is a Koranic reference ("those who pretend to have faith") and carries great significance in the Shiite symbolic universe: Sunnis are hypocrites who refused to recognize Imam 'Ali's rightful leadership. However, in Khomeini's rhetoric, the term came to stand for enemies more generally, in particular the *Mojāhedin-e khalq* (MEK). During the ethnic unrest, officials often casually employed this term, such as in the Minister of Defense's statement that "there are no hypocrites or counterrevolutionaries among the Arabs; the Arabs of Khuzestan will not act against a government which is Shiite."[101] In this sense, the minister managed to allude to both an abstract Sunni enemy and an internal enemy, without naming or specifying either. Such rhetoric was aimed to tell apart good from bad citizens, "real" Iranians from traitors.

THE PEOPLE AND THE EVIL

A key point in the official rhetoric on the ethnic unrest was thus that the protesters and militants did not represent a significant segment of Iranian society or public opinion. As such, ethnic unrest was often described in terms of crime rather than politics, and especially the unrest in Khuzestan and Kurdistan were portrayed as the violent acts of mindless mobs. State media detailed the damage inflicted upon state and private property and claimed that the troublemakers were "hoodlums" (*arāzel-o-owbāsh*), "agents of disorder" (*'avāmel-e āshub*), unemployed youths and disgruntled individuals who had gone on the rampage and targeted ordinary citizens.[102] Officials even portrayed protesters with almost parental concern: the protesters were misguided and frustrated teenagers gullied into making trouble.[103]

The term *sharir* (pl. *ashrār*), which translates into "bandit" and "evildoer" (and is related to the noun *sharr*, "evil," which describes satanic motives as opposed to *kheyr*, "good"), was a prevalent idiom of otherization in the official denunciations of ethnic unrest. During the Baluchistan unrest, officials and media employed *sharir*, as an agentive noun and adjective, to describe *Jondollāh*.[104] In the media imaginary, drawing on popular and historical perceptions of Baluchistan as a sort of "Wild East" with arid deserts roamed by fiercely independent tribes, *Jondollāh* was thus associated with drug gangs and violent smugglers operating across the borders. By portraying the militants as mere mercenaries and criminals (and not even "counter-revolutionaries" or "separatists"), any political legitimacy or ethnically framed motivation for the violence was implicitly dismissed.

More generally, official rhetoric tended to depict the instigators of unrest as morally depraved people.[105] During the unrest in Khuzestan and Azerbaijan, officials claimed that there were drug addicts, thieves and robbers among the protesting crowds. In some cases, news items in state-run media announced mass-arrests that included, indiscriminately, both rioters and petty criminals. A state-affiliated media outlet also claimed that the Arab ethno-nationalists who had allegedly orchestrated the Khuzestan unrest had "no religious beliefs" and that their "daily lives are brimful with corruption, alcohol consumption and debauchery." The Kurdish activist whose death triggered the 2005 Kurdistan unrest was described as having a criminal track record, including killing a child, and it was stated that he was, in fact, caught by police during an alcohol binge. Attempts to connect Baluchi insurgents with moral depravity included rumors in state-affiliated media about the *Jondollāh* leader Abdolmalek Rigi being infected with HIV.

Narratives about instability and insecurity cemented these images of dangerous immorality. In one news item, PJAK were accused of abducting men and women from a village in Kurdistan, beating them up, stripping them naked and letting them loose in the mountains in blatant violation of traditional mores and local sensitivities.[106] In Baluchistan, a high-ranking official warned that if locals did not cooperate with the state in crushing *Jondollāh*, their *nāmus* (family members protected by a traditional code of honor, especially women) could no longer travel safely from one village to another.[107] Thus, officials played on the fear of marauding, pillaging and raping bandits—and implied that resisting groups such as PJAK and *Jondollāh* was the only way to secure the traditional order and tranquillity of local communities.

Officials also portrayed ethnic unrest as an attack on the ostensible democracy of the Islamic Republic.[108] During the Khuzestan unrest, officials explained the unrest as a deliberate attempt by enemies to sabotage public participation in the upcoming presidential elections. It was even suggested that the riots had been timed to coincide with the beginning of a new calendar year that the Leader had named "The Year of National Solidarity and Public Participation." Thus, "the people" (*mardom*) and their participation in the supposedly democratic mechanisms of representation in the Order were presented as contrasts to the elements of disorder.

News items about the Kurdistan unrest portrayed a situation in which "normal" people were utterly dissatisfied with the riots and demonstrations;[109] in fact, state-run media claimed, the Mahabad bazaar strikes had occurred only because militant groups had threatened shopkeepers. The state-run news agency quoted "the people of Mahabad" stating that they had had enough of this disturbance of their civilian lives. PJAK's tactic, another outlet claimed, was to "kill and hurt the people and then blame the Islamic Republic." The Kurdish protestors were simply dismissed as "enemies of the people" or, harking back to the rhetoric of Khomeini's war against his domestic rivals, *zedd-e enqelāb* (counter-revolutionaries).

However, "the people" was not just portrayed as a victimized, passive agency. One recurrent theme in official rhetoric was the notion of voluntary civilian resistance against unrest and riots.[110] Clerics and officials called on the people to take matters in their own hands, and quash (*khatt-e botlān keshidan*) or apprehend the troublemakers and foreign agents. In Baluchistan, an official reminded his audience that during the revolution, vigilantes had confronted counter-revolutionaries, and that today they could do the same. After the Azerbaijan unrest, former president Rafsanjani made similar allusions to popular resistance during the revolution and the Iran–Iraq War.

Sometimes, these encouragements carried implicit threats. In the case of the Azerbaijan unrest, officials felt it necessary to express a measure of understanding with the outraged masses. Yet even here, the rhetoric altered ambiguously between laudatory and admonitory. One MP stated that the "heroic and intelligent people of Azerbaijan should be alert" to the divisive actions of the enemy scheming in their midst: "There is no longer any need for discussion or for organizing rallies," the MP warned.[111] Another official argued that the protests of "Order-loyal and morally sound forces" in Azerbaijan were legitimate, but that the protest had now been corrupted by a small number of individuals, who were attacking public property and creating mayhem. These elements were "not from the people" but rather "foreigners" and "opportunists."[112] A state-run daily claimed that pan-Turkist ethno-nationalists had treated the demonstrations as "a mere excuse for creating unrest and riots," but that "some demonstrators," that is "the people," had "confronted the riotous elements."[113]

The violence, then, was attributed to nihilistic vandals and foreign agents, and contrasted with "the people," who were loyal to the Order even when demonstrating against the state. With this language, officials portrayed the ethnic unrest as the work of "agents of disorder" that threatened not so much the political system but society as a whole. Hooliganism, vandalism, sabotage, crime, anarchy, moral decay, psychological terror, and in one word, evil, was evoked to simultaneously demonize protestors and praise those who did not participate in the radical phases of unrest.

Concluding such statements were the ritual, rhetoric routine: that the Order would prevail against all threats and challenges. Indeed, the ubiquitous use of terminology such as *āshub-e zehni* ("mental unrest"), *tashvish-e azhān-e 'omumi* ("provoking the minds of the public"), *bi-nazmi* ("disorder") and *nā-ārāmi* ("unrest") carried with it the implicit antidote to such unnatural, undesirable states of mind and society: the Order.

SACRED DEFENSE OF THE ORDER

In the state discourse, "The Order" implies a range of things: the person of the Leader (the *vali-faqih*); the theological-republican underpinnings of the Islamic Republic (the *velāyat-e faqih*); the ruling establishment, namely the clergy and the Revolutionary Guard; the regime in its totality; or simply Iran in a general sense. Thus, as a flexible but powerful term, "the Order" was used in the state response to ethnic unrest as a rhetorical yardstick or point of reference for audience loyalty: being loyal to the Order meant being loyal to Iran, while resisting the Order meant being a traitor and an enemy.[114] An example is from a speech by a high-ranking official that placed the Khuzestan unrest within a heroic history of loyalty toward Iran:

> The people [of Khuzestan] stood their ground with empty hands [*dastān-e khāli*] in the face of British colonialism and gave [the British] an unforgettable lesson ... The Arab people of Khuzestan played a matchless role in the Islamic Revolution's victory and consolidation ... and they love the Islamic Order [*be nezām-e eslāmi 'eshq mi-varzand*] ... The [Iran-Iraq War] was a heavy burden on their shoulders, and the tombs of martyrs witness this; their unparalleled and magnificent reception of the Exalted Leader of the Revolution proves their love for the *velāyat*[*-e faqih*] ... The enemy has completely miscalculated if he thinks he can exploit the Shiite Arab population of Khuzestan; [they] are not only supporters of the Order, they see the Order *as their own.*[115]

Referring to the Khuzestani Arabs' being Shiites, to their defense of Iran's territorial integrity against the British and the Iraqis, and to their alleged allegiance to the Order, the tone of this statement is significant: it seems almost to *defend* Arabs, to clear them of some sort of accusation in order to prove their loyalty. A so-called Unity Rally after the Khuzestan unrest concluded with a high-ranking cleric reading out the text of a written "renewal of the covenant" re-affirming the Arabs' commitment to the Order and the revolution.[116] The statement proclaimed that "the people" had "again proven their solidarity with the Islamic Order." In this fashion, officials, in all the cases of unrest, seemed to put on display the collective credentials of ethnic groups in order to confirm these groups' allegiance to the Order.

The Iran–Iraq War contained crucial symbolic capital upon which officials regularly drew for this purpose. The so-called Sacred Defense (*defā'-e moqaddas*) is the object of an elaborate popular mythology and the subject of a vast state-sponsored cultural industry in Iran today. Khomeini and his successors thoroughly instrumentalized the Sacred Defense and its correlations with Shiite martyrdom narratives in order to consolidate the revolutionary state and ideology.[117] The Sacred Defense also played a special role in the official response to unrest in Khuzestan: this province was the scene of many important battles, and most Khuzestani Arabs rejected Saddam's calls for an Arab front against Iran. Officials routinely evoked this testament to Arab loyalty, claiming that in 2005, the Arabs had again repelled the enemy by not letting the unrest spiral out of control.[118]

Officials promised that the Order would reward ethnic groups for their loyalty. After the Khuzestan unrest, officials and state-affiliated media expressed their sympathy with Arabs suffering under economic, social and environmental problems.[119] They reminded the national audience that Khuzestanis still endured problems related to the Iran–Iraq War. It was thus implied that the resentment was rooted in these conditions, and not in any deeper ethnically framed issues.

In the words of the Minister of Defense at a meeting with Arab tribal elders, "The Holy Order of the Islamic Republic pays special attention to Arab tribes" and "recognizes them as among the ethnic groups most loyal to the Islamic Revolution."[120] Dressed in his gaudy white naval uniform embellished with medals, the minister (who is himself an ethnic Arab) represented a living example of ethnic equality: "The Order," he declared, "places no kind of limitation on the Arab people's advancement, and there is no boundary for our progress within the administrative system and the armed forces."[121]

Obviously, laudatory statements about loyalty also carried within them implicit threats. An example was when the Attorney General, visiting Baluchistan, issued a warning to "the great men of the province" that they should cooperate with the state in driving out crime, poverty and militants like *Jondollāh:* "It is unacceptable to the Order," he announced, "that the people of Sistan[-Baluchistan] must always give martyrs and experience great suffering."[122] Here, and in the above address to the Arabs, the Order as "the center" is issuing simultaneous cautions and promises to "the periphery," flagging both the potential dire consequences of disloyalty and the rewards of loyalty.

At the end of the day, officials always maintained that in its effort to destabilize Iran by provoking ethnic tensions, the enemies had miscalculated. "Their attempts are doomed to fail," Khamene'i announced after the Azerbaijan unrest, in a speech where he connected the issue of Iran's drive toward nuclear power with that of foreign conspiracies exploiting Iran's minorities. "Azerbaijan has always been unmatched in its vigorous defense of the Islamic Revolution and the territorial integrity and independence of the country," the Leader stated.

During another sermon, a high-ranking conservative cleric chimed in, stating that the Azeris had "slapped Global Arrogance hard in the face" by not falling prey to US schemes during the unrest.[123] Other officials declared that the enemy and its grand scheme for the Middle East was facing defeat, and now it was acting out of feverish desperation.[124] The enemies were ridiculed as being envious of Iran's status as role model for the global *Ummah,* and as a nation moving toward independence, nuclear energy and regional supremacy.

The notion of loyalty to the Order, however, was presented as something more spiritual than political. Thus, officials regularly stressed that the Iranian people saw itself as being on a revolutionary and spiritual mission in the world and that all Iranians were united under Islam.[125] In the words of president Ahmadinejad, "the great, God-worshipping Iranian nation" would convince the enemy to stop its malicious schemes of inciting ethnic hatred, and instead "return to the way of the Prophets, that is, the road to salvation for human kind."[126] As a representative of the Hidden Imam and of God, and as the embodiment of the Order, the Leader was presented as a guardian of civil and religious life, a protector of tradition and society. The Order, in turn, was projected as a God-sanctioned bastion in the cosmological, Manichean battle between good and evil, security and danger, purity and impurity.

HARMONY AND UNITY

Even though officials strove to present the ethnic unrest as marginal and limited in scope, as the work of foreign powers or as the unfortunate result of socio-economic problems, the inflamed ethnic sentiments undoubtedly caused concern. In the words of one high-ranking cleric, "ethnic sensitivities are like a time bomb that might explode any minute."[127] A rhetorical response was to portray Iran as endowed with an unshakeable multi-ethnic equilibrium.

One way to achieve this was to emphasize the role of ethnic groups in defending Iran's territorial integrity. During the Azerbaijan unrest, officials habitually evoked the role of Azeris in Iranian national history, such as when former president Rafsanjani declared that the medieval, Turkic-speaking Safavid dynasty was "the founder of national unity" and that, today, it was still "the love of these kind of people"—that is, the Turkic-speaking Iranians—that kept Iran united.[128] Some officials even referred to Azeris as a *qabile* ("tribe" rather than *qowm*, "ethnic group"), stating that the Azeri tribe was firm on showing foreign enemies that Azerbaijan is inseparable from Iran.[129] Officials claimed that separatism "carries no meaning" among Iran's Azeris[130] and that "Azerbaijan has always been Iranian, all ethnic groups of the country are all Iranian, and they have all protected the borders and frontiers of the country for centuries."[131]

In the case of Khuzestan, officials lauded the province and its people by quoting Khomeini's statement that "Khuzestan is the gateway for Islam and Shiism into Iran."[132] The Minister of Interior stated that "whatever language or dialect they may speak, and whatever sect they may adhere to," Khuzestanis were "firm on one principle: protecting Iran's borders and being Iranian."[133] The Minister of Defense assured his audience across Iran that "the Order is not worried about the borders of Khuzestan and that is because of the presence of Khuzestani Arabs."[134] In the words of a parliamentarian, Khuzestanis, whether Arab or non-Arab, were "the border guards of Iran" who would "not allow one inch to be separated from the soil of the homeland."[135] With such rhetoric, ethnic groups were portrayed with an evocative image of tribal border guards grounded in Iranian ancient and medieval history, thus assuring audiences of these groups' eternal loyalty to Iran and its territorial integrity.

Another way for state-run media to underscore minority loyalty to the central state was to insinuate that signs of this loyalty could also be expressed in the non-Persian languages spoken by these minorities. It was reported that after the unrest, National Unity rallies had taken place across Azerbaijan under the (Azeri-language) banner of "Self-Sacrificing Azerbaijan will never part from the Revolution!" (*āzarbāijān-e jānbāz enqelāb'dān āyrilmāz!*). During National Unity rallies in Ahvaz, statements were read out in both Arabic and Persian, and the Minister of Defense declared that there were no restrictions on speaking the Arabic language in Khuzestan. The message was that the Order is tolerant of ethnic and linguistic diversity.

The official response to ethnic unrest also gave Iranian politicians a rare opportunity to put on display their nationalist credentials and patriotic sentiments in blatant, bombastic ways. Every imaginable and emotional connotation of the country was evoked: Iran as a mental geography was described as *irānzamin* ("the Land of Iran"), *khāk-e pāk-e irān* ("the Pure Soil of Iran"), *marz-o-bum* ("Border and Homeland") or *marz-e porgowhar* ("Country of Diamonds"). Ethnic groups were praised as patriots in terms that would previously have sounded suspiciously like the rhetoric of secular nationalists, ranging from *vatan-khāh* ("one who wants the homeland") over *vatan-dust* or *mihan-dust* ("one who loves the homeland"), all the way to *vatan-parast* ("one who worships the homeland"). Every possible word for "nation" and "country" was used, including *vatan*, *khāk*, *zādgāh*, *mellat*, *bum* and *mihan*. Politicians even evoked Iran's pre-Islamic past, such as in this particular succulent speech by reformist MP Mehdi Karubi after the Khuzestan unrest:

> All of Iran's ethnic groups must know that Iran is for all Iranians and that a nation, which is rooted in a history and an ancient civilization, can never lose its identity due to foreigners' [attempts to] sow discord . . . Arabs, Turks, Turkmen, Lors, Baluch, Bakhtiyaris, Kurds, and all Iranian ethnic groups have defended the ancient civilization, the traditions, the values and the territorial integrity of our country for ages, and they have paid for it with the blood of their youths; therefore they will never separate from Iran . . . I have met the enduring and brave people of the homeland, boasting a wealth in the values of five thousand years of history and civilization; pure and patriotic humans, fertile lands overflowing with natural resources—and they have had a very important role in guarding our country.[136]

At the heart of such a speech was the idea that ethnic unrest was threatening Iranian civilization, traditions, values and territorial integrity, or, in one word, *identity*. However, the officials claimed over and over again that despite the unrest, *vahdat-e melli* ("national unity") would prevail because the individual tiles of the multi-ethnic mosaic of Iran were glued together by history and faith. Rafsanjani warned that "if tribes and ethnic groups feel injustice," national unity would be weakened, but that "in the shade of Islam, national unity can undoubtedly be protected and strengthened."[137] All of Iran's ethnic groups have always lived in harmony, he emphasized. During the same parliamentary session, another official stated that "even though they have different cultures," all Iranian ethnic groups will always understand themselves as Iranians above anything else: "they see themselves as essentially Iranian."[138]

In this way, the official line was one of praising diversity and unity while warning of discord: its congratulatory narratives of minority loyalty carried within them implicit admonitions against political dissidence.

DISCUSSION

While few scholars have ventured to explain nationalism as a form of religion,[139] many others have at least noticed the many similarities, and have brought back religion as a key factor in understanding nations and nationalism.[140] They have made a timely call for reconsidering the "well-worn, ahistorical and Eurocentric opposition of modernity and tradition," and the presumption that there is a fundamental rupture between the two.[141] Taking a cue from such new directions, scholars have also questioned the extent to which nationalism in Iran should be interpreted as a departure from religion. Afshin Marashi, for example, has argued that as opposed to the examples used by modernist thinkers such as Hobsbawm and Anderson of nationalisms that "invoked a religious spirituality in an age of growing secularism," Iranian nationalism did not develop as "a new spirituality to fill a void left by one fast receding."[142]

Anthony D. Smith has noted that "neo-traditional" Iranian intellectuals (including, I suggest, the Islamo-nationalists that rule Iran today) have tried to wrest the nation out of the hands of secular nationalists and westernizing assimilation. This, Smith correctly notes, is more than a mere "tactical alliance of nationalism with traditional religion," which was what Elie Kedourie previously suggested in regards to Iran.[143] With this in mind, Smith argues:

> there is a more fundamental reason for questioning the thesis of the purely secular nature of nationalism, and that has to do with its role as a species of public culture, with its own political symbols, codes, rituals and practices. Considered strictly as a political doctrine, nationalism may be secular; but, seen as a set of reiterated cultural practices, it appears in a new guise, as a form of religion . . . [144]

Since nationalism did not grow in Iran in opposition to religiosity, and since nationalism can appear as a new form of religion, the contemporary proponents of Islamo-nationalism do not see the amalgamated ideology as self-contradictory. The main rupture between traditional Iranian nationalism and the post-revolutionary Islamo-nationalism lies primarily in the different views on what role should be played by the clergy. The "national constant," including both the nation-state framework, within which the state necessarily functions, and the politicized fragments of culture singled out and institutionalized as constituent elements of Iran's national identity, has ensured that this rupture did not appear as a fundamental paradigm shift—despite its outward appearance as such.

The novelty of a religious regime such as the Islamic Republic should thus not blind us to a historically fluid relationship between religion and state, nor should the secular opposition's insistence on being the keepers of true Iranian national identity blind us to the nationalist nature of the religious regime. Having compared Iran's Constitution with the speeches of Khomeini, Malesevic concludes:

> Unlike the normative level of ideology which speaks in the voice of universality, rationality, and superior ethics, that is in the name of Universal Islam, the operative layer of ideology is profoundly particularistic and appeals to affect and group self-interest among a specific and exceptional social entity—the Iranian nation.[145]

Despite theocratic underpinnings that make it seem an obscurantist anomaly, the Islamic Republic, as a political regime in a nation-state, is part of an international system of regimes and nation-states. In this sense, Iran is no exception, and in many ways similar to other regimes that were essentially nationalist despite professed internationalist solidarity. This includes Russian, Chinese, Cuban and North Korean nationalisms under various communist regimes, or American civil and liberal democratic idealism under various war-mongering, messianic presidents presenting Americans as God's "chosen people."[146]

The Islamic Republic has defaulted to nationalist rhetoric when pan-Islamist rhetoric failed to mobilize support because, in the words of Sami Zubaida, "the logic" of the regime "is pan-Islamic, but its reality is often particular."[147] This does not mean that the ideology of the Islamic Republic is more "untrue" or deceitful than any other ideology. The founders of the Islamic Republic were not blind to social realities, and therefore they did not deny the existence of minorities; they were not any less saturated in the nation-state framework than their monarchic predecessors, and therefore could not abandon nationalism.

Ideology is a "complex, multi-faceted and messy process," Malesevic argues.[148] Thus, the power of the Islamic Republic's ideology is exactly in its amalgamate nature. In the words of Malesevic,

> The potency of nationalism comes from its ability to adapt and metamorphose so as to dovetail with distinct and often contradictory official doctrines. In other words while normative ideologies may be transient and ephemeral, and many change or proliferate in different directions, operative ideologies, in the age of modernity, tend to remain stable and endure, couched in the dominant narrative of nationalism.[149]

While nationalism is not the only ideology in the world, an ideology must be "articulated in a nation-centric way" in order to "resonate with the desires, projects, and aspirations of the general public."[150] In post-revolutionary Iran, the official language has not only shifted from an emphasis on the *Ummah,* the global Muslim community, to the nation, *mellat;* the boundaries of language with which one can praise the nation have also been expanded well beyond those originally established by Khomeini. These semantic, symbolic and aesthetic shifts facilitate an image of *the Order = the Nation* that is supposedly more appealing to the Iranian middle classes and their proclivities toward nationalism rather than pan-Islamism.

This does not mean that religion is unimportant. When combined with Shiite symbolism, Islamist rhetoric and traditional, conservative values, the state narrative projects a vision of *the Order = the Islamic Republic*—a God-given guardian of honor, morality, security, sanctity, peace, law and order in a world increasingly beset by the globalized horrors of Western secular modernity with its imperialism, capitalism, materialism and moral decay. The Islamic Republic, in this projection, is the spiritual order deriving its legitimacy from the revolutionary leaders and the clergy through to the Imams, the Prophets and God. Being a good Muslim means being a good Iranian, and vice versa: *the Order = divine destiny.*

While Iran's leaders would certainly disagree with Smith's argument that the nation is now the "exclusive divinity," it does not change the fact that they treat the Order exactly as a "sacred communion," as the object of the cult of Iranian Islamo-nationalism.[151] Threats to Iran's territorial integrity, culture and civilization, and to the messianic mission bestowed by God on the Iranian nation, including those materializing as ethnic unrest, are thus confronted in epic battles of a "sacred defense."

All this notwithstanding, it is important to keep in mind that the Islamic Republic is not a unanimously unified, internally coherent entity separated from society. Despite recent years of centralization of powers in the hands of Supreme Leader Ayatollah Khamene'i, the regime is still a maze of competing institutions negotiating interests that often conflict. It is a complex state apparatus manned by a diverse elite representing different layers of society even when it does not represent all layers. Khamene'i has since the late 1990s been more or less successful in driving out rivals and marginalizing challenges to his power, and in doing so, has striven to project a vision of *the Order = the Leader*. Yet despite this personification of authority, and despite the general militarization of Iranian politics, there is still room for a certain degree of dissent and divergence. The appearance first of an Islamist-reformist movement in the late 1990s and then of a broad civil society movement against authoritarianism in the aftermath of the 2009 elections has underscored the fact that Khamene'i's vision is in no way uncontested.

As one manifestation of a long history of democratic struggles, the reformist narrative of *the Order = all of Iran's citizens* has planted deep roots in Iran's political soil. Even Ahmadinejad's speeches show that the reformist governments, if nothing, did succeed in de-tabooing the minority issue. However, since the improvements gained by minorities under Khatami's government were mostly in the sphere of cultural policy and not in that of economic progress, and since the reformist narrative of Unity within Diversity did not translate into actual and fundamental reforms, many minority members have become disillusioned. It remains to be seen if state reformism can ever become an ideological narrative that unites all segments of society again—and, if the idea of *the Order = all Iranians, including the minorities* will ever come to be universally accepted.

CHAPTER 4

A NATION DEFENDED

Mayangiz fetne, mayafruz kin
kharābi mayār irānzamin.
[Do not spread sedition, do not incite hatred
Do not bring destruction to the land of Iran.]
— Nezami, *Sharafnāme*, late twelfth century

MINORITY DEMANDS AND ETHNICIST DISCOURSES ON CULTURAL DIFFERENCE represent a profound challenge to the common nationalist notion of what it means to be an Iranian. The issues discussed in this chapter point to a discursive gap between nationalists and ethnicists: the question of how to define "the ethnic" and "the national," whether such terms are mutually exclusive or reciprocally reinforcing, and what role they play in defining the identities of those living in Iran.

In this chapter, I will outline three histories: that of traditional Iranian nationalism, that of the minority issue as a topic in Iranian social sciences and that of the minority issue as an ideological battlefield in post-revolutionary academia. I will show that the key nationalist myth, originating in the late nineteenth and early twentieth centuries, of an *essential homogeneity despite superficial diversity* persists in much writing about Iran today.

As Craig Calhoun has shown, "nationalist visions of internally uniform and sharply bounded cultural and political identities often have to be produced or maintained by a struggle against a richer, more diverse and more promiscuously cross-cutting play of differences and similarities."[1] Anthony Smith has indeed used Iran as an example of how a multi-ethnic country was much more heterogeneous than nationalists and nation-builders would have wished, and that they thus had to make a "careful selection of popular ethnic traditions, symbols and memories," and then elevate "some of them to the exclusion of others."[2] The "intolerance of difference," Michael Billig has pointed out, is an essential characteristic of modernity with its insistence on nation-state congruence: new states were to be "centralized polities, which flattened traditional regional, cultural, linguistic and ethnic differences."[3] National unity came to equal "uniformity" and difference "threat."

To traditional Iranian nationalists, "Iranian-ness" was an identity that stretches across millennia and is defined by a particular language, culture and mindset. In order to defend their definition of Iranian-ness, the nationalist scholars insisted on the nation-state congruence principle, and castigated the expressions of ethnic minority identities. These two aspects are universal to nationalisms everywhere, and not unique to Iran. As the scholar of minority studies, Stephen May has pointed out, modernist thinkers tend to see nation-states as

> something to which we can legitimately give our allegiance... but ethnic groups are not. Nation-states are embracing and cohesive whereas ethnic groups are exclusive and divisive. Nation-states represent modernity while ethnic groups may simply represent a harping, misinformed and misguiding nostalgia.[4]

These binary distinctions, May argues, are based on a pejorative view of ethnicity as a parochial and "anti-national" form of communalism.[5] Nationalism is based on "the claim that the people of a country constitutes a socially integrated body, a meaningful whole," Calhoun argues:[6] national identity becomes the overarching commonality to which unwavering loyalty is demanded, whereas to forward a claim on behalf of a minority becomes a "challenge" to the "presumptive goodness of the nation."[7] As Calhoun has shown, such narratives are often tied up with a claim to a primordial national identity, which is portrayed as a "nearly fixed" identity "moving through history rather than constructed within it."[8] As such, the dominant identitarian discourse conflates progress, unity, stability and peace with the nation-state, and minorities with backwardness, balkanization and destabilization.

In the first half of the chapter, I will show how traditional nationalists portrayed nationhood and national identity, and how they approached the minority issue as an "Internal Other," and then how social sciences took form as a discipline in the context of an authoritarian, Western-inspired monarchic state apparatus and a society undergoing rapid changes, modernization and conflicting ideologies. Nationalism, I will argue, dominated these social sciences up to the Islamic Revolution, and again from the 1990s. This obviously impacts the way the minority issue is understood and studied. Similarly, the political and social changes after the revolution have had a detrimental impact on social science research that still mars the study of minorities today. This first half of the chapter draws on a range of works in Iranian Studies and examples from some primary sources.

In the second half of the chapter, I analyze the semantics of the nationalist backlash against minority mobilization and ethnicist discourses that appeared in the 1990s, as formulated by scholars and public intellectuals united in concern with the minority issue. In particular, I will examine how this nationalist backlash at once draws upon a deep legacy of nationalist discourses and at the same time differs from traditional nationalism in key, fundamental aspects—most importantly, in the question of religion and how the Islamic Republic and its cultural policies are perceived. This second half of the chapter draws on a broad range of scholarly works published in Iran since the death of Khomeini—primarily within the fields of history, sociology, anthropology and political science—and on the statements and writings of a handful of leading nationalist intellectuals and activists—some framed academically but most highly polemical.

The debate over the minority issue, this chapter will show, is indicative, on the one hand, of the persistence of nationalism, and on the other, of broader concerns and ideological battles over Iran's future. This is reflected in an instrumental use of history writing and social sciences for the purpose of defending "the nation" not only against minority mobilization and ethnicist discourses, but also against a state that many nationalist-minded scholars believe is detrimental to Iranian society, and indeed Iranian identity.

THE DEEP LEGACY OF NATIONALISM

ANIMATING THE NATION BODY

Around the turn of the nineteenth century, Iranian intellectuals brought new life to a society that had stagnated under a century of Qajar despotism. These often Western-inspired, sometimes Western-educated, intellectuals crafted a language of nationalism through which they sought to formulate a modern Iran with a strong state and a unified society capable of facing the challenges of a rapidly changing world. In order to understand the ideological and discursive dimension of the minority issue in Iran today, one needs to trace the genealogy of nationalist semantics back to the early modernist thinkers. An obvious point of departure for such an exercise is in the word *mellat*. Even though often translated as "nation," Ludwig Paul captures the versatility of the word:

> English "nation" is usually rendered by Persian *mellat*. In addition, *mellat* also covers part of the meaning of (Engl.) "people"; used in this sense, it competes with another Persian word, *mardom*. In expressions such as *mellat-e mosalmān* or *mellat-e Eslām*, *mellat* is also sometimes used in the sense of "community (of Muslim believers)". In this usage it interchanges with the more prototypical word of this meaning, *ommat* [*Ummah*], which in turn sometimes is used in the sense of "nation/people."[9]

Indeed, the original Koranic *mellat* simply meant "religion," while the Ottomans employed the Turkic variant *millet* to denote various religious communities within the empire. Due to the manifestly religious roots of the term, Paul proposes that "Iranians cannot even think of, or "imagine" themselves as a political community in purely secular terms."[10]

Avoiding such stark generalizations, several scholars have shown that since the eighteenth century, Iranian intellectuals have sought to infuse *mellat* with the Western-inspired, modern sense of "sovereign nation" and "nation-state." From the 1890s, and particularly during the 1905–11 Constitutional Revolution, Iranian intellectuals thus brought about a new modality of perceiving society and subjectivity by transforming the popular meaning of *mellat*: from signifying a Shiite religious community to a political entity and agency encompassing all citizens.[11] Similarly, the related concept of *melliyyat* came in this period to refer to "national identity," "nationhood," "national or ethnic group" and even "nationalism"[12] or "race."[13] Today, *melliyyat* in the juridical sense renders the meaning of "nationality," and thus citizenship: it is the category in a passport that identifies an individual as Iranian.

During the Constitutional Revolution, Mohammad Tavakoli-Targhi notes, there were tensions between French-inspired, often secular-minded intellectuals who understood *mellat* as the total citizenry "without regard to professional, social and religious status," and the clergy, which rejected this definition as heretical.[14] The Shiite exceptionalism witnessed in Iran today is rooted in this contention: as we saw in Chapter 2, the Iranian constitution today still discriminates against non-Shiites. Similarly, Persian-centrism—a key doctrine of traditional Iranian nationalism—also arose out of the chaos and instability of this period. Modernist intellectuals brought from Europe the idea that a nation should have only one national language in order to counter the centrifugal forces of regionalism.

Only few minorities (mostly Armenians and Azeris) were active in the political currents that shaped the Constitutional Revolution, and with it, modern Iran. Some (including certain Kurdish tribes) were even opposed to the revolution, even though not necessarily out of ideological convictions. While the Constitutional Revolution thus popularized new notions of democracy and the rule of law, it also carried within it the seed for future tensions between the centralized state apparatus and the minority periphery. All this notwithstanding, the reconceptualization of *mellat* was key to reframing Iranians as citizens (*shahrvand*) rather than subjects (*ra'iyat*) of the shah.

In the 1870s, Iranian nationalists had also co-opted the Islamic notion of *hobb-e vatan* ("love for the *vatan*"), in which *vatan* originally referred to an individual's faith and birthplace ("the spiritual home"), and eventually turned it into a signifier of the territorial homeland ("the national home").[15] The dialectic processes of centripetal state consolidation and a paradigmatic shift in popular notions of loyalty from traditional and local to those framed as modern and national were also mirrored in the change in the understanding of "Iran": from signifying a loosely knit conglomerate of "protected domains" (*mamālek-e mahruse-ye irān*) under the shah to a modern, unified nation under the state.

In these early nationalist processes of spatial, territorial reification, nationhood became bound up with, on the one hand, an abstract geography of Greater Iran as it "used to be" before foreign powers had diminished the empire—an idea that was at the heart of pan-Iranism (see later in text), and on the other hand, nationhood was understood, in a more pragmatic and urgent sense, to be bound up with the actual physical territory of the modern nation-state. As brilliantly documented by Kashani-Sabet, spatial conceptions of an Iranian homeland (*sarzamin, mihan, vatan*) played a key role in cementing nationalist narratives of identity, in fueling oppositional movements and in consolidating the state.[16] As borders were demarcated amidst intense geopolitical rivalry and imperialist aggression, nationalist intellectuals imbued *vatan* (and its synonym, *mihan*) with a sense of sanctity.

To these intellectuals, "Iran's pure soil" (*khāk-e pāk-e irān*) seemed under perpetual threat by greater military powers that had encroached upon, torn apart and encircled Iran. They developed a siege mentality, and inscribed their territorial fears and ambitions on maps, in pamphlets, poetry and print media. The loss of territory under incompetent Qajar shahs was condemned as *vatan-forushi* ("homeland-sale"), and by the early twentieth century, love for the *vatan* had become a "natural law" of Iranian national politics.[17] The doyen of modern Iranian Studies and Western-educated founder of the intellectual journal *Āyande*, Mahmud Afshar (1893–1983), forcefully expressed this "law":

> The homeland [*vatan*] is the primary collective basis for the solidarity of the people of a nation [*mellat*]. All the people of a homeland must, like the people of one household, strive towards protecting it. What is a homeland? A homeland is a country in which peoples [*mardomān*] have lived for centuries, have together experienced joy and sorrow, good and bad, pain and comfort... The people that live in this collective geographic and historical homeland may have different languages and religions. But if the enemy attacks this homeland-house [*khāne-ye vatani*], it is the duty of all to defend it.[18]

Afshar was a key proponent of what I term *traditional nationalism*, which was to a certain extent secularist. Afshar thus viewed Iranian nationhood as something above and beyond religion: the homeland existed well before the advent of Islam. In accordance with the core nationalist principle of nation-state congruence, the homeland was seen as the prerequisite for the modern nation-state: homeland equals nation equals state. The subordinate clause about "peoples" and "different languages and religions" indicates an awareness of cultural diversity. However, the bottom-line was that the homeland-nation is the overarching entity to which all loyalty must be directed.

Afshar was one of the intellectuals who informed and inspired the state nationalism that was institutionalized under the Pahlavis. In that period, the image of Reza Shah as *vatan*-saver was promoted in the education system and in state propaganda as a counter-image to the *vatan*-selling Qajars, while *vatan* came to equal "one race, one language and one religion."[19] In this exclusivist narrative of national uniformity, *vatan* came to signify the geophysical embodiment of a Persian-speaking Shiite Iranian people. The state and its supporters evoked narratives on national culture to counter the potential threat emanating from tribes and minorities (the Internal Other) and from abroad (the External Other). In the words of the eminent scholar of Iranian social history, Ervand Abrahamian:

> The modernizing intellectuals, even those originating from the non-Farsi minorities, associated linguistic diversity with oriental inefficiency, regional autonomy with administrative anarchy, and tribal nomadism with rural gangsterism. They planned to transform their multi-tribal, multi-lingual, and multi-cultural empire into a unified state with one central authority, one language, one culture, and one nationality.[20]

As Reza Shah campaigned in Iran's far-flung peripheries, quelling tribal and minority insurgencies, subduing autonomist local rulers and forcibly settling nomads, Iranian politics were militarized in a way different from previous political regimes. Whereas before, Iran was ruled as a network of tribal alliances and clientelist autonomies, the state now demanded full loyalty to one source of centralized power backed up by the monopolized use of force.

However, when Reza Shah had finally quashed all resistance and brought the entire territory under his command, the new dictatorship needed to glue together the new entirety. For this end, Reza Shah could utilize the notion of a distinct, homogeneous "national identity" that modernist intellectuals had forged out of selected

124 MINORITIES IN IRAN

cultural traits in a heterogeneous society, and thus to merge the disparate, disjointed fragments into a coherent whole. In the words of Rouzbeh Parsi,

> This is the official line which every nationalist must tow: on the one hand the nation exists and does not need to be conjured into existence; on the other hand it is in danger and its primordial cohesion must be strengthened. Its members must be "reminded" of who they are, educated as to their true identity.[21]

As in classical European nationalism, the temporal and emotional reification created an anthropomorphic depiction of the nation as an organic entity. The animated nation-body could sense and remember both existing and deceased members, and it naturally instilled loyalty in all its members. The nationalists thus sought to endow Iran as an entirety with a unified national spirit, and a single national culture.

ROOTED IN COMMON GROUND

In deciding what should constitute the national culture, nationalists took it upon themselves to write new histories of the nation. In the words of Afshin Marashi, they used the pre-Islamic past as a "convenient template" for this creative reinvention of "Iranian culture in a modern form."[22] Conceptions of Iran as a territorial entity were dug out from ancient and medieval texts, particularly from Iran's national epos, the *Shāhnāme,* and recast in a modern light. Romanticizing pre-Muslim invasion Iranian empires and yearning for ancient grandeur, the nationalists sought authenticity in an undiluted, "true" Iranian civilization set apart from its surroundings. This pre-Islamic civilization was enlightened, and not, as Islamic history writing claimed, an era of ignorance (*jāheliyyat*).[23] Out of Iran's antiquity, the nationalist intellectuals created for the nation a narrative of an exceptional identity.

However, this portrayal was more profound and nuanced than a shallow chauvinist nostalgia. The nineteenth century saw a surge in literary and artistic creativity as well as in philological, linguistic, historical and archaeological interests and discoveries, all augmented by a rapidly evolving dialogue with scholars in the West. Pre-Islamic myths and folkloristic tales were recast as social and political critique of the present in diaspora writing; new histories were written in a simplified language and medieval works republished; interest in masterpieces such as the *Shāhnāme* grew among both aristocrats and commoners; the state ordered excavations and commissioned the weaving of national carpets and new movements rekindled public interest in pre-Islamic Zoroastrianism.[24]

This wave of endeavors and interest in the past in turn bolstered a call for sweeping top-down societal reform to bring Iran back on its course and into the future.[25] A linear, national history became the key thread in the modernist tapestry of "Iranianness," which was woven to inspire progress: the national history conveyed a narrative of development and refinement despite setbacks and obstacles. According to this history, Iranian nationhood and national identity date at least to the Median Empire (625–549 B.C.), and certainly to the Achaemenid Empire (549–330 B.C.). Today, this myth of national genesis still dominates in lay public discourse and flourishes in authoritative works of scholarship.

In his 1993 talk on "Persian identity," Ehsan Yar-Shater (see Introduction) thus argued that the rise of the Medes against Mesopotamian domination was a "very early affirmation of Iranian identity," and that this identity was "clearly asserted in the inscriptions of Darius the Great (522–486 B.C.), who as an Aryan and a Persian was fully conscious of his racial affiliation and proud of his national identity."[26] When the Muslim armies ("the Arabs") invaded Iran in the seventh century A.D., this identity was, according to Yar-Shater, confronted with its gravest threat ever:

> The response that emerged after decades of struggle [against "the Muslim Arab armies"] was a compromise: adoption of Islam on one hand and preservation of the Persian language and cultural heritage on the other. The dichotomy implicit in this compromise has confused and bedeviled the Persian psyche to this day, but it has also invigorated and uplifted the spirit of the Persian intellectual elite.[27]

In this historicized narrative, Iranian national identity is understood to predate the emergence of the modern nation-state, and reified to the extent of becoming a "psyche." Islam is seen as the religion of "Arabs," and the Iranian conversion as a forced choice. Islam is presented as the root cause of an identity crisis, "bedeviling" Iranians throughout the centuries. This line of argument exemplifies the traditional, secular nationalist understanding of history. Moreover, when Yar-Shater identifies Darius the Great as an "Aryan," he weaves into the nationalist tapestry another key piece: that of "race."

The 1786 linguistic establishment of an Indo-European language family that included Persian, combined with the emergence of racialized ideology in Europe, had a profound impact on Iranian intellectuals.[28] The conflation of linguistic and archaeological findings with racial hypotheses of ancestry and superiority brought about the notion of Iranians as an "Aryan" people that is fundamentally different from, and superior to, surrounding peoples such as the Semite Arabs, "Yellow" Mongols or Altaic Turks. The equation of the European concept of "Aryan" with certain words in Vedic, Old Persian and Avestan sources fortified the idea that "Iran" simply *meant* "the home of Aryans." This, Reza Zia-Ebrahimi argues, created "one of history's less-researched—albeit most impactful—malapropisms."[29] From the 1870s onward, nationalists popularized this imagined nexus between language, culture and race, spreading Aryanism in the literate strata of society as if a scientific fact.

Recent research shows that such notions of racial superiority were not, as Mostafa Vaziri has suggested,[30] simply "planted" in Iran by Orientalists and European imperialists (see Chapter 5). Rather, the racialized fetishization of everything pre-Islamic was used to appropriate, not merely simulate, European modernity.[31] Nonetheless, Aryanism afforded certain nationalists an imagined ladder of civilizational superiority on which to elevate Iranians, moving them closer to the "White" European utopia of modernity.[32]

As Benedict Anderson has noticed, language is to the patriot what the eye is to the lover,[33] and it was in the Persian language that nationalists saw the richest repository of symbols to bolster their narratives on Iranian-ness. Early nationalists argued that a common language was a vital prerequisite for a people to turn into a modern nation;[34] indeed, to some, a nation simply meant "a people [*ommat*] speaking in one language."[35] The outstanding scholar Shahrokh Meskoub (1925–2005) articulated this significance of language.[36] According to Meskoub, Iran existed as a nation centuries before the coming of Islam but took the shape of a nation-state (*hokumat-e melli*) four centuries after the Muslim invasion:[37]

> Only in two matters were we, the Iranians, set apart from other Muslims: in our history and language... It was exactly upon these two factors that we built our national or ethnic [*qowmi*] identity. One (history) was our support, provision for the road to be traveled, our refuge[;] and the other (language), was the foundation, the base and soul sanctuary, the stronghold in which we stood firm.[38]

Meskoub, and many other historians of his generation, thus claimed the Persian language and literature was the prerequisite for the existence of an independent Iranian nation.[39] Indeed, "the blessing" of Persian language, he argued, was the glue that holds together not only Iranian society but Iranian-ness itself. Works such as the *Shāhnāme* provided nationalists with a vast repertoire of symbolism with which to portray Persian language as "the soul" of Iran. This Persian-centrism has influenced much academic writing on Iran for a century, and it is echoed all the way up to the 1990s, when Ehsan Yar-Shater wrote the following:

> A more promising defense against the sense of anonymity that accompanies a submerged identity is a restorative and sustaining element that Persia has cherished and preserved against all odds: the shared experience of a rich and rewarding past. It finds its expression primarily through the Persian language, not simply as a medium of comprehension but also as the chief carrier of the Persian world view and Persian culture. The Persian language (not Farsi, please) is a reservoir of Iranian thought, sentiment, and values, and a repository of its literary arts. It is only by loving, learning, teaching, and above all enriching this language that the Persian identity may continue to survive.[40]

This quote succinctly summarizes the identitarian worldview of Persian-centric Iranian nationalism: the Persian language equals the Persian (i.e., Iranian) identity (in singular). This identity—a reified, indeed almost tangible, entity—has been "submerged" and must be restored to its true state, and for this, it is completely dependent not just on its Persian speakers but on the very language itself. There is, in short, a sense of exigency and crisis: Persian language must survive and flourish, for without it, Iranian-ness cannot be sustained in the face of the cultural, religious and political onslaught of foreign-ness.

Yar-Shater's view on language and identity is in direct continuation of the traditional nationalist view. In the words of Kashani-Sabet, the early nationalists in effect used language to draw up a "Persian perimeter" with which to distinguish their territorial-spatial unit and cultural-temporal identity from that of the Other.[41] As Kashani-Sabet shows, language was used in the nineteenth century "to justify Iran's irredentist crusades in claiming territories that had come to represent Iranzamin,"[42] or "The Soil of Iran." Indeed, many nationalist histories begin with a lengthy exposition of the historical importance of Persian and a lamentation over its loss of regional status.

An example of this is provided in a book on the old *āzari* language by Naseh Nateq (1901 or 1905–1984), an influential nationalist writer, translator and poet. In this book, Nateq claims that since ancient times, Iran's enemies have schemed to progressively eradicate Persian from Central Asia and the Caucasus, replacing it with other languages, all with the ultimate aim of wiping out Iranian identity.[43] Indeed, Nateq argues, it is nothing but a miracle that Iran still exists and that this miracle can be explained by the Persian language and its literature. In short, language was and is a matter of life and death to traditional Iranian nationalists: for keeping alive the Persian cultural sphere and for consolidating the nation-state with all its fragments.

The focus on language materialized in a twentieth-century purification drive to root out words considered foreign and to replace them with equivalents in earlier forms of Persian, or with neologisms with a "Persian sound." This purist restyling reflected the desire to disassociate Iran from Arabic culture by distilling a supposedly undiluted "pure" or "sweet Persian" (*pārsi-ye serre, qand-e pārsi*) free of Arabic loanwords. While this literary and linguistic drive sometimes produced, in Marashi's words, "a somewhat stilted literary style,"[44] it also spawned creative processes and "inventions of tradition" that influenced the development of modern Persian literature.

The language purification drive, Persian-centrism and Aryanism were all related to the often contentious relationship of traditional secular nationalism with Islam. As Mehrdad Kia has argued, while Iranian nationalists had ceded European superiority in the material realm, they still retained "the spiritual realm" as a "domain of sovereignty."[45] However, since Islam dominated this spiritual realm, nationalists had to challenge the hegemony of the Shiite clergy by associating it with regression, conservatism and Arab culture—a challenge that we will see later in text has recently been revived in a wholly different context.

It was in the works of these secular-minded traditional nationalists that the various narratives merged: that of Iranians belonging to one race, which happened to be the same as Europeans (Aryanism); the notion of pre-Islamic splendor and the eternal Iranian nation (perennialism and "ancientism"); and the emphasis on "pure" Persian language and culture (Persian-centrism)—sometimes to the extent that other languages and cultures should be subdued or eradicated.

By the time of Reza Shah's ascendancy to power, the nationalist intellectuals and scholars had brought about the narratives needed to bolster a modern state, to curb the power of the clergy and to instill in the population a sense of pride and superiority. The Pahlavis established a Language Academy to remove Arabic words from Persian while they issued orders for the renaming of cities, places and regions, and stipulated how Iranians should dress. The increasingly megalomaniac shahs wrote themselves into the history of imperial grandeur,[46] the symbolic culmination of which was in Mohammad-Reza Shah's opulent 1971 celebration of "2,500 years of monarchy."

The nationalist fetish for the past was not regressive, but rather part of negotiating nativist modernity in Iran. Yet while nationalist intellectuals had provided the broader populace with a sense of historical continuity, they had also, even if unwillingly, endowed the Pahlavis with a history befitting tyrants. Even though the same intellectuals soon fell prey to the monarch's paranoid suppression of dissent, they had

128

equipped a new state with all the identitarian tenets required for an authoritarian regime.

THE INTERNAL OTHER

In writing a streamlined national history and in canonizing a uniform, standardized national culture, Iranian nationalists were forced to deal with the ambiguous topic of ethnic diversity. This presence of an Internal Other did not always fit these narratives on the homogeneity. In the words of Kia, only by "denying the existence of non-Persian identities could this nationalist discourse portray Iran as an ancient and unified nation with one history, one culture and one literary language."[47] With Reza Khan's crowning as shah in 1925, these denials of diversity, the fixation on the Persian language and the glorification of the "Aryan" myth were institutionalized as policies of cultural homogenization that had wide-ranging impact on Iran's minorities.

This change occurred at a very sensitive time in Iranian history. In the first three decades of the twentieth century, Iranians had experienced revolution and state repression, regionalist rebellions and tribal insurgencies, socialist-inspired movements and nascent industrial labor action, the rapid expansion of the oil industry, the imperialist division of the country into spheres of interest, as well as foreign occupation. From afar, the Russian Revolution, the disintegration of the Ottoman Empire, rebellions in India and wars in Afghanistan sent reverberations through the region. Following World War I, nationalist feelings gathered momentum in Iran. The fear of territorial disintegration, foreign power machinations and the rapid spread of new ethnicist ideologies such as pan-Turkism and pan-Arabism galvanized the popular demand for centralization of power, strengthening of the military, curbing of tribal forces and, in short, a modern social order.

A main domestic obstacle to attaining this order, nationalists argued, was the existence of unruly tribes and minorities in Iran's periphery. In journals such as *Irānshahr, Āyande* and *Farangestān,* they stressed that in order to make all citizens identify as Iranians, local, regional and minority languages and dialects, customs and traditions had to be reformed or eliminated. Homogenization, intellectuals such as Mahmud Afshar argued, was the only solution:

> By national unity is meant that Persian should become customary throughout the country, that regional differences in clothing, mindset and so on be stamped out, that traditional tribal power [*moluk-ot-tavāyefi*] be completely eradicated, that there should be no difference between Kurd, Lor, Qashqa'i, Arab, Turk, Turkmen, etc. and that each of these should no longer wear a one kind of attire and speak one kind of language [other than Persian]. It is our belief that until Iran is endowed with national unity in terms of language, mindset, dress etc., there will always be a potential threat to political independence and territorial integrity.[48]

Indeed, in order to make all inhabitants "Iranian in the fullest sense," society should be made "uniform" (*yek-navākht*), and this could be achieved through development schemes in education and transport infrastructure, through scientific and literary endeavors, by changing non-Persian place names to Persian and by facilitating demographic shifts and ethnic inter-mixing. Writing in 1925, the same year Reza Khan became Reza Shah, Afshar warned that if these changes did not take place, Iran would face total disintegration.

Minorities were thus portrayed, on the one hand, as a threatening element. On the other hand, nationalists sought to downplay or even reject the existence of cultural diversity by insisting on Iranian-ness: minorities were inseparably bound to Iran through shared linguistic, racial and cultural roots, and any attempt at "forging" distinct identities was an act against Iran's national unity. Naseh Nateq, for example, argued that those who advocated minority and cultural rights "may be well-wishers," but that they were in fact pursuing goals that would benefit Iran's avaricious neighbors.

In the case of the Azeris, Nateq maintained that never in history had they "seen themselves as different from other Iranians" and that they furthermore had always "shared destiny with Iran's people."[49] Turkic-speaking tribes had proved their loyalty by defending Iran against the Turkic-speaking Uzbeks and Ottomans, and today they would defend Iran against pan-Turkism out of pure *shur-e irāndusti* ("Iran-loving passion"). Anyone who imagined that Azeris could or would want to have a "life, way of thinking or culture" separate from that of "the mass of Iranian peoples" was clearly unaware of "historical rationality" and "geographical reality."[50] Indeed, Nateq explained, an Azeri "thinks Iranian, writes Persian but speaks Turkic," and only ignorant people would assign the Azeris to the Turkic "race" of nomadic tribes.[51] Contrasting the rough barbarians of Central Asia with the refined pioneers, poets, prophets and heroes of Iranian high civilization, Nateq thus presented Turks as a race less magnificent than the Iranian—only to underscore that the Azeris of Iran were no longer Turks but simply Iranians.

About Khuzestan, Nateq wrote that Iranians loved and respected the Arabic-speaking minority, *as long as* members of this minority would "feel Iranian and view Iranian culture as their own culture."[52] However, Nateq modified with a warning, stating that Arabs "must keep in mind that they are guests in the country of Iran."[53] The "family of Iran" here seemed somewhat dysfunctional: Iran's Arabs should not take the nation's love, or even their existence on Iranian soil, for granted. Arabs, and other minorities, were thus turned by certain nationalists into Internal Others—balancing on a knife's edge between being accepted and internalized in the National Self or rejected and alienated as subversive foreign elements. This was particularly true of minorities such as the Arabs who perceived themselves, or were presented as, belonging to a different "race" than the Persian-speaking core.

In the Aryanist discourse, the "noble" Aryan Self was contrasted with a barbarian Other that was portrayed by nationalists, retrospectively and contemporarily, as the source of Iran's misfortune, as obstacles to Iran's renaissance or as diseases that had struck the nation body.[54] Nationalists such as Afshar claimed that in terms of "its proud history of several millennia and the outstanding Aryan race," Iran was "distinguished from its yellow-skinned neighbors in Turan" (a concept Afshar borrowed from the *Shāhnāme* to denote Altaic peoples), and from "the Semitic Arabs."[55] Indeed, Afshar warned, Turks and Mongols constituted a "Yellow Peril" and Arabs and Semites a "Green Peril" to Iran: these were Iran's eternal enemies, more dangerous than European powers. This portrayal obviously had contradictory effects on the national unity narrative vis-à-vis minorities that were not deemed Aryan and/or spoke Altaic and Semitic languages.

Afshar tried to dodge this contradiction by mentioning minorities only in passing, or by claiming that "the mixture of different peoples in the Iranian stock has not resulted in any difference in the homogeneity of the Iranian race."[56] In this way, the social fact of diversity was tabooed, denied or distorted to fit a myth of homogeneity and to bolster what was seen as an Iranian identity under threat. The idea that Iranians belong to a "true/noble/pure race" (nezhād-e asil) figured prominently in the nationalist discourse because it fitted the nation-state congruence narrative of one people, one polity. This was also reflected in the question of language.

In the spirit of Persian-centric Iranian nationalism, several social reformers and intellectuals called for the "Iranization" of minorities through Persian language. In 1929, Afshar stated that Iran's national unity was "impaired" due to its linguistic diversity and that since religion was not necessarily going to hold together the population any longer, much effort was needed in promoting Persian as the source of cohesion. Being the largest minority language, and a non-Indo-European one at that, Azeri was often the focus of calls for linguistic homogenization. As early as 1906, modernist intellectuals had claimed that "our present misfortunes can be traced to the Mongol and Tatar invasions, when a foreign language was imposed on our beloved Azarbayjan, and our population was sharply divided into Farsi and Turkish speakers."[57]

The national poet Aref-e Qazvini (1882–1934) used his popular concerts to call on Iran's Azeris to abandon Azeri Turkic on the grounds that this language was "a shameful reminder of the Turkic and Mongol domination." Qazvini implored his Azeri audience to instead embrace "the beautiful and sweet Persian."[58] The founder of Iran's major communist Tude Party, Taqi Arani (1903–1940), championed the total obliteration of Turkic language. Nateq demonized languages such as Azeri Turkic and Arabic as zabān-hā-ye tahmili ("imposed languages") that had been employed against Iran by enemies at various historical stages. While Nateq did not demand total linguicide, he nonetheless called on ethnic minorities to "honor the Persian language and its precious literature" and to make sure that their own languages did not "open the roads for foreign influence into the country" by providing enemies with a pretext to intervene.[59]

A key claim to justify Persian linguistic hegemony was that Persian was allegedly more sophisticated than any other language spoken in Iran. Nateq claimed that Turkic could have replaced the ancient "Azari Persian" only because it was a "very simple and easy language" that "fitted the lives of Azerbaijan's peasant masses" with its lack of the stylistic grace and grammatical complexities that characterized Persian and Arabic.[60] Furthermore, it was only through "the power of the sword" that Iranians in Azerbaijan had succumbed to Turkic, letting this language of the invaders cover Azerbaijan "with a metaphorical cloth":[61] Turkic was the language of a violent, occupying enemy from a lower culture, and Persian the high tongue of a cosmopolitan, refined civilization.

Thus, nationalists under Reza Shah—after centuries of monarchic rule by bilingual Turkic—and Persian-speaking dynasties, and despite the multi-lingual, multi-ethnic diversity of the population—declared that Iran could henceforth only have one national language and one national culture. They had created a nationalist discourse—or, more precisely, a set of identitarian narratives on culture—that would shape not only Iranian politics but also social science research, history writing and public debate for the century to come.

GAZING INWARD

The ways in which public intellectuals and scholars today discuss the minority issue in Iran are, as elsewhere, closely connected to the political and social context in which their academic centers of learning and knowledge production are placed. The history of social sciences in Iran is intertwined with the history of the Iranian state apparatus and dominant ideologies of modernity.

While a form of indigenous Iranian ethnography can be traced back to medieval travel accounts, nineteenth-century scholars were the first to employ ethnography in its modern sense. Under the Pahlavis, from the 1930s onward, the nascent field of anthropology was dominated by positivism and the idea of social science as natural science. The scholar was posited as a champion of modernity against tradition, and social sciences as tools for state-building. Anthropologists and sociologists were used to develop human power for the new bureaucracy, propagate state ideology, facilitate policies, assist reforms and internalize ideology in the populace.

This view on social sciences amounted to what anthropologist Ne'matollah Fazeli has called a "military approach to culture,"[62] and rare was the social scientist who had the opportunity and means to work independently. Fazeli has comprehensively documented the "reciprocal and intimate" relationship between modernist-nationalist discourse and early Iranian anthropology.[63] As elsewhere, early social sciences and folklore studies in Iran were rooted in nationalist romanticism and the identitarian quest for "authenticity" in the National Self, while at the same time wedded to a modernist pursuit of enlightenment and reform against traditionalism and backwardness. Sociology was dominated by Durkheimian notions of solidarity and "collective consciousness," and Aryanist (and sometimes Nazi-inspired) notions of racial primacy and supremacy were embedded in genealogies of identity.[64]

Scholars in general were pushed to focus on mythology and the role of common cultural traditions such as *Nowruz,* and on restoring and presenting in museums ancient culture and relics of national heritage. The Pahlavis saw social science research institutions as instrumental in strengthening national culture over minority cultures. The state obstructed the publication of folklore materials gathered in non-Persian-speaking communities and expected anthropologists to assist in the state's program of forcibly settling nomads. This first generation of Iranian anthropologists adopted the European and American social theories and methods they encountered, often through studying abroad. From the 1950s onward, Iranian anthropology was also partly shaped by the foreign anthropologists who came to Iran for fieldwork and through university exchange.

Iran provided many researchers with a unique arena for ethnography, empirical surveys and participant observation.[65] This research contributed significantly to the later development of ethnicity studies in the west: Fredrik Barth's work on Iranian and Afghan tribes is today required reading for students of anthropology in Europe and the United States.[66] From the 1960s, and with renewed energy since the 1990s, anthropologists associated with Iranian Studies have expanded their field considerably with issues pertaining to women, urban communities, religion, language, law, memory, youth culture and broader questions of the encounter with modernity. Yet studies of modern and non-tribal minority communities have been preciously rare in the body of literature.

In the 1960s, reactions against the Iranian state approach to social science, history and folklore studies surfaced through counter-discourses to Pahlavi secular, Westernizing nationalism and monarchic authoritarianism.[67] Intellectuals sought to envision an alternative, native Iranian modernity, and to rediscover an authentic Self. Intellectuals such as Ehsan Naraqi, Gholamhosein Sediqi, Mahmud Ruholamini and Abolqasem Anjavi-Shirazi strove to establish an indigenous anthropology free of the typical Western research agendas and their underlying ideologies. Political thinkers such as Jalal Al-e Ahmad and 'Ali Shari'ati used ethnography, travel writing and social critique to imagine a spiritual and culturally authentic modernity that would set Iranians free from their increasing addiction to anything Western. These intellectuals also paved the way for a new generation of Iranian scholars who were engaged in documenting their own non-Persian minority cultures within Iran.

However, as Fazeli points out, the various strains of nativist intellectualism had self-realization as common goal rather than objective research or rigorous academic explorations.[68] Whether they and their successors currently active in Iranian academia have succeeded in establishing an indigenous anthropology remains an open question.[69] Yet their contributions to a more diverse understanding of Iran were significant and far reaching, as were their contributions, directly and indirectly, to the intellectual and ideological aspects of the revolutionary movement that swept away the Pahlavi regime in 1978–9. However, the consolidation of the post-revolutionary regime had far-reaching and largely detrimental consequences for social sciences.

Khomeini deemed much of the research produced in social sciences and the humanities to be part of Western colonialist, anti-Islamic crusades of the West against Iran and the Muslim world, and after 1979, Iranian academia was engulfed in the so-called Cultural Revolution and the drive to Islamize Iran's universities. Scholars not deemed to conform to revolutionary ideals were expelled or accused of acting as a fifth column, students and staff screened for ideological commitment, research policies and university structures changed, curricula revised and the physical space of campuses symbolically Islamized. The revolutionary clergy demanded that research and teaching be framed by Islamist ideology, and state intervention curtailed academic freedom while universities were forced to cooperate with religious seminaries and comply with the recommendations of clerical supervision.

As an antidote to research rooted in evolutionary theory, Marxism and cultural relativism, the Islamic Republic has sought to promote an Islamic social science that is epistemologically antithetic to secular philosophy. Instead of empirical research, scholars are often required to focus on sources in Islamic history and religious texts,[70] and except in natural sciences and medicine, cooperation with foreign scholars is often discouraged. In addition to the general post-revolutionary clampdown on dissident intellectuals, the eight-year war with Iraq also impacted negatively on universities and academia. In the name of national unity, critical research was shelved and resources spent elsewhere.

However, with the relative political relaxation following Khomeini's death in 1989, social sciences experienced a number of positive developments: new research centers, academic organizations and museums were established; the numbers of researchers, students and courses offered increased; new journals and publications appeared; numerous books were translated into Persian and the scope of anthropological discussion was broadened considerably.[71] Much of this progress, in tune with the rapid expansion of higher education, was initiated or accelerated by the reformist governments of 1997–2005.

However, the expansion of research into topics that were deemed unnecessary or were tabooed under Khomeini also points toward an increased appreciation within the state apparatus of certain aspects of social sciences. In line with its normative ideology of spiritual and material independence and self-sufficiency, the state has invested in projects that utilize local knowledge (*dānesh-e bumi*), and it has also used anthropological research to shape more sustainable policies toward the nomadic communities.[72] Yet the state drive to Islamicize social sciences has not translated, so far at least, into a paradigm shift from nationalism to Islamism.

The study of Iran's minorities is today disadvantaged by two sets of problems, one that is general to all social science research in Iran and another that is specific to the minority issue. Among the former, critical scholars point to the lack of overall state vision and planning. According to Fazeli, the state views expansion of higher education as a goal in itself, which is why disciplines such as anthropology remain immature and lacking in basic research, qualitative approaches and critical perspectives.[73] Fazeli argues that post-revolutionary restrictions, a negative state attitude and the fact that pro-regime and Islamist-oriented scholars receive the bulk of funding impede the development of scholarly critique and self-critique. It has also contributed to a drastic decline in the quality of research, teaching and learning, while research institutions are often managed by lesser-qualified bureaucrats, and rarely by outspoken scholars.[74] Fazeli and Naser Fakouhi, Head of Tehran University's Department for Anthropology, both argue that amateurs outweigh professionals in terms of publishing.[75] Fakouhi has also shown that male authors dominate social science research output.[76] Despite revitalization, many key areas of social inquiry are still taboo,[77] and students often see anthropology as the study of archaic topics rather than issues of contemporary relevance.[78]

Social sciences also suffer from a lack of a comparative and cross-cultural perspective that is caused by Iran's political isolation and the lack of exchange and cooperation with scholars abroad.[79] While anthropologists are forced to work within Iran and focus on national concerns, they are also constrained by the regime's "red lines" that obstruct the critical application of anthropology "inwards." Fazeli explains that "many social scientists have been directly or indirectly put under pressure to consider the political priorities of the state" in order to attain or keep a job.[80] The ideological monitoring breeds self-censorship, and has discouraged many scholars from engaging with sensitive issues such as ethnicity, and instead present only "what is good about Iranian society and the country in general."[81] Fazeli concludes:

> [T]he political and social cost of doing independent research has always been high. Under these circumstances only pro-regime scholars, those who seek economical and political rewards, and anti-regime scholars who heroically accept myriad political and social pressures, have succeeded in working. Accordingly, a scholar may be a hero or a servant of the state. The third way, namely the life of an independent scholar who seeks to critically elucidate society and culture is difficult if not impossible.[82]

This untenable situation is arguably very evident to those who choose to study minorities in an independent and critical manner. While recent years have seen the topic of ethnic minorities return to academic research and public debate, the research is often coupled with a broader secular nationalist agenda. Since the 1990s, several institutions have also expanded their focus to include the minority issue. The political objectives of some of these institutions, I will argue later in text, are connected not only to reformist currents, but also to resurgent state nationalism.

THE PERSISTENCE OF NATIONALISM

A NEW, OLD BATTLEGROUND

The late-1990s reformist wave brought about new spaces for discussion about the minority issue in Iran. Apart from making it possible to publicly express ethnicist views and minority demands, these new spaces—in media, in universities and in intellectual and political circles—also made room for the expression of nationalist views that were more or less unheard of in the years prior to Khatami's presidency.

Together with independent public intellectuals, political activists and journalists, a broad range of scholars expressed such nationalist views through scholarship, often produced in research bodies that were either established by Khatami's government or had been re-staffed with reformists. These scholars obviously had to observe the official and unofficial limits to what can be said and written within the official institutional framework. Nonetheless, while benefitting from it, they were able to address what they perceived as a negative outcome of this relatively freer political atmosphere: the emergence of minority mobilization, ethnicism and ethno-nationalism. They expressed a common concern with what was described as an identity crisis— an "ethnic identity crisis" or a "national identity crisis." To inform the public of this crisis, these scholars are today dealing head-on with the sensitive topic of ethnic diversity.

Indeed, the nationalist paradigm that shaped the early twentieth century modernist visions of Iran still holds sway over the spheres in which the minority issue is discussed today: in the knowledge produced in universities and in the statements of public intellectuals. Nationalist-minded scholars and intellectuals approach the minority issue with a combination of myths of unity and notions of threat similar to those early nationalists used to demand a strong, centralized state and the repression of rebellious and non-conforming societal elements: on the one hand, they evoke and embellish narratives of common racial ancestry, linguistic affinity, shared mythology and certain stereotypical portrayals of minorities; on the other hand, they evoke the image of foreign enemies and conspiracies. At stake, the nationalists argue, is the very existence of Iran.

This serves a particular purpose: using the prism of "identity crisis," the nationalists are discussing the minority issue within the context of a broader national concern with the direction in which the ruling elite is taking Iran. These scholars and intellectuals together represent the hitherto most evident attempt at bringing back overtly nationalist identitarianism in Iranian public discourse after two decades of post-revolutionary representations of nationalism as one of the great evils of Western civilization, antithetical to Islam and directly opposed to the Islamic Republic. Today, the new research and debate about ethnic diversity and national identity is re-appropriating the language, aesthetics and ideology of nationalism. As such, the new research and debate at times complements the Islamo-nationalist discourse, and at other times it directly challenges its Islamist element.

However, while some nationalist-minded scholars and intellectuals are critical of, or even opposed to, the Islamic Republic, not all of them are. Between the lines of the books, articles and interviews, one can discern opinions of a factional spectrum that spans from secularist (particularly people associated with the *Jebhe-ye melli* or National Front) over so-called religious-nationalist (*melli-mazhabi*) and reformist (*eslāh-talabān*) to the populist neo-conservatives associated with president Ahmadinejad. Thus, while some use the minority issue as a discursive ground for a nationalist critique of Islamist policies, others use it to present new vistas of a future Islamic Republic. This latter category thus represents a partial shift in the objectives of state research policy: when these scholars are able to use their positions in state-funded research bodies to express certain nationalist views, they are sometimes indicating internal differences within the state apparatus.

Yet even with Iran's political arena in a state of flux, with perpetual re-alignments and a multiplicity of small and big differences in ideological stance, the nationalist-minded scholars and intellectuals have something in common that is more stable than their nominal political affiliations and professional positions: the project of bringing back nationalism, in one way or another, to counter-balance the power of the conservative clergy and the idealist pan-Islamism of the revolutionary fathers. This project is reflected in the two interrelated domains of public debate and academic research.

The following analyses will be based mostly on the works of important commentators who differ in professional and political affiliation. I will add some biographical detail throughout, and here just introduce one key person and a key institution. Professor Hamid Ahmadi of Tehran University is Iran's foremost expert on national identity, ethnicity and the history of minority mobilization. Born in 1957, he was educated in political science at Tehran University and received his doctorate from Carleton University in Canada in 1995. Ahmadi's doctoral dissertation was later published in Iran, and since then, he has written numerous books, articles and interviews.[83] In these works, Ahmadi has pursued two goals in particular: to dismiss the key arguments of radical ethnicists and warn the public of the threat of ethnonationalism and to criticize both radical Islamist state policies and radical strands of secularist Iranian nationalism. In this sense, Ahmadi appears to be inspired by, if not aligned to or supported by, reformist and religious-nationalist circles in Iran. This is underscored by the fact that his key works appeared during the reformist government. Ahmadi, I will argue, is at the forefront of the new wave of nationalistic scholarship.

The National Studies Institute (*mo'asase-ye motāle'āt-e melli*) is, according to its website, founded in 1997 as a "non-profit, non-governmental" entity, a "scientific, research-based, cultural and specialist institution in the field of... Iran's national identity." The caveat in Chapter 3 about Iranian media—that such claims to NGO status should be taken with a pinch of salt—also extends to research institutions. Any such body can operate only under the generally quite strict control of the state and with the approval of relevant ministries. This is particularly so when the topics of research are as sensitive and important as those of the National Studies Institute: national unity, societal cohesion, ethnic groups and Iranian identity. Within these fields, the Institute has a quite remarkable record of publication: more than 30 monographs, edited volumes, translated works and poetry collections as well as a periodical, *Motāle'āt-e melli* (National Studies), which first appeared in 1999, received recognition as a scientific journal by the Ministry of Research in 2006 and is still running at the time of writing.

While the websites of the institute and the journal contain overviews of members and editorial boards, no information is given on the founders. According to unconfirmed reports, however, one of the founding members is a controversial advisor of Ahmadinejad.[84] Whether or not this is true, the fact that the institute not only remained open while other research bodies founded during the Khatami years were shut down by Ahmadinejad in 2005, but also received official recognition in 2006 shows that the Institute serves purposes aligned with the interests of some forces in the ruling elite. This is remarkable since the institute's output is often characterized by nationalistic views contrary to much of the established, state-supported research.

In the following subsections, I will outline the key arguments of scholars such as Hamid Ahmadi and those associated with state-sanctioned academic institutions, as well as of influential nationalist-minded intellectuals, with the purpose of analyzing the impact of resurgent nationalism on the debate about the minority issue. I will show that some of the arguments made and conclusions drawn in this literature are based on exclusivist notions of Iranian-ness and often stereotypical views on minorities. This critique, however, should not be understood as a wholesale indictment of all scholarship on the minority issue today, nor of the individual scholars whose work I examine. As Chapter 5 will show, there are numerous promising signs of constructive, balanced and non-nationalistic research in this area. That, however, does not mean that we should neglect or belittle the heavy legacy of Persian-centric nationalism in contemporary academia.

NATION SINGULAR

The nationalist discourse on authenticity and identity has been somewhat semantically reformed since the revolution but nonetheless draws on the legacy of early Iranian nationalism. The key objective with the discourse is to discredit ethnicist revisionism and counterdiscourses by cementing the claim to the historical, sometimes even primordial, superiority of what nationalists understand to be Iran's national culture and Iranian-ness. The object of the nationalist cult, of course, is the nation itself. That the nation is the highest point of reference of social life, thought and action is a core belief among nationalists everywhere, and Iran is no exception.

Nationalist-minded scholars routinely refer to Iran as a unique and singular case in order to cement the place of "the national" (*melli*) above "the ethnic" (*qowmi*) on an imagined hierarchical ladder of universal identity markers. Sometimes this is expressed very bluntly—such as when Hamid Ahmadi claims that "national identity is the highest layer of identity of any human individual."[85] At other times, it is expressed indirectly, such as when minorities are referred to as "sub-national" (*foru-melli*) units, when minority cultures are described as "sub-cultures" (*khorde-farhang* or *pāre-farhang*), or when minority identity is deemed to be "sub-identity" (*khorde-hoviyat*).[86] While not denying the existence of various forms of self-identification, nationalist-minded scholars using such vocabulary nonetheless imply that at the end of the day—and as the result of a teleological historical process, if not a natural and inevitable evolution—all Iranians have and will have one overriding identity. This means that despite cultural differences, all ethnic groups in Iran are intrinsically loyal to and part of Iran as a nation: nation and ethnic groups are two sides of the same coin.

The nationalists thus consider the claim of some ethnicists—that ethnic groups should be considered as nations or nationalities or that ethnic identity in and by itself can be a national identity—as the erroneous, malignant claims of a harmful political force that can have detrimental consequences for Iran as a society and as a nation-state. These scholars, intellectuals and political activists instead argue that since Iranian ethnic groups have merged together through centuries of coexistence, they all have a stake in the Iranian nation. The ultimate attachment of all ethnic groups is and must be to the nation, the nationalists argue, and in propagating a deceitful conception of identity, ethnicists have targeted Iran as an independent nation-state and Iranian-ness as the true overriding identity of all Iranians.[87]

Ahmadi thus criticizes a recent propensity to give ethnicity "as much weight as" its national superior.[88] Ahmadi argues that "from a scientific point of view," ethnic groups can be designated as nations only when they have established an internationally recognized nation-state—which makes talk about the minority issue as a national issue nonsense. Ahmadi instead argues:

> Those who place ethnic groups and ethnic identity in opposition to national identity are in fact entering a political and ideological discussion, not a scientific discussion. For example, talk of a [Azeri] Turkic nation, a Kurdish nation or a Persian nation is meaningless... From a scientific point of view, there is only one nation within the framework of a country's recognized borders, and [in Iran] one can only talk of the Iranian nation.[89]

The "unscientific" talk is a reference to ethnicists using nationalist vocabulary. Ahmadi's constricted use of *mellat* in the singular—in both a grammatical and a political sense—reflects the nationalist belief in nation-state congruence: that there can be only one nation in a country, because a nation must have a state. Such efforts of disambiguation and monopolization of key vocabulary is not a new phenomenon, nor is the use of claims to "scientific truth" to prove the superiority of the nation.

However, it seems that these arguments have recently taken on new urgency with
the rise of an ethnicist counterdiscourse to the nationalist hegemony. The recent literature on the minority issue is characterized by retorts and rejoinders to ethnicist
claims, stressing before the audience that there can be only one nation and one
nationality, and that ethnic attachments will always be less important and salient
than attachments to the nation. The literature thus conveys a simultaneous insistence that "the ethnic" be separated categorically from "the national" and that ethnic
minorities are inseparable from the nation.

Iran's nature as a multi-ethnic but solidly unified entity is explained with the
alleged singularity of its history. Since nationalist-minded scholars present loyalty
toward one nation above all other attachments as natural and ultimately unavoid-
able, the political mobilization of ethnicity among minorities is then explained as
something that goes against the ingrained logic of history. Indeed, in order to dismiss the legitimacy of ethnicist claims to "nationhood," nationalist-minded Iranian
scholars point to "the outside" and abroad, blaming Western academia and foreign
state powers. They argue that foreigners have misunderstood Iranian society, and
with their essentially incompatible theories or wrongly translated concepts, they have
given ammunition to the ethnicist barrage against Iranian national identity.

Ahmadi thus argues that existing conceptual frameworks for understanding ethnicity do not fit the case of Iran. As the three main actors behind the rise of
ethno-nationalism, he singles out (1) the modern, secular and centralized Pahlavi
state, which confronted tribes and destroyed traditional bases of power in the early
twentieth century; (2) elites, which Ahmadi describes as "political and intellectual,
both ethnic and non-ethnic,"[90] who have "manipulated" religious and linguistic differences in order to construct ethnic identities; and finally (3) "Western Orientalists
and external forces" who, Ahmadi claims, have disseminated the notion of ethnic and
national identities among Iranian minorities.[91]

Among the misdeeds of Western scholars is the erroneous conflation of tribes with
ethnic groups—an argument for which Ahmadi invokes Richard Tapper's refutation
of a state-tribe dichotomy. Ahmadi thus points out that tribes and state have not
been locked in an antagonistic cycle of mutual resistance, but rather have co-existed
and mutually reinforced each other. Indeed, tribes were not "proto-nations," simply
because their struggles against the Iranian state were about survival and never about
independence. For this argument, Ahmadi refers to Anthony D. Smith's concept of
an *"ethnie"* that can turn into, or form the basis of, a modern nation-state—which
was *not* the case of Iran's tribes.[92] It was only with foreign powers' infiltration and
the diffusion of Western Orientalism among Iranians that certain tensions took the
form of ethno-national struggles, inducing power-hungry regional elites to incite or
galvanize regional movements with alien notions of minority rights and self-rule.

Through this anti-imperialist prism, Ahmadi claims that he can present the cases
of Kurdish, Azeri and Baluchi ethno-nationalisms as Hobsbawmian "invented traditions": that "ethnic groups with distinct cultural and political identities" in Iran are,
in Anderson's terminology, "imagined communities"—not just in the communities'
own imagination but also in the minds of Western researchers who have labeled
them "ethnic."[93] Western approaches to tribalism and ethnicity, then, are inca-
pable of explaining Iran's cultural diversity since "the Iranian linguistic and religious

minorities ... do not represent ethnic groups if these groups are to be defined as unified racial and cultural identities." Ethnic groups are, in short, "states of mind" and
ethnic minority identities are "imagined" (in the sense of "faked"), while the nation
is very real and very old[94]—a significant argument to which we return shortly.

Ehsan Hushmand and Nahid Kuhshekaf—both of whom are researchers, journalists and political activists associated with the religious-nationalist (*melli-mazhabi*)
currents—have spelled out this critique of Western scholarship. They argue that since
the study of ethnicity traditionally centered on recent immigrant communities in new
countries such as the United States, the theories produced in the West cannot explain
ethnicity in a place such as Iran that have several millennia of history. In fact, they
argue, all ethnic groups in Iran have contributed to the creation of the Iranian nation:
none of them have been adjoined to Iran through conquest. They allege that "there is
no precedence in Iranian history of discrimination against a [particular] group," and
that Iran's ruling establishment has at all times been a compound of "at least the elites
of *all* Iranian groups" as no group has been excluded "due to race or language."[95]

To prove this selective reading of history, the authors point to the high degree of
ethnic intermingling and intermarriage, and to the claim that there has been relatively little ethnically framed inter-group violence in Iranian history. The conclusion
is that Iran is different to other cases and that in order to understand this, scholars
must take into consideration "the commonality in historical co-existence, culture,
myths and homeland" that unites all ethnic groups—despite "linguistic and religious differences."[96] Such differences, Hushmand and Kuhshekaf claim, "have never
stood in opposition to Iranian-ness, nor have they brought about social rifts between
the Iranians"—indeed, the differences are to be "considered as part of Iranian-ness"
itself.[97] The bottom-line then is that *aqvām* should not be understood as the same
as "ethnic groups" elsewhere; rather, it should be understood as a substrata of the
Iranian nation.

A similar critique centers on the concept of minority (*aqaliyyat*). Hushmand and
Kuhshekaf are joined in this critique by another scholar, Mohammad-Reza Khobruye
Pak, a lawyer and independent scholar based in France who is associated with nationalist circles and has published several articles and books inside and outside Iran
about issues pertaining to ethnic minorities and Iranian history. Pak argues that "the
feeling of being a national minority has no precedence in Iran" since such a sentiment comes into being only when "a national group's homeland is conquered by
another group." Iran, however, "is the homeland of ethnic groups that have been
left untouched since the beginning of history," Pak claims.[98] He concludes that since
"ethnic groups" are not threatened, and neither seen as inferior nor discriminated
against by the majority, there is no reason to call them minorities. Indeed, unlike
other multi-cultural countries, Iran simply does not have a problem of co-existence
between ethnic groups.[99]

If neither "ethnic" nor "minorities" are correct descriptions of Iran's non-Persian-
speaking communities, the question then is: what are they? Ethnic minority identity
claims are treated in the nationalistic literature as the expression of certain sub-
national social identities (*hoviyat-e ejtemā'i*, which appears less contentious than,
say, political identities). In one example of this, a scholar makes the sweeping
claim about Iran's ethnic groups that "their national identity is Iranian and their

social identities are Baluch, Turkmen, Khorasani, Kermani, Persian, Khuzestani, etc."[100] As such, it is assumed that a national identity is not a social identity, but something qualitatively different. Another way is to stress that minority identities are "local identities" (*hoviyat-e mahali*).[101] By making, say, Kurdish identity a "local" phenomenon, Kurdish identity as a transnational ethnic phenomenon is ruled out, as is of course the potential of Kurdish identity claims to be framed as "national." Indeed, it seems that the word "ethnic" is often omitted due to its political connotations.

The most extreme form of rejection of ethnic identity, however, emanates from political activists associated with nationalist currents such as the National Front. A representative of this is engineer and intellectual Kurosh Za'im, who in 2006 and 2008 gave two interviews that created a stir in ethnicist online communities. In reaching the conclusion that "there is no such thing as ethnicity" in Iran, Za'im claimed to draw on "internationally recognized definitions."[102] Yet he implied that Iran, being an "ancient country," was somehow exempt from these definitions:

> In my view, *mellat* (Nation), has an international definition: that is, a people that lives within the defined borders of a country, and have a collective language, constitution, and state [*dowlat*]. A country is what one calls an entity with clear boundaries, which has a population and an internationally recognized state . . . However, *qowmiyat* or (Ethnicity) denotes immigrant peoples, who have migrated from their ancestral country to another country, who are in the minority and who have languages and cultural customs different from that of the host nation. Until they are assimilated into the nation's culture, one can call them a minority or an ethnicity.[103]

Obviously, Za'im does not think any of this applies to Iran, which is why he argues that

> today, it is ridiculous to state that the Baluch, Khorasanis, Gorganis, Gilakis, Lors, Azerbaijanis and Kurds are ethnic groups different from the body of the Iranian nation—unless, of course we have suspicious political motives. That would be like claiming that in France, Franks and Gauls are ethnically separate or that in Britain, Angles and Saxons.[104]

Za'im proceeds to declare that with the possible exception of Arabs, Turkmen and some religious minorities, all other claims to ethnic identity should be uniformly rejected as the work of traitors with foreign support. While this argument—"there is no such thing as ethnicity in Iran"—represents an extreme view, there is nonetheless ample evidence throughout the academic and polemical literature of various degrees of rejection of ethnicity. This, I will argue, is tied up with the nationalistic view on Iran as a singular, exceptional unit in the world, which is exempt from many of the dynamics and phenomena that characterize modernity elsewhere.

LOYALTY OF AN ANCIENT CLAN

Schooled in modernist social sciences, most Iranian scholars today agree that the world system of nation-states is a modern, largely European invention, and that a nation is a social construct. However, many scholars depart from this social constructionist paradigm by claiming that due to its history, Iran is unique and exceptional. As an "ancient nation," they claim, Iran is incomparable to most other nations in the world.

Earlier in text we saw how Ahmadi employs Benedict Anderson and Eric Hobsbawm's concepts of "imagined communities" and "invented traditions." From this, it appears that Ahmadi subscribes to social constructionism. Yet the deconstruction extends only to minority communities, and not to the community of the Iranian nation. Ahmadi thus focuses on the historical specificities unique to Iran to advance the argument that while minority claims are social and political fabrications of recent date, Iranian-ness is an ancient phenomenon.

In order to explain how Iran differs from surrounding Arab and Central Asian societies, he argues that these areas did not have the same coherent, unified political formations of a country (*keshvar*) and a state (*dowlat*) that Iran had in ancient times.[105] Establishing a connection between territory and sovereignty, Ahmadi in effect argues that Iran is an ancient nation-state. Unlike Arab and Central Asian societies, factors such as history, mythology, geography, state traditions, cultural legacies and religion came together in Iran to form a national identity at a very early stage: indeed, "Iranian identity," Ahmadi claims, "has at least some two thousand years of antiquity."[106] As evidence of this pre-modernity "traditional national awareness" (*āgāhi-ye sonnati-ye melli*), Ahmadi argues that mythical history is just as important as actual history: "the mind and identity to which Iranians have attached themselves," he explains, "existed within the mythical tales of the pre-Islamic period"—among other things, in the concept of *irānzamin* as articulated in the *Shāhnāme*.[107]

In other words, Ahmadi seeks to liberate the semantics of "the nation" from its Eurocentric context.[108] A key argument in his critique of Western-inspired theories of ethnicity is that the juxtaposition of ethnic and national identity has created a "methodological fallacy" in Middle Eastern identity politics: a person is forced "to choose between attachment to national, religious or ethnic identities," each presented as "contrary and antithetical to each other."[109] This artificial, forced choice is even more problematic, Ahmadi claims, in "ancient nations" such as India, China, Egypt, Greece and Iran, which all have "a history of civilization and a very ancient state and culture" that have persisted, even when ethnic groups have come and gone.[110] The notion of civilization is tied together with the nation-state congruence paradigm: Iran is a civilization while ethnic minorities are, in their own capacity, not; minorities can only be a civilization when they are part of the Iranian nation.

This idea was elaborated upon in a 1992 editorial for the prominent journal *Nashr-e dānesh*, by the distinguished Tehran University professor emeritus of Islamic philosophy, Persian literature and Iranian history, Nasrollah Purjavadi:

> Despite all the differences in dialect and traditions, and even in artistic and literary taste and style, as well as in way of thinking, Iran's ethnic groups are all children of a pure, ancient Iranian civilization ... Just like members of a family are naturally connected to each other, Iranian ethnic groups are also united from the bottom of their hearts. The link that ties together Iranian ethnic groups is a cultural and spiritual matter, and that is indeed the soul of Iranian-ness itself.[111]

Here, the notion of an emotional, almost biological, bond to Iran is tied together with a selective reading of history that places civilization and nation above any other possible affiliation. Iranian-ness becomes more than a question of political loyalty: it is a question of spiritual identity and belonging, all tropes familiar to nationalist languages around the world.

There are several such tropes with which nationalist-minded scholars seek to portray Iran's ethnic minorities as historically loyal to Iran, essentially attached to the rest of the population and harmonically integrated in society. A key one is that of organic unity: the argument, flagged above, that Iran is the outcome of the voluntary co-existence of several ethnic groups, and not, as is the case of many empires, of annexation and forced integration.

Scholars often invoke ancient and medieval concepts that are popularly seen as directly equivalent to the modern nation-state of Iran, such as the *iranvej* and *Aryanem vaeja* of the Avesta, or *irānshahr* of the *Shāhnāme*.

Pak, for example, argues against the ethnicist demand for federalism by stating that in the ancient and medieval concepts of state and sovereignty, Iran already had the recipe for voluntary and equal co-existence of various ethnic groups in one "conglomerate of homelands"—and, hence, no need for federalism or other "foreign" concepts.[112] It is thus a prevalent argument that the only way the emotional, organic bond of minorities to Iran can be broken is by the intrusive force of outside manipulation. As a typical example of this, one scholar argues that despite a "secret ambition for autonomy, Iran's Kurds have a burning desire to remain within the framework of Iran's political geography."[113]

Another prevalent trope is in the claim that ethnic minorities are not just intrinsically Iranian but in fact "more Iranian than the rest." With such a trope, nationalist-minded scholars and activists push specific lexical buttons: *asil* (pure, genuine, authentic, pureblooded, highborn), *esālat* (authenticity) and *asliyyat* (descent, origin)—all related to the same word stem, *asl* (root, essence). Scholars thus claim that "we can find the purest/most authentic dimensions of Iranian culture among Iran's ethnic groups," that "Kurds and Azeris are more Iranian than we are," that "Kurds and Azeris are the oldest and most authentic of Iranians" or that the Baluch and the Kurds are "the true owners of Iran."[114] As part of the political struggle over semantic meaning and claims to identity, the suggestion of separateness or distinctiveness for minorities is rejected with a rhetorical endowment of ownership and superlative authenticity.

A third trope centers on the role of traditions, rituals, symbols and myths that are common to all Iranians. Foremost among these is *Nowruz,* the Iranian New Year at spring equinox, which originated in pre-Islamic culture. Since practically all ethnic groups in Iran observe this holiday and its associated traditions, scholars argue that it is more than a symbol of cultural affinity: it is a sign of a national unity and identity that transcends mundane cultural differences.[115] Ahmadi, for example, argues that "the power of Iranian mythology" has "facilitated the Iranization [*irāni kardan*] of immigrant ethnic groups such as the Turkic tribes."[116] Similar praise is extended to the phenomenon of *naqqāli,* the tradition of singing verses of the *Shāhnāme* popular among many Iranians, and especially the Kurds. Sometimes, legends are even evoked as a sort of hard proof of the Iranian identity of the minorities, as in an article by Mojtaba Maqsudi (see Chapter 3), who is a key figure in the National Studies circle:

> All Iranian ethnic groups such as the Kurds, Baluch etc. are all Iranian at root [*irāni-ol-asl*]. For example, the Kurds are Iranians who fled into the mountains out of fear of Zahhak Snakeshoulder, and settled down there.[117]

Zahhak is a brain-devouring demon from the *Shāhnāme*. Though this legend does figure prominently in Kurdish folklore, it is nonetheless awkward to find it uncritically replicated in an academic article such as the one quoted above. An extension of the trope is the argument that, historically, minorities have "chosen" Iran over the External Other. An example is the somewhat dubious claim that, in the early medieval period, the majority of the Baluch chose the Hanafi school of Sunni Islam because the founder of that school was considered an "Iranian at root" (*irāni-ol-asl*).[118]

A fourth trope flips the fear of an Internal Other collaborating with the foreign enemy on its head, and presents the opposite: an idealized vision of ethnic minorities as a layer of natural defense against attacks on Iran's territorial integrity. With this trope, minorities are described as border guards that have historically defended the frontier against perpetual threats from abroad. This trope may hark back to Iran's imperial history, when the shah would demand tribal levies *in lieu* of taxes and as a sign of loyalty. The minorities' loyalty to Iran is today thus repeatedly proven and reaffirmed, and their metaphoric oath of allegiance to Iran renewed by references to fictional tribal armies ready to serve the nation when called upon.[119]

This frontier guardian trope is also projected onto modern history: tribal revolts against the British in nineteenth century Baluchistan, the Bakhtiyari participation in the Constitutional Revolution, the Qashqa'is' participation in the oil nationalization movement of the 1950s, the Khuzestani Arabs' resistance against Saddam's invasion in the 1980s, and so on.[120] As Ramezanzadeh (see Chapter 3) puts it, the "Arab community's strong resistance to the Iraqi army led to their acceptance as true Iranians."[121] In a study of ethnic groups and national security, a scholar thus claims that these groups have "always" been at the frontline of defense. As such, they should be regarded as "part of the dynamic human resources of resistance against foreign violations."[122] In short, the various fears about the Internal Other acting in unison with the External Other are reassuringly inverted, and Iran as a national whole is reaffirmed.

A fifth and important trope is of course that of race. Despite the fact that the Aryan myth has been subject to numerous rebuttals and debunking—including in Iranian academic literature—and despite the fact that most scholars of ethnicity in contemporary Iran agree that today's Iranians are the product of centuries of ethnic intermingling, the myth persists. The notion that all or most Iranian ethnic groups can trace their roots to "Aryan" ancestors is still often evoked as a sort of historical and genetic "proof" that these groups are inseparably bound to the modern nation-state of Iran. The most blatant and consistent use of the Aryan myth is unsurprisingly to be found among the more or less secular-minded nationalist intellectuals. In one of his controversial interviews, Za'im defines Iranians as being like a sweet-pastry dough, all the ingredients of which have been blended over thousands of years. That handful of Aryan tribes that entered Iran, [consisted of] the Medes, Persians and Parthians as the core tribes, as well as the Kurds and Azeris ...—all of whom have spent thousands of years in this homeland, and have intermingled. Therefore we cannot separate Parthians from Persians, or [Parthians and Persians] from the Baluch, Gilakis, and others ... These tribes came from one race.[123]

Thus, while acknowledging the historical reality of ethnic intermingling and migrations, Za'im downplays the importance of diversity by maintaining that all Iranians are from one race. These arguments are found in various shapes and forms in the writings and statements of public intellectuals, historians and scholars. It is even found in academic writing that aims to counter ethnicist claims: such as when one scholar argues that although Kurdish language and culture, as the key focus of autonomist movements, is different from Persian, "the Kurds' being Aryans and Iranians cannot be denied"; or that even though socio-economic deprivation and a sensitive geographical location may lead to a divide between Iran and the Baluch, then the Baluch remain "Iranian in race."[124]

A more subtle example of this underlying racial logic is from an interview with professor of sociology at Imam Sadeq University, Kavus Seyyed-Emami. In the interview, Seyyed-Emami claims that apart from the Persian language, the second key factor shaping Iranian identity is the ability to incorporate cultural elements from outside and into the "indigenous cultural complex." This shows, Seyyed-Emami continues, that "the inner core" of Iranian identity cannot be sought out "*only*" in the Aryan cultural element."[125] It is clear that from this definition of Other and Self (*khod*, here translated as "indigenous") that despite ethnic blending and cultural mixing, the Self is still "Aryan": "we," the Iranians may have been *influenced* by the Other, but remain Aryan. Even when scholars expressly dismiss the validity of the Aryan myth as an explanatory factor of Iranian-ness, and even when they reject the exclusivist racism behind the myth, they still readily use the concept of "the Aryan race" in their writings about Iranians.[126]

Despite concluding that Iranian culture is the outcome of amalgamation and intermingling, there is still an underlying contrasting of elements that come from "the outside" and elements that are considered part of an "inner core"—a distinction for which "Aryan," "more Iranian than Iranian," "family members" and other tropes are still employed in the academic writing on the minority issue.

DISMEMBERING THE NATION BODY

According to the nationalist understanding of modern Iranian history, there have been and are several foreign conspiracies that, by way of exploiting the minority issue, are targeting Iran's territorial integrity. The ultimate aim, it seems, is to gain control of Iran's resources and to diminish its regional power. For this, foreign powers have striven, it is argued, to *forge* belligerent "anti-Iranian identities" among the minorities. Several scholars, including Ahmadi, trace this in the dual processes of modern, Western-inspired and Western-dominated state building and the dissemination of liberal and Marxist notions of self-determination and autonomy in the twentieth century—both processes that were tied up with geopolitical rivalry. A key area for this rivalry, nationalist-minded scholars argue, is Azerbaijan.

These scholars claim that Russian and Soviet agents as well as pan-Turkists and Azerbaijani nationalists have all employed ethnicists as tools and weapons against Iran. They trace the history of Russian aggression and malignant policies towards Iran: from the tsar's annexation of Iranian territories in the Caucasus through the Soviet occupation of northern Iran to the creation of a fifth column of ethnicists within Iran. Already in the twentieth century, the nationalist-minded scholars argue, Baku Azeris "descended upon Iran with the intent of exporting their own identity and ideals into Iranian Azerbaijan."[127]

Today, the pan-Turkists are still scheming to create sedition within Iran, and Israel and the United States are now involved in the scheming.[128] These foreign agents have planted the seed of pan-Turkism among Iran's apparently credulous Azeris, intent on "creating a Turkic identity" (*hoviyat-sāzi-ye torki*).[129] Taking their cues from Baku, Iranian Azeri ethnicists are "distorting history, creating a fake identity and alienating Azeris from the rest of the Iranians and from *irānzamin* [Soil of Iran]."[130] According to Ahmadi, the aim of these moves is nothing less than the total destruction of "Iran's national unity, civilization and identity."[131]

Similar arguments about other groups abound. Regarding Baluchistan, the tirades are aimed at the ethnicist claims that the Baluch are in fact ethnic Arabs, or that their identity as Sunnis has alienated or separated them from Iranian national identity. Nationalist-minded scholars dismiss the first instance as a pan-Arabist conspiracy concocted by Saddam Hussein; and in the second instance, the culprits are said to be Wahhabists who force upon Baluch clerics a "non-Iranian" version of Sunni identity.[132] The well-documented history of foreign power involvement in Kurdistan nurtures similar claims: one is that "we did not have an issue called Kurdistan" before World War II, when the Soviets propagated ethno-nationalism among Iran's Kurds.[133] Again, the Soviet Union, and at other stages, the United States or Saddam's Iraq, are blamed for inventing a modern Kurdish identity as a way of contesting Iranian sovereignty.

Nationalist-minded scholars thus claim that ethnic identities, as they are promulgated today, were invented by foreign powers and then passed on to "local elites" who have found in them handy instruments for political advancement. The argument goes that the sons and grandsons of former tribal leaders, deprived by Reza Shah of their ancestors' traditional power, have turned to notions of ethnic identity as a new source of political legitimacy and authority. Viewed through this prism, the creation of ethnic identity (*khalq-e hoviyat-e qowmi*) is partly an outcome of elite competition.[134] In other words, ethnicity did not play into politics prior to the interaction of geopolitical rivalry and local-level elite politics in the twentieth century.

The same arguments are mirrored in the rejection of ethnicist claims to nationhood for minorities. Nationalist-minded scholars point out that the whole idea of "ethnic groups as nationalities" originated in communist Russia and spread into Iran via Caucasus with the aid of leftist propaganda and regional elites who, eyeing the possibility to gain or regain local power, were imitating Europe.[135] There is a sense that the political utilization of cultural differences can only be a foreign phenomenon since these differences have, allegedly, not played a part in politics prior to Iran's contact with the West.

In his 1992 article, Purjavadi too lamented the infatuation among some Iranian ethnicists with notions of minority self-rule inspired by ethnic politics in the crumbling Soviet Union. He argued that this infatuation has been compounded by the fact that some of Iran's ethnic groups have co-ethnics in neighboring countries, including some that were, at the time of his writing, breaking away from the Soviet Union. Purjavadi warned:

> Until the day when these ethnic groups are turned into "nationalities," the Baluch and the Kurds can protect their Iranian identity. However, when these ethnic groups emerge as a nation outside of Iran's borders and [thus] attain a political-geographic dimension, and when foreign powers or some of our neighbors strive to exploit some of the characteristics shared [between an ethnic group's members inside and outside Iran] . . . then Iran's national unity and territorial integrity will suffer.[136]

In other words, the transformation of an ethnic group (*qowm*) into a nationality (*melliyyat*) or a nation (*mellat*) can only, in this interpretation, be understood in terms of geopolitics and foreign relations. Calling one's own ethnic group a nation or nationality is, in the words of one political activist, "poisonous" and "will plant the seed of hatred between Turk and Persian":[137] the very act of appropriating the vocabulary, codified and institutionalized by the nationalist intellectual elite during the consolidation of the modern, centralized Iranian state, is thus seen as tantamount to treason. The Iranian identity of the various ethnic minorities must, the present-day inheritors of this nationalist elite argue, be protected against the onslaught of numerous sophisticated and far-reaching foreign plots.

Nationalist-minded scholars such as Pak thus dismiss the call for federalist solutions to the minority issue because they are stepping-stones toward separatism. According to Pak, self-appointed community leaders, "regional chauvinists," are deliberately exaggerating socio-economic grievances among the minorities, distorting otherwise legitimate criticism of the political system into an illegitimate demand for independence. They are, Pak argues, oblivious to the fact that their words and actions will only lead to more state repression, prejudice, ghettoification and ethnic conflict.[138] He details numerous cases of "failed attempts" at federalism, from Yugoslavia to Malaysia, and argues that there is no evidence that federalism can lead to democracy: indeed, Iran cannot prosper or progress by blindly imitating foreign models.[139]

To understand this pervasive anxiety with the separatist potential of ethnicist politics, one obviously needs to take into consideration the nationalist reading of Iranian history. In this reading, Iran is a nation-state that has been territorially reduced and politically, economically and militarily humiliated by belligerent neighbors and imperialist superpowers for more than 200 years. One also needs to appreciate the nationalist notion of a Greater Iran that is projected into pre-modern times. This is not just an expansionist fantasy but also a sense, prevalent in academic works and public discourse, that Iran is the center of a sphere of historical, cultural affinity that runs throughout Western and Central Asia. In this pan-Iranist sense, it is Ideal Iran, which as a cultural space encompasses vast swathes of Asia with boundaries drawn from Achaemenid-era, Safavid-era or simply imagined geographies—and not Iran's actual, present boundaries—that matter.

When a nationalist-minded scholar such as Pak discusses the Kurdish issue, it is thus perfectly possible and permissible to claim, in passing, that "Iran lost 68% of the Kurdistan homeland in the Chalderan War" in 1514, or even to talk of "Iran's *extraterritorial* Kurdistan."[140] When another scholar discusses "geographic units" that used to "belong to Iran," he can claim (without referring to any sources) that the separation of these units was not the "natural wish" of the people who lived in these units but rather the result of the enemy's "policy of reducing Iran."[141] In this line of thinking, it appears historically defensible and academically acceptable to consider vast areas, inside and outside modern Iran, as "naturally" indivisible parts of an ideal Iran—and, in extension, to consider illegitimate the rule of these areas by any other nation-state than the Iranian. Foreigners have dismembered the nation body many times before, and this time, its constituent parts must rise in its defense.

PANDORA'S BOX

These views on ethnicism as more or less equal to separatism, and ethnic mobilization as synonymous with threats to Iran's territorial integrity, I will argue, are shared by a broad variety of scholars. It is part of what has been criticized recently as "the security view" (*negāh-e amniyyati*) on the minority issue (see Chapter 5). This view is particularly pronounced among scholars in military and security studies, where the minority issue is often analyzed in terms of a risk calculation between opportunities and threats.

In this genre,[142] ethnic mobilization is sometimes understood as connected to domestic socio-economic problems, but very rarely to discrimination or disrespect for human and civil rights. Rather, the analyses focus on the sensitive geographic location of minorities, and on the possibility of foreign military and intelligence infiltration, or on the influence of foreign media and propaganda machineries. These scholars frame the minority issue as a risk/opportunity calculus: if used correctly as a national asset, the presence of minorities that have co-ethnic populations across the borders can be utilized to spread Iran's cultural and political influence abroad; if exploited by avaricious powers, the presence of minorities become a liability.[143] In such a reductionist, instrumentalist analysis, minority communities can potentially be manipulated to function as a Trojan Horse for foreign enemies. Sometimes, the enemy is not even specified since the perpetual infiltration of foreign powers is taken for granted.[144]

It is interesting that the regime-affiliated "security view genre" shares this pervasive tendency to view demands for minority rights in terms of security threats with the regime-critical discourse on the minority issue. An example is from National Front member Za'im's statement that ethnicists are nothing but

> a very small but loud [group] with foreign financial and propaganda support—in particular the support of some ungrateful neighboring countries—[a group,] which is duping discontented people into creating a fake identity and preparing the ground for notions of separateness by telling lies and making provocations, by distorting history and by stealing from Iranian national identity.[145]

Hence, those who present demands for minority rights in ethnic terms are by definition agents of foreign conspiracies, and such rights should be reserved for religious minorities only. In the words of another National Front member, "it has been totally proven that ethno-nationalist movements" in modern Iranian history "could not have come into existence without the interference of foreign powers."[146]

In short, whether in regime-funded security studies or in regime-critical comments, a siege mentality characterizes the nationalist approach to ethnic minorities. Minorities are depicted as pawns in a geopolitical game—not as independent agents of social thought and action. However, sometimes, the blaming finger is also pointed at the rulers of the Islamic Republic. Since the late 1990s, the minority issue has become an ideological theatre of contention between many different strains in Iranian politics and public debate. The sympathy of some scholars, including Ahmadi, toward nationalist and religious-nationalist strains in Iranian politics is most obvious in the criticism they have directed at the Islamic Republic.

The key point of this critique is that after the revolution, Iranian political leaders have abandoned nationalism in favor of internationalism, neglected Iranian national culture in order to propagate Islamism and nurtured a close relationship with Arab rather than Iranian thinkers.[147] This flawed approach to ideology and culture, the nationalist-minded scholars argue, is manifested in an overemphasis on the broader Muslim world, on Islamic culture and on Arabic language, all to the detriment of Iranian national culture and identity. In short, the interests of the *Ummah* have overtaken national interest as the primary focus of the state, creating an unnatural imbalance in Iranian citizens' dual identity as Muslims and Iranians.

This does not mean that these scholars are secularist nationalists. According to Ahmadi, for example, the alleged contradiction between Iranian-ness (*irāniyyat*) and Islamicity (*eslāmiyyat*) is rooted in a Western-imitating extremist strain of Iranian "ancientist" (*bāstān-garā'i*) nationalism that went too far in the attempt to disassociate Iran from the Arab and Muslim world. Ahmadi argues instead that Iranian literature, folklore and mythology testify to a historically harmonic coexistence between religion and nation, and to natural balance between Islamic and Iranian aspects of national identity. By "Iranizing" Islam with pre-existing symbols, heroes and spiritual traditions, Iranians have in fact fully embraced and internalized Islam as compatible with their core identity.[148]

Ahmadi and the post-revolutionary religious-nationalists thus depart from the traditional nationalist legacy by arguing that until the Pahlavi regime instrumentally exploited "ancientism" in an attempt to curb Shiite oppositional discourses and clerical power, Iranian anti-Arabism rarely translated into hatred of Islam. The opposition of Islam and national identity, then, was the product of Western-inspired secularist nationalism and Pahlavi state propaganda, and never a reflection of what the broad population of Iranians truly believed. The battle between secularism and Islamism eventually came to a head during the revolution, which led to the expulsion of nationalist forces from the political spectrum.

Ahmadi argues that radical Islamists have since imposed upon Iranians a forced choice between religion and nation. This has caused an identity crisis, forcing some to keep their views to themselves in order to gain entry into educational institutions and secure jobs. Ahmadi states that "pure and authentic Iranian nationalism" (*jariyān-e asil-e nāsiyonālism-e irāni*) has historically been freedom-seeking, anti-colonialist and not, as Islamists accuse it of, pro-Western and imperialist.[149] This "authentic" nationalism, he argues, does not negate religion but stresses the continuity of the Iranian nation despite the seventh century conversion to Islam, and despite the current regime's overemphasis on the Muslim world community.

This overemphasis on religious over national identity, Ahmadi argues, has opened the floodgates for ethno-nationalist currents cultivated by Iran's foreign enemies. Here, Ahmadi differs significantly from the general pro-regime literature, including even that of state-affiliated reformists such as those analyzed in Chapter 3: religious-nationalist scholars such as Ahmadi are critical of the state because they view Islamism as a failed policy that has fuelled the emergence of both supra- and sub-national identity discourses, each in their own way detrimental to Iranian unity.

Since the ruling elites are engaged with international concerns, focused on religious matters and embroiled in factional rivalries, they have failed to properly grasp the ethno-nationalist threat, and to counter it with the tools already available in the Iranian citizenry: patriotism, popular Shiism mixed with pre-Islamic traditions, and national culture. The state, in short, has—unintentionally, perhaps, but nonetheless effectively—created a breeding ground for "anti-Iranian identities."[150] Ahmadi contends that despite their superficial and erroneous readings of history, ethnicists have been able in this situation to strike a chord with young Iranians suffering from the "identity crisis" caused by the said failed state policy.[151]

This way of using the minority issue as a prism through which to criticize state policy and overall ideological direction is a significant development in post-revolutionary Iranian academia and public discourse. Between the lines of many works on the minority issue, one can find both subtle and explicit regime critique. Nationalists aligned with the National Front, for example, have often connected the minority issue to its general critique of the government, claiming that what has been wrongly characterized as ethnic mobilization is in fact Sunni-Shia sectarian tensions exacerbated by the government's overemphasis on religion.[152]

During Khatami's presidency, several key National Front figures voiced their critique in open letters. In a 2000 letter to Khatami, the prominent archaeologist and intellectual Parviz Varjavand (1934–2007) referred to his own background as a nationalist activist and politician, who was imprisoned both by the Pahlavis and the Islamic Republic.[153] Speaking on behalf of "all national and freethinking forces in Iran," Varjavand warned of an extensive conspiracy aimed at Iran's national unity, territorial integrity and independence through the utilization of ethnicists inside Iran by hostile governments in the Republic of Azerbaijan, Turkey and the US. This conspiracy was unfolding, Varjavand stated, at a time when the Iranian state was paying no attention to national culture in the education system. Indeed, the conspiracy had even managed to extend its sway to state-run media.

Varjavand complained that while authorities were cracking down on reformist organizations and media, they did nothing to stop ethnicists with foreign support who were busy creating "deceitful identities" and spreading "anti-national" propaganda inside Iran—namely through bilingual and Turkic-language local media. Varjavand wondered whether Khatami was aware of the connections between Azeri ethnicists and foreign governments, and whether Iran's intelligence agencies and ministries had even reported to the president about these dangerous developments.

A similar letter from a number of National Front activists in 2004 warned of "attacks against the root of the great Iranian nation's existence"—the latest of which had been a Ministry of Education decree that primary and secondary schools throughout the country were now allowed to use schoolbooks focused on regional cultures and histories.[154] This, the National Front members argued, was unprecedented in the world, and could only lead to the deterioration of public knowledge about national culture and history, and thus, the "alienation" of a whole generation. Indeed, they claimed, such a policy constituted "a great treason in modern Iranian history" that would only help foreign powers in dismembering Iran, and eventually lead to civil war.

In their various statements, National Front members have warned about the danger that giving into minority rights demands—opening the proverbial Pandora's Box—would eventually result in Balkanization or horrible scenarios such as those unfolding in neighboring Iraq and Afghanistan. They have called on the state apparatus to use its repressive mechanisms to curb ethnicist agitation and minority mobilization—paradoxically, despite the fact that the National Front itself has been the victim of these very same mechanisms numerous times in recent history.[155]

FIXED GAZE OF A LOVER

The arguably most contentious issue between ethnicists and nationalists is that of language. Nationalist-minded scholars champion the necessity of one national language in order to keep Iranians united, and often present their scholarship in terms of a defense against what are seen as unreasonable minority demands for linguistic rights, historical distortion and anti-Iranian propaganda. The question of language is thus tied up with issues of unity and identity.

In the first of three slightly different but mutually compatible approaches to the issue of minority languages, nationalist-minded scholars and intellectuals present language/dialect as the *only* factor that differentiates minorities from the Persian-speaking majority, that is, that the only basis of minority distinctiveness is linguistic, and that there is thus not enough substance, so to speak, to ethnicist claims and demands. In the second approach, certain nationalists trivialize, downplay or even ridicule minority languages, presenting them as inferior to and subordinate of Persian. In the third approach, specific languages are presented as foreign imports, alien to native, Iranian culture and thus as the side effects of an unfortunate history that could or should ultimately be discarded. These three approaches are paths to the same goal: legitimizing Persian as superior and as Iran's only possible national language, while countering ethnicist claims to an identity different than the dominant one.

As an example of the first approach, Hamid Ahmadi argues that

> [e]xcept for language, Azaris [*sic*] share with Persians many other commonalities, including Shi'ism and cultural heritage. Despite the fact that the question of Turkish [*sic*] language in Azarbaijan has been a factor of distinctiveness vis-à-vis the dominant

Farsi—(Persian-) speaking Iranians, this has not prevented many Azari and other Iranians from considering the people of Azarbaijan culturally and historically Iranian.[156]

The existence of a separate Turkic ethnic identity for the Azeris (which is the ethnicist claim) is thus rejected, reducing "minority identity" to a question of linguistic difference. The argument that only language differentiates minorities from the rest of the population can also lead to somewhat self-contradictory statements, such as the following from Abdollah Ramezanzadeh's description of Tehran's sizeable Azeri community. He explains how migration and industrialization led to the

> integration of Azeris among the Persian speaking population in the sense that at least one third of the population of Tehran are Azeri speaking. There is no special feature, which can be used as a distinguishing factor between the Azeris and the others in the capital, and intermarriage is common.[157]

Claiming that there is "no special feature," Ramezanzadeh forgets that he, in the previous sentence, identified these people as Azeri speakers, and thus at least distinguishable in linguistic terms. In nationalist-minded scholars' accounts of the Azeris, the cultural elements and history shared between Persians and Azeris are enhanced in order to trivialize the Azeri-specific elements. Scholars such as Ramezanzadeh and Ahmadi conveniently overlook the fact that Azeris across the political borders do share a language, but also, to use these scholars' own arguments, Shi'ism, cultural heritage and the territorial history of the Arran-Azerbaijan region. Yet these links are routinely presented as recent or artificial fabrications. Hence, Ahmadi argues that ethnicist publications seek to "*create* a sense of proximity" between Iran's minorities and "fellow language speakers abroad":[158] when put this way, "proximity" is reduced to a linguistic, and not cultural, political or historical relationship, and furthermore, it is implied that this proximity did not exist prior to its recent creation by ethnicist agitators.

Another aspect of the reduction of cultural difference is when commentators in the minority issue debate argue that members of minority communities should be described as "Iranians speaking a particular language": that is, "Kurdish-speaking Iranians" instead of simply "Kurds" or even "Iranian Kurds." The view contained within such a formulation is that these ethnic groups are essentially Iranian, and the only thing that distinguishes them from the rest of the (Persian-speaking) Iranians is the fact that they speak a minority language: instead of an "ethnic" identity, the minorities are ascribed a sort of linguistic sub-category of the overriding national identity. This is also reflected in the tendency to describe minority languages as "dialects"—an issue to which we will shortly return.

A third aspect is found in the laudatory terms with which linguistic affinity between many of Iran's ethnic groups is described. Nationalist-minded scholars tend to emphasize the fact that Baluchi, Kurdish and other minority tongues are Indo-European languages of the Western Iranian languages branch, and thus related to Persian. This linguistic fact is in turn used to prove a historical and political "fact": that these ethnic groups are allegedly bound inseparably to the modern Iranian nation-state. This argument is pushed through by endowing the languages of certain ethnic groups with the power of "authenticity." Thus, Baluchi is often described as "more genuine and authentic (*asil-tar*)" than Persian due to the fact that it relies on fewer loanwords than Persian.[159] In the case of the Kurds, it is often argued that since Kurdish language is "genuinely" Iranian, and even more "pure" than Persian, Kurds are "genuinely and purely Iranian": the broad population in Iran "feel a sense of kinship" with the Kurds, and see them as "natives"[160]—indeed, it is due to this sense of kinship that Kurds allegedly "enjoy their cultural freedom" in Iran, as opposed to in Turkish-speaking Turkey or Arabic-speaking Iraq.[161]

Nationalist-minded scholars and intellectuals routinely accentuate the argument that Persian is the one and only common historical medium of communication between all the people inhabiting Iran. They stress this by pointing out that minorities have often used Persian in political, scholarly or artistic expressions.[162] Persian is thus presented as the "high" language of the national, literary and educational sphere, and non-Persian languages the "low" vernaculars of the local, provincial, parochial and sectarian sphere. Ahmadi, for example, claims that non-Persian languages historically were more "colloquial than literary and educational," and that Persian has always been Iran's lingua franca:

> Right now, ethnic groups are very sensitive to the issue of language. Naturally, economic and political problems as well as elite-related problems are reflected in the issue of language. [Yet] we cannot escape the fact that we must have a national language. Our national language, Persian, has a very ancient history[. A]ll Iranian ethnic groups...have their literary heritage written in Persian and have used that language as medium of education throughout the post-Islamization period. That does not mean that we should ignore other languages, no one wants that.[163]

Non-Persian languages are thus associated with contemporary minority elite dissatisfaction, political and economic problems, and not with a sense of historical injustice, which is how ethnicists portray it; Persian, conversely, as an "ancient" language is associated with both a sense of heritage and with the practical necessity of a national language.

Ahmadi refers, for example, to the founder of the Safavid dynasty, Shah Isma'il (1487–1524), who in his writings presented himself as an inheritor of mythical heroes from Persian literature. However, Ahmadi fails to mention the fact that Shah Isma'il also wrote in Turkic—indeed, he is considered a pioneer of Turkic poetry in Iran. This omission—which, with Ahmadi's knowledge of Iranian history, must be on purpose—exemplifies the Persian-centric view of history. Ahmadi privileges Persian as the sole carrier of Iranian-ness to the extent that the historically multi-lingual nature of Iranian society is obscured. This historical interpretation is then used to justify the role of Persian as the sole national language today and in the future.

An aspect of the language issue that is of great importance to ethnicists is the use of the word "dialect" (*guyesh, lahje*) instead of "language" (*zabān*). By describing minority languages as "dialects," nationalist-minded scholars implicitly—whether deliberately or unconsciously—belittle the importance of these languages, questioning their historical legitimacy and societal value while endowing primacy and importance on Persian as "*the* language."[164] The most radical approach to this

"dialectization" is to simply deny that non-Persian languages are significantly different than Persian: that Kurdish, Baluchi and even Azeri are actually dialects of Persian
or some imagined "Iranian" (or "Aryan") prototypical mother language.

This type of argument is not uncommon among Persian-speaking lay Iranians.
When articulated by scholars, however, it constitutes a deliberate confusion of
concepts: on the one hand, the concept of an Indo-Iranian sub-branch of the
Indo-European language family to which Baluchi, Kurdish and Persian all belong,
but in which there is no hierarchical subordination of one to the other, and, on
the other hand, the nationalist concept of Persian as a mother of all Iranian languages. This is why one scholar claims that Kurdish is "*today* no longer understood
by Persian-speakers,"[165] as if it necessarily used to be; why a nationalist activist
calls Baluchi a "sub-branch" (*zir-shākhe*) of "the national language";[166] or why a
political scientist states that "despite the difference in dialect," Azeris "have never
wavered in their [loyalty] towards their collective identity with the other peoples of
Iran."[167]

To hammer through the idea that minorities are inseparably bound to Iran,
nationalist-minded scholars and intellectuals thus conflate linguistic affinity with
national loyalty, sometimes demoting languages that are not even remotely related
to Persian (such as Azeri) to a "dialect." The most blatant examples of this tendency
are again found among nationalist activists, such as in Za'im's statement that "if we
removed the *foreign* words from Kurdish and Azeri, it is the same [language] that
we are speaking [i.e., Persian], of course with different dialects."[168] Such a statement
ignores key facts: while Kurdish, as an Indo-Iranian language, is indeed related to
Persian, it is certainly not Persian; nor is Azeri, which is a Turkic language with
a structure and content wholly different from Persian, despite loanwords (just as
Persian is not in its essence Arabic despite the huge common vocabulary).

Za'im's claims is a particular type of nationalist propaganda based on the premise
that there is such a thing as a pure language, and that all Iranians, rooted in the
same racial and cultural ground, should be speaking one language. As Max Weinreich
once said, "a language is a dialect with an army and navy," and the "dialectization"
of languages is a discursive show of strength: the proverbial forces of the national
language against a poorly armed, inferior "dialect." Radical nationalists sometimes
even seem to ridicule these languages, showing them to be less sophisticated than
Persian.[169]

A related tendency is to present minority languages as foreign. Also in this aspect
is there a direct continuation of language and perceptions from the early modernist-
nationalist thinkers who argued that Persian as a language is threatened. As such,
certain non-Indo-European languages, namely Turkic languages and Arabic, are portrayed as recent, alien, non-native additions to Iranian society. Some nationalists
directly claim or indirectly insinuate, for example, that Turkic languages have been
"forced" or "imposed" upon Iranians in Azerbaijan; or that minority elites are using
language rights as an excuse in their political ploys.[170] Ahmadi claims that these
elites have politicized the question of language, turning it into a "tool" to be used
"against the territorial civilization and cultural unity of Iran" with the ultimate goal
of "weakening Persian," "manipulating the historical and cultural identity of Iran"
and "destroying national unity."[171]

Such views, in turn, are often connected to the "security view" described earlier in text: that minority languages, reified as containers of political action, can be exploited by foreign powers, which makes minority language demands suspect. In a pronounced example of this, Mohammad-Reza Qamari of the University of Law Enforcement Sciences argues that language either strengthens national unity and endows a country with national identity or functions to the detriment of social cohesion as an instrument of neo-imperialism and a harbinger of ethnic crises. Qamari outlines various international and UN resolutions against ethnic discrimination, but then argues:

> What is important is that these resolutions and international, humanist thoughts have often been co-opted as tools and instruments in the hands of foreign hegemonic powers pursuing their political, economic and military interests by creating riots, unrest and ethnic upheavals. In this . . . two-pronged game, [the foreign powers]—while supporting ethnic protests and movements—are actually facilitating an increased suppression and suffocation of ethnic groups.[172]

The articulated fear is that Western powers will use Iranian ethnicist discontent as tools to undermine the Islamic Republic. Qamari warns that if "the language factor" is not employed and utilized by Iran itself in a constructive fashion, then it will cause instability and conflicts in the future—such as, Qamari explains, during the 2006 Azerbaijan unrest. He argues that minorities must be made aware that "they can be both Azeri-speaking *and* Iranian" at the same time, "the same way that a person can be a Hispanic-speaker but American." Indeed, "local and ethnic languages must be respected and given attention," but not "with the aim of weakening the national language."[173] In other words, ethnic minorities are bound by national duty to remain alert that their own languages are not abused in the ploys of the enemy.

Nationalist-minded scholars thus view the recent wave of interest in minority languages as very suspicious. Ahmadi argues that proponents of this wave are propagating "anti-Iranian identity" while hiding behind a facade of "being supporters of the Islamic Republic."[174] Another scholar claims that Azeri ethnicist students in Tehran University have invited "anti-Iranian" speakers to campus,[175] and a third claims that these ethnicists are influenced by "lurking pan-Turkism" and anti-Persian "Grey Wolves" who seek to remove Persian as the official language of Iran and eventually break Azerbaijan away from Iran.[176] Za'im similarly claims that the call for Azeri-language instruction in elementary schools should be condemned as part of "the long-term strategies of certain neighboring countries, which is being executed by disoriented compatriots, who might be traitors."[177] Sometimes, these fears are also expressed through concern about the choice of alphabet or particular ways of spelling place names in ethnicist writings,[178] or about "foreign-sounding" names in vogue in certain parts of the minority societies.[179]

Nationalist-minded scholars and intellectuals thus read into the ethnicist discourse—indeed, into the minority languages, into the alternative practices of naming and even into the letters with which ethnicists choose to express themselves—a far-reaching, complex and multi-pronged conspiracy against Iran as a country and

Iranian-ness as an identity. In this respect, language is seen as perhaps the most formidable threat arising from the minority issue.

DISCUSSION

There are tempting comparisons to be made between the early twentieth century when Iranian nationalists wrote against regionalism, tribal power and foreign intervention, and the present-day debates about the minority issue. The fear, it appears, is still that Iran as a country and civilization will succumb to the onslaught of envious neighbors, avaricious imperialists and opportunistic domestic traitors. However, the difference is that unlike the calls for centralization of state and strengthening of national unity that proceeded and coincided with Reza Shah's rise to power in the 1920s, the Iranian state is today consolidated, independent from imperialist powers, in command of powerful mechanisms of coercion and legitimized by quasi-democratic processes of public participation—however fundamentally flawed these might be.

The fear of territorial disintegration, however, persists. Today, ethnicist demands for federalism, autonomy or minority rights are key concerns, tainted by historically grounded suspicion towards foreign powers. The precarious situation of Iran in a region marred with conflict and foreign interference, and in a post-9/11 world of psychological war and tension, obviously frames the ways that scholars, intellectuals and politicians perceive Iranian society, and thus also the minority issue.

A crucial difference, it appears, is the role of religion. As Parsi has shown in his work about interwar Iranian political thought, nationalist discourse in Iran has never been "one easily organised along religious-secular lines."[180] Shabnam Holiday has argued that it is impossible to clearly separate two distinct discourses of "Islamic-ness" and "Iranian-ness,"[181] and as we saw in Chapter 3, the state is today propagating an amalgamated ideology of Islamism and nationalism. However, the advent of a clergy-led political regime and an Islamo-nationalist hegemony in Iranian post-revolutionary politics, society and academia has undeniably created circumstances different from those of pre-revolutionary Iran. Subtle semantic differences and a sometimes surprisingly frank critique of the state all reveal discursive frictions between competing visions of Iranian-ness underlying the public debate.

Thus, some nationalist intellectuals today balance between opposition to the state apparatus, or the Islamist clergy, and resistance to foreign intervention. In the words of one National Front member, echoing a substantial diaspora opposition of secularist forces, Iran's "suffering" has nothing to do with "the Azeri ethnic group, the Kurds, the Persians . . . it is the pain of not having a democratic, secular state."[182] As we have seen, however, not all nationalist-minded scholars and intellectuals are secularists, and most of those able and willing to publish within Iran give prominent place to religion.

Then what unites these disparate voices is the supra-factional project of nationalist group-making, drawing upon the traditions of Iranian nationalism to create, consolidate or re-envision an allegedly singular entity called Iran by defending dominant notions of identity against the types of ethnic group-making that are perceived as threats—that is, ethnicism.

There is, throughout the nationalist writings on the minority issue, often a sense of an omnipresent "we," the National Self, looking at "them," the ethnic element on the periphery, the Internal Other. Even though this element is rhetorically endowed with the honor of being more Iranian than the rest, it is at the same time seen as something external that "we" must relate to or pass judgment on. In the words of Purjavadi, aspects of ethnic minority cultures "only make sense when they are used to protect and strengthen the national culture and not to weaken it." Thus, the "ethnic element" is objectified as something "we" can decide as to whether is nonsensical or beneficial. It is not an independent agency. The superior "we" is looking at the ethnic groups from an elevated position of the National Self, at once otherizing and internalizing the minorities as something among which "we" can, in turn, find pieces of the true, authentic national culture and a potential enemy or traitor.

Thus, the "more Iranian than the rest" trope, I will argue, is symptomatic of the centripetal and centrifugal processes of the nationalist discourse. It is not necessarily an inclusive statement of tolerance; it does not really mean that the minorities are the true owners of Iran. It is a symbolic gesture of appeasement, contingent upon the minorities' full cooperation and full acceptance of the dominant definition of Iranian-ness and national culture. This conditioned offer of inclusion comes with an implicit threat of exclusion and the branding as "anti-Iranian."

These notions are used not only to create a Self-image different from surrounding countries, but also to argue that minorities are "naturally" part of the Iranian nation-state. The outcome of these self-contradictions is that nationalists on one hand grudgingly admit the existence of various modes of ethnic self-expression within Iran while at the same time they negate this diversity by stressing the coherence, uniformity and homogeneity of the Iranian nation.

Several of the scholars whose works and statements I have analyzed in this chapter also share in common what I term "selective ethno-symbolism": the use of particular modernist theories on nation and ethnicity in order to push what is essentially a nationalist agenda. These scholars trace the ethno-genesis of the Iranian nation to antiquity, while at the same time treating ethnicist minority identities as modern, sometimes even very recent fabrications. While concepts such as "imagined communities" and "invented traditions" are evoked in the discussion of minority mobilization as an un-historic or non-native phenomenon, these scholars conversely use theories such as those of Anthony D. Smith to buttress the argument that Iran is incomparable to modern European nations.

Through a critical examination of Anthony D. Smith's famous works on nations and nationalism, Sinisa Malesevic has deemed ethno-symbolism to be highly identitarian. This is evident, Malesevic argues, when Smith's work is understood as expressions of a Durkheimian view of the social world: indeed, Smith's genealogy of nationhood as something that begins with *ethnies* and ends with full-fledged nations, his focus on nations as moral communities and on the notion of ethnic sacredness all parallel Durkheim's theories of solidarity, morality, religion and collective consciousness.[183] The problem with the academic use of terms such as "destiny," "historical mission" and "chosen-ness" to explain collective social action, Malesevic argues, is that the resulting analysis "tends to coalesce with the views of the subjects" of study, "so that it slips into advocacy for their cause":[184]

Instead of providing an explanation as to why and how actors reify their group membership and perceive other actors as homogeneous entities (i.e., "Christian peoples" and such), neo-Durkheimian identitarians simply accept folk concepts and treat large-scale social actors as if they have singular and recognisable wills.[185]

As such, "holistic epistemologies of the neo-Durkheimian type," Malesevic argues, "are prone to the reification of group action":

> Hence instead of viewing inter—and intra-group relations as dynamic processes, through which groups emerge and change, collectivism [such as ethno-symbolism] often ends up ascribing individual qualities to entire groups.

I have argued in this chapter that some nationalist-minded scholars today abuse such an ethno-symbolist approach in order to legitimize and rearticulate what is in essence Herderian nationalism: anthropomorphizing the nation, endowing it with a "soul" and claiming that, because of its antiquity and singularity, every human being born within is spiritually or organically attached to it; and expressing perennialist notions of an "eternal Iran" and anachronisms about pre-nation-state national identity when in fact, to quote Malesevic, there was no "significant degree of congruence between polity and culture" in the ancient world.[186]

Resorting to notions of "collective consciousness," to truth-claims about "authenticity" and to arguments about Iran being exceptional, some scholars push for a highly essentialist definition of Iranian-ness. Essentialism is as a basic feature of nationalism understood here as "a reduction of the diversity in a population to some single criterion held to constitute its defining 'essence' and most crucial character."[187] In the case of Iranian nationalists, this "essence" is based on a Persian-centric (and at times Aryanist and/or Shiite exceptionalist) discourse of identity that at once alienates and internalizes minorities. In invoking concepts such as "the Iranian mind" or "the national spirit," this crude essentialism is laid bare: scholars using such concepts seem to believe in the existence of a singular, socio-psychological reality for everyone who happens to be born in the territory known as Iran. In its crudest shape, this exceptionalist chauvinism is manifested in the claim that Iran's collective memory is stronger than that of other nations.

This view is reflected in the academic denunciation of "ethnicity," "ethnic group" and "minority" as concepts that cannot correctly depict realities in Iran. The argument that the Persian word *aqvām* should not be understood in the sense that the word "ethnic groups" is understood elsewhere, however, does not bring about any solid knowledge about either Iran or human societies in general. Indeed, there seems to be a pervasive tendency not to call a spade a spade: instead of "ethnicity" or "ethnic," two terms that are perceived as dangerous or divisive, scholars routinely refer to "local," "sub-national" or "sub-identity" phenomena. The discussion is distorted while the discussant beats around the proverbial bush.

While it is true that Western scholars originally devised these concepts to describe particular phenomena in particular societies, it is nonetheless a dubious claim that none of them can be adapted to sociological descriptions of Iran. Indeed, scholars such as Ahmadi, Hushmand, Kuhshekaf and Pak base their definitions on a very narrow understanding of the concepts and a very selective reading of history. The claim that the Iranian ruling elite has always incorporated representatives of all ethnic groups is simply not supported by historical evidence, and it is certainly not the case today. Similarly, the argument that there are more bonds binding these ethnic groups to Iran than to co-ethnics abroad is based on a particular historicized understanding of what "bonds" mean, and how different bonds can be strengthened or weakened in particular phases of history.

To be sure, contemporary scholars do not normally emphasize the Aryan myth to the same extent and for the same purpose as pre-revolutionary nationalists did. Scholars such as Ahmadi criticize the traditional nationalists for exaggerating the importance of racial origins. Yet even so, there is still a tendency to use "Aryan" in a sense broader than its linguistic one, and thus, to perpetuate the primordialist idea that Iranians are racially related *even* when ethnic diversity is admitted. Similarly, the fixation with Persian language hampers the realization that Iran is a multi-lingual country and that languages are "'created' out of the politics of state-making, not— as we often assume—the other way around."[188] As elsewhere,[189] minority languages are seen in Iran to have less worth, and minority language rights proponents are dismissed as nostalgic nationalists or separatists. In short, ethnic identity as a linguistic difference is seen as a potential threat to the essence that defines national identity, Persian language, because it is seen as a threat to the nation-state-congruence principle.

The "siege mentality" or fixation with foreign threats allows nationalists to reduce minority mobilization to a one-sided affair of outside infiltration in which minorities become passive chessmen manipulated from abroad. No room is left for the possibility that minorities could have an independent cultural and political agency. As gullible pawns, easily manipulated due to their disadvantaged socio-political and geographical position, or their lack of knowledge of the outside world, minorities *receive* "faked" and "distorted" identities, fed to them by foreign propaganda. This instrumentalist view focuses on rational choice (in a sphere that is often dominated by non-rational behavior) and on particular, "easy" targets such as "local elites" or the cold calculations of self-interest of a few. In the words of Rogers Brubaker:

> Elite discourse often plays an important role in the constitution of interests, but again this is not something political or cultural elites can do at will by deploying manipulative tricks. The identification and constitution of interests—in national or other terms—is a complex process that cannot be reduced to elite manipulation.[190]

The scapegoating of minority elites is, as May has argued, often no more than a "red herring": "a useful stick, in effect, with which to beat proponents of minority-language rights."[191] As Malesevic has pointed out, overemphasizing one group of social actors will lead to a distorted view of the larger context, denying "the masses" any significant agency, will or diversity. It is in this way that nationalists can use elite theory, such as that of Paul R. Brass, to dismiss the legitimacy of a broad, diverse movement for minority rights. Furthermore, since nationalist scholars only apply the instrumentalist view on minorities, it does not move us closer to an understanding of the majority.

Viewing minorities through a security prism, which is a legacy of the "military approach" to culture under which social sciences was founded in Iran, allows nationalists to draw reductionist conclusions in the name of national unity and security. These conclusions entail the wholesale criminalization of ethnic sentiments and minority demands. In such an atmosphere, any Iranians expressing political thoughts in minority languages or through ethnicist demands can be condemned as traitors. Hence, the minorities who will not accept the dominant definition of identity—the ethnicists—become "anti-citizens": they are "undemocratic" since they will not accept the majoritarian notion of citizenship. They are labeled and castigated, stigmatized and alienated as "anti-Iranians" by nationalists who simultaneously invoke the authenticity of an ancient nation and the democratic principles of a modern nation.

CHAPTER 5

A NATION RE-ENVISIONED

THE ETHNICIST DISCOURSE ON THE MINORITY ISSUE TODAY BUILDS on a heritage that consists of, on the one hand, the leftist discourses on oppression and resistance among particular socialist organizations and, on the other hand, the 1960s and 1970s literary and social critique of Pahlavi authoritarianism.

While the constitutionalist movement (see Chapter 4) had introduced the idea of citizenry and democracy to a significant part of the population in central and northern Iran, the leftist movement introduced the idea of social justice to a much broader audience—including minorities in the periphery. Whereas regionalist movements such as the Jangalis of Gilan (1914–1921) and that of Colonel Pesiyan in Khorasan (1921) did not represent particular minorities, the demands raised in the first revolt of Shaykh Khiabani in Azerbaijan in 1919 contained significant ethnic framing. This created a rift in the broader movement for social reform: between those who believed regionalism was antithetical to modernism and those who believed that the modernist elite of Tehran was out of touch with realities in the periphery. From that point onward, the latter segment of the movement gravitated toward a socialist language attentive of minority demands and concerns.

In the communiqué issued by the 1927 congress of the Communist Party (*ferqe-ye komunist,* abolished in 1937), for example, it was stated that "discrimination against and oppression of the minority nations (*melal-e aqaliyat*)" was one of Reza Shah's great misdeeds.[1] Although one could discuss what was exactly meant by *melal,* the use of the plural "nation*s*" was nonetheless significant: during the same period that nationalist intellectuals were striving to monopolize and singularize the meaning of "nation" in accordance with the nation-state-congruence principle, it opened the possibility of thinking of Iran as the home of more than one nation. However, this interpretation was at odds with the one that came to dominate the leading Iranian communist organization, the Tudeh.

Whereas the Tudeh Party, established in 1941, was mostly led by young Persian speakers and Persianized Azeris in Tehran who adhered to orthodox Marxism and had little understanding of or sympathy with minority grievances (among them also extremist Persian-centrics such as Taqi Arani, see Chapter 4), the Azerbaijan Democrat Party was led by Azeri Leninists who were primarily influenced by fellow Turkic speakers and their experiences with tsarist ethnic policies in the Caucasus.[2]

The Democrat Party was originally a wing of the Tudeh but gradually broke ranks with the party after a 1944 congress had descended into disagreement over the issue of local autonomy. This happened after a period of mounting inter-ethnic tensions in areas of socialist mobilization, including between Arabs and Persian speakers in the oil industry of Khuzestan and between Azeris and Persians in the coalfields of northern Iran.[3] These tensions also created deep divisions among the leading cadres of the socialist movement.

Thus, the Democrat Party, which declared Azerbaijan autonomous at its establishment in 1945, represented an alternative to the orthodox Marxist interpretation of Iranian society as only divided by class. According to this alternative interpretation, ethnic minorities were "peoples" (khalq-hā) oppressed not only by the forces of capitalism but also by ethnic discrimination. What had started with Azeri critique of the Persian- and Tehran-centric approach of the Tudeh Party and its ambiguous stand on the minority issue had thus spawned a new wave of regionalism and ethnicism, demands for local autonomy and linguistic rights. Instead of "the nation," to which the Tudeh addressed its official party program, the Azeri socialists addressed "the nations" (melal) of Iran.

When the Democrat Party took over control of Azerbaijan, they presented a declaration of autonomy that identified "the people of Azerbaijan" with "distinct national, linguistic, cultural, and traditional characteristics."[4] While the Party clearly stated that they had "no desire to separate" from Iran, they referred to the 1941 Atlantic Charter that promised all nations freedom and autonomy. Apart from autonomy, the Party demanded that Azeri Turkic, as the "national and mother tongue" of the Azeris, should be instituted in the education system and in local government. The declaration was thus a written testament to the perception among some people in Iran's periphery of constituting a nation with a national culture distinct from that of the Persian-speaking core.

The reaction to this development was strong and harsh: the Tudeh called for national unity and sought to ignore the ethnic dimension of the autonomist movement, and nationalist intellectuals condemned the Democrat Party for unleashing a potentially unstoppable cycle of regionalism and separatism that would lead to Iran's disintegration. After less than a year, the Iranian military moved in to crush the movement in Tabriz. However, the Azeri autonomists—and to some extent the Kurdish equivalent in the Mahabad Republic of 1945—had opened the possibility of ethnically framing regional discontent, and thus laid the seed of modern-day ethnicism. While the Democrat Party and the Tudeh eventually merged in a united front, ethnicist discourse had gained a life of its own.

The demand for administrative autonomy, linguistic rights and cultural independence in the name of oppressed peoples in the periphery was again launched during the 1978–9 revolution, resulting in inter-ethnic clashes and a regionalist uprising in Kurdistan. Various socialist-inspired armed movements at odds with Khomeini fled to areas such as Kurdistan and Turkamansahra, where they instigated an insurgency in the name of oppressed peoples. Regionalism and ethnicism came to equate, in the eyes of the ruling elite in Tehran, with socialism and separatism.

However, by that time, the ethnicist movement had also found a number of other ideological reference points. Inspired by developments all over the post-colonial

Third World, ethnicists had gained a keen awareness of ideologies of resistance and national liberation. With various socialist movements facing defeat in post-revolutionary Iran, and with the subsequent dissolution of the Soviet Union, ethnicist movements instead embraced international discourses on human, civil and minority rights. However, the leftist legacy is still evident in the way some ethnicists frame their demands and claims to identity.

In this chapter, I will first outline these core demands and claims, and how they challenge the Persian-centric nationalist paradigm in history writing and social sciences outlined in Chapter 4. For this purpose, an appraisal of new directions in Iranian Studies is needed. In the 1990s, a number of scholars took bold steps to deconstruct dominant definitions of Iranian-ness in the academic literature. These developments were congruent with the emergence of a new ethnicist movement in Iran; indeed, the two currents were to some extent aware of each other. In the first half of this chapter, I will thus present the key points in prominent ethnicist and revisionist works published inside and outside Iran.

In the second half of the chapter, I will attempt a tentative appraisal of the current state of the minority issue in Iranian society. First, I will outline crucial events relating to minorities up to and immediately after the Green Movement of 2009. Next, I will summarize the fundamental issues facing the ethnicist movement today. And finally, I will briefly discuss the salient points of what appears to be an emerging critical and inclusive understanding of the minority issue among scholars and public intellectuals in Iran today.

REVISIONISM AND ETHNICISM IN POST-KHOMEINI IRAN

A NATION DECONSTRUCTED

In 1994, Mostafa Vaziri[5] published *Iran as Imagined Nation*, a highly controversial critical inquiry into the formation of Iranian national identity. Vaziri argues that this identity is a modern creation based on a distorted, biased, linear vision of history. Borrowing the term from Benedict Anderson, Vaziri presents Iran as an "imagined community" in order to "challenge the conservative academic literature" and its "unfortunate impact on national and racial stereotyping."[6]

Vaziri argues that Iranian modernists were heavily influenced by European nationalism and Western Orientalist scholarship, and that the ideas projected into Iran from the West brought about a particular kind of Aryanist nationalism and the construction of a false national history. Indeed, the very name of Iran was "forged," Vaziri claims, by Orientalists in order to signify both a modern nation-state and an allegedly homogenous and singular civilization.[7] This idea of Iranian-ness was bolstered by Western scholars' philological and archaeological discoveries: by "linking the literature (Farsi) to a national tradition," Orientalists gave nationalists the necessary "dynastic connection" to create an exclusivist and anachronistic history. *In lieu* of direct colonial domination, this Orientalist "academic domination"—an "European intellectual authoritarianism over the Orient"—continues today.[8]

In fact, Vaziri argues, Iranian elites did not conceptualize Iran as a homogenous entity before they were inspired to do so by European secular thinkers: until the late

Qajar era, the terms "Iran," "Iranshahr" and "Fars" did not have any political, ethnic or national meaning at all. Since it was only with the Pahlavis that Iranian national identity took shape, the idea of cultural continuity from pre-Islamic to modern times, Vaziri argues, amounts to "nationalist mumbo-jumbo."[9] Most importantly for the topic of this book, Vaziri argues that in trivializing the non-Persian element, nationalist history writing has not been able to adequately answer the question "Who is Iranian?":

> What does a Kurd have in common with a Gilaki, given that their languages, traditions, and histories have been totally dissimilar? The philological answer provided was that they both belong to an Iranian language family. But this ignored the fact that neither Kurds nor the Gilakis ever used the term Iranian in their tradition. Furthermore, the classification of the Iranian language family was a recent academic undertaking; thus, the proposition that an Iranian consciousness had existed among the speakers of these language families in the past is improper and anachronistic. Obviously, many of these obscure views were swept under the rug by the Orientalists or were answered in the form of common citizenship and patriotic propaganda by the modern centralized state.[10]

These aspects of Vaziri's critique are often neglected by mainstream scholars who focus on his more spectacular claims: his argument that Iran, as a name and an entity, is "forged" is indeed both a threat to Iranian nationalist self-perception and a serious accusation against prominent scholars of Iranian Studies. Even though Vaziri claims that he did not intend for his work to "transmit any political message nor to deny the reality of the modern Iranian nation-state,"[11] this is nonetheless how his detractors perceived it. Yet Vaziri's work is hard to ignore for a new generation of students of Iranian Studies.

When it appeared in the 1990s, reviewers argued that Vaziri's critique was based on a selective reading of history, inconsistent and reductive historical arguments, omissions of crucial events and simplistic views on the relationship between Europe and Iranian intellectuals. They argued that Vaziri misapplied Benedict Anderson's concept, taking "imagined" to mean "fake," and thus completely rejecting any legitimacy for Iranian national identity.[12] One reviewer argued that critical historical thinking "requires that Iranologists such as Vaziri free themselves from the martyrdom syndrome of claiming innocence and blaming others for all that appears undesirable and unfashionable," and listen to the "creative voices of Iranian intellectuals" instead of reproducing "a Eurocentric paradigm that constitutes Orientals as passive subjects of European analysis and gaze."[13] All this notwithstanding, reviewers concluded that, polemics aside, Vaziri had managed to challenge received wisdom about Iran.[14]

There are, however, also less radical and more convincing attempts at deconstructing nationalist truth claims in Iranian Studies. In his groundbreaking 1998 article, "Contesting nationalist constructions of Iranian identity," Mehrzad Boroujerdi shows how secularist intellectuals have "fallen victim to an ahistorical definition of authentic 'Iranian identity'":

> These intellectuals have anchored their conception of identity on the matrices of language, selective historiography, and a Persian-centered nationalism that ignores ethnic minorities.[15]

Boroujerdi argues that nationalist historians have "taken refuge in the belief that Iran enjoys the blessing of God, the angel of history, and prodigious heroes and sages," failing to realize that "the conceptual capital inherited from the ancestors is depleted, if not already overdrawn."[16] He criticizes "heritage-ism," the tendency among secularist nationalists to fetishize the past and to neglect "anomalies, inconsistencies, transmutations, and ruptures" to the extent that it creates a "lethargy" and "cultural rigidity."[17] Criticizing the "mytho-poetic" world-view, Boroujerdi singles out the works of scholars such as Yar-Shater and Meskoub (see Chapter 4). In praising the Persian language in "romantic rather than factual" terms, these scholars, Boroujerdi argues, have conveniently forgotten that the Persian hegemony was facilitated by a "morbid" Pahlavi ideology.[18]

Boroujerdi speculates that at the advent of the modern Iranian nation-state, "close to 80 percent of Persian-speakers themselves were illiterate," that "perhaps no more than 50 percent of Iranians actually spoke Persian" and that even with Persian as national language, it never really "replaced the local languages."[19] Yet despite this, the nationalist scholars have disregarded the multi-lingual nature of Iran. In extension, Boroujerdi criticizes the portrayals of minority demands as "treasonous" and non-Persian rebellions in Iran as "a matter of foreign conspiracy and manipulation." In conclusion, Boroujerdi calls on his peers to correct the imbalance of focus in Iranian Studies by taking serious "the legitimate demands and plight of ethnic and religious minorities in Iran by studying their genealogy, customs and beliefs."[20] Thus, Boroujerdi has raised some highly contentious issues and helped facilitate a long overdue debate that this book, as mentioned in the Introduction, should be seen as a part of.

Joya Blondel Saad's 1996 *The Image of Arabs in Modern Persian Literature* is another, though quite different, example of 1990s revisionist Iranian Studies. Saad argues that the largely negative and often racist image of Arabs in modern Persian literature is crucial to nationalist discourses on Iranian-ness: an Arab Other is needed, in the formation of a modern nation-state in a multi-ethnic society, as a "reverse" image of the "authentic" Self. The Aryanist and primordialist notions of "linguistic/racial purity" and an "unchanging spirit of a people" naturally precluded "a multi-ethnic nationalism," she argues; instead of representing Iran's diversity, the Pahlavi regime sought to "change the ethnic identity" of all non-Persians into "Iranians."[21]

The specific case of Iranian attitudes toward Arabs, Saad admits, however, is more complex than a question of mere one-sided prejudice. There is nothing inherently anti-Arab or racist about Iranian culture, she stresses—rather, negative stereotypes of the Other are used selectively to criticize certain domestic cultural features deemed uncivilized or ignorant, such as superstition and conservatism. However, Saad also explores the explicitly anti-Arab sentiments among some Iranians, including many of the early modernist thinkers that founded Iranian nationalism. She explains this as follows:

> Iran was Islamicized; in the eyes of some Iranians, Islam is essentially Arab, and therefore non-Iranian. Others, however, hold that Shi'i Islam is an Iranicized Islam, essentially Iranian, and an essential part of Iranianness. Anti-Arab feelings may go hand in hand with anti-Islamic feelings, or one may give rise to the other, or there may be anti-Islamic

sentiments without anti-Arab bias, or the reverse. Writers may hold one view or the other; indeed, to some extent, the Pahlavi regime reflected one view, and the Islamic Republic the other.[22]

Saad seeks to demonstrate this complexity through examples from Persian literature in which she sees nationalist sentiments ranging from xenophobia over Persian chauvinism to virulent anti-Semitism and anti-Arabism.

Although Vaziri's, Boroujerdi's and Saad's works differ in aim, scope and focus, they are nonetheless all part of an undercurrent among scholars that started to question the "received knowledge" in Iranian Studies in the 1990s. This undercurrent of deconstruction is conterminous with a more nuanced approach in the mainstream of Iranian Studies, which aims to depart from the highly Persian-centric and nationalist reading of history and society, but not necessarily with the same sweeping revision as that of Vaziri. The most important change in Iranian historiography, it seems, is the discarding of nationalist truth claims about continuity. In the words of social historian Ahmad Ashraf, a prominent scholar of Iranian Studies at Columbia University and managing editor of *Encyclopaedia Iranica*:

> [S]ome Iranian intellectuals naively think that "Iranian national identity" in the modern sense has a past of several thousand years[; a]s if since Creation and the beginning of Iraj's rule (attributed in myths as the first legendary Shah who founded the country of Iran) up until today, all the people of Iran, from each ethnic group, tribe and clan, from cities, villages and tribes, from the educated to the uneducated, have been aware of this [national identity], and seen themselves as part of its framework.[23]

Ashraf argues that there *was* such a thing as Iranian-ness in ancient times, but that this does not necessarily translate into a national identity or collective consciousness. This is a critical distinction, and it testifies to the emergence of a less nationalistic approach in contemporary Iranian Studies as seen from abroad. This new approach is parallel with a new movement within academia inside Iran. These new scholars, I will argue, are keenly aware of ethnicist perspectives and minority discontent, and are currently seeking to reform Iranian anthropology and sociology. Before we return to the proponents of this movement in the final part of this chapter, I will now briefly turn attention back to the roots of the contemporary ethnicist perspective.

WRITING BACK

Apart from the political organizations on the Iranian left mentioned in the beginning of this chapter, an important source of inspiration for pre-revolutionary ethnicism came from three proponents of the critical literary school: Gholam-Hossein Sa'edi, Samad Behrangi and Reza Baraheni, all Azeri Iranians associated with the Marxist-inspired circle of nativist anti-establishment intellectuals around Jalal Al-e Ahmad.

Although a trained psychiatrist, Sa'edi (1936–1985) is famous as one of Iran's most prominent writers of fiction and screenplays. Sa'edi had found an interest in Azeri rural life at a young age, and he was active in the Azeri socialist movements before establishing himself in the leftist intellectual milieu. Apart from three ethnographic works on Azeri, Shahsevan and south Iranian communities, his fiction was also inter-woven with thick ethnographic description and detail that had an impact on many thinkers and artists of his time.

Behrangi (1939–1968) is today mostly famous for his children's books, but in his native Azerbaijan, he was also an avid ethnographer, folklorist and educator. Along-side scholars such as Nader Afshar-Naderi and Amir-Hushang Keshavarz, Behrangi made an important contribution to ethnography as a discipline in Iran. However, he also played a role in giving a voice to Azeris. Dedicated to preserving Azeri culture, he struggled with Pahlavi authorities to publish poems and tales translated from Azeri to Persian. Behrangi was also prevented from publishing in Azeri, and his folk tale col-lections have only recently appeared in their original language. Eventually, Behrangi died in a swimming incident that some leftists blamed on the shah's agents.

Of these three, the most important, however, is the literary critic, poet, writer and human rights activist Baraheni (b. 1935). Now in Canadian exile, Baraheni wrote about his experiences as a prisoner of the Pahlavi regime in the book *Crowned Cannibals*—among other things about "the Shah's racism":

> The Shah considers all Iranians to be Aryans, thus overlooking the ethnic diversity, which exists in the country. Everyone has to learn one language, Persian. This is a great injustice to the other nationalities. I belong to the Turkish-speaking Azerbaijani nationality. The men and women of my generation were told by the Shah to forget about their language and to read and write everything in Persian. When I write a poem about or a story about my parents, my mother, who is alive and doesn't know how to read or write or speak Persian, cannot understand it. I have to translate it for her so that she can understand.[24]

Baraheni was one of a handful of prominent literary voices who raised the question of ethnic discrimination in an explicit fashion before a national audience in pre-revolutionary Iran. Though in exile today, his Internet writings are still read in Iran and circulated on ethnicist online platforms. In the following subsections, we will return to his views on the minority issue.

Two of the most comprehensive recent attempts of ethnicist "writing back" are from two scholars based in North America. Ali Al-Taie is a US-based professor of sociology who has described himself as "an Arab by roots, Arab-Iranian by cir-cumstance, and naturalized Arab-American by desire."[25] His 1999 book *Bohrān-e hoviyat-e qowmi dar irān* ("Ethnic Identity Crisis in Iran"), which is a collection of earlier writings, appeared in Iran in 1999. The Azeri-Iranian, Canada-based soci-ologist 'Ali-Reza Asgharzadeh published his monograph *Iran and the Challenge of Diversity: Islamic Fundamentalism, Aryanist Racism and Democratic Struggles* in North America in 2007.

Although written within an academic framework, with outlines of methodolo-gies, sources and theories, the two books can also be read as personal histories of being a member of an ethnic minority in Iran, which is presented as a sometimes painful and confusing experience. Al-Taie describes his frustration as a pupil in the "alien" environment of a majority-Persian elementary school where he was ridiculed for his "thick Arabic accent."[26] He explains the impact of racist jokes, mockery and popular sayings that "Arabs are donkeys" or "Arabs eat grasshoppers." Despite these negative experiences, he turned out a very good student of Persian, Al-Taie recounts. This, however, did not mean that he became "Iranicized," "wanna-be-Persian" or "Aryan-ish."[27]

Asgharzadeh's work is also in many ways personal and emotional, with numerous descriptions of ethnic discrimination in Iran and in exile communities presented in the first person plural:

> Notwithstanding the fact that we Azeris, Kurds, Arabs, Baluchs, Turkmens, and others constituted the numerical majority in the country, the government sought to supplant our languages, cultures, and histories with those of the Persian minority. As non-Persian citizens of Iran, we were subjected to open and shameful acts of linguicide, cultural annihilation and forced assimilation.[28]

This use of hyperbole ("linguicide," "annihilation"), emotive language ("shameful," "forced," "subjected") and dubious claims ("numerical majority") marks the text throughout. The book comes across as a harsh counter-attack on the criticism and intimidation that Asgharzadeh claims he has experienced as an ethnicist. When working on a bilingual Azeri/Persian journal in Canada, Asgharzadeh explains:

> The mere fact that these journals were partly written in the Azeri language was reason enough for members of the dominant language to brand me and my colleagues as traitors, secessionists, and separatists. Without even reading the journal and knowing its content, former friends and acquaintances began to isolate me, considering me a dangerous, radical element disloyal to Iran's territorial integrity.[29]

Al-Taie too recalls the experience of being branded a separatist for even "*mentioning* Kurdistan, Azerbaijan, Khuzestan or Baluchistan."[30]

Asgharzadeh places his work in a post-colonial studies tradition that seeks to liberate oppressed peoples, whether from imperialism or from internal colonization, which he deems an apt expression for the situation of non-Persian-speaking ethnic groups in Iran. While Asgharzadeh's monograph is thus presented as a typical work of ("Western") sociology, Al-Taie's method is somewhat alternative: he seeks to explain complex concepts of social science for the uninitiated Iranian reader through the extensive use of Persian and Arabic poetry, philosophy, parables and examples from everyday life.

In the following subsections, I will present the grievances and demands expressed by the ethnicist movement, relying on Asgharzadeh and Al-Taie as well as a number of other ethnicist scholars, intellectuals and political activists as representatives of this movement. Among these are also the aforementioned Baraheni and another important figure: Yusef-Azizi Bani-Torof (b. 1951). Bani-Torof is an Arab-Iranian intellectual, journalist, translator and scholar of ethnicity now residing in exile in London. He is an outspoken critic of state ethnic policies and discrimination against minorities, and he has published extensively on this matter in political journals and websites. He was also a key figure in the attempt during the 1990s to establish an Arabic-language local press in Khuzestan.

As a central figure in the wave of social and political critique after the election of Khatami in 1997, Bani-Torof was harassed, intimidated and arrested by authorities on several occasions. In 2005 he was detained by security forces for his alleged implication in the Khuzestan unrest (see Chapter 2), and in 2008, after being handed a five-year prison sentence for political activities, he escaped from Iran. Nonetheless, like Baraheni, he continues to be an important voice in the ethnicist movement inside Iran.

The four authors that I will refer most to in the following discussion are thus all based abroad, whether by choice or not. The reason why they are influential and important voices is clear: since the moderated cultural policy of the reformists was rolled back in the beginning of the new millennium, very few explicitly ethnicist works have been published inside Iran. While there is still a prolific industry publishing fiction, poetry and folklore in various minority languages, critical works such as those introduced here are exceedingly rare. Instead, most ethnicist critique has been relocated to cyberspace where writers can shelter behind online anonymity.

A HISTORY DIVERSIFIED

Through their writings, the ethnicists seek to present a vision of Iran as essentially and historically diverse: there is no one race, one language, one culture or even, according to some, one nation in Iran. With this vision of Iran as a plurality, the ethnicists attack the Persian-centric nationalism with its inherent Aryanism, negation of ethnic identities and disrespect for linguistic diversity. The ethnicists seek to "de-Persianize" the conventional definitions of Iranian national identity and the histories that underpin these definitions, demanding a place and respect for the contributions of minorities to Iran as a whole.

In Asgharzadeh's case, the primary aim is to prove "once and for all that racism does exist in Iran." This is necessary, he warns, in order to prevent "the cultural annihilation" of non-Persian-speaking ethnic groups and their languages.[31] Asgharzadeh maintains that the peaceful coexistence characterizing pre-modern Iran was ruined by the emergence of a non-inclusive, "Fars-centered" (i.e., Persian-centered) proto-nationalism around the time of the Constitutional Revolution (1905–11). This nationalism "failed to include in a democratic manner the non-Persian groups and nationalities within an emancipatory discourse" and it has created a sense of "Farstoxification": a feeling of resentment among the minorities toward the Persian-centric cultural and political hegemony.[32]

A target of the ethnicist critique is thus the role of modernist intellectuals in Iran's last 100 years of history. Bani-Torof blames key Iranian intellectuals, including "chauvinist theoreticians" (such as Afshar and Kasravi, see Chapter 4) and authors with "Arab-hostile, anti-Turk ideas" (such as the famous writer Sadeq Hedayat and the historian Abdolhossein Zarrinkub). From these thinkers, a "Reza Khani supremacy discourse" (goftemān-e bartari-talab-e rezā-khāni) spread down through society to become a "mass-culture" of "insult, abuse and ridicule against non-Persian ethnic groups."[33] In this fashion, modernist intelligentsia helped destroyed the "historical unity, brotherhood, solidarity and co-existence of Iranian ethnic groups and nations."[34]

To counter the Persian-centric linear histories of a homogeneous national entity moving uninterrupted through time, ethnicists instead portray Iran as a society molded historically by repeated immigrations. Following the revisionist line of Vaziri, Al-Taie uses the *Shāhnāme* to prove that Iran's "geographical reality" before and after Islamization was mired in "ambiguity." Al-Taie also argues that important Iranian cultural figures, such as Hafez, actually professed a "regional" rather than a national identity, and that others were actually Arabic, not Persian, speakers.[35]

Asgharzadeh places great emphasis on towering figures in Iranian history that were actually native Turkic speakers, including Bagher and Sattar Khan of the Constitutional Revolution. Baraheni similarly reminds his audience that it was Turkic-speaking dynasties that nurtured Persian literature in the medieval ages, not "Persians."[36] Al-Taie laments that despite all this, Iran's people, culture and artifacts are still known as "Persian" to the outside world: Persian Heritage, Persian cat, Persian rug, and so on. In this fashion, ethnicists use the symbols most dear to the nationalists—the poets, heroes and famous artifacts—to prove the point that Persian-centrism is a recent anomaly, and not a part of Iran's historical reality.

Ethnicist writers often point out the contributions their respective communities historically have made to Iran as an entirety, such as resisting the Muslim invasions, protecting Iran's borders against Sunni powers, restoring Iran to its place as a regional power after various setbacks and defending it against colonial aggressors.[37] In fact, these are quite similar arguments to those made by the nationalists: that Iranian minorities have "always" stood up in defense of the homeland. However, in the ethnicist discourse, the aim is clearly different: to underscore that the majority should respect the cultures and languages of the minorities, not the other way around.

In order to highlight the existence of non-Persian ethnic groups in Iran, ethnicist commentators often make statistical statements based on dubious sources or with no references at all. Some writers state that "the Persians" are in fact a minority. However, others are aware of the problematic paucity of data. As Al-Taie also points out, this allows for "unrealistic estimates" and "the construction of demographic myths" among members of the state apparatus, nationalist intellectuals and minority proponents alike. Thus, the state acts "as if there were no Arabs in Khuzestan" while, on the other hand, Arab ethnicists regularly come up with imaginary, heavily inflated estimates.[38] Al-Taie calls for a census:

> Indeed, in a future census in Iran, while asking "Who is your father? Who is your mother? What is your occupation?," why not also "Sir, to which ethnic group . . . do you belong?" The results of such findings would both put the governmental leaders in a favorable position with regards to economic planning and to conjectures of "security matters" (!); and [the results] could [have the effect of] cold or hot water poured on the heads of this or that ethnic group, making them realize that their demographic "weight" is, in reality, this light or that heavy.[39]

Since the Aryan myth is today at once rejected academically and yet sustained in popular discourses on identity and ancestry, Aryanism is an obvious target for the ethnicist critique.

Asgharzadeh singles out Aryanism as a main constituent in state ideology under the Pahlavis *and* the Islamic Republic: a racist ideology based on European Orientalism that places Persians in a superior position to "minoritize" the non-Persians. Colonial powers dug up, restored and redistributed the works of ancient Orientals for the consumption of modern Orientals, inspiring modern nation-statism and Aryanism, which was only to the advantage of Persians.[40] Direct foreign meddling, in particular that of Britain and its alleged responsibility for enthroning Reza Khan, also played a key role in the spread of Aryanism, as did the connections between Nazi Germany and Pahlavi Iran. Asgharzadeh presents the claim, though without substantial elaboration, that "the Islamic Republic, like the Pahlavi regime before it, has sought to equate Fars/Persian with Iranian."[41]

Some ethnicists extend the specific critique of Aryanism to a broader critique of the very idea of racial purity. Of 2,500 years of monarchy, Al-Taie claims, Iran was for 1,500 years in the hands of "non-Aryan dynasties," including Arabs, Turkmen, Turks, Mongols and Afghans:[42] the idea of an "Aryan Iran" or that these groups have ruled "like Aryans" (*āriyā'i-vash*) is mere "sophistry." Al-Taie provides examples from history: that Alexander the Great made his soldiers marry local Iranians, thus mixing in "Greek" blood; that Iran has thousands of *seyyed*s, descendents of relatives of the Prophet Mohammad, who must necessarily have an "Arabic gene" and can thus not be "pureblooded" Aryans; and that the Qajar Fath-'Ali Shah (1797–1834) left behind 786 children and grandchildren from his 157 wives of Persian, Turkic, Arabic, Georgian, Jewish and Armenian stock, making a huge "contribution" to Iran's racial/ethnic melting pot.

Al-Taie's point is broader than merely calling on nationalist historians to abandon the "Aryan" myth and accept that Iran is and has always been a multi-ethnic society: the idea that any race can be pure is simply nonsense. In short, the myth of essential homogeneity is denied in order to give room for ethnic and racial diversity.

PLURALIZING THE NATION

In their project of "writing back," the ethnicists today demand that we understand Iran as a multi-ethnic (*kasir-ol-qowmi*) if not multi-national (*kasir-ol-melle*) country inhabited by a diverse population and characterized by a multiplicity of identities. As we saw in Chapter 4, a major nationalist concern with ethnicism is the demand for a federal structure in Iran, which nationalists fear will pave the way for Iran's territorial disintegration. However, this is actually not reflective of the demands as they are voiced in most ethnicist works. Rather, many of the ethnicist intellectuals, branded as separatists by the state apparatus or by nationalist intellectuals, are in fact staunch supporters of Iran's territorial integrity. They differ from the nationalists, however, on the crucial issue of how to understand "nation."

The spectrum of narratives on "the national" and understandings of *mellat* (nation) and *melliyyat* (nationality/nationhood) is broad. At one end of the spectrum are ethnicists who clearly frame and conceptualize their demands as "national" issues: they see themselves as nations, either as part of a "multi-national" (*kasir-ol-melleh*) Iran or as nations that should have been independent but are colonized and suppressed by "the Persian nation." At the other end of the spectrum, we find ethnicist intellectuals who do not necessarily see their ethnic groups as nations, and certainly not as nation-states in the making. They stress that their *qowm* (ethnic group) is part of an Iranian nation, which is unjustly dominated by another group, the Persians, leaving little room for expressions of diversity.

In the first category we also find radical ethno-nationalists, generally writing in online forums and under what are probably pseudonyms. Some have very elaborate schemes for dividing Iran's population into nations, nationalities and national minorities. These diverse national communities are only tied together, the radicals argue, by a voluntary accord. In other words, the nations could or should be independent, and whether or not this independence should be achieved within the framework of a federation depends on what the populations of these nations choose the day they are presented with the opportunity to choose.[43]

Detractors can of course dismiss such views as the far-fetched delusions of a small group of separatists—they certainly summarize the stuff of nationalist nightmares: that minorities not only have the right to, but will eventually, establish their own state, "with or without" the rest of Iran, so to speak. Such arguments represent a fundamental challenge to the nation-state-congruence principle. These radical visions are, however, outweighed by more realistic demands and less provocative voices, among them Ali Al-Taie.

Al-Taie defines *mellat* historically as an equivalent of *qowmiyat*: "an ethnic nation." However, he crucially emphasizes that in the modern sense of a "nation-state," *mellat* is a recent construct.[44] He also argues for two separate and simultaneous functions of *melliyyat*: a citizenship-based concept pertaining to a modern nation-state and an ethnic concept that can transcend territorial borders. Thus, Al-Taie argues that a Khuzestani Arab is just as much an Iranian citizen as a Kermani, or someone from the city of Kerman: they share *melliyyat* in the sense that they belong as citizens to the Iranian nation-state. However, the Arab also shares *melliyyat*, based on ethnic kinship, with Arabs in other countries.

It seems that most ethnicists have yet to make up their mind on how to define their own community within a plural Iran. Asgharzadeh, for example, constantly fluctuates between "nationality" and "ethnic group."[45] Other commentators argue that Iran's various communities must together agree on how to define themselves and each other. In the words of an Azeri Iranian commentator:

> Iran's Persians must define themselves. Whatever they are called, we too [will be defined as such]. If they are "the Persian ethnic group" [*qowm-e fārs*], we too are the ethnic groups of Turks, Kurds, Arabs, Lors, Baluch, Turkmen, and so on. If they are a "nation" [*mellat*] or a "nationality" [*melliyyat*], then we are too.[46]

Arguably the most important aspect of the ethnicist discourse is that it questions taken-for-granted truth claims about Iranian history and Iranian-ness. The aim of "writing back," then, is to return agency to marginalized peoples in the periphery. Yet, apart from such abstract discussions, most ethnicists instead spend their time and energy on a more immediate, pressing and practical demand: the call for a decentralization and re-distribution of power based on what is presented as a historically homegrown Iranian systems of government. They propose to solve the ethnic crisis by instituting a federal structure, which they insist has a long precedence in Iranian history: the medieval *moluk-ot-tavāyefi* ("Kings of Tribes") system, which Al-Taie claims persisted until Reza Shah replaced it with a centralized state, or the historical concept of *mamālek-e mahruse-ye irān,* which Asgharzadeh translates as "independent kingdoms of Iran."

With concepts such the *mamālek,* Asgharzadeh claims, the Qajar state governed a "multiethnic, multicultural and multilingual society" by way of "a loose form of federalism where all ethnic groups were free to use, study, and develop their languages, literatures, cultures, traditions and identities."[47] Al-Taie argues that the political elites of today must move to the logical conclusion and include all ethnic groups in a revived federal system.[48]

Apart from these pre-modern concepts for visualizing future solutions to the minority issue, numerous ethnicists have looked into more recent history—specifically to the concept of *anjoman-hā-ye iyālati va velāyati* ("Provincial and Regional Councils") enshrined in Iran's first constitution. Some ethnicists argue that the authors of this 1906 constitution had the foresight to accommodate demands for regional autonomy and were keenly aware of the minority issue—among other things by not specifying a national language at the expense of other languages.[49]

Thus, while nationalists hail the Constitutional Revolution as a crucial step in safeguarding Iran against territorial disintegration, ethnicists on the other hand interpret it as an attempt at decentralizing power. Some ethnicists refer to the fact that during the revolution, the various regions of Iran often communicated with Tehran in the name of *mellat*s, such as the *mellat-e āzarbāyjān.* It is clear that *mellat,* in the dominant discourse, has taken on another meaning today. Yet the ethnicist reference simultaneously underlines the independent agency of minorities as "nations" *and* their historical role in the modern project of state-making common to all Iranians.

The ethnicists lament that the provisions for regional autonomy were never implemented, and that with the coming to power of Reza Shah, all hopes for ethnic equality were quashed. Bani-Torof argues that the policies of the Pahlavis, and subsequently in the Islamic Republic, have forced Iranian society toward homogenization, assimilation, centralization and the notion of "mono-nationality" (*tak-melliyyati*) in a country that is historically "multi-nationality" (*chand-melliyyati*). This, in turn, has ignited minority radicalism and created a dangerous tension between center and periphery. The solution, then, is a return to a historically grounded federal structure, in which minorities are granted self-rule under the umbrella of the Iranian nation-state.[50]

Bani-Torof calls for a total overhaul of the political and social order of Iran, and for the wholesale disavowal of nationalism, whether in the form of Aryanism, Reza Khanism or even the more progressive, democratic nationalism of Mosaddeq. These nationalisms, Bani-Torof contends, insist on a "straightjacket definition of "Iranian identity" and the negation of the existence and rights of Iranian ethnic groups."[51] Bani-Torof and his peers thus call on scholars and intellectuals to live up to their responsibilities as critical thinkers and break with the discourses of the past.

DILUTING THE MAGIC POTION

The one point shared by practically all ethnicists is the concern with the issue of language. Ethnicists argue that the hegemony of Persian language in modern Iranian state and society has created a dominant definition of Iranian-ness in which Iranian identity is equaled with Persian proficiency, and where literacy (*savād*) is equaled with the ability to write and read in Persian. A key strategy for ethnicist writers is thus to routinely remind their audiences of the simple fact that the mother tongue (*zabān-e mādari*) of many Iranians is not Persian, and to demonstrate their love for these mother tongues.[52]

Ethnicist writers often share their personal experiences with the ridicule and discrimination they have faced due to their linguistic difference with the majority, to their accents when speaking Persian and to the embarrassment of not being able to read and write in their mother tongues. Al-Taie, for example, explains in a sarcastic tone:

> The fundamental oppression [lies within the fact that] since 1925 they have forced us to put aside our mother tongue, that is the Koranic language of Arabic, and only learn Persian, which, even though it is [like] sugar, sweet and honey-like, was a foreign language to us.[53]

In this fashion, Al-Taie challenges in a witty way the well-established literary notion and popular saying, *qand-e pārsi* (Persian Sugar), and its implied consequences: that the melodious, poetic Persian is "sweeter" than other languages. This challenge does not dispute the sweetness of Persian, but rather aims to show that other languages are just as "sweet"—at least in the ears of those who hear and speak them as mother tongues. "No language is bitter," Al-Taie reminds us: that "Persian is sugar" (*fārsi shekar ast*) should not be an excuse to prevent minorities from learning and cultivating their own languages.[54]

In order to further challenge Persian supremacy, Al-Taie questions the notion of a "pure Persian" (*pārsi-ye sarreh*), which Iranian nationalists maintain has been preserved in works such as the *Shāhnāme*. He points out that the veneration and glorification of the *Shāhnāme* in this sense contradicts the equally profound love for later works, such as those of Sa'di and Hafez—works written in a Persian heavily reliant on a huge vocabulary borrowed from Arabic. Al-Taie cleverly enforces his point by using Arabic and Turkic loanwords to describe the linguistic interbreeding that characterizes the Persian language (*makhlut, momzaj, qāti-pāti*). "Pure Persian," Al-Taie claims, is just a political myth. Instead of the *Shāhnāme*, which is "rich in racist expressions," the "impure Persian" of later poets should be hailed, he argues.[55]

Ethnicists thus argue that the fact that Persian is an extremely rich literary language—nurtured over centuries by Persians and non-Persian alike, celebrated by Muslim artists and poets, and studied in fantastic detail by eminent scholars across the globe—should not prevent the realization that Iran is a multi-lingual country. They argue that the fact that a language such as Baluchi only recently became a literary language, and that languages such as Kurdish and Azeri have received comparatively little scholarly attention, should not be used as an excuse to reject the legitimacy of these languages and their speakers—indeed, all of these languages should be officially recognized.

The basic formulation of the language right demand takes shape within the context of the Islamic Republic Constitution's Article 15, which promises minorities that their languages can be used in media and public schools. Since the ratification of the constitution, minority spokesmen have complained that this article has never been implemented in actual policy. Ethnicists such as Bani-Torof argue that through constitutional noncompliance, the current regime is in fact a major destabilizing factor in society, damaging national unity and causing the same radicalization it so fears.[56] Bani-Torof proposes that the regime allows for the teaching of minority languages in elementary schools, re-opens minority language journals that have been banned, gives permission to new journals currently barred from activity and (re-)legalizes minority rights organizations currently outlawed. Such measures would "contribute to national reconciliation."[57]

Within the framework of law, the ethnicists present a plethora of arguments: that as tax-payers, minorities should benefit from public education in the languages they prefer; that teaching minority languages would develop human resources since many of these languages are also spoken in neighboring countries with economic and political importance to Iran; that resources spent on teaching Koranic Arabic in public schools should be diverted to serve more immediately important purposes and so on.[58] Apart from Iranian law, they also refer to international conventions and declarations. A major site of contention between ethnicists and nationalists, in both physical-political and intellectual-discursive domains, thus revolves around International Mother Language Day.

For several years, ethnic activists have staged small protests throughout Iran on this UN-designated day. They report that authorities seek to disrupt and prevent the gatherings and that Iranian media do not pay attention to their demands. One activist voiced his grievance with these rhetorical questions:

> I am an Iranian but I am not Persian. I am Baluch, Turk, Arab, Kurd, Turkmen. Why won't you allow me to study in my mother tongue? What difference is there between your mothers and my mother since her language has been removed from the educational system?[59]

The writer laments that his language has been ridiculed, marginalized and censored but maintains that as long as there are "mothers" of different ethnic origins, their languages will survive.

A similar site of opposition to the nationalist hegemony centers on the politics of naming. Ethnicists argue that the state-ordered practice of re-naming of minority areas, cities and landmarks is part of a particular policy and discriminative mentality and that it causes both confusion and inter-ethnic tensions.[60] As examples of Tehran's alleged divide-and-conquer strategy, they mention the splitting up of Azerbaijan into two and then three provinces (Western, Eastern Azerbaijan and Ardabil provinces); of designating only a small portion of the Kurdish-inhabited areas as Kurdistan; of merging (Shiite, Persian-speaking) Sistan with (Sunni, Baluch) Baluchistan; and of changing the names of Torkamansahra to Golestan and Arabestan to Khuzestan.

All these peripheral areas have been (re-)designated by the ruling center in order to manipulate minorities and prevent internal unity among them, Al-Taie argues.[61]

Regarding the change of Torkamansahra into Golestan, he writes:

[O]ur compatriots from "Torkamansahra" have been placed within the framework of a province called "Golestan." Yet we do not know if we should congratulate them that they have become an *ostān* ["province"] and a *golestān* ["garden"], or not[:] their *sahrā* [desert] may have become a garden, yet "Turkmen" has disappeared from the map.[62]

The issue of personal naming is equally crucial. Al-Taie explains how Iran's Arabs are not free to choose their own personal names, and prevented by bigoted bureaucracy from changing the Persian-flavored names they are given by authorities.[63] He argues that it is a basic right, in Islamic culture, of a mother and father to name their child. Al-Taie and other ethnicists thus see "imposed names" as a strategy to undermine ethnic cultures: part of a state-run and intellectual-endorsed drive toward cultural homogeneity that is particularly evident in the language domain.

"Talking back," ethnicists insist on their own traditions of naming. This includes regular use of the names of cities, places and provinces as they are known in local languages, or as they were known before the Pahlavis or the Islamic Republic changed them. It also includes using spelling that differs from the standard Persian spelling, employing different alphabets than the Perso-Arabic or using pseudonyms that have a distinct non-Persian sound to them.

At the heart of the ethnicist discourse on language rights is the fear that minority languages are withering away under the Persian linguistic hegemony. Al-Taie likens the effects of the modern state's discriminative language policy to an environmental disaster, turning ethnic communities into barren wastelands with nothing but a mirage left of their cultures: when minorities are denied the right to teach their own languages, they are denied the very foundation of their nature or essence (*zāt*), he argues.[64] Similarly, Baraheni explains that when minority children go to state schools, they are torn away from their parents, especially the mothers, by the mono-lingual education policy, which creates a "schizophrenia in each and every one" belonging to "an oppressed nationality."[65]

There is a sense of life and death in much of the ethnicist writing on the topic of language. This is most tangible in a statement by Shirin Alamhooli, a Kurdish activist sentenced to death in 2010 for her alleged affiliation with the PKK:

Why have I been imprisoned and why am I going to be executed? For what crime? Is it because I am Kurdish? If that's the case then I must say I was born a Kurd and my language is Kurdish; the language that I use to communicate with my family, friends, and community. It is also the language I grew up with. However, I am not allowed to speak my language or read it. I am not allowed to go to school and study my own language and I am not allowed to write it. They are telling me to deny my Kurdish identity, but if I do, that means I have to deny who I am.[66]

SEEKING IDENTITY

In order to further explore the symbolic dimension of the ethnicist discourse, a look into the *hoviyat-talab* or Azeri student ethnicist literature is enlightening. Two years after the 2006 Azerbaijan unrest, students from the Research Centre of the

Azerbaijani University Students Society (*ābtām*) at the Science and Technology University in Tehran published a special edition of their bi-lingual journal *Günash* ("Sunshine" in Azeri Turkic).[67] The journal presents a distinctly ethnicist account of the background and events of the unrest. In this account, the writers touch upon many themes and narratives key to the ethnicist agenda.

The special issue itself is comprehensive (179 pages) and elaborately designed, and it was available for free download from numerous websites. The editor, Sina Jahanbakhsh, who was forced by the authorities to step down following its publication, states that one of the key problems facing "the nation of Azerbaijan" is the dearth of history writing. He thus presents the special edition as a first step toward historically documenting the 2006 unrest. He also sets the tone for the rest of the publication:

> Why is the third biggest living language in the world, the second biggest language in the world of Islam [i.e., Turkic languages], not officially recognized in Iran? Is this lack of recognition only to be blamed on chauvinists, the Pahlavi state apparatus and so on? Don't you think that the nation itself, and in particular its intellectuals, are guilty in this respect?[68]

He proceeds in the opening article with a comprehensive day-by-day chronology of events that unfolded during the unrest, seen through a distinctly ethnicist lens.

Jahanbakhsh explains that the 2006 unrest was in fact an explosion of long-standing discontent and that the outrage with the caricature in *Irān* daily depicting Turkic speakers as cockroaches was merely an excuse to vent frustrations with 100 years of Persian-centric discrimination. He notes that in the first written condemnation of the caricature, students of Tabriz University had also protested the choice of name for the Iranian national football team, *Setāregān-e pārs* ("Stars of Persia"), which the ethnicists deemed a blatantly Persian-centrist decision. Jahanbakhsh also argues that the presidential New Year address to "Persian-speakers" of the world had caused Azeri outrage in the period leading up to the unrest.[69]

The alleged mentality behind the caricature, the ruling elite, the intellectual elite, the government and the forces that crushed the 2006 unrest are associated, throughout the journal, with apartheid, chauvinism, racism, fascism and Aryanism. Ahmadinejad's government is blamed for espousing "Pan-Farsism," and a range of cultural figures—from comedians over Pahlavi politicians to secular nationalists—are lambasted for ridiculing the Turkic language and Azeri culture. The cockroach caricature is even compared to the cartoons of the Prophet Mohammad published by a Danish newspaper in 2005, and the attacks on Azeri protestors are likened to Israeli repression of Palestinian intifadas.

Azeris are labeled as *turk* (not *tork* as it is usually rendered in Persian), and the writers clearly take offense to use of the term *āzari*. They believe that the word *turk* should be cleansed of its stigma and that *āzari* is a recent historical fabrication aimed at disassociating Azeris from their Turkic heritage. As Jahanbakhsh notes, a key slogan on the streets of Tabriz was indeed *hārāy, hārāy man turkom*, "Hey! Hey! I'm Turk!." Similarly, the writers routinely use local Azeri names instead of official names and spellings, such as *Urmiye* or *Urmu* instead of Orumiye, *Qushachay* instead of

Miandoab and *Solduz* instead of Naqde. The Azeris are constantly referred to as a nation and a nationality, and rarely as an ethnic group. There is a heavy emphasis on the fact that protest communiqués during the 2006 unrest were translated into Azeri, and there is a whole article dissecting and analyzing the numerous Azeri-language slogans brandished during the demonstrations.

There are also numerous references to distinctly Turkic symbols of Azeri culture, depicted as signs of a movement of resistance. An example is from Jahanbakhsh's article:

> The blood of Sattar Khan and Babak gives away a scent of resistance all over Azerbaijan. The pens of the Behrangis, Shahriyars and Zehtabis of Azerbaijan is dipped in blood, and the words of Dede Qorqud is bringing the news of liberation and freedom to our hearts.[70]

Sattar Khan is a reference to the Azeri hero of the Constitutional Revolution, and "Babak" to the legendary Babak Khorramdin who in the ninth-century A.D. rebelled against the Abbasid Caliphate. Like Behrangi and Zehtabi, Mohammad-Hosein Shahriyar is a renown Azeri literary figures, while the Dede Qorqud (or Dede Korkut) is a famous medieval epic popular in most Turkic-speaking countries.

To further situate the 2006 unrest in a history of Azeri resistance, Jahanbakhsh refers to the state repression of the 1946 autonomist movement as "the genocide of December 12." Tabriz is referred to as "the city of revolutions," and in describing the 2006 unrest, words such as *qiyām* ("uprising") are used. It is claimed that members of the security forces deployed to crush the unrest actually joined the protestors and that there were fights between supporters and opponents of the movement within the ranks of the security forces. The ethnicist writers also hint at simmering inter-ethnic conflict in the region: Armenian "Dashnak" militants mobilizing against Azeris in Tehran; the state deploying security forces from Lor, Gilaki and Arab regions to Azerbaijan; and rumors of impending war between Azeris and Kurds. In accounts of the violent repression of the movement, the writers allude to an "Aryan army" as synonym for the security forces.

Crucially, the accounts in the journal run counter to those of most Iranian exile political groups who maintained that the Azerbaijan unrest was an uprising against the Islamic Republic or a reaction to religious despotism. Indeed, there are several indications that the Azeri ethnicists behind the journal are not necessarily opposed to the Islamic Republic, at least not on religious-ideological grounds. Often, the narrative contains Shiite symbolism and allusions to religious beliefs, and there are numerous references to the self-sacrifice of pious Azeris during the so-called Holy Defense against Iraq—including how Azeri veterans in the aftermath of the war felt shortchanged for their efforts.[71]

At the same time, however, the writers are clearly critical of the official reaction to the unrest, in particular accusations that separatists, pan-Turkists or foreign agents had infiltrated the Azeri movement. Indeed it is clear, from the articles in the journal, that the Azeri ethnicists consider themselves completely detached from the ordinary factional spectrum inside and outside Iran: they are equally critical of the government and the opposition, of conservatives and reformists, of secular nationalists and even their peers in pro-democracy student organizations. Indeed, one of the authors simply refers to all existing political organizations in Iran as *fârs*.[72]

There is a sense throughout the journal of emboldening. The authors are keenly aware of the power that collective action by millions of Turkic-speaking Iranians can harness, and the devastating effect a full-fledged uprising would have on the country as a whole. This is reflected, among other things, in mentions of the fact that authorities, out of fear of the uprising, had to appease public sentiment such as by playing Azeri music on state-run television and even broadcasting an Azeri Turkic translation of official announcements. The ethnicists express awareness of the fact that the Islamic Republic cannot persist without the support of the highly religious segment among the Azeris—many of whom are serving in the military, bureaucracy and clergy.

The accounts, narratives and symbolism presented in the journal reflect an aspect of society that is often overlooked in representations of contemporary Iran. It is an aspect that has arguably been misunderstood, misrepresented or demonized in most of the small but growing literature on ethnicism. Although the factual side is undoubtedly often distorted, with exaggerations and understatements to fit the overall narrative, these ethnicist accounts represent a remarkable insight into a new generation of political and socio-cultural activists.

The narrative is marked by a high degree of ethnic framing: the minority Self is situated within a particularistic history of local folklore and symbolism, ripe with words, names and images that are deliberately differentiated from the dominant history; the Other is criticized and blamed for willingly or unwillingly sustaining a discriminative social order; thus, the minority Self is given political agency in a narrative of historical resistance to injustice. Most important, perhaps, is the sense of dashed hopes that lurks underneath the texts.

STEPPING STONES AND TRAPS

As the preceding subsections have shown, there are a number of common points that unite the disparate minority voices into a shared ethnicist discourse: the resistance against Persian-centric history writing and discrimination in state policy; the demand for recognition, increased influence and autonomy; the importance of language rights; and an identitarian quest for belonging, self-expression and societal change. However, there is no general agreement on terminology and no overall ideological program. One pivotal point of difference is the role of religion.

In Asgharzadeh's view, the conflict is between an Islamic Republic, which is both religious fundamentalist and Aryanist-racist, and the "majority," which is slowly but surely regaining its "authentic" ethnic Self by expressing an identity in response to oppression. Since he believes the Islamic Republic is facilitating the persistence of racism in Iran by linking religious ideology with Aryanism, Asgharzadeh's solution is secularist: the clergy must leave politics and the Islamic Republic must be abandoned in favor of a new democratic regime.

In contradiction to Asgharzadeh, Al-Taie's conclusion is that Islam and the Koran could, if understood and employed correctly, provide society with a complete discourse of unity and equality. He states, for example, that Iran's Arabs are asking themselves why they do not benefit from the same circumstances as other Arabs elsewhere and why they do not enjoy the same status as other ethnic groups in a society such as the Iranian, which is ostensibly based on Islam and in which the Koran has granted them the same rights as other Muslims.

Yet Al-Taie claims that "royalists," "nationalist Persian Iranians" and "their Zionist and Baha'i friends" have managed to prevent a popular realization of how Islam could eradicate discrimination.[73] Al-Taie emphasizes that Iranian nationalists have abused religious concepts such as *vatan* to justify their excessive love for an exclusionary nation-state at the expense of Islam's inclusionary message. "Young Iranian Muslims," Al-Taie warns, "should not be deceived by the glitter and gleam of everything 'Western'" but should rather look to their own cultural, religious and ethnic heritage for guidance.[74]

Al-Taie's writings are clearly not those of a separatist: his constantly expressed praise and love for his country and its cultural legacy are testament to his patriotism. He even sees in the ethnic identity crisis an opportunity for Iranians to save themselves from the threats of imperialism, territorial disintegration and national disunity. Al-Taie does not promote Islamism either; indeed, his subtle criticism of the Islamic Republic confirms this—yet he maintains that Islam is the only sound and coherent framework for addressing inequality in Iran.

As we have seen, religion plays a central role among at least some of the most outspoken Azeri ethnicist students, and, as we have seen in chapters 2 and 3, also among Sunni Muslim minority activists. There is thus no reason to claim that the ethnicist movement is inherently opposed to the Islamic Republic, anti-Islamist or necessarily secularist. While some ethnicists, particularly those in exile, and leftist segments in the Kurdish population demand secularist solutions to the minority issue and an overthrow of the Islamic Republic, others have at times aligned themselves with Islamist-reformist currents working within the political system. What unites a significant number of ethnicists is the opinion that the key problem facing minorities is Persian-centrism and racism.

An important point in the ethnicist critique of state, opposition, politicians and intellectuals, is to "decriminalize" the minority issue and to defend minorities against the accusation of separatism. An example of this was in the many responses to Kurosh Za'im's controversial interviews in 2006 and 2008 (see Chapter 4). In one of these responses, an ethnicist commentator stated that Za'im suffers from a "conspiracy delusion," and that just as government representatives, Za'im is in denial of Iran's real problems.[75] When confronted with the ugly truth of ethnic oppression, Za'im and his nationalist cohorts merely blame minority activists for being on the payroll of Iran's enemies abroad, including otherwise "friendly" neighboring countries. One ethnicist commentator, himself a Kurdish journalist and political activist, wrote back to Za'im with the following rhetorical questions:

> What neighbors are Mr. Za'im talking about[?] As a Kurd, everywhere I look, I cannot find a friendly neighbor...In the pockets of which Kurd can you find Iraqi Dinars or Turkish Lira?...What a conspiracy delusion! Why do we think that the whole world...has nothing to do but to sit, day and night, plotting against our Islamic Republic? Why do we blame others for our inability to run the country? Why do we see the people's quest for justice as a foreign conspiracy? Why do we always take a defensive

position by creating a hypothetical enemy, and then using it as an excuse for censoring others and ourselves?.[76]

A new generation of ethnicist commentators is attempting to break with this siege mentality and its images of "foreign stooges" and "conspiracies"; instead of foreign intervention and manipulation, they demand that the minority issue be understood in relation to Iran's domestic culture and politics.[77] Within the discussions about redistribution of power, however, is of course also an implicit warning: if the state does not live up to the promises of freedom and equality enshrined in the constitution, it will force minorities toward separatism.[78] Rather than endorsing such a process, the majority of the ethnicist writers are warning against it. In the words of Baraheni,

> Only with equality in democratic rights among all the nationalities and ethnic groups in the country can the perseverance of a country called Iran be secured.[79]

In the student journal about the 2006 Azerbaijan unrest, Jahanbakhsh finishes his account with a lengthy personal recollection from one of the participants in a demonstration in front of the parliament in Tehran on May 28, 2006. This participant describes the massive security presence in front of the parliament and, coming face to face with one of the police officers, she recollects:

> A strange fear and terror gripped my body. I felt a deep sense of alienation. As if there were miles of distance between me and this officer. I don't understand his language, and he doesn't understand mine. Two estranged nations!

The narrative then turns into a reflection on what it means to be Iranian:

> Is this Iran? Am I Iranian? Is this the same parliament that has as its most important purpose to institute justice in the Iranian society but has allowed all kinds of insults and abuse against us, and taken from us even the right to protest? Why? Doesn't the 27th Article of the constitution give Iranians the right to non-violent protest? So what has happened? I don't hope that this means I am not Iranian? But, I *am* Iranian. Didn't my father spend the prime of his life in the frontline to protect this soil and these borders? Didn't my nation, Azerbaijan, give thousands of martyrs for the victory of the Islamic Revolution of "Iran"? . . . Enough! Persian-speaking compatriot, brother officer, parliament: I have come here today to say: Turks have a noble and true culture, civilization and history, Turks have pride, Turks have dignity, Turks have a language, Azerbaijani Turks have a nation and a homeland![80]

She then recollects hearing the "*Hey! Hey! I am Turk!*" slogan ringing out in the air above parliament, which to her was "the song of my identity."

WRITING BACKWARD, WRITING FORWARD

While critical Iranian Studies and ethnicist narratives on Iranian society have all contributed to an overdue questioning of some key assumptions and truth claims deeply embedded in Persian-centric writing on Iran, they have also exhibited a number of problematic aspects. In the following, I will outline some of these aspects with an eye to the next half of the chapter. The reason is that these aspects, I will argue, have an impact on how the debate takes shape now and where it can lead Iranian Studies in the future.

Parallel to the emergence of ethnicist literary voices in the decades up to the Islamic Revolution was a radical trend of historical revisionism within Iran. A notable example of this trend with importance for Azeri ethnicists is Mohammed Zehtabi (1923–1998),[81] whose main hypothesis was that Turkic peoples have more than 6,000 years of history in Iran, thus predating Indo-European immigrations. In line with nationalist historians in Turkey, Zehtabi thus claimed that now extinct peoples such as the Elamites, Sumerians and Urartians were in fact Turks.[82] He also claimed that Persian chauvinism flourished from the Sasanian dynasty (224–651 A.D.) onward, obliterating all traces of the pre-Persian Turkic civilization. These claims obviously have no basis in historical evidence, and Zehtabi's writings have attracted a lot of critique over the years.[83]

Another more recent example of the radical historical revisionism is the works of Naser Purpirar (b. 1940), who claims that established historiography covering pre-Islamic to Safavid times is fundamentally and deliberately flawed: the Parthian and Sasanian dynasties simply did not exist, but have rather been invented by Jewish and American historians in a conspiracy to cover up the actual facts of the Purim, which, according to Purpirar, was a Jewish-led genocide against indigenous Iranian peoples.[84] The Achaemenids (550–335 B.C.), Purpirar argues, were the Jews' Slavic mercenaries, and practically all legacies from Iranian history between 600 B.C. and 1500 B.C. are either modern forgeries or leftovers from other cultures such as the Greek.

With these bizarre, sensationalist and wholly unsubstantiated claims, writers such as Zehtabi and Poorpirar could be dismissed as eccentric and marginal were it not for one fact: they are used by a growing number of ethnicist commentators, together with scholars abroad such as Vaziri, as respected sources of factual information. As such, the radical revisionists are part of a broader trend to challenge established Iranian history writing with extremist counter-theories.

This trend is also evident in works such as those of Asgharzadeh and Al-Taie. In the effort to "de-Persianize" Iranian history, Asgharzadeh constantly leans toward "Turkification." For example, when discussing the thinkers who revolutionized Iran's social and cultural sphere in the early twentieth century, Asgharzadeh mostly cites Azeri figures, generally omitting important non-Azeri figures. Asgharzadeh also tends to leave out trendsetting Iranian nationalists of Azeri origins who were generally opposed to the use of non-Persian languages, as well as important religious figures.

The selective amnesia in regard to recent history is compounded by the fact that Asgharzadeh relies on the works of Vaziri, Zehtabi and Poorpirar as key sources for a far-reaching deconstruction of pre-modern history. Indeed, Asgharzadeh's book encompasses such distant historical events as those surrounding King Cyrus, and he even attacks ancient and medieval texts such as the Avesta and the *Shāhnāme* as evidence of "Persian chauvinism"—surely an anachronistic application of this concept. Asgharzadeh argues that there is a "conspiracy of silence" on the topic of pre-Aryan civilizations in Iran and that this censoring away of Iran's pre-Persian past has "culminated in the denial of difference and diversity in the country both historically and at the present time."[85] This conspiracy theory, unsurprisingly, includes the highly dubious claim that Turkic-speaking peoples lived in Iran before Persian speakers did.

To back up these conspiracy theories and claims, Asgharzadeh introduces Zehtabi as a "well-respected Azeri scholar" and "outstanding professor."[86] Even more baffling is that Asgharzadeh relies heavily on the works of Purpirar and his anti-Jewish speculations. Asgharzadeh's work and scholarly integrity is opened up to criticism when he thus employs a fiercely racist writer to support an ostensibly anti-racist deconstruction of history. A similar concern can be raised about Al-Taie, who expressly believes in a "Zionist conspiracy" against Islam.

While not aiming to prove the primordial presence of his own ethnic group in Iran, Al-Taie's book nonetheless also exhibits a tendency toward "historical mudslinging." In response to the statements of an Iranian nationalist who had used the adjective "wild/barbaric" (*vahshi*) about seventh-century Arabs, Al-Taie counters with a long catalog of historical events stretching from the Achaemenid King Cyrus's attacks on Babylon over the Sassanid King Shapur's attack on the Arab Peninsula to the Zand shah Karim Khan's destruction of a watermill in Khuzestan and so on.[87] All of these distant events, Al-Taie argues, are evidence of "Persian" chauvinism.

Such far-reaching projects of historical revisionism with the aim of justifying a present-day ethnicist demand naturally entail many contradictions and inconsistencies. Even though Al-Taie criticizes nationalists' anachronistic, ideological exploitation of the *Shāhnāme,* he does exactly the same, arguing that since Ferdowsi talked of "the countries" (*keshvar-hā*) of Kerman and Khuzestan, Iran may not have been a country itself.[88] Unconvincing claims and deliberate provocations abound: Asgharzadeh alleges that non-Persians "have always constituted the numerical majority in Iran, from ancient times up to present."[89] Such truth claims about the statistical reality of distant epochs seem out of place in a book aimed to refute anachronistic history. It seems the "minoritized" are in fact minoritizing the oppressive Other.

Another ominous tendency among radical ethnicists is to champion "reverse" hypotheses of linguistic and racial primacy. In this approach, the ethnicist demand for the recognition of linguistic diversity today is framed by selective and distorted views on historical precedence that are just as speculative and chauvinist as those of the Persian-centric nationalists. Ethnicists seek to counter the nationalist argument about Azerbaijan: that before Turkic invasions, the inhabitants here spoke an ancient, pre-Turkic *āzari* language, an offshoot of Middle Persian, and thus, modern Azeris are actually ethnically and racially "Aryan" and "Iranian" though mixed with Turkic blood.[90] However, to do this, the radical ethnicists present Zehtabi's absurd countertheory: that of an ancient, pre-Indo-European Turkic civilization in Azerbaijan. One example is from Sadr-ol-Ashrafi (henceforth Sadr), an Azeri ethnicist in exile, who in the Khatami years published a short book about the minority issue inside Iran.

In this book, Sadr carves out four supposedly universal ethno-linguistic categories of which "the agglutinative languages" is one.[91] Sadr claims that within this category, Urartian, Elamite and Sumerian belong to "the dead languages," and Turkic, Mongolian, Manchurian, Korean and Finnish to "the living languages." While Sadr rejects the Ural-Altaic hypothesis (a discredited concept, with which some linguists sought to prove the affiliation of Finno-Ugric with Altaic languages), he nonetheless subscribes to its fundamentals: a historical affinity between all agglutinative languages, which in turn allows for pure speculation about extinct languages such as the Elamite, on which there is no scholarly consensus.[92]

Most problematic, however, is that Sadr suggests a connection between ethnicity/race and language, arguing that "agglutinative-speaking ethnic groups" (*aqvām-e eltesāqi-zabān*) predate Indo-European speakers.[93] The implicit notion—which seems to be inspired directly or indirectly by Turkish nationalist 'Sun Language' theories—is that since Iranian Turks speak agglutinative languages, they should be considered Iran's original inhabitants. Sadr (as well as Asgharzadeh and other Azeri ethnicists) claims that Western and Iranian scholars have deliberately "forgotten" about the Elamite civilization because it does not fit the Persian-chauvinistic reading of Iranian history. In the process, Sadr claims, these scholars have censored away Iran's allegedly ancient Turkic past.[94]

To present the Elamites as the forefathers of the Turkic peoples, to claim that the Parthians were "Turks" or to state that "the Azerbaijani Turkic nation has more than 7,000 years of history in Iran" are highly problematic claims with no support in any sober historical research. Nonetheless, these scholars are presented, in their own works and in those of other ethnicists quoting them, as academic authorities. Hypotheses such as those of Sadr's can be seen as "historical-distortion-in-reverse": they are symptomatic of an enveloping obsession with primacy—at once a reaction to and a reflection of a pervasive cult of authenticity.

WAYS FORWARD, STEPS BACKWARD

THE AFTERMATH

In the aftermath of the 2005–7 unrest, ethnicist groups as well as international organizations reported a broad-ranging clampdown across the affected minority regions. In Khuzestan,[95] scores of people accused of participating in the demonstrations were detained, and several prominent ethnicist activists, journalists and human rights defenders such as Bani-Torof were arrested. A group of 180 MPs protested to Khatami, urging the release of detainees not found to have committed any crime. International organizations reported that authorities also arrested family members of suspects in order to intimidate activists and that fugitives have been arrested in Syria when attempting to obtain refugee asylum abroad.

Since the 2005 unrest, unknown activists have carried out a series of sabotage missions: four bombs exploded in Ahvaz and Tehran in June 2005 before the presidential elections, killing ten and wounding 90; in September and October 2005, "armed attacks" were launched against oil installations in Khuzestan; and in October 2005 and January 2006, bombs killed at least 12. Since, at least a dozen of people have been executed for their alleged involvement in these bombings, some in public, some after giving televised confessions and all, according to international organizations, without fair trials. Authorities sometimes announce that they have uncovered "separatist gangs," often during fights in which suspects are killed. In short, there has been a militarization of parts of the ethnicist movement in Khuzestan.

There have also been numerous signs of tensions between the general Arab population and the security forces. In November 2005, scores were arrested during Ramadan
festivities, after which locals clashed with security forces in Ahvaz, allegedly killing
two civilians. A similar case occurred in January 2006. In April 2011, marking the
sixth anniversary of the April 2005 unrest, riots broke out in Ahvaz and outlying
townships, reportedly spreading to other cities. According to exile media and international organizations, numerous people died in clashes with anti-riot forces and
Basij units using live ammunition.[96] Hundreds were reportedly arrested, many during
arbitrary, random house searches in Arab-inhabited areas.

The state enforced a news blackout and arrested local bloggers. Government
reports were few and vague, and generally referred to the rioters as separatists with
foreign backing, and to the role of international Arabic media in fanning the unrest.
Throughout April, there were scattered reports of clashes between police forces and
armed insurgents. There were also numerous reports of heavy security measures,
house searches and the collection of satellite TV receivers. In the aftermath, authorities carried out mass arrests of local ethnicists, including some who were apprehended
after showing public expressions of sympathy with the Arab Spring.[97] Numerous
Arabs were executed for their alleged role in the unrest.

According to Amnesty, the 2005 unrest in Kurdistan "marked the start of a new
wave of state repression."[98] Since the unrest, several prominent Kurdish journalists, bloggers and writers have been imprisoned or exiled, while NGOs have been
shut down and new ones denied state licenses to function. Poets, intellectuals, journalists, academics, local historians and cultural, environmental and human rights
activists work under tight state surveillance, and are often arrested and tried under
national security laws. Some activists have also "disappeared" under mysterious circumstances, and numerous Kurds have been executed following unfair trials behind
closed doors. Human rights groups provide a constant flow of reports on harassment
and imprisonment of Kurdish activists, civilians and Sunni clerics. Since much of
Iranian Kurdistan is off-limits to foreign observers and international organizations,
it is impossible to verify many of these reports; however, it is clear that repression is
widespread in particular areas known for dissent.

The armed insurgency also continues, and there have been numerous reports of
bloody clashes between Kurdish *pishmergas* and Iranian forces since 2005. One of
Barack Obama's first actions as US president in 2009 was to place PJAK on the
US Department's terrorist list, which was welcomed by conservatives in Iran. PJAK's
leader was arrested in Germany, and the organization signaled a change of strategy toward political settlement. During spring and summer 2009, and again during
summer 2011, it appears Iranian forces dealt serious blows to *Komele* and, most
importantly, to PJAK.[99] In September 2010, during a state-organized celebration
in Mahabad, a bomb was detonated. The Iranian state accused PJAK, who refused
involvement, and then Sunni militants. This bombing indicates a possible new direction for the Kurdish insurgency at a time when the guerilla organizations appear to
have suffered setbacks.

Since the 2006–7 unrest in Baluchistan, there have been several attacks and
counter-attacks, executions and hostage-takings.[100] In 2008, *Jondollāh* allegedly executed 16 hostages, while Pakistan handed over four key *Jondollāh* members to

prosecution in Iran. The same year, there were ambushes and fighting outside of Zahedan, as well as the assassination of an official. In December 2008, *Jondollāh* perpetrated its first suicide bombing, signaling a change in strategy.

In May 2009, a Shiite mosque was bombed, claiming 19 casualties, while militants attacked the offices of Ahmadinejad's election campaign. In February 2010, *Jondollāh* leader Rigi was apprehended by Iranian intelligence, either inside or outside Iran, under mysterious circumstances and amidst conflicting media reports. While constituting a significant publicity success for Ahmadinejad, *Jondollāh* continued its campaign with a yet another twin suicide terror bombing of a Shiite mosque in Zahedan in July 2010. In the continuing state clampdown, there have been unconfirmed reports of extrajudicial killings, torture, harassment and civilian casualties from anti-insurgency operations, as well as numerous official reports on arrests, trials, televised "confessions" and executions.[101]

There is also a steady flow of mostly unconfirmed reports of tensions between, on the one hand, Baluch citizens and tribes, and on the other, security forces and Shiite locals. Baluchistan is still more or less off-limits for researchers and journalists. Apart from *Jondollāh,* there are numerous websites, probably maintained by exile Baluch, claiming to represent various groups within Iran. These are quite active online and in exile, but their measure of support within Iran is far from certain. Reports from Iranian state media also seem to suggest that *Jondollāh* is not the only militant group operating in Baluchistan, although these reports are deliberately vague on distinctions between drug gangs and political groups.

During the clampdown following the 2006 Azerbaijan unrest, scores of ethnicists, journalists and human rights advocates were intimated and given heavy prison sentences.[102] Some ethnicists were held incommunicado for acts against national security, distributing illegal pamphlets, relations with foreigners, propaganda against the Islamic Republic and spreading ethnicism; at least one died in jail. Numerous websites, weblogs and student newsletters that had followed and covered the events were closed or received warnings from the authorities.

In 2008, security forces arrested 20 activists gathered to break the Muslim fast. Students have been arrested in groups, some held in prison for months without trial and some sentenced up to eight years in prison. There have been reports of the use of torture against imprisoned ethnicists. In August 2008, over 700 regime critics demanded the release of student activists, followed by a similar call in December 2008. Azeri ethnicists complain that they are labeled separatists, traitors and secessionists by authorities for simply articulating their legitimate demands.

THE GREEN MOVEMENT

The minority issue figured high in the agenda of practically all political factions in the 2009 presidential election campaigns. The two major reformist candidates, Mehdi Karubi and Mir-Hossein Musavi, both delivered highly articulate, detailed promises of an increased share of power for minority representatives and respect for cultural rights. The conservative candidate Mohsen Reza'i promised governmental positions to minority politicians, and even Ahmadinejad seemed attuned to ethnic demands. The incumbent president addressed Azeri crowds with Turkic greetings, and he personally attended a meeting in the Supreme Council for Cultural Revolution a few months before the election to oversee the passing of a resolution that permitted and encouraged the establishment of university courses in minority languages.

The reformist faction seemed particularly keen on attracting minority votes. Various organizations issued statements on how the minority issue should be considered part of the struggle for civil rights, calling for greater participation of minorities in all affairs of the country and condemning Ahmadinejad's approach to ethnic minorities.[103] The leading reformist candidate, Mir-Hossein Musavi, routinely addressed the minority issue, and minority audiences in Kurdistan, Azerbaijan and Turkmensahra. Musavi even issued a communiqué detailing specific promises,[104] namely that his government would protect minority rights, reform and strengthen the City and Village Councils, change the mindset of those administering the country, eradicate discrimination in media and in the political system, revise the distribution of resources and launch new development policies. Musavi stated that it was in the interest of all Iranians to give minorities freedom and equality and that diversity was a "God-given asset," not a threat. All the promised changes were framed within the constitutional framework of the Islamic Republic.

Karubi, however, outdid Musavi on this front.[105] During his extensive campaigns and through statements, communiqués and his representatives, Karubi promised to revise the constitution and to institute "local parliaments". One of his spokesmen promised to redistribute oil wealth according to the size of various ethnic communities and to end the tendency, within the security establishment, to treat the minority issue as a security threat. He also stated that it would be best if a "non-Persian" was elected—presumably a reference to Karubi's ethnic background as Lor. The most outspoken ethnicist during this period, however, was Akbar A'lami of Tabriz. Before the 2009 presidential elections, the local politician and former MP used his website and a series of speeches to lambast Persian chauvinism and promote ethnicist demands. A'lami explicitly stated that he did not belong to any of the existing political factions in Iran. His candidature was eventually rejected.

Anger with what was perceived as the fraudulent presidential elections in June 2009, which saw Ahmadinejad as a declared victor, generated a broad-based mass movement. This movement was against Ahmadinejad, in support of Musavi and Karubi and, more generally, demanded civil rights, reform and democracy in Iran. During this uprising, Iran saw the most widespread demonstrations, violent clashes and brutal clampdown in its post-revolutionary history, and nowhere was left untouched by the so-called Green Movement and the repression of its activists. Yet there are still discussions about the extent to which minorities participated in and supported the Green Movement. This is a crucial question since the Green Movement constitutes the most comprehensive challenge to Ayatollah Khamene'i, the ruling conservative elite and Ahmadinejad's faction to date.

Although the Green Movement contained a wide range of social and political forces, and although there was no clear overall ideological program, some of the general key demands were more or less congruent with those of the ethnicist movements: moderation toward opposition and dissidents, reform of cultural policy, easing of restrictions placed on media and society, as well as an opening of Iran toward the world. These were in fact distilled and more plainly expressed versions of the demands originally championed by reformists in the 1990s, and by the student movements of 1999 and 2003. Furthermore, the two symbolic leaders of the movement, Musavi and Karubi, both hailed from minority backgrounds, and had both spent considerable time and energy on addressing the minority issue.

However, the Green Movement vanguard's association with the reformists may also have been its Achilles Heel: the disillusion over broken promises of the Khatami era may have kept minority expectations toward the Green Movement very low, making minorities place little faith and trust in leaders such as Musavi. None of the Green Movement leaders had spoken out in clear defense of the minorities in their previous careers, nor had they defended minorities during the ethnic unrest of 2005–7. Furthermore, despite the rhetoric and communiqués regarding the minority issue during the election campaigns, none of the candidates had associated with ethnicist organizations. One possible reason was that such an association would provide conservatives with further ammunition in the bombardment of slander and accusations of foreign backing against the Green Movement. Another is that public opinion in Tehran, particularly after the violent events in Baluchistan, was highly guarded toward ethnicist activities.

On a more general level, it seemed that the gap between Tehran and the periphery had grown deeper during Ahmadinejad's first four years as president. Indeed, minority regions saw comparatively little in terms of dissident activities associated with the Green Movement. Despite some unrest in Tabriz, Ahvaz and Zahedan, most minority regions, including Azerbaijan, was largely silent during the 2009–10 post-election unrest. This, some observers have speculated, was a clear indicator of a deep fissure between Tehran and the periphery, and between Persian speakers and the minorities, and more generally, a feeling that the current political system cannot be reformed—even with the Green Movement.

Contrary to this analysis, others have argued that the repression and militarization of minority regions following the 2005–7 unrest had left no avenues open for expressing discontent or support for the Green Movement, and that state clampdown had spared no media to report on any such events. According to this interpretation, minorities did participate in the Green Movement whenever and wherever possible. It is, for example, pointed out that even if protests were largely limited to Tehran, the sheer size of the Green Movement demonstrations shows that ethnic minorities, many of whom reside in Tehran, must have been present.

However, it is quite clear that minority rights spokesmen were hesitant and undecided on whether to support the Green Movement. In February 2010, a group of Azeri activists criticized the movement for not being inclusive. While calling on the Green Movement to embrace Azeri ethnicist demands, they asked it to specify which form of democratic system was envisioned for future Iran.[106] Bani-Torof, the Arab ethnicist spokesman, initially claimed that the Green Movement was a continuation of the minority protests in Khuzestan and Kurdistan in 2005.[107] However, he subsequently criticized the movement and its proponents, especially in the Iranian diaspora, for not taking minorities into account. Other ethnicist commentators have argued that the Green Movement demand for civil rights did not attract minorities because it lacked a direct reference to the minority situation.

No matter the truth about minority participation in the Green Movement, the post-2009 uprising has had a far-reaching impact on all of Iranian society. It taught the broad population a lesson about the power of civil disobedience and protest, and a bitter lesson about state repression. While the minority issue was a key focus in election campaign propaganda, the elections also showed that this focus rarely extends beyond rhetoric. During the 2012 parliamentary elections, ethnic diversity was again a central feature of campaigns and in state-run TV. The local dances, colorful clothing and traditional crafts of ethnic minorities were displayed together with slogans about national unity and Iranian identity, while minority music—sometimes in minority languages and sometimes even that of previously outlawed artists—was played. Ethnicity, in short, had become a commodity in Iranian election politics. It remains to be seen whether this will translate into actual changes.

FREEDOM CURTAILED

Ethnicists share with political activists all over the country a crucial obstacle: the repression of freedoms of assembly and speech, and a lack of representation within the political system. As we have seen, the ethnicist movement is in many ways the outcome of the socio-economic, educational, infrastructural, welfare and political developments ushered in by the Islamic Republic. Under Khatami, a number of political representatives were able to voice minority region grievances in parliament, while a range of minority organizations were able to function, either with the tacit accept of authorities or with official recognition.

Despite the violent unrest and repression of 2005, the non-military Kurdish movement is still alive. In 2006, a former MP established the Kurdish United Front (*Jebhe-ye mottahed-e kord*), advocating civil society activism to empower Kurds within the framework of the Islamic Republic, and with respect for Iran's territorial integrity.[108] Alongside outspoken Kurdish journalists, human rights activists and writers, the Front is a new face of Kurdish ethnicism that appeared together with the 1990s reformist movement but has since gone its own way. These ethnicists seek to document and publicize breaches of Kurdish human, civil and ethnic rights; they argue for the implementation of already existing laws; and they work to raise the number of Kurdish representatives in administration.

However, it seems that much of the progress made under Khatami has been rolled back under Ahmadinejad. This has affected the non-violent civil society movements. In order to curb what is seen as dissident activity across the country, Ahmadinejad has created new councils to oversee the activities of NGOs. According to Human Rights Watch, this has severely obstructed and curtailed NGO operations—especially in Kurdistan:

> The government increasingly applied a "security framework" in its approach to NGOs, often accusing them of being "tools of foreign agendas"... This trend is particularly evident in minority regions, including Kurdish regions, where the government often denies permits or prevents the registration of NGOs. Organizations that are able to register and obtain permits still face harassment and worse.[109]

This approach to NGOs has severely hampered the operation of peaceful organizations such as the Organization for the Defense of Human Rights in Kurdistan, which has seen limits imposed on its channels of communication, including website filtering, as well as numerous arrests, torture and even death sentences against its members.

Human rights defenders are particularly worried about the plight of minority women who are oppressed on several levels.[110] Amnesty, for example, has pointed out the widespread practice of honor killing among Kurds. Baluch and Arab societies are marred by the widespread practice of polygamy, gender discrimination and the lack of access to education and welfare. Although there are state-sanctioned efforts to combat these problems, it seems that the security apparatus is particularly wary of NGOs that combine a women's and minority rights agenda. Finally, as elsewhere in Iran, minority student organizations face a host of juridical measures and accusations of cooperation with insurgents. Student activists have been arrested, newsletters shut down and state-sanctioned disciplinary committees are active in campuses with large minority student bodies.

"Once a Kurdish activist is targeted," a Iran Human Rights Documentation Center report explains, he or she is subject to a "pattern of mistreatment and deprivation of due process safeguards" while his or her family and relatives are subject to threats, intimidation and harassment.[111] The arrests of Kurdish activists, the Center reports, carry a number of similarities: "Many are arrested without charges or are not informed of the charges against them until months into their detention; sometimes the charges against them are modified numerous times without adequate notice or additional case files created."[112] Hundreds of Kurds have allegedly been arrested for cooperating with outlawed parties and organizations under the broad, threadbare allegation of "acts against national security."

Cultural repression in the name of national security intensified under Ahmadinejad. Since the 2005 unrest in Kurdistan, numerous bi-lingual publications have been shut down and journalists and editors harassed, arrested and convicted of offenses ranging from disturbing public opinion, over aiding illegal groups and inciting to inter-ethnic hatred, to slandering Khomeini and smuggling drugs. Authors have been denied permits or otherwise obstructed from publishing works, including fiction and history, or translating political works between Kurdish and Persian. Works critical of the state policy are categorically denied publication license and are confiscated from bookshops found to carry them. Cultural activities, even traditional dancing, music and theater, are monitored by authorities and often met with a heavy security presence. People engaged with preserving Kurdish culture and heritage face numerous obstacles and suspicions.[113]

Similar patterns are evident in Baluchistan. Today, the handful of civil society organizations and cultural centers remaining from the Khatami years can operate only under strict state control, and their activists are often subjected to severe repression.[114] In 2007, members of a local youth group were arrested and their leader allegedly tortured, convicted of *mohārebe* ("fighting against God") and eventually executed in August 2008. A year later, 15 Baluch teachers in Saravan were arrested, most likely for political activities. Many of the gains the Baluch made under Khatami, including cultural and civil society activities, have thus reportedly been rolled back under Ahmadinejad.[115]

With the opening up of the political climate under Khatami, there were numerous attempts by ethnicist spokesmen to enter provincial and parliamentary politics, and despite many setbacks, they were able to gain some recognition. Azeri, Arab and Sunni Kurdish and Baluch representatives were able to voice minority concerns in parliament. However, this recognition has so far not generated any actual changes. In the three decades that have passed since the revolution, the parliament has not passed one single piece of legislation to safeguard the cultural rights of ethnic minorities.

It is also hard to gauge if minorities feel better represented in local and provincial administration. While a handful of Kurds were appointed to key positions in the Kurdish regions under the reformist governments, there are few today. Similarly, ethnicists in Khuzestan and Sistan-Baluchistan claim that they are still severely underrepresented, when state officials claim that the number of Baluch and Arabs in higher administrative positions has increased. Conversely, the size and importance of the Azeri community also means that it has had relatively higher chances of pushing through localist and regionalist agendas in parliament. However, while Azeris are historically well represented on all levels of administration, the experience of ethnicist politicians such as Chehregani and A'lami shows that there are clear boundaries to what popular representatives of minority regions can express and demand.

More generally, it appears that the association of most minority parliamentarians with reformist currents that are now castigated by the ruling elite as "seditionist" have had a detrimental consequence. With the unelected, conservative-run Guardian Council's hostile approach to reformist forces, numerous parliamentarians have been barred from running or re-running in elections. While the level of participation in the 2012 parliamentary elections was higher in Sistan-Baluchistan than in the rest of the country, it was lower in Kurdistan. There were reports that many ethnicist candidates had been rejected, including the Kurdish United Front members. Similarly, the City and Village Councils may have local importance, but their impact on overall legislation and planning is negligible.

It is outside the scope of this book to enter the still heated debates over whether the 2009 elections were rigged in favor of Ahmadinejad. However, if the official results were correct, and minority voters in many regions chose Ahmadinejad, this would indicate a number of developments in regard to the minority issue: that minorities are generally disillusioned with the reformists and perceive the extensive attention to the minority issue as insincere PR stunts; or that Ahmadinejad's populism, years of touring the periphery and promises of redistributing wealth in society have had the desired effect. Yet even if the official results are true, they may still indicate minority discontent with the government: apart from Tehran and Yazd, the 46 districts won by Musavi were all minority strongholds.

Conversely, if it is true that the 2009 presidential elections were rigged or significantly manipulated, it could possibly indicate something more drastic: that the ruling elite feared that the combined power of Green Movement agitation in the urbanized center and minority dissatisfaction in the periphery would become the first force in post-revolutionary Iranian history to prevent a president from re-election, and that out of this fear, they decided to steal the election. It is, however, impossible to ascertain the truth about the 2009 election. What is certain is that many of the pundit musings about regional voting patterns and the role of minorities in the elections that surfaced after the 2009 uprising were characterized by a fundamental lack of knowledge about the minority issue in Iran.

It also remains a fact that while the Islamic Republic since the death of Khomeini has seen a number of developments with positive impact on minorities specifically—a pronounced attention to the minority issue during election times, an increased volume of minority-language media, diversified depictions of culture in schoolbooks and so on—there have been few significant improvements or structural changes. Minority activists still face numerous obstacles, and ethnicists are actively repressed. With the broad clampdown on dissidents and oppositional activity after the 2009 Green Movement, many Iranians appear disillusioned with the possibility of change under the current ruling elite.

NEW TACTICS, RENEWED REPRESSION

It seems that in the years following the 2005–7 unrest, the situation has deteriorated in Sunni regions. Since the 2005 unrest in Kurdistan, there have been numerous reports of repression of Sunnis and signs of sectarian tension. In the Ramadan of 2007 and again in January 2008, security forces attacked and arrested followers of the Sunni *Maktab-e qor'ān* movement.[116] The Iranian state, Kurdish activists claim, routinely harasses and intimidates Sunni clerics. In February 2008, a prominent Sunni cleric went missing after having delivered a "critical sermon."[117] During protests in Sanandaj, the cleric's supporters were arrested, intimidated and beaten. In December 2011, Sunni MPs in parliament called on Khamene'i to amend Article 115 in the Constitution to safeguard the religious rights of the Sunni minority.

It appears that Sunni Kurdish organizations have become radicalized. Iranian authorities have blamed "Salafist" and "Wahhabist" organizations for the 2009 assassination of a local cleric and politician and for the deadly attacks on security forces in Mahabad and Sanandaj. Following a series of hostage-takings, bank-robberies and armed attacks on police forces in 2011, authorities blamed a group identified as the Society of Towhid and Jihad for carrying out "terrorist operations"—including the killing of clergymen and the planned bombing of a meeting for visiting members of the cabinet.[118] Authorities have even suggested that Iraq-based Al-Qa'eda is involved in the sectarian violence.

Following the first ever suicide bombing in Iran in December 2008, which was carried out by *Jondollāh*, it appears that militants in Baluchistan too have changed tactics. In October 2009, a suicide bombing in the city of Sarbaz claimed 41 lives, including that of high-ranking commanders in the Revolutionary Guard and local tribal leaders attending a Sunni-Shia solidarity conference. Iran blamed the usual suspects, including the United States, UK and Pakistan. These events followed the 2008 bombing of a Shiite mosque in Shiraz by the previously unknown Jihadi Movement of the Sunna People of Iran. All this points toward a radicalization of Sunni militants.

It is uncertain whether the militants have broad backing. According to one report, the arrest of Rigi was "widely welcomed" by people in Sistan-Baluchestan—mainly because the operations of *Jondollāh* have disrupted local business and trade.[119] Yet it is also possible that the combination of ongoing repression of peaceful Sunni activists and the silence of many state-sanctioned *mowlavi* clerics in the area is pushing some Baluch toward militancy.

In 2007, a Sunni mosque was bulldozed and a theological school raided near Zabol, causing tensions in the region. In 2008, the arrest of a prominent cleric set off a wave of protests, and the same mosque was once again razed while local Sunni activists were arrested. In June 2008, human rights activists reported that Special Forces had attacked a village near Sarbaz to arrest a local *mowlavi*, and when locals had resisted, several were injured and scores arrested. There were also simultaneous attacks on two other villages near Iranshahr, with several arrests.[120] In June 2009, street clashes broke out in Zahedan following a demonstration, and authorities reported an armed attack on a bus.

Since, there have been continued reports of new arrests and sentences and the establishment of new military and Revolutionary Guard bases. Authorities have vowed to retaliate and revenge inside and outside Iran's borders, and to arm local tribes against smugglers and insurgents. These reports stem from news agencies connected to the security apparatus, and they rarely contain detailed information. Indeed, media coverage is characterized by contradictory reports, ambiguous language and unsubstantiated rumors. This in itself seems to indicate that Baluchistan remains unstable.

A related issue is the continued militarization of border regions such as Baluchistan and Kurdistan. Following the 2006–7 unrest in Baluchistan, there have been reports of heavy security measures, including the installation of fences, canals, cameras, radars and other equipment along the borders, as well as the ambiguous announcement on September 5, 2006, of a "plan to expel illegal immigrants" from Baluchistan.[121] In Kurdistan, observers claim that the state is using the sensitive border position as a pretext to harass locals. They claim that Iranian security forces target and kill petty smugglers in the border area and even that the Revolutionary Guard is involved in the flourishing drug trade.[122] It is impossible to verify such accusations, but it is possible to state with certainty that Kurdistan is ridden with tensions, and that these tensions affect ethnicist activists in a direct fashion.

The result of these developments is that the state increasingly tends to use terrorism as an excuse to curb civil society movements and ethnicist activism. The most evident aspect of this toughened stance is the use of execution as a way of warning others from joining insurgent organizations. However, this has also created a backlash by bringing new attention to the plight of minorities, inside and outside Iran. In 2007, the death sentence against Kurdish journalist 'Adnan Hassanpur for speaking to foreign journalists sparked a "political strike" among Kurdish activists. In February 2008, Farzad Kamangir, a teacher and allegedly PKK member, was sentenced to death. When Kamangir and five other Kurds were hanged in May 2010, following two other executions of Kurdish political activists in November 2009 and January 2010, it drew worldwide condemnations.

There were reports of a broad strike in most Kurdish cities, as well as reports of clashes with security forces and numerous arrests.[123] The protests over these executions spread across the country, and leading reformists voiced their outrage. Musavi, for example, questioned the basis of the sentences, after which he himself was threatened with prosecution. These shows of sympathy indicate a growing awareness among dissidents in the center of minorities in the periphery. However, they have not stopped the state from executing activists it deems to be insurgents. There were reportedly at least 14 Kurds on death row in April 2012.[124]

While repression in Azerbaijan has been decidedly more restrained than in Kurdistan, Khuzestan and Baluchistan, there are nonetheless numerous reports of an ongoing clampdown on ethnicists.[125] Yet in comparison, the ethnicist movement in Azerbaijan has been significantly more successful in marking its causes in public space. A key topic, as already mentioned, is language, and one example of Azeri ethnicist passive resistance is the boycott of Iranian public schools in Azerbaijan on the first day of the school year in protest against the lack of right to education in the Azeri language.[126] Furthermore, there are demonstrations marking International Mother Tongue Day every year, always followed by the arrest or intimidation of participants or organizers.

Another example is the annual gatherings at Babak Castle, where ethnicists celebrate what they consider an ancient Azeri hero. The gatherings grew until June 2005, when scores of participants were allegedly arrested and 21 persons charged with "spreading propaganda and establishing organizations against the system."[127] Since then, the annual gathering has met numerous obstacles, but nonetheless persists. The tendency to celebrate local heroes such as Sheikh Mohammad Khiyabani, Sattar Khan and Baqer Khan, as well as imbuing local landmarks such as Mount Sabalan and the mythic hill *Heydar Bābā* with ethnic sentiments, is still expressed through a lively press and new literature, as well as at public gatherings.

A third example is the almost fanatic worship of the *Terāktorsāzi* (locally *Tirākhtursāzi*) football team of Tabriz. At this team's games and on Internet forums, fans openly flaunt Azeri Turkic ethnicist and ethno-nationalist symbols and gestures such as the pan-Turkist Grey Wolves' greeting. Slogans in Azeri Turkic are of a decidedly ethnicist nature, and the football club enjoys a huge following. Due to the team's popularity, the police do not seem to intervene in what has by now become a ritual mass manifestation of Azeri ethnicism.[128]

A final example of the different ways in which ethnicist demands are expressed is the Lake Urmia movement. In 2010 and 2011, thousands of Azeris marched on the Lake Orumiye in Azerbaijan, which is currently threatened by increased salinity and evaporation as a result of drought and the construction of a dam. Numerous protestors were arrested and wounded in clashes in Orumiye, Tabriz and Tehran in September 2011. Although pro-democracy and environmentalist groups more generally have sought to present the Lake Orumiyeh disaster in terms of a national concern, ethnicists have nonetheless made it a rallying point for local and ethnic sentiments. Furthermore, as experiences in Azerbaijan (as well as Kurdistan) show, authorities view environmentalist activism with just as wary and suspicious eyes as they do more typical ethnicist activities.

In short, the various Azeri ethnicist movements have so far been generally peaceful, seeking to operate within the framework of the law, and predominantly focused on cultural and civil rights rather than sensitive issues such as autonomy or independence.[129] The sheer numerical strength of the Azeri community and its broad influence over Iranian politics and economy has so far meant that the occasional flagging of ethnicist symbolism is met with more lenient reactions from the security apparatus. The space for expressing cultural identity provided by the reformists in the 1990s also raised expectations, and when the reformist movement failed in significantly bettering the lives of the generations entering the universities, many young Azeris were left with what appeared to be few prospects of personal advancement and collective influence. As is quite clear from the writings and actions of the Azeri student ethnicist movement, this situation created a sense of identity crisis, feeding into a radicalization of rhetoric, and finally, an outburst of anger.

The relative success of ethnicists in placing their symbolism in the Iranian public sphere may also be the reason for increased suspicion and apprehension in the ruling elites and the broader population. Indeed, as we saw in Chapter 4, many Iranians are concerned with the rising number of Azeri publications with ethnicist agendas. Such fears of "Turkicization" may be augmented with the appearance across Azerbaijan of Turkic-language signs on shops that now also cater to businessmen from Turkey and ROA, and with the profound popularity of Turkic-language foreign media.

There are numerous questions about the phenomenon of ethnicism and minority mobilization in post-Khomeini Iran that need research attention—questions that this book has only been able to hint at. One of them is the role of new media. International organizations and ethnicists in exile maintained that during the 2011 unrest in Khuzestan, social media such as Facebook, Twitter and YouTube played a significant role in mobilizing young Arabs. There have been numerous indications that the same is true in other minority regions. Simple searches on these media reveal large and highly active online communities of Azeris, Kurds and even Baluch—communities that appear to be in direct contact with co-ethnics across the borders. In response to this rising online socializing and activism, the Iranian state has filtered websites and arrested bloggers. In cases of unrest, such as the 2011 unrest in Ahvaz, authorities reportedly disrupted Internet and mobile phone access.

This leads us to the question of whether the Arab Spring has influenced ethnicists. There were scattered reports that leading up to the 2011 Khuzestan unrest, unknown activists had spray painted slogans in support of the Arab Spring on city walls. Despite mass confiscations of satellite dishes, many Iranians still have access to international media, and in Khuzestan, this includes Arab-language media such as *Al-Jazeera* that provided extensive coverage of the fall of dictators in the Arab Middle East. Indeed, these Arabic media followed the 2011 unrest in Khuzestan in a daily and comprehensive manner, at a time when few Persian-language media, state-run and exile alike, found these events newsworthy. According to Bani-Torof, there was a total "boycott" of the 2011 Arab unrest in Khuzestan among Persian-language media. This points toward a potentially very harmful trend: that minorities, unlike the Green Movement, which received extensive coverage in exile and oppositional Iranian media, only see their struggles and grievances reflected in foreign media.

NEW RESEARCH AND NEW VOICES

As argued in Chapter 4, nationalistic tendencies in Iranian academia dominate the study of the minority issue. However, there have in recent times been numerous attempts at a new approach to research on ethnicity. First, there seems to be a more nuanced and critical trend growing within Iranian Studies globally. This includes calls for approaching Iranian identity as a cultural phenomenon rather than in terms of a national phenomenon and to abandon the Aryan myth altogether in histories of Iran; to understand that one can have multiple, overlapping identities; that pre-modern states in Iran were based on patrimonalism, not nationalism;[130] or to see nationalism, racism and a uniform national identity within the context of a capitalist Western modernity enforced upon a country that traditionally had a diversity of identities and cultures.[131] In the beginning of this chapter, we saw several examples of revisionist and critical research challenging the Persian-centric paradigm.

Second, there also seems to be a slowly but steadily evolving new school of minority research inside Iran. This includes not only critique of the state approach to social sciences, but also self-critique among scholars. One of Iran's leading anthropologists, Ali Bulookbashi, has criticized the lack of distinction in Iran between local folkloristics and actual ethnic studies; he adds that there is also a problematic lack of a common academic language with which to understand phenomena such as ethnicity.[132] Another prominent anthropologist, Shahnaz Nadjmabadi, argues that since ethnography has traditionally focused on "local groups and villages," there has been precious little "comparative analysis of indigenous discourses or the expression of ethnic identities."[133] Head of Department for Anthropology at Tehran University, Naser Fakouhi, adds that even within the preponderant folkloristic studies, the main focus is on Persian-speaking Iranians and Azeris, while other groups are underrepresented. Fakouhi has nonetheless also noted a growing movement of local history writing, indigenous ethnography and collection of folklore among the minorities. Much of this literature, however, is "underground": it is published without official permission, or outside the country.

When the minority issue emerged as an academic topic of study in the 1990s, it was primarily dominated either by sociologists employing positivist theories and quantitative methods or by political scientists who tend to view minorities only in terms of geopolitics and security concerns. In contrast, the new generation of scholars argue that in analyzing the minority issue, the state should not perceive of ethnicist movements as inherently violent;[134] that the state needs to respect religious rights in order to prevent radicalization;[135] and that the state should use its power to influence TV programming and prevent negative stereotyping of minorities and instead use media as a source of unity and inclusivity across ethnic divides.[136]

Scholars that would be categorized as nationalist-minded in this book have also presented numerous constructive suggestions for solving the problems that ethnicists claim to suffer under. Indeed, even academic works that exhibit a vehemently anti-ethnicist stance contain generally fair depictions of the socio-economic problems facing many minorities. Within instrumentalist research, for example, it seems that there is now a focus on how to change the state's view on minorities from one of "threat" into one of "opportunity." One could thus argue that negative attention has been better than no attention, as it brings the minority issue into discussion. Furthermore, critical scholars from a broad range of disciplines are now seeking to engage in a dialogue with the state apparatus, and to offer recommendations for future policies and approaches to the minorities. These scholars have brought "the security view" approach under scrutiny.[137]

Perhaps the most influential of these critical voices in contemporary Iranian anthropology is Fakouhi. Regarding the "security view" approach, he has stated:

limiting ethnic studies to political aspects has had a profoundly negative effect on anthropological studies in this field by trying to push them towards addressing only the folkloristic and historical dimensions of any ethnic entities, thus ignoring their actual problems and situation.[138]

Fakouhi argues that today, scholars in Iran's universities still believe that "the less there is talked about the ethnic phenomenon, the better,"[139] which is why "there is practically no serious research" on the minority issue.[140] Indeed, Fakouhi's project is even broader than a challenge to the "security view" genre: in his writings, there are far-reaching calls for reform clad in the language of research. In an article about the relationship between trade and regional and national identities, for example, Fakouhi argues that the state and the business elites have overlooked potentials for marketing regional specialties, for catering to particular ethnic groups or for exploiting the tourist potentials in minority regions. The main reason, Fakouhi argues, is the unease with addressing cultural difference and the prevailing taboos about the minority issue. Fakohi explores the source of such concerns and taboos:

There is a very evident tendency to argue that any kind of effort for strengthening ethnic cultural elements will result in the weakening of national identity, and that it is possible that it will cause an intensification of inter-ethnic tensions and harmful ethnicisms. Notwithstanding the fact that they contain nothing in terms of a correct understanding of the ethnic phenomenon in Iran, such analyses prevail.[141]

Instead of these erroneous approaches, Fakouhi calls for a re-conceptualization of Iranian national culture as the sum of all the regional and ethnic cultures of the country. Hence, Fakouhi argues that "insisting on Persian language as the only determinant of national culture is a mistake."[142] Fakouhi offers the state a range of recommendations in different aspects, ranging from the very broad and substantial (such as officially recognizing, spreading literacy in and creating media content for minority languages) to the very specific (such as promoting eco-tourism in minority regions, encouraging the use of ethnic cuisine in fast-food chains and reviving the caravanserai system to serve as hotels with regional décor). In this fashion, Fakouhi manages to argue for very significant reforms within the framework of a quite specific research topic.

In another research project,[143] Fakouhi delivers a sharp criticism of the Islamic Republic's educational policy and of the Persian-centric discourse: he claims that instead of belittling minority cultures and languages, Persian speakers could benefit from learning these languages; he argues that languages such as Kurdish should be acknowledged officially as a language, and not be treated as dialect; he even suggests that minority children could be taught their mother tongues in elementary schools—which, as we have seen in Chapter 4, is what nationalist-minded scholars have fervently rejected.

There are also several overlapping tendencies shared across the whole spectrum from nationalist-minded scholars over critical researchers to ethnicist advocates. The most important of these overlaps is the demand that any future solutions to the minority issue must be grounded in Iranian history. Regarding decentralization, scholars across the spectrum evoke a broad range of historical concepts, from the satrapies of the Achaemenids over the early modern *mamālek-e mahruse* to the Iranian constitution's provisions for provincial councils. Even though the suggestion that these concepts are somewhat analogous to contemporary provincial units or ethnic regions is anachronistic, and although the aim with employing these concepts may differ, there is a clear convergence in arguments: scholars that otherwise disagree on many points all treat these concepts as "authentic" and indigenous, and therefore, legitimate solutions.

It is also striking that most of the writers, ethnicist and nationalist alike, portray pre-modern Iran as a society bound together by peaceful, voluntary co-existence. These idealized visions of the past could easily become mutual vistas for the future. Thus, while nationalists seem to fear ethnicism and its demands for federalism and language rights among minorities, they may not have much reason to fear—there may be a common ground for finding a solution.

There are also indications of a fundamental change under way in the broader society. The 2005–7 ethnic unrest, and in particular the Azerbaijan unrest, seems to have brought about a new understanding of certain minority concerns in the majority. Compounded by the emergence of the minority issue in election campaigns, by the increased attention toward ethnic diversity in state media and by the new discourses of civil and human rights embedded in the 2009 Green Movement, this may lead to a change in the ways ordinary people tend to understand and portray non-Persian-speaking communities. There has, for example, been a broad call for abandoning jokes that are perceived as discriminative against minorities. Indeed, activists in the Green Movement even turned this call into an instrument of government critique: in social media, they called on their fellow Iranians to replace the minorities portrayed in jokes as ignorant and backward with the various militant arms of the Islamic Republic.

Although much more research is needed in this respect, there seems thus to be a number of domains in which there is a growing sense of mutual understanding and respect between different groups in Iranian society, as well as among different political forces and intellectual elites. It remains to be seen whether this is enough to deflate rising discontent and create a common ground for resisting authoritarianism and the violation of human and civil rights.

DISCUSSION

It is difficult to deduct any broad conclusions about an emerging field of voices so wide and disparate as the critical, revisionist and ethnicist discourses. However, it appears that a core issue to some Iranian intellectuals, and in particular the nationalists, is that the deconstructions embedded in these discourses pose a challenge to the nation-state-congruence principle. The threat, in other words, may not actually be separatism, but rather that the logics of a Persian-centric understanding of Iran is being questioned.

The Holy Grail of the nationalist discourse, so to speak, is of course national identity, which is treated by scholars and laymen alike as an axiomatic, universal and inevitable aspect of human life. In the words of Malesevic,

> Quite often it is simply and incorrectly assumed that individual human beings, by virtue of being categorised as members of certain institutionalised or state reinforced collectivities automatically express a strong sense of attachment to those collectivities or are otherwise somehow predetermined to act on the basis of that collective membership. In other words using national identity as a semantic equivalent to nation, nationality or nationalism suggests incorrectly that group designation inevitably implies a personal sense of belonging or generates social action.[144]

Instead of treating national identity as a residual concept that social actors use to "make objective material order consistent with their subjective experience of that order," as Malesevic proposes,[145] most nationalists—including nationalist-minded Iranian scholars—treat national identity as if it was a vital part of the human organism. This does not mean that claims to national identity, as ideological devices, are deceitful and propagandistic: "On the contrary," Malesevic argues, "many individual claims to a particular ethnic, national or gender identity are profoundly sincere." However, that social fact should be separated from the scholar's obligation to objectively study phenomena through the language of social science rather than the language of the object of study.

At the same time, it is clear that ethnicists share with nationalists a number of problematic basic assumptions and ontological beliefs. The most evident of these is a pervasive groupism—that is, the conviction that humanity can be subdivided into distinct, well-defined and neatly bordered groups. Whereas the nationalist project of group-making aims to cement the idea of national identity as the highest marker of any individual identity, ethnicists are prone to the same form of essentialist reification of ethnic identity. In this sense, it does not matter whether the point of reference is a nation-state or a minority: groupism is the attempt to argue for the existence of identities to which people "naturally" or inevitably belong, even if they are not necessarily aware of this fact themselves. Thus, the rhetorical question to the "Persians" of Iran, mentioned earlier in this chapter—"how do you define yourself?"—may never receive an answer, simply because many Iranians do not identify as "Persians", or as belonging to any particular group. Indeed, when ethnicists quote Mostafa Vaziri as an academic source of legitimacy for their claims about ethnic identity, they tend to overlook the following quote:

> It is a question whether, among the Kurds or any other ethnic group in Iran, the sense of identity established under its tribal system (if it involved anything besides a common language) was created as a result of contemporaneous events or whether it had a material historical basis that can be proved. How such ethnic identities were incorporated

into a larger (and territorial) Iranian identity is also an acute issue that demands adequate analysis. In attempting to address these questions without becoming entangled
in a priori assumptions about the sense of historical identity possessed by members of
linguistic minorities, as well as in the whole construct of national identity elaborated by
the Western Orientalists, one should seek out other parameters and criteria in order to
construct an unbiased research methodology.[146]

The specific problem with ethnic identitarianism and ethnically framed mobilization
is thus that if successful in placing "ethnic identity" on the public agenda, it can
potentially force everyone to identify in ethnic terms—even people for whom such a
categorization did not seem important to begin with.

However, the most dangerous aspect is arguably the essentialism inherent in
ethnicism: in challenging taken-for-granted truth claims about national identity and
culture, most ethnicists respond with other truth claims that are no less contentious
and problematic than those of the nationalists. Often, this essentialism entails primordialist claims of the exact same kind as revisionist historians have sought to
challenge in the nationalist discourse: claims to primacy and thus, potentially or ideally, the superiority of one group in a particular geographic area. In feverish acts of
historical mudslinging, anachronistically applied concepts are hurled back and forth
in a competition over "who came first."

It is certainly relevant to question whether concepts and words derived from
Avestan texts or from the *Shāhnāme* should be seen as proof of Iran as an ancient
nation-state, and thus to challenge the linear, teleological conception of history that
traces Iranian nationhood from antiquity to modern times. The problem that revisionists have rightly, if sometimes indirectly or provocatively, pointed out is the
conflation of ancient notions with modern concepts such as a nation-state that
demands a particular form of loyalty and homogeneity from its citizens. However,
it seems unnecessary to dispute the fact that concepts such as *Ērānshahr* have been
used at least since Sasanian times to indicate a discrete territorial entity; it seems even
more pointless to simply dismiss all historical indicators of this territorial entity as
elaborate, modern fabrications.

While the ethnicist discourse is thus, on the one hand, indicative of a budding,
healthy debate and skepticism toward received knowledge, it is, on the other hand,
also a reaction to racial-linguistic extremism that sometimes gives way to another
extremism: more half-baked essentialist hypotheses based on dubious sources, distortion and reductionism. Even if aimed at re-envisioning Iran as a heterogeneous and
diverse country, the radical ethnicist arguments tend to polarize proponents of the
debate. When such new notions of ethnic supremacy appear, nationalist suspicions
and public fears are confirmed, and a cycle of chauvinist reaction, backlashes and
mudslinging set in motion.

While nationalists read the minority issue into a history of conflict with the outside world, ethnicists see it as symptomatic of historically entrenched prejudices
inside Iran. Thus, while nationalists routinely stress the antiquity of the Iranian
nation-state and the uniqueness of Iranian-ness as a way to defend the nation-state's
territorial integrity, some ethnicists have proclaimed the end of the Westphalian
sovereignty paradigm and the nation-state-congruence idea: the beginning of a new,

globalized era in which a citizen can easily have more than one identity and in which cultural borders are not necessarily coterminous with territorial borders of nation-states. Indeed, they may in fact be calling for Iran to become a state-nation rather than a nation-state.

These academic and abstract debates, I will argue, have a direct bearing on the public debate. The reformist focus on the minority issue in 2009, for example, outraged nationalists in Iran, and members of the National Front issued a condemnation of presidential candidate Mehdi Karubi's attempt to garner minority votes with the aid of "suspicious, anti-Iranian currents" and at the expense of national unity. In the letter of condemnation, they stated:

> These actions of Mr. Karubi's election committee shows more than anything the lack of sufficient scientific knowledge about Iran's national identity, which is a great shame... Mr. Karubi and his advisors do not have sufficient knowledge of concepts such as "ethnicity" and "nationality" in Iranian society. Unfortunately, Mr. Karubi's committee is unaware of the opinions of renowned Iranian and foreign experts on this sensitive topic. For example, Anthony Smith, the noted theoretician of nationalism, believes that "the phenomenon of nation" in Iran has reached completion despite the existence of various ethnic groups. Yet the people active in Mr. Karubi's committee have shown, with their efforts to ethnically divide this nation, that they still do not believe in "Iranians becoming a nation."[147]

The academic debates about how to understand "the national" and "the ethnic" are thus not insignificant abstractions. They are key to the ideological battles over "identity" in Iran today in which academic knowledge is evoked, distorted or forgotten to suit particular political purposes.

All this notwithstanding, this chapter has also presented a number of potentially constructive points of convergence. This hints at something more profound than a glib assertion about the advantage of nationalists and ethnicists reading the works of each other: it has to do with the power of solidarity. Malesevic points out that the close connection of ethnicity and culture clearly shows that ethnicity is not a collective asset of a group or simply a political instrument of a small elite. Yet ethnicity is also *not* a mere synonym for culture:

> Firstly, unlike culture, which is a particular way of collective living, expressed in the universal human ability to articulate symbolically, classify, and communicate common experience, ethnicity entails only a small fragment of this huge gamut. Ethnicity could not possibly be a mere synonym for cultural difference as there are hundreds of thousands of diverse practices, "sentiments and attitudes" that crisscross ethnic boundaries, the great majority of which never become an object of collective action.[148]

In other words, even in the most radical of ethnicist writings, there is always an allusion to this "huge gamut" called Iran. While recent years have seen the state apparatus willing to mobilize many resources in stifling dissent and controlling Iranian citizens' access to information and exchange, and while there have been numerous setbacks for all civil society activists critical of the regime, Iran is in no way a stagnant, moribund society. In the daily interactions of societal groups that would not interact had it not been for the many structural changes brought about by the Iranian state in the past three decades, and in exchanges on social media and within student organizations, NGOs and environmental movements, Iranians are facing cultural difference every day. At least among the tech-savvy generation of young Iranians, the prevailing views on "the huge gamut" are steadily but surely changing.

CHAPTER 6

CONCLUSION

IN THIS BOOK, I have argued that there are a number of important issues demanding further study and discussion within the burgeoning field of critical Iranian Studies. Even though the "ethnic commonsense" prevalent in general works on Iran is in many ways "nonsensical" or at least simplistic, ethnicity is nonetheless experienced as very real and important to significant segments of Iranian society. Ethnicity *happens,* so to speak—whether in the explicit shape of ethnically framed minority mobilization or in the less obvious shape of an ostensibly supra-ethnic notion of majority identity. In other words, scholars need to take ethnicity into consideration even when a given collective claims not to be "ethnic."

Current minority mobilization is both a product of and a reaction to the Islamic Republic. On the one hand, the post-revolutionary state has managed to usher in a vast expansion of welfare, infrastructure and education; it has witnessed, and sometimes encouraged, the rapid spread of information and communication technology, and it has overseen the incorporation of a large segment of the population, previously excluded, into a project of state-building. The latter also includes attempts at engaging the whole population in electoral politics. Even though the Islamic Republic has not brought genuine democracy, it has provided the participatory mechanisms that eventually set off the late 1990s reformist wave and it has brought many previously excluded minority voters into an arena of nationwide politics. Thus, the emergence of the ethnicist movement cannot be reduced to a case of "civil society against the state": as a "nationalizing" force of change, the Islamic Republic has also empowered and emboldened segments of Iranian society that were completely marginalized under the Pahlavis.

On the other hand, the Islamic Republic has not managed to level out the deep socio-economic gap between center and periphery; it has institutionalized Shiite exceptionalist discrimination in the constitutional core of Iranian politics, and it has repeatedly launched campaigns of repression against critical and dissident voices, including those working within the boundaries of the law and the political system. In short, while it has had significant success in nationalizing Iranian politics, the Islamic Republic has proven to be inherently undemocratic and authoritarian, scared of the same diversity it hails and praises, and violently opposed to any alternative ideological vision of Iran.

The contradictory dynamics generated by these populist, authoritarian, Islamist and nationalist policies of the post-revolutionary state, combined with the sense of relative deprivation in minority regions and the changes in the geopolitical landscape, eventually generated an ethnically framed minority movement different from that of the revolutionary days. Despite clampdown and repression, the emergence of ethnicist discourses in Iranian politics, I have argued, is significant and irreversible: any Iranian politician and state leader will now have to calculate with not just an "ethnic variable," but a "minority constant" alongside and within "the national constant."

I have shown in this book that nationalism and Islamism are in no way incompatible and that not even an Islamic Republic can do without nationalism in its ideological discourse. Yet I have also shown that religion, particularly the political role of the clergy, remains a key site of contention. This is why the minority issue has become a prism through which a wave of nationalist-minded intellectuals and scholars seek to criticize state policy or even the nature of the quasi-democratic/quasi-theocratic regime. They use the emergence of much-feared radical ethnicism as an evidence of how the regime is a "bad" agent of state-building because it relies on a traditionalist and heavily Islamist discourse: with "good" nationalism, the nationalist-minded intellectuals argue, the state could instead usher in modernity and elevate Iran to a place in the world hierarchy of countries more befitting of such an ancient nation-state.

Despite their differences, it appears that the regime and some of its nationalist critics—constituting two different segments of one dominant elite—share a fear of their own surroundings. Instead of extending the laudatory rhetoric of multi-ethnic harmony and perennial solidarity into a new paradigm of a genuinely inclusive Iranian-ness, they focus on demonizing ethnicists and minority rights activists. The fear of balkanization is obviously augmented by the increased pressure of Western powers against Iran; however, this pressure is certainly also exploited in order to criminalize minority demands. While the actions of Western powers toward Iran impact on how state and intellectuals will approach the minority issue in the future, the minority issue will obviously still have to be solved by changes within Iranian society.

Nationalist-minded scholars play an important role in this respect. We saw in the final part of Chapter 5 how Iranian nationalists, outraged by a reformist politician and his promises of local autonomy and cultural rights to minorities, reacted by invoking a sociological authority such as Anthony D. Smith. This instrumental use of social science and history legitimizes a reification and sanctification of the nation. Instead of explaining complex phenomena, these scholars, intellectuals and activists simply claim that Iran is unique and that social dynamics that they deem detrimental must be the result of foreign machinations. Such skewed interpretations of theory and history are potentially harmful because they help to maintain a discriminative status quo, to reject the legitimacy of minority demands or even to justify the violent repression of ethnicists.

While the nationalist-minded Iranian scholars are seeking to liberate the semantics of the nation from its Eurocentric context, some seem to have been caught between, as Khomeini famously promised, "Neither East nor West." In their simultaneous critique of the Islamic Republic and Western powers, some have ended up devising a highly Iran-centric approach that is prone to essentialism, primordialism, exception-alism and reductionism. Insisting that Iran has a deep-seated history of tolerance, these scholars gloss over the fact of discrimination today; they omit the fact that the modern nation-state in Iran has been shaped by the same violently homogenizing forces as other nation-states. Indeed, if minorities needed historically to be "Iranized," then the notion of Iran as being the total sum of its different ethnic groups cannot be correct.

The question is whether the ruling elites of future Iran, with or without an Islamic Republic, will choose an inclusionary approach to state-making and nation-building—or whether the exclusionary aspect of Persian-centric nationalism and Shiite exceptionalism will continue to hold sway as a dominant discourse on national identity. The civic ideals of the Green Movement seem to suggest an alternative, albeit one that has so far not yielded a fully articulated re-interpretation of Iranian-ness beyond the general demand for an end to despotism. As in any other multi-ethnic and multi-cultural country, even the progressive, democratic discourse of civic nation-alism in Iran is still ambiguous on the question of tolerance of difference. The question then is to what extent will the nation-state-congruence principle remain a key demand in the nationalizing project. Indeed, who should define what it means to be Iranian?

While in this book, I have warned fellow scholars against the tendency to uncrit-ically internalize the arguments of those studied, I will nonetheless venture to emphasize one aspect of nationalism that may carry the promise of an inclusionary Iranian-ness. As it was suggested in the beginning of this book, it sometimes appears as if nationalism is *everywhere* in Iranian society. A reason for this is undoubtedly the sheer wealth of symbols and traditions handed down through history and nur-tured by scholars, enhanced in popular culture, adapted to political discourses and utilized by the modern ruling elites. Nationalists today can draw upon very elabo-rate *longue-durée* repertoires with emotional importance to many Iranians, whether Persian speaking or not. Within this reading of history, nationalists envision a cos-mopolitan, multi-ethnic Iranian cultural sphere boasting many shared traits and collective assets.

The realization that Persian has been *lingua franca* for centuries in this multi-ethnic cultural sphere should not be used to justify the hegemony of Persian language in the framework of a modern nation-state. However, it *is* a significant asset of inter-cultural exchange and understanding, and this aspect is often lost in the narratives of more radical ethnicists, who are single-mindedly obsessed with stating their own primordial authenticity. Even with the politicization of certain distinct and diver-gent traits among minorities, the shared traits are still potent symbols and narratives for building inter-ethnic solidarity. Any such project of solidarity-building, how-ever, demands an appreciation of the fact that one can espouse different identities at different times—without that necessarily resulting in national disunity, territorial disintegration or an existential threat to Iranian-ness.

These arguments are all reflected in the writings of a new generation of Iranian social scientists, historians and intellectuals who have acknowledged that cultural difference, ethnic diversity and minority demands are parts of societal reality in Iran today—facts that cannot be tabooed or wished away. They are also reflected in certain segments of Iran's oppositional spectrum, where activists seem to have realized that no democratic movement can succeed without the participation of the minorities.

The struggle for freedom, democracy and human rights continues in all spheres of Iranian civil society, and Iranians are in the process of defining the place and role of minorities within these struggles.

NOTES

INTRODUCTION

1. The most comprehensive is Sanasarian 2006.
2. Malesevic 2011a: 68.
3. Brubaker 2004: 11.
4. Ibid.: 11, 65.
5. Malesevic 2006a: 27.
6. Malesevic 2011a: 78.
7. Brubaker 2004: 28.
8. Ibid.: 38.
9. Ibid.: 18.
10. Anderson 1983, Gellner 1983, Hobsbawm 1991.
11. Billig 1995.
12. Calhoun 1997: 3, 8.
13. Ibid.: 99.
14. Brubaker 2004: 32–3. Hence the use of the terms "ethnic group," "communities" and "collectivities" throughout this book is necessary since these are the lay and academic idioms and understandings in focus. Indeed, even those sympathetic to Brubaker's deconstruction of identity have noticed that Brubaker himself (indeed, perhaps any scholar) cannot completely abandon groupist language—if nothing then for stylistic reasons. See, for example, Malesevic 2006b.
15. Brubaker 2004: 29.
16. Ibid.: 32.
17. Ibid.: 44.
18. Malesevic 2006a: 4.
19. Brubaker 2004: 11–12.
20. Malesevic 2006a: 5.
21. I have borrowed this term from Richard Jenkins (1997: 87), who classifies ethnicism as an ideology based on identification with ethnicity, while nationalism is based either on ethnicity/nationality or on ethnicity/"race."
22. Hushmand & Kuhshekaf 2007: 212–3.
23. PhD project funded by the Danish Research Council, 2006–10.
24. Hegland 2004; see also Tapper 2009 for a personal and historical perspective on doing research on Iran.
25. Abdi 2001: 51, Ashraf 2006: 529.

CHAPTER 1

1. This term is borrowed from Hirschfeld 1996 via Brubaker 2004: x.
2. Boroujerdi 1998.

3. Tapper 1998: 397.
4. Brubaker 2004: 41.
5. Ibid.: 12.
6. A similar distinction is in the anthropological division between *emic* and *etic* views: the former being how people label themselves and others, the latter how scholars, looking from the outside or "above," label different people. Social anthropologist Richard Jenkins operates with "nominal" and "virtual" to distinguish the act of external categorization from the internal experience of belonging. Jenkins 2008: 83.
7. Tapper 2008a: 100.
8. Ibid.: 106.
9. Tapper 1998: 395.
10. Tapper 1988: 27.
11. CIA 2011. Accessed April 28, 2011. Based on July 2011 estimate.
12. CIA 2007. In 2012, the CIA changed the estimates to something closer to that of the Library of Congress, but added that this was based on its 2008 estimate.
13. Library of Congress 2008.
14. Estimated, respectively, at around 150,000–200,000 and 16,000–18,000 in 1992. See Sanasarian 2000: 36, Table 2.
15. Estimated at perhaps around 20,000–30,000.
16. Estimates ranging, respectively, from 0 to 350,000; around 50,000; and 5–10,000. See, for example, Sanasarian 2000 and Hassan 2008.
17. Since official statistical reports lump together Shiites and Sunnis in one category of "Muslim," it is impossible to verify the estimates presented by Sunni activists.
18. CIA 2011, ISC 2006.
19. Library of Congress 2008.
20. Compare, for example, Amirahmadi 1987 with Amanolahi 2005. For reference tool examples: Stokes 2009 and Shoup 2011. Ramezanzadeh (1996: 129) includes Gilakis, Bakhtiyaris and Lors together with "Persians"—which makes his category of "Persians" a clear majority (65 percent of the population).
21. CIA 2007.
22. See Doerfer 1989. The "1% Turkish," referring to the language spoken in Turkey, points to an error or misunderstanding in the CIA report: even if Turkish was spoken in Iran, then why not include it in the umbrella category of "Turkic"?
23. Paul 2008.
24. One scholar who has noted this problem with using "ethnic," "linguistic" and "religious" interchangeably without highlighting the crucial differences is Hamid Ahmadi (see Chapter 4). Ahmadi (1995: 37) complains that some scholars seem only to apply the term "ethnic" to communities that have framed political demands (such as for autonomy) in connection to their religious self-identification.
25. For statistical information on nomad tribes, see ISC 2008.
26. Conversely, some argue that *Iranian Turks* is the correct ethnonym for all Turkic speakers in Iran, whereas Shahsevan, Afshar, Qashqa'i and so on are tribal sublabels.
27. Tapper 1988: 29.
28. See, for example, Eriksen 2002: 8.
29. Ittig (1989) thus describes "gypsies" in Iran (the Dom people) as those who "make sieves, carding combs, spindles, etc."
30. Kazemi 1988: 211–2.
31. Amanolahi 2005: 38–9.
32. An example of this is in the work of US-based scholar and minority activist 'Ali Al-Taie (see Chapter 5). Al-Taie's key argument is that since the concept of "race" has been

academically discredited and since Iranians are mixed, claims to ethnic or racial purity are invalid. Nonetheless, Al-Taie himself defaults to the concept of "race" when he divides Iranians into "White," "Yellow" and "Red" races (1999: 166–7).

33. See, for example, Doane 1997, Gladney 1998, Kaufman 2004.

34. The eminent anthropologist Lois Beck (2009: 159) has criticized the failure of most non-anthropologist scholars of Iranian studies to recognize the difference between "Iranian" and "Persian."

35. Yar-Shater 1993: 141.

36. Hanaway 1993: 147–8.

37. Tapper 2008a: 102.

38. For example, see Amirkhosravi 2006: 9; Ashraf 2004: 160; for an example in English, see Amanolahi 2005: 37.

39. Himself an Azeri, Amirkhosravi is a former Tudeh Communist party member; while currently living outside Iran, he nonetheless has published articles inside Iran.

40. Amirkhosravi 2006: 14.

41. Oberling 1999.

42. Hushmand 2007: 3

43. Ibid.: 4

44. Rezakhani 2003.

45. Bosworth 1984, Perry 2009.

46. Tapper 2008b: 74–5.

47. Maqsudi 2003: 77.

48. Ibid.: 129.

49. See, for example, Bonakdar 2009.

50. Rezakhani 2003.

51. Amanollahi 2005: 37.

52. Amanolahi 2005: 39.

53. Hushmand & Kuhshekaf 2007: 219–20. For other examples of similar arguments, see Ahmadi 1995: Chapter 1; Kaviyanirad 2007: 101. See Chapter 4 in this book for an elaborate discussion of this aspect.

54. Hushmand 2007: 5.

55. Doane 1997.

56. "The Idea of Iran" is borrowed from a book series of that name, edited by Vesta Sarkhosh Curtis and Sarah Stewart.

57. Key English-language works on modern Azeri history includes Atabaki 2000, Clark 2006, Nissman 1987 and Swietochowski 1995.

58. Throughout this book, "Azerbaijan" refers to this historical region in Iran; "the Republic of Azerbaijan" refers to the independent post-Soviet republic.

59. Amanolahi 2005: 37.

60. For example Shaffer 2002: 222–3, Riaux 2008: 46.

61. Bosworth 1986.

62. See, for example, Entessar 1994, Izadi 2004 and Reza 2006. It was in fact anti-Russian Azeri separatists who adopted the name Azerbaijan for Arran, using the name "Caucasian Azerbaijan" in their foreign correspondence.

63. A seminal work on the Shahsevan is Tapper 1997.

64. For an example of the view that Azeri ethno-nationalism in Iran was the product of Soviet policies, see Entessar 1993.

65. See Atabaki 2000 and L'Estrange 2009; for a critique of Pishevari, see Morshedizad 2001.

66. Compare, in order, CIA 2011, Price 2005, Yildiz & Taysi 2007. Again, the numbers—not the percentage estimates—are based on the latest total figure for Iran's population (77.8 million).
67. Kurdistan in this book refers to the area inhabited by Kurds that stretches across approximately six provinces, and Kurdistan Province to the administrative unit.
68. Madih 2007: 11.
69. Key works on modern Kurdish ethno-nationalism in Iran include Entessar 1992, Koohi-Kamali 2003, Natali 2005 and Vali 2011.
70. McDowall 2004: 9.
71. Koohi-Kamali 2003.
72. See McDowell 2004, Van Bruinessen 1991.
73. McDowell 2004: 15.
74. Paul 2008.
75. Compare, in order, Yildiz & Taysi 2007, Keddie 1995, Salehi-Amiri 2006 and Price 2005.
76. For example, Limbert 1968; rejected by other scholars (e.g., Asatrian 2009).
77. Van Bruinessen 1983.
78. McDowell 2004: 245.
79. Compare, in order, Library of Congress 2008, CIA 2007, Qayem 2005: 65 and Bani-Torof 2005.
80. Qayem 2005: 63, 65.
81. Bani-Torof 2005.
82. Among the few studies of modern Khuzestani Arabs are Gharayaq-Zandi 2008 and Purkazem 2006.
83. For example, BAFS 2007.
84. For example, Chalabi & Janadele 2007.
85. Ibid.: 85–6.
86. Qayem 2005: 67–8.
87. For example, Maqsudi 2003: 71.
88. For example, Gharayaq-Zandi 2008, Qayem 2005.
89. On early Arab history in Iran, see Bosworth 1986; Daniel 1986; Oberling & Hourcade 1986.
90. For example, Gharayaq-Zandi 2008: 75.
91. Soucek 1984.
92. See Ansari 1974 and Strunk 1977.
93. Mann 2010.
94. Elling Forthcoming.
95. For example, CIA 2011, Library of Congress 2008.
96. In this book, "Baluchistan" will, unless otherwise specified, refer to the Baluch-inhabited parts of southeastern Iran.
97. *Sistan va Baluchestan* 2009.
98. Ahmadi 2004c. This is disputed, see SunniOnline 2010.
99. Spooner 1988, Fabietti 2009.
100. Elfenbein 1988.
101. Spooner 1988.
102. Hosseinbor 1984.
103. Ibid.: 83.
104. Hosseinbor 1984: 136–7.
105. Amanolahi 2005: 37.

CHAPTER 2

1. Brubaker 2004: 12.
2. Key works on the Kurdish uprising include MacDowell 2005, Koohi-Kamali 2003. In addition, I draw on some primary sources, including National Archives: FO973/40, FCO 8/3394, FCO 8/3647; Moradbeigi 2004; and Pasdaran n.d.
3. Ahmadzadeh & Stansfield 2010: 18.
4. Entessar 2010: 41.
5. MacDowell 2005: 276.
6. See, for example, Razmi 2000.
7. Hosseinbor 1984: 156. See also National Archives: FCO 8/3574.
8. *Hezb-e ettehād-e moslemin.*
9. Hosseinbor 1984: 159.
10. For these discussions, refer to Salehi-Amiri 2006: 342–6.
11. *Jebhe-ye vahdat-e baluch.* Ahmadi 1999: 261.
12. National Archives: FCO 8/3575;
13. Including the Ba'thist Arabistan Independence Front, *Jebhat-ot-tahrir 'arabestān.*
14. *Kānun-e farhang-e khalq-e 'arab.*
15. Nabavi 2004: 504–5.
16. Haghayeghi 1990: 37.
17. For example, Price 2005: 305–6
18. For an elaborate discussion, see Sanasarian 2006.
19. A possible exception is Kurdistan Province. However, since the state has never carried out a census on religious parameters, it is hard to see how Article 12 could ever be institutionalized on a provincial level.
20. Salehi-Amiri 2006: 346.
21. See, for example, Mojab & Hassanpour 1995, HRW 1997, Tohidi 2009.
22. Mehran 2002.
23. SCCR 2010. For a discussion, see Fazeli 2006: 167–9.
24. Speech by Ayatollah Taleqani as quoted in Salehi-Amiri 2006: 349–50.
25. Proceedings of the constitutional drafting process as quoted in Salehi-Amiri 2006: 348–9.
26. Farzanfar 1992: 412.
27. See Aghajanian 1983, Haghayeghi 1990, Kazemi 1988.
28. Amirahmadi 1987, Amirahmadi & Atash 1987, Amirahmadi 1989.
29. Farzanfar 1992: 436.
30. HRW 1997.
31. Haghayehi 1990: 44–5.
32. See, for example, Amirahmadiyan 2005.
33. Sultan-Qurraie 2008: 64.
34. Hushmand & Kuhshekaf 2004: 462–4.
35. Amirahmadi 1987: 105.
36. Amirahmadiyan 2005: 168, 170.
37. Salehi-Amiri 2006: 239.
38. Harris Forthcoming.
39. Ibid.: 78–80.
40. Changiz Pahlavan quoted in Morshedizad 2001: 241; Salehi-Amiri 2006: 386.
41. Bani-Torof 2005.
42. 'Abbasi-Shavazi & Sadeqi 2005.
43. Yusefi 2005: 204. Note that Arabs were not included in this study.

44. Chehabi 1997; see also Kaviyanirad 2007.
45. Chehabi 1997: 248.
46. Via Salehi-Amiri 2006: 423.
47. Maqsudi 2006: 94.
48. Godarzi 2005b.
49. Ibid.: 94.
50. Khamene'i quoted in Izadi 2004: 411.
51. Samii 2000: 129.
52. See, for example, Baztab 2005b, Kayhan 2005a, Mehr 2005d.
53. See Hamid Ahmadi quoted in Azadi 2005 and Seyyed-Sa'idi 2005.
54. See, for example, Pak 2007b, Kaviyan & Hosseini 2008.
55. Gerecht 1997; James Woolsey quoted in Glazov 2006.
56. Peters 2006.
57. Hersh 2006a: 3.
58. For example, *Financial Times* 2006, Hersh 2006b & 2008, Lowther & Freeman 2007, Malbrunot 2012, Oppel 2007, Perry 2012, Ross & Isham 2007.
59. See, for example, Olson 2002, *Washington Times* 2003.
60. Riaux 2008: 47.
61. For sources on post-revolutionary Azeri ethnicism, refer to Atabaki 2005, Brown 2004, and Riaux 2005. For Azeri ethnicist accounts, see Asgharzadeh 2008, Nazmi-Afshar 2005. For a representation broadly criticized for its pro-ethnicist and ahistorical approach, see Shaffer 2002. For nationalist Iranian accounts, refer to chapters 4 and 5.
62. Key figures include Mohammad-'Ali Farzane, Javad Hey'at, Hamid Notqi, Hossein Sadeq, Hossein-Qoli Katebi and Mohammad Zehtabi.
63. *Azerbaijan Khalq Jebhesi.*
64. Bani-Hashemi 2002.
65. Riaux 2005: 52.
66. EurasiaNet 2008.
67. S. Bosnali's PhD dissertation *Patrimoine linguistique et littéraire turcophone de l'Iran (une etude sociolinguistique),* quoted in Riaux 2005: 57, note 6. Azeris read and write either in a modified Arabo-Persian alphabet or in one of the two Latin-based alphabets used in Turkey and ROA.
68. Eslami 2006: 199.
69. HRW 1997. Chehregani was arrested, held in solitary confinement and prevented from re-running in 2000. After leaving Iran in 2002, Chehregani formed GAMOH (South Azerbaijan's Awakening Movement, *Güney Azerbaycan Milli Oyanis Herekati*), which maintains that Azeris are an oppressed majority in Iran and that the Azeri language is being exterminated. While Chehregani has claimed not to be a separatist, the name of his organization (and some of his statements) suggest otherwise (see GAMOH 2010: 1, and Chehregani quoted in Brown 2002). Due to its underground nature, it is impossible to estimate the number of sympathizers inside Iran. It is also impossible to verify GAMOH's allegations of state repression, systematic harassment and extrajudicial killings of its supporters, or to verify the Iranian state's allegation that GAMOH assassinated a government employee in 2005.
70. Protests were also heard in Parliament, and during a 1993 tour in Azerbaijan, Khamene'i held a rare speech in Azeri, which included symbolic warnings to the Armenian government. There were also tensions between Armenians and Azeris in Iran. Tehran-based Armenian clergy sought to defuse the situation by condemning Armenian aggression in Nagorno-Karabakh. See Chehabi 1997: 246 and 253, note 92; and Riaux 2005: 57, note 9.

71. Olson 2002: 64.
72. During the 2006 protests, neither Ankara nor Baku expressed any official sympathy. On the contrary, president Aliev actually persecuted some ROA journalists for "divisive and offensive" cartoons of the Iranian Leader, and then deported Chehregani from Baku. See Tohidi 2006: 3.
73. For example, Eftekhari 1999: 39.
74. UNDP 1999.
75. Salehi-Amiri 2006: 241.
76. Samii 2000: 134.
77. UNCHR 2005.
78. On disrespect for the human, civil and cultural rights of Iran's Kurds, see Ahmadzadeh & Stansfield, Amnesty 2008, Gresh 2009, HRW 1997, IHRDC 2012, Mojab & Hassanpour 1995, Samii 2000, Yildiz & Taysi 2007.
79. These include KDPI's Paris-based *Tishk*, the PKK-run, Denmark-based *Roj TV* as well as *Komele*'s *Roj Helat* and PJAK's *Newroz*, both based in Sweden. See Ahmadzadeh & Stansfield 2010: 24.
80. Sarajzade & Adhami 2008 shows that Kurdish university students are attracted to critical student unions rather than the religious bodies such as University Basij.
81. Ahmadzadeh & Stansfield 2010: 21.
82. Compare Ahmadzadeh & Stansfield 2010: 24–5 with Brandon 2006: 2.
83. Zambelis 2011. Some observers originally reckoned that Iran was secretly supporting PKK against NATO-member and once Israel-allied Turkey (Olson 2001: 75). Yet this strategy seemed contradictory by 2004 when PKK-affiliated PJAK started its guerilla operations and terrorist attacks against Iran. Since then, Turkey and Iran have often coordinated their actions against PKK/PJAK.
84. On PJAK activities, see Brandon 2006, Kaussler 2007, Zambelis 2011.
85. See BBCPersian 2005a, 2005c, RFE/RL 2005.
86. See, for example, Lahsaeizadeh et al. 2009, Navah & Taqavi-Nasab 2006.
87. For example, in 2004, a local health official pointed out that 80 percent of the children in the Dasht-e Azadegan area suffered from malnutrition. Dr. Balali quoted in *Jomhuri-ye eslāmi* daily, May 30, 2004 (via Azadtribun 2004).
88. See Chapter 5. For an ethnicist view on the socioeconomic factor, see Bani-Torof 2005 and Khaz'al 2008; for reports from international organizations, see FIDH 2010 and IRIN 2005; for a sociological survey among Arabs in Ahvaz using quantitative methods, see Lahsaiezadeh et al. 2008.
89. IRIN 2005.
90. Rabihe n.d.
91. Khaz'al 2008: 21; see also Bani-Torof 1999.
92. *Hezb-e vafāq-e eslāmi* or *Lajnat-ol-Wafāq.*
93. Al-Tamimi, the Concord leader, withdrew from the reformist coalition, and wrote an open letter to Khatami complaining about the reformists' inattention to Khuzestan. Al-Tamimi was later arrested.
94. Athanasiadis 2005.
95. Khandaniha 2009.
96. See, for example, Abedin & Farrokh 2005.
97. In 1991, a flooding left some 50,000 Baluch homeless. Another flooding caused widespread damage to agriculture in 2007. See Amnesty 2007.
98. Kamal-od-Din Qorab quoted in Farzanfar 1992: 445–6.
99. See, for example, Amnesty 2007, Eta'at & Musavi 2011: 80.
100. 'Abbasi-Shavazi & Sadeqi 2005: 35.

101. Farzanfar 1992: 442; Hosseinbor 1984: 110; Piran 2000: 26.
102. See Kaviyanirad 2007: 111. One observer in 1985 claimed that 70 percent of the population was engaged in smuggling (Kamal-od-Din Qorab quoted in Farzanfar 1992: 445–6).
103. On Baluch militancy, see Amnesty 2007, Vatanka & Aman 2006, Zambelis 2006.
104. See, for example, Eta'at & Musavi 2011, Kaviyanirad 2007.
105. LCMM 2010.
106. See Amnesty 2007, Houleh 2007.
107. Amnesty 2007: 19.
108. On cultural repression in Baluchistan, refer to Amnesty 2007, Jahani 2005, RSF 2007.
109. For example, HRW 1997, Athanasiadis 2005.
110. See HRW 1997, Amnesty 2007 and Fars 2009b.
111. One example of this is the fact that many young Baluch evade military service, allegedly since they prefer not to subject themselves to the Shiite indoctrination processes institutionalized in the military. See Kaviyanirad 2007.
112. Kaviyanirad 2007: 112.
113. In 1994, riots broke out in Zahedan when locals protested against the destruction of a Sunni mosque in Mashhad; in 1996, two clerics were killed during parliamentary election campaigns; in 1997, a Sunni cleric was killed under mysterious circumstances in Bandar 'Abbas; in 1998, two Sunni clerics were murdered and a Sunni mosque was bombed; in 2000, a Sunni seminarian was set on fire and killed in Zahedan; and in 2008, a cleric was assassinated in Saravan. In 1990, a Shiite cleric was killed, and in 2000, a bomb hit a Shiite mosque in Zahedan.
114. Iran 2006a.
115. Rooz Online English 2006.
116. See for example Hafezniya & Kaviyani 2006: 33–4; Kaviyanirad 2007.
117. For details, see Baztab 2005a & 2005c, Gooya 2005, Iran 2005a, IRNA 2005a, Jomhuri-ye eslami 2005a. For ethnicist accounts, see AHRO via SAHR 2005. For reports from international organizations, see Amnesty 2006b, HRW 2005.
118. AHRO via SAHR 2005.
119. Compare ISNA 2005a and ILNA 2005a with BAFS (via UNPO 2005).
120. Hamshahri 2005a.
121. For state-affiliated media reports, see Hamshahri 2005b, IRNA 2005b, Kayhan 2005a & 2005b, Mehr 2005a, 2005b and 2005g.
122. Sharq 2005b.
123. Mehr 2005c, Iran 2005b.
124. Amnesty 2006c.
125. See Aftab 2005, BBCPersian 2005d & 2005e, CPPE 2005, Jomhuri-ye eslami 2005b, Iran 2005j, ISA-Amir Kabir 2005, Shahrvand 2005.
126. Baztab 2005e & 2005f, Iran 2005d, 2005e, 2005f, 2005g, 2005h, 2005i.
127. Iran 2005c & 2005d, ISNA 2005d.
128. For official reports in state-affiliated media, see Baztab 2006a, Fars 2006a, 2006b, 2006c, 2006d, IRANEWS 2006, IRNA 2006a, ISNA 2006a, 2006b, 2006c & 2006d; for reports in international media, see BBCPersian 2006a, 2006b, 2006c.
129. A Revolutionary Guard commander, for example, told officers to be lenient in their dealings with locals, reminding them that smugglers were often the sole breadwinners of impoverished families left with no alternatives to crime. See BBCPersian 2006c.
130. For official reports on this event, see Aftab 2007, Entekhab 2006b, 2006d, 2006f, 2006h, Fars 2007c, 2007d & 2007e, ILNA 2007a, IRNA 2007, ISNA 2006f,

Kayhan 2007. Authorities also claimed that they seized a ton of drugs during the intial operations, though it was unclear whether these drugs had been in *Jondollāh*'s possession.

131. Baloch Front 2006.
132. BBCPersian 2007.
133. Iran 2006b.
134. For official reports in state-affiliated media, see Baztab 2006b & 2006c, ISNA 2006g, Kayhan 2006c. For reports from reformist media, including official statements, see Farda 2006, Farhang-e ashti 2006a, ILNA 2006, ISA-Zanjan 2006. For ethnicist media, see Shams-e Tabriz 2006, Tabriz News 2006. For reports from international media, see BBCPersian 2006d.
135. Shams-e Tabriz 2006; see also Chapter 5.
136. Aftab 2006a, b, Entekhab 2006i.
137. ISNA 2006i, Kayhan 2006c.
138. Rooz Online Persian 2006.

CHAPTER 3

1. Arjomand 1989, Dabashi 2005, Keddie 1962 & 2006.
2. Malesevic 2006.
3. Ibid.: 72, 78.
4. Ibid.: 75–6.
5. Ibid.: 77.
6. Ibid.: 94.
7. Malesevic 2011b: 286.
8. See Zia-Ebrahimi 2011a: Chapter 2.
9. For numerous examples, refer to Kashani Sabet 1999; also Kian & Riaux 2009: 192.
10. Moaddel 2005: 184.
11. Vahabzadeh 2011.
12. Motahhari quoted in Salehi-Amiri 2006: 337.
13. Bazargan quoted in Ashraf 2006: 528.
14. Chubin 1990.
15. See Hunter 1992, Menashri 1990.
16. See Menashri 2001, Mashayekhi 1993.
17. Ram 2009: 46; see also Elling 2012.
18. Ram 2009: 47.
19. Amirahmadi 1996.
20. Holliday 2007.
21. Esteqamat 2010. Masha'i allegedly proclaimed in 2004 that "the age of Islamism is over." See Jahan News 2008.
22. Khamene'i quoted in Paul 2010: 82.
23. Hunter 1992.
24. See, for example, Parsine 2010, Asr-e Iran 2010.
25. Moin 1999: back cover.
26. See, for example, Davari 1980.
27. Babai-Zarech 2004, Toyserkani 2006; for a detailed analysis, see Elling 2012.
28. Menashri 1988: 216.
29. Khomeini as quoted in Atabaki 2005: 38.
30. Menashri 1998: 218.
31. Islamic Republic Party as quoted in Morshedizad 2001: 269–70.

32. Khomeini quoted in Toyserkani 2006: 178.
33. Khomeini in ibid.: 180.
34. My paraphrasing of Khomeini as quoted in ibid.: 181.
35. Toyserkani 2006: 67.
36. Ibid.: 68.
37. Ibid.: 70–1.
38. Ibid.: 71.
39. Ibid.: 166.
40. Ibid.: 166, 175.
41. Ibid.: 131–2.
42. Ibid.: 181.
43. Ibid.: 166.
44. Maqsudi 2003, Mo'azzampur 2004.
45. Maqsudi 2003: 129.
46. Ibid.: 129.
47. Ibid.: 316–7.
48. Mo'azzampur 2004: 139, 184–5.
49. Ibid.: 184–5.
50. Ibid.: 249.
51. The Expediency Council has mentioned minority rights and development of minority regions in several of its key strategic documents, has organized conferences and has published reports about national unity and ethnic identity. It has even established a so-called Committee for Elites, Ethnic Groups and Subcultures (*komite-ye nokhbegān, qowmiyat-hā va khorde-farhang-hā*). See www.maslahat.ir.
52. Ramezanzadeh 1996: 115, 156.
53. Ibid.: 94.
54. Ibid.: 119.
55. Ibid.: 148.
56. Ibid.: 101, 104–13.
57. Ibid.: 121–2.
58. Ibid.: 121, 236.
59. Salehi-Amiri 2006: 432.
60. Ibid.: 431.
61. Ibid.: 123.
62. Ibid.: 167–8.
63. Ibid.: 169.
64. Ibid.: 361.
65. Ibid.: 445.
66. Ibid.: 447–8, 455–6.
67. Ibid.: 450–2.
68. For example: Tabnak 2010.
69. Khamene'i 1991, 2006, 2009.
70. See, respectively, President 2005, 2006, 2007, 2009a.
71. See, respectively, President 2009b, 2010a, Fars 2007b, 2009a.
72. See, for example, President 2010b, 2011a, 2011b, 2011c, 2011d.
73. See, for example, President 2009a.
74. See Shahidi 2007, Khiabany 2008. The entire press is dependent on state-controlled licenses, paper supplies and subsidies. Furthermore, various state bodies apply a broad range of political, judicial and extra-judicial tools of repression to intimidate and censor journalists and editors. This demands attention to detail and small differences in

wordings, headlines and emphasis that may convey widely differing positions and lively debates within the ruling elite.

75. For this task I have received kind help from journalists and experts such as Hossein Bastani and Majid Mohammadi. Also see, Menashri 2001, Semati 2008, Shahidi 2007.

76. Among these factions, I distinguish between the four main camps at the time of the unrest: the "conservatives" (*mohāfezekārān,* associated with Khamene'i), "neo-conservatives" (*osulgarāyān,* Ahmadinejad), "pro-reformists" (*eslāhtalabān,* Khatami) and "centrists" (*kārgozārān,* Rafsanjani). This political landscape has changed significantly since then, particularly after the 2009 president election and uprising.

77. Under the admittedly ambiguous label "officials," I include the Leader, the President, ministers, MPs and parliamentary spokesmen; administrators in local governance, municipalities and city councils; spokesmen from extra-parliamentary institutions including the Expediency Council and the Guardians Council; state-employed clerics such as Friday Prayer Leaders and members of organizations such as the Islamic Propagation Organization and the Leadership Foundation; the Judiciary, including the Attorney-General and judges; and high-ranking officers of the Army (*artesh*), the Revolutionary Guard (*sepāh-e pāsdārān*), the paramilitary *Basij* force, the police or Disciplinary Forces (*niru-ye entezāmi*), and the intelligence agencies.

78. Kayhan 2005f.

79. For examples of the state reaction to the Khuzestan unrest, refer to Kayhan 2005b, 2005d, IRNA 2005c, ISCA 2005.

80. 'Ali Yunesi quoted in Kayhan 2005d.

81. Ashraf 1992, Abrahamian 2004.

82. See Kayhan 2005h, ISNA via MEW 2005a, Fars via MEW 2005b.

83. See BBCPersian 2005b, ISNA 2005c, Mehr 2005f & 2005h.

84. See Kayhan 2005h, Mehr 2005f & 2005g.

85. Beeman 2005, Slavin 2007.

86. See, for example, Hamshahri 2005c, IRNA 2006b, ISNA 2006k, Mehr 2005h, Miras 2006.

87. See, for example, Baztab 2005h.

88. A state-run newspaper even put a number to the pay, alleging that *Jondollāh* received up to 1 billion Iranian Rial for each operation: Iran 2006a. For other examples, see ISNA 2006e.

89. Brigadier-General Ahmadi-Moqaddam quoted in Entekhab 2006a.

90. Baztab 2007.

91. See Baztab 2005a, Fars 2005b, Mehr 2005c, 2005f, 2005h.

92. Baztab 2005b; see also Kayhan 2005e.

93. Baztab 2005d; see also Mehr 2005c.

94. Dorri-Najafabadi quoted in ISNA 2006a. Also see BBC Persian 2006/3b, Iran 2006a.

95. See, for example, Fars 2006b, ISNA 2006a. Iranian reformists even used the word "Taliban" as a derogatory term to condemn their conservative rivals. See for example Iran-e emruz 2005.

96. Mehr 2005c.

97. Dorri-Najafabadi quoted in ISNA 2006a.

98. Judge Hojjatoleslam Nekunam quoted in Entekhab 2006c.

99. 'Abbas-'Ali Soleymani quoted in ISNA 2007.

100. Baztab 2005i.

101. Admiral Shamkhani quoted in Iran 2005a.

102. See, for example, Baztab 2005c, Hamshahri 2005b, Iran 2005b, IRNA 2005d, Jomhuriye eslami 2005a.

103. See, for example, ILNA 2005a.
104. See, for example, Fars 2006a, 2006f, 2006g, IRNA 2006a, ISNA 2006l, Kayhan 2006a, Mehr 2007.
105. See ILNA 2007b, Iran 2005k, Mehr 2005f & 2005h.
106. Baztab 2005g.
107. Entekhab 2006c.
108. For example, IRNA 2005a, Kayhan 2005d.
109. See Baztab 2005i, IRNA 2005d, Jomhuri-ye eslami 2005a & 2005b, Kayhan 2005a & 2005f.
110. See Entekhab 2006c & 2007, Farhang-e ashti 2006b, Kayhan 2005a & 2005/4g, Resalat 2007.
111. IRNA 2006c.
112. ISNA 2006i.
113. Kayhan 2006b.
114. See Entekhab 2006e & 2006g, ISNA 2007.
115. Ahvaz MP Seyyed Ahmad Musavi quoted in IRNA 2005b; my emphasis.
116. Kayhan 2005g.
117. See Aghaie 2004, Gieling 2006.
118. See, for example, Kayhan 2005a, Fars 2005a.
119. See, for example, Fars 2005a, Mehr 2005d.
120. Shamkhani quoted in Fars 2005a; see also ILNA 2005b.
121. Shamkhani quoted in Fars 2005a.
122. Dorri-Najafabadi quoted in Fars 2006e.
123. Ayatollah Nuri-Hamadani quoted in ISNA 2006k.
124. See BBCPersian 2006/3b, Iran 2006a, ISNA 2006j & 2006k.
125. For example IRNA 2006c, Kayhan 2006f.
126. Ahmadinejad quoted in Fars 2006h.
127. Mehr 2005f.
128. Rafsanjani quoted in Farhang-e ashti 2006b.
129. MP Bahonar quoted in Kayhan 2006e.
130. Aftab 2006b.
131. ISNA 2006h.
132. See, for example, Mehr 2005e.
133. Yunesi quoted in IRNA 2005b.
134. Shamkhani quoted in Fars 2005a.
135. MP Hamid Zangene quoted in Sharq 2005a; see also Kayhan 2005b.
136. Karubi quoted in ISNA 2005b.
137. Rafsanjani quoted in Kayhan 2006d.
138. Bahonar quoted in Farhang-e ashti 2006b.
139. Marx 2005.
140. See, for example, Juergensmeyer 1993, van der Veer 1994, Smith 2003.
141. Mihelj 2007: 265.
142. Marashi 2008: 113. On the other hand, another "classical" modernist, Ernest Gellner (1981), observed early in his career that Islamism ("Muslim fundamentalism") is underpinned by the same mechanisms as nationalism.
143. Smith 2009: 76.
144. Ibid.: 76.
145. Malesevic 2006a: 99.
146. Ibid.: 150.
147. Zubaida 2004: 409.

148. Malesevic 2006a: 88.
149. Ibid.: 99.
150. Ibid.: 106–7.
151. Smith 2009: 77.

CHAPTER 4

1. Calhoun 1997: 19.
2. Smith 2009: 72.
3. Billig 1995: 130.
4. May 2008: 20.
5. Ibid.: 52.
6. Calhoun 1997: 77.
7. Ibid.: 79.
8. Ibid.: 53.
9. Paul 1999: 192.
10. Ibid.: 194.
11. See Ashraf 2006, Kashani-Sabet 1999, Tavakoli-Targhi 2001.
12. Ashraf 2006: 254.
13. Kashani 2007.
14. Tavakoli-Targhi 2001: 40.
15. Kashani-Sabet 1999: 174–5; Tavakoli-Targhi 2001: 119–23.
16. Kashani-Sabet 1999.
17. Kashani-Sabet 1999: 139; see also ibid.: 108, 125.
18. Afshar's foreword in Nateq 1980: 7–8.
19. Kashani-Sabet 1999: 203.
20. Abrahamian 1970: 293.
21. Parsi 2009: 175.
22. Marashi 2008: 136.
23. Tavakoli-Targhi 2001: 102.
24. See Abdi 2001, Ashraf 2006, Kurzman 2005, Marashi 2008, Parsi 2009. Tavakoli-Targhi 2001.
25. Tavakoli-Targhi 2001: 102.
26. Yar-Shater 1993: 141.
27. Ibid.
28. Kian & Riaux 2009, Zia-Ebrahimi 2011a.
29. Zia-Ebrahimi 2011b: 449.
30. Vaziri 1994; see Chapter 5.
31. Tavakoli-Targhi 2001: 102–3; Parsi 2009: 372–3.
32. Marashi 2008: 75; Parsi 2009: 350.
33. Anderson 1991: 140.
34. Kashani-Sabet 1999: 216.
35. Mirza Aqa Khan Kermani quoted in Sadr 1998: 50. See also Marashi 2008: 65.
36. Meskoub 2008.
37. Ibid.: 17, 29.
38. Ibid.: 19.
39. Ibid.: 10.
40. Yar-Shater 1993: 142.
41. Kashani-Sabet 1999: 217.
42. Ibid.: 58.

43. Nateq 1980: 17–9, 59, 89–90.
44. Marashi 2008: 64.
45. Kia 1998: 9.
46. Bayat 2009.
47. Kia 1998: 9–10.
48. Afshar quoted in Salehi-Amiri 2006: 248–9.
49. Nateq 1980: 56.
50. Ibid.: 58.
51. Ibid.: 26.
52. Ibid.: 84.
53. Ibid.: 85.
54. See Tavakoli-Targhi 2001, Kian & Riaux 2009, Parsi 2009.
55. Afshar quoted in Mo'azzampur 2004: 148–9.
56. Afshar quoted in Parsi 2009: 178.
57. Editorial in *Habl-ol-Matin,* November 12, 1906, translated and quoted by Abrahamian 1970: 293.
58. Kia 1998: 33, note 29.
59. Nateq 1980: 64.
60. Ibid.: 42.
61. Ibid.: 26.
62. Fazeli 2006: 106.
63. Ibid.: 11–14.
64. Mostafa Vaziri; Fazeli 2006.
65. See Bulookbashi 2009. The key focus of foreign anthropologists was on "primitive," isolated tribal societies, which Tapper (1998: 390) explains with "the ethnographer's romantic notions about pastoralism, nomadism, and warrior tribes," and with a "concern to conform with the traditional conventions" of anthropology.
66. Barth 1961. Other prominent scholars worked on Iran's Bakhtiyaris, Baluch, Kurds, Shahsevan, Turkmen and Qashqa'is. See also Spooner 1985 & 1998, Tapper 2009.
67. See Fazeli 2006: Chapter 4.
68. Fazeli 2006: 115.
69. See Fazeli 2006: 97; Fakouhi 2009.
70. Fazeli 2006: 149–57.
71. See Fazeli 2006, Fakouhi 2009.
72. Fazeli 2006: 182–190.
73. Ibid.: 91–2, 198–9.
74. Ibid.: 137, 162–3.
75. Fakouhi 2009: 106; Fazeli 2006: 211.
76. Fakouhi 2009: 97; one scholar has pointed out the detrimental effects of social sciences being a gendered space: Shahshahani 2009.
77. Bulookbashi 2009: 26.
78. Fazeli 2006: 199.
79. Shahbazi 2009: 153–5.
80. Fazeli 2006: 162–3.
81. Ibid.: 182; see also Shahbazi 2009.
82. Fazeli 2006: 210.
83. Ahmadi 1995, 1999, 2001, 2003, 2004a-d, 2007.
84. See the conflicting reports on Masha'i's relation to the institute—or to another institute, under the Intelligence Ministry, with a similar charter—in Parsine 2008, Shomal News 2009.

85. Ahmadi 2003: 9.
86. See, for example, Eslami 2006, Izadi 2004, Maqsudi 2001, Motallebi 2008, Salehi-Amiri 2006.
87. See, for example, Ahmadi 2003, Amirkhosravi 2006, Sabbaghpur 2002, Nassaj 2009.
88. Ahmadi 2003: 9.
89. Ahmadi 2004d: 194.
90. Note the use of ethnic and non-ethnic. As elsewhere (Jenkins 2008: 15, May 2008: 26), there is in Iranian academic works often a tendency to relegate ethnicity only to minorities.
91. Ahmadi 1995: iii, iv, 15.
92. Ibid.: 42, 45, 50.
93. Ibid.: iv.
94. Ibid.: 5.
95. Hushmand & Kuhshekaf 2007: 230–2. For a similar view, see Sabbaghpur 2002 or Nassaj 2009.
96. Hushmand & Kuhshekaf 2007: 234.
97. Ibid.: 233–5.
98. Pak quoted in Hushmand & Kuhshekaf 2007: 236.
99. Pak quoted in Nassaj 2009: 138.
100. Eslami 2006: 197.
101. For example, Izadi 2004.
102. Bahrami 2008.
103. Za'im in Bahrami 2008: 1.
104. Ibid.
105. Indeed, some nationalist-minded intellectuals claim that Iran was the first country in the world to establish a state: Amirkhosravi 2006: 4.
106. Ahmadi 2004d: 195.
107. Ibid.
108. For another pronouncedly nationalistic interpretation of Iranian history, refer to Mo'ini-'Alamdari 2004, who argues that the "narrations" that created Iranian national identity can be dated back to pre-modern times, which means that Iran as a nation is not a modern but an ancient construct.
109. Ahmadi 2003: 9–10.
110. For another example of this view, refer to the introduction of Qamari 2006.
111. Purjavadi 1992: 3–4.
112. Pak quoted in Hushmand & Kuhshekaf 2007: 236.
113. Motallebi 2008: 9.
114. Purjavadi 1992: 4; Za'im in Rahimirad 2006: 3; Pak 2007b: 6; Ramezanzadeh 1996: 178.
115. See, for example, Amiri & Samimi 2007, Sheikhavandi 2005. There are also numerous references to other pre-Islamic rituals such as the *Sadeh* and *Mehregan* festivals.
116. Ahmadi 2003: 16.
117. Maqsudi 2001: 222.
118. Salehi-Amiri 2006: 145–6.
119. The folklorist Zand-Moqaddam (Ahmadi 2004c: 314), for example, refers to a local Baluch cleric's stratement that the Baluch have been present in "the Iranian army" throughout "all wars in Iran," from Xerxes' campaigns against Greece (480 B.C.) to popular resistance against the Mongol invasion (thirteenth century A.D.). Indeed, the Baluch are indefatigable "border guards" (*marzdārān*), Zand-Moqaddam argues, thus omitting

the fact that historically, culturally, linguistically and religiously, Baluch "borders" were and are not necessarily congruent with the territorial borders of present-day Iran.

120. See, for example, Amirkhosravi 2006, Eslami 2006, Maqsudi 2001, Maqsudi 2003, Motallebi 2008, Ra'is-Tusi 2006.
121. Ramezanzadeh 1996: 206.
122. Farrokhi 2005: 77–8.
123. Za'im in Rahimirad 2006: 1.
124. Eslami 2006: 200–2; for other examples of Baluch and Kurds described as Aryan, see Eftekhari 1999, Motallebi 2008, Salehi-Amiri 2006: 149.
125. Seyyed-Emami 2004: 165.
126. See, for example, Ahmadi 2004d: 197, 212.
127. Izadi 2004: 356–7; for other examples, see Morshedizad 2001, Salehi-Amiri 2006.
128. See, for example, Ahmadi 2001, Farrokh 2005, Izadi 2004.
129. Izadi 2004: 405.
130. Ibid.: 407–8.
131. Ahmadi 2004b: 91.
132. See, for example, Zand-Moqaddam in Ahmadi 2004c: 312.
133. Pak 2007b: 6.
134. See, for example, Ahmadi 1999, Shabani 2006.
135. For example Maqsudi 2001: 225, Pak 2004: 172–3.
136. Purjavadi 1992: 4.
137. Amirkhosravi 2006: 8; see also Za'im in Rahimirad 2006 for similar arguments.
138. Pak 2004: 182–4.
139. A similar critique of minority elites as oblivious not only to Iranian history and political culture but also to the international world of politics is found in Izadi 2004: 412.
140. Pak 2007b: 7, my emphases.
141. Motallebi 2008: 6–7. For a similar view, see Nassaj 2009: 138.
142. See also Baharlunezhad 2006, Divsalari 2009, Eftekhari 1999, Farrokhi 2005, Qamari 2006.
143. Motallebi 2008: 16.
144. See, for example, Eftekhari (1999: 36), who states that "widening the gap between Turks and non-Turks is one of the basic goals of foreign powers."
145. Za'im in Bahrami 2008: 1.
146. Rahmani 2008: 2.
147. For example Ahmadi 2004b: 84–7.
148. Ahmadi 2004b: 96.
149. Ibid.: 83–4.
150. Ibid.: 89.
151. Ahmadi 2004a: 12.
152. See, for example, Bahrami 2008 or Rahmani 2008.
153. Varjavand 2000.
154. National Front 2004.
155. For other examples, see Izadi 2004, who has hailed measures such as the banning of the Azeri-language press in the 1980s.
156. Ahmadi 1996: 147.
157. Ramezanzadeh 1996: 147.
158. Ahmadi 2004b: 112, my emphasis.
159. Zand-Moqaddam in Ahmadi 2004c; Salehi-Amiri 2006 142.
160. Pak 2004: 173.

161. Ramezanzadeh 1996: 218; Zaʻim (in Rahimirad 2006: 3) even argues that if Kurds were to secede from these two countries, they would do so only because they see themselves as Iranians, rather than as Turks or Arabs.
162. For example Ahmadi 2003: 41.
163. Ahmadi 2004d: 212.
164. For examples, see Izadi 2004, Motallebi 2008, Purjavadi 1992.
165. Eftekhari 1999: 39.
166. Zaʻim in Rahimirad 2006: 2.
167. Izadi 2004: 356.
168. Zaʻim in Bahrami 2008: 2.
169. An example of this is from Pak (2007b: 10): "If the Persian language was not obligatory in education, what would have happened to those who fled the war between Iran and Iraq and migrated to the Persian(!)-inhabited areas? How would "Bashu, the Little Stranger" from Khuzestan be able to play with his peers in northern Iran? And, by the way, if the teaching of Persian was not compulsory, how could our local elites reach the level of literacy they have today? And finally, what treasure trove of knowledge and culture have you found beyond Iran's borders since you wish to learn local languages to access it?" The first reference here is to Khuzestan's Arabs who fled the war and settled in mainly Persian-speaking areas; and the second is to Bahram Beyzaʻi's 1986 movie about a child refugee, Bashu, from southern Iran who settles among Gilaki-speaking people in the north. The third statement, clearly sarcastic, alludes to ethnicists ("local elites"), and their attainment of literacy in an Iranian education system based on Persian. The final statement seems to indicate that Iran's neighboring countries cannot possibly have a more enriching and refined cultural and literary heritage than that of Iran—and hence, there is no reason to learn "their" languages.
170. See, for example, Ahmadi 1996, Rahimirad 2006.
171. Ahmadi 2003: 21–2.
172. Qamari 2006: 97.
173. Ibid.: 100.
174. Ahmadi 2004b: 112.
175. Izadi 2004: 410.
176. Bonakdar 2009.
177. Zaʻim in Bahrami 2008: 1.
178. For example, Arab ethnicists use the name "Mohammerah" instead of "Khorramshahr" for an important city in Khuzestan, and some Arab ethnicists refer to Khuzestan as "Arabistan" or "Al-Ahwaz." Izadi laments about the Azeri-language magazine *Ārāz* that "pan-Turkists" behind the magazine chose to spell the name with *z* instead of *s* and the long vowel *ā* instead of short *a*. As several other scholars, Izadi is also worried about the use in bi-lingual Azeri magazines of the alphabet used in the Republic of Azerbaijan. See Izadi 2004.
179. Bonakdar (2009), for example, condemned a 2009 communiqué from Azeri ethnicists on the occasion of International Mother Language Day that was authored in both Persian and Azeri (in the Latin-based alphabet), and signed with what Bonakdar claims is "strange and hostile pseudonyms such as Attila, Ilghar, Kublai and Okhtay"—testaments, Bonakdar believes, to the authors' "obsession with rotten racial meta-narratives". Actually, names such as Attila and Ilghar—even Genghis (*changiz*)—are common among Iranians, but it appears that in an ethnicist context, they are perceived as threats to Iran: the revived ghosts of Huns and Mongols.
180. Parsi 2008: 379.
181. Holiday 2007.

182. Rahmani 2008: 3.
183. Malesevic 2006a: 110–1, 113.
184. Ibid.: 129.
185. Ibid.: 131.
186. Ibid.: 145.
187. Calhoun 1997: 18.
188. May 2008: 5 with reference to Billig 1995.
189. See May 2008: 143, 147.
190. Brubaker 2004: 291–2.
191. May 2008: 37.

CHAPTER 5

1. Quoted in Mahmudi & Sa'idi 2002.
2. Abrahamian 1970.
3. Abrahamian 1970, 1981.
4. The Democrat Party's declaration for autonomy, published in *Azerbaijan,* November 25, 1945, translated and quoted by Abrahamian 1970: 309.
5. Today, Vaziri is a lecturer at University of Innsbruck, Austria.
6. Vaziri 1994: 11.
7. Ibid.: 3.
8. Ibid.: 213.
9. Ibid.: 8.
10. Ibid.: 5.
11. Ibid.: 218.
12. Matin-Asgari 1995, Tavakoli-Targhi 1994.
13. Tavakoli-Targhi 1994: 317.
14. Matin-Asgari 1995: 262.
15. Boroujerdi 1998: 43.
16. Ibid.: 47.
17. Ibid.: 45–6.
18. Ibid.: 50
19. Ibid.
20. Ibid.: 44.
21. Saad 1996: 10, 12.
22. Ibid.: 18.
23. Ashraf 2004: 135.
24. Baraheni 1977: 11–12.
25. Al-Taie 1999.
26. Al-Taie 1999: 144–5, note 1.
27. Ibid.: 144–5, note 1, 239, 248.
28. Asgharzadeh 2007: x.
29. Ibid.: x.
30. Al-Taie 1999: 230–1.
31. Asgharzadeh 2007: 6.
32. This term refers to Jalal Al-e Ahmad's *gharbzadegi* ("Westoxification," which denotes Iranian infatuation with and then hatred toward everything Western).
33. Bani-Torof 2006: 3.
34. Ibid.: 3.
35. Al-Taie 1999: 80

36. Baraheni 2008.
37. For examples of ethnicists emphasizing the major contributions of Turkic-speaking dynasties to Iranian history, see Baraheni 2008, Sadr 1998.
38. Al-Taie 1999: 171.
39. Ibid.: 172.
40. Asgharzadeh 2007: 3.
41. Ibid.: 114.
42. Al-Taie 1999: 190.
43. See: Gerdizi nd.a, nd.b, 2007.
44. Al-Taie 1999: 117.
45. See, for example, Asgharzadeh 2007: p. 94.
46. Sadr-ol-Ashrafi in Shahrvand 2007: 6.
47. Asgharzadeh 2007: 11.
48. Al-Taie 1999: 204.
49. Ja'fari 2007: 67–71.
50. Iranian federalism, Bani-Torof argues, should be the first step toward a confederate structure for the whole Middle East: an entity resembling the European Union in which Iran would be the axis.
51. Bani-Torof 2006: 6.
52. See, for example, Sadr (1998) for an elaborate ethnicist critique of a Persian-centric, nationalist definition of Iranian-ness.
53. Al-Taie 1999: 239.
54. Ibid.: 191–2; see also Savalanli 2008.
55. Al-Taie 1999: 191.
56. Bani-Torof 2006: 3.
57. Ibid.: 3–4.
58. See, for example, Ahangari 2008, Payedar 2008.
59. Tabrizi 2009: 1.
60. Al-Taie 1999: 174, 182; Asgharzadeh 2007: 122–3.
61. Al-Taie 1999: 174, 181–2.
62. Ibid.: 174.
63. Ibid.: 173.
64. Ibid.: 71.
65. Baraheni 2008: 81.
66. Shirin Alamhooli quoted in IHRDC 2012.
67. *Günash* appears to have been published since 2003, and in 2008, it had 40 issues. It is uncertain whether or not it is still published.
68. Jahanbakhsh 2008a.
69. Jahanbakhsh 2008b.
70. Ibid.: 15.
71. See Tabrizli 2008.
72. Saveli 2008: 145.
73. Al-Taie 1999: 12.
74. Ibid.: 19.
75. Kermanshahi 2008: 4.
76. Ibid.: 4.
77. See, for example, Ja'fari 2007.
78. See, for example, Sadr 1998: 45–6.
79. Baraheni 2008: 85.
80. Anonymous protestor quoted in Jahanbakhsh 2008b: 74–5.

81. After having experienced the short-lived stint at Azeri autonomy and cultural revival in 1946, Zehtabi left Iran for a lengthy exile in the USSR and Iraq. He returned after the revolution to work at Tabriz University, where he conducted research on Turkic linguistics and history, and published several books. Zehtabi died under what fellow ethnicists claim was mysterious circumstances.
82. This claim runs counter not only to established Iranology but also to Turcology, linguistics and archaeology. See Golden 1992, Johanson & Csató 1998.
83. Many thanks to Dr. Touraj Atabaki for sharing an unpublished manuscript debunking Zehtabi's work.
84. Poorpirar nd.
85. Asgharzadeh 2007: 47–8.
86. Ibid.: 177.
87. Al-Taie 1999: 241–2.
88. Ibid.: 159.
89. Asgharzadeh 2007: 13.
90. For example Izadi 2004: 395–6.
91. Sadr 1998: 9.
92. Grillot-Susini 1998.
93. Sadr 1998: 26.
94. Ibid.: 28.
95. Amnesty 2006a & 2006c, BAFS 2007, HRW 2005, HRW 2007.
96. See, for example, Akhbar-e Rooz 2011, Amnesty 2011, HRW 2011, RSF 2011.
97. HRW 2012.
98. Amnesty 2008. See also Amnesty 2008, DW—World 2007, IHRDC 2011, Mizan 2008b; Mukrian 2007a-k.
99. See Fars 2009a & 2011.
100. See AFP 2008, Fars 2008, Fathi 2008, Zambelis 2009.
101. See Amnesty 2007. For the ethnicist groups' perspective, refer to Balochistan People's Party website (www.balochpeople.org), Balochistan National Movement (*Zrombesh*)'s website (www.zrombesh.org) and the *Jondollāh* website (www.junbish.blogspot.com)
102. See Advar 2008, AKU 2007, Amnesty 2006b, CHRA 2008, CHRR 2008, Ghahreman 2008, Gooya 2006, 2008a & 2008b, ILNA 2007b, Mizan 2008a, Rooz 2008, Rooz Online Persian 2006, SCHRR 2007.
103. See, for example, Mosharekat 2008.
104. See Hammihan 2009, Musavi 2009, QalamNews 2009. Musavi in particular seemed to pay attention to issues raised by the Sunni community.
105. See AdvarNews 2009, Bigdeli 2009, ILNA 2009, SahamNews 2009.
106. Afary 2010.
107. Shaykhi 2010.
108. Fars 2007a.
109. HRW 2009: 19.
110. Amnesty 2008.
111. IHRDC 2012.
112. Ibid.
113. Ibid.
114. See, for example, HRANA 2009, Amnesty 2007: 10.
115. Amnesty 2007: 7.
116. HRW 2009.
117. Mukrian 2008.
118. Zamaneh 2011.

119. Soghdi 2010.
120. BHRW 2008.
121. ISNA 2006m.
122. IAS 2005.
123. RAHANA 2010.
124. IHRDC 2012.
125. For example Ghahreman 2008.
126. Fifteen people were reportedly detained in September 2006 for complicity in a call for this boycott. See FIDH 2010: 15.
127. Amnesty 2006b.
128. Whereas the urban *hoviyat-talab* student organizations that were key in mobilizing the masses for the 2006 unrest are based in universities, it seems that *Tirākhtursāzi* draws on a rural populations with a relatively lower educational background. More research is needed, however, to prove this hypothesis and, more generally, to map the Azeri ethnicist movement.
129. Bani-Hashemi 2002.
130. Bashiriyeh 2004: 115–7.
131. Ravasani 2004: 115.
132. Bulookbashi 2009: 21, 25.
133. Nadjmabadi 2009: 10.
134. Bani-Hashemi 2002.
135. See, for, example Hafezniya & Kaviyani (2006: 38–9) on Baluchistan's Sunnis.
136. See Nurbakhsh 2008, Reza'i & Kazemi 2008 & Seyyed-Emami 2008. There are indications that some of these scholars themselves hail from minority regions. If this is the case, the expansion of higher education and research under the Islamic Republic, combined with the restrictions and impediments for doing research abroad and with growing ethnic awareness, seems to have created an interesting cocktail.
137. For two good examples, see Lahsaiezadeh et al. 2009 and Navah & Taqavi-Nasab 2006.
138. Fakouhi 2009: 89–90.
139. Fakouhi 2010: 224.
140. Ibid.: 224.
141. Ibid.: 206.
142. Ibid.: 211.
143. Ibid.: Part Two, Chapter 3.
144. Malesevic 2006a: 47.
145. Malesevic 2011: 273.
146. Vaziri 1994: 217.
147. National Front 2009.
148. Malesevic 2011a: 70.

BIBLIOGRAPHY

Abbasi-Shavazi, Mohammad-Jalal & Sadeqi, Rasul. 2005. 'Qowmiyyat va olgu-hā-ye ezdevāj dar irān', *Pazhuhesh-e zanān*, Vol. 3, No. 1, (Spring), pp. 25–47.

Abdi, Kamyar. 2001. 'Nationalism, Politics and the Development of Archaeology in Iran', *American Journal of Archaeology*, Vol. 105, No. 1, (January), pp. 51–76.

Abedin, Mahan & Farrokh, Kaveh. 2005. 'British Arabism and the bombings in Iran', *Asia Times Online*, www.atimes.com, November 3.

Abrahamian, Ervand. 1970. 'Communism and Communalism in Iran: The *Tudah* and The *Firqah-i Demokrat*', *International Journal of Middle Eastern Studies*, Vol. 1, pp. 291–316.

Abrahamian, Ervand. 1981. 'The Strengths and Weaknesses of the Labour Movement in Iran, 1941–53', in Bonine, Michael E. & Keddie, Nikki R. (Eds.). *Continuity and Change in Modern Iran*, Albany: State University of New York Press, pp. 181–202.

Abrahamian, Ervand. (Ed.). 2004. *Jostār-hā'i darbāre-ye te'ori-ye towte'e dar irān* [*Studies on Conspiracy Theories in Iran*], 3rd Ed., Tehran: Nashr-e ney.

Afary, Frieda. (Transl.). 2010. 'Azeris and the Green Movement', reproduced on PBS Tehran Bureau (www.pbs.org), April 15.

Aghaie, Kamran Scott. 2004. *The Martyrs of Karbala: Shi'i Symbols and Rituals in Modern Iran*, Washington: University of Washington Press.

Aghajanian, Akbar. 1983. 'Ethnic Inequality in Iran: An Overview', *International Journal of Middle Eastern Studies*, Vol. 15, No. 2, pp. 211–224.

Ahangari, Kave. 2008. 'Cheshm-hā-rā bāyad shost, jur-e digar bāyad did (javābiye'i be āqā-ye kurosh-e za'im) [Rinse the eyes and see in another way (an answer to Mr. Kurosh Zaim)]', from the website *Iran Global* (www.iranglobal.info), November.

Ahmadi, Hamid. 1995. *The Politics of Ethnic Nationalism in Iran*, Doctoral Thesis, Ottowa: Carleton University.

Ahmadi, Hamid. 1999. *Qowmiyyat va qowm-garā'i dar irān: afsāne va vāqe'iyyat* [*Ethnicity and Ethno-Politics in Iran: Myth and Reality*], Tehran: Nashr-e ney.

Ahmadi, Hamid. 2001. 'Esterātezhi-ye novin-e pān-torkism: esterātezhi-ye "khatne" [The New Strategy of Pan-Turkism: The "Circumcision" Strategy]', originally published by Aran Cultural Institute of Orumiye, December 19. Here from reproduction on *Ruznāmak* online, www.ruznamak.blogfa.com, posted September 22, 2008.

Ahmadi, Hamid. 2003. 'Hoviyyat-e melli-ye irāni: bonyād-hā, chālesh-hā va bāyeste-hā [Iranian National Identity: Foundations, Challenges and Imperatives]', *Nāme-ye pazhuhesh*, Vol. 7, No. 6, (Summer), pp. 5–51.

Ahmadi, Hamid (Ed.). 2004a. *Irān: Hoviyyat, Melliyyat, Qowmiyyat* [*Iran: Identity, Nationality, Ethnicity*], Tehran: Mo'asase-ye tahqiqat va towse'e-ye 'olum-e ensani.

Ahmadi, Hamid. 2004b. 'Din va melliyyat dar irān [Religion and Nationality in Iran]', in Ahmadi, H. (Ed.). 2004a: *Irān*, pp. 53–114.

Ahmadi, Hamid. 2004c. 'Baluchestān-e irān: hoviyyat, tārikh va degar-guni [Iran's Baluchistan: identity, history and change]', interview with Mahmud Zand-Moqaddam in Ahmadi, H. (Ed.). 2004a: *Irān*, pp. 305–342.

Ahmadi, Hamid. 2004d. 'Hoviyyat-e melli-ye irān: vizhegi-hā va 'avāmel-e puyā'i-ye ān [Iran's national identity: its dynamic characteristics and factors]', interviewed by Davud Mir-Mohammadi in Mir-Mohammadi, D. (Ed.). 2004: pp. 189–212.

Ahmadi, Hamid. 2007. 'Vā-kāvi-ye padide-ye qowmgarā 'i dar sepehr-e jahāni-shodan (tajrobe-ye mantaqe'i-ye irān, torkiye va 'arāq) [An Inquiry into the Phenomenon of Ethno-Nationalism at the Dawn of Globalization (Iran, Turkey and Iraq's Regional Experience)]', *Siyāsat-e dākheli*, Vol. 1, No. 3, (Summer), pp. 9–33.

Ahmadzadeh, Hashem & Stansfield, Gareth. 2010. 'The Political, Cultural and Military Re-Awakening of the Kurdish Nationalist Movement in Iran', *Middle East Journal*, Vol. 64, No. 1, (Winter), pp. 11–27.

Al-Taie, Ali. 1999. *Bohrān-e hoviyyat-e qowmi dar irān [Ethnic Identity Crisis in Iran]*, Tehran: Nashr-e Shadegan.

Amanolahi, Sekandar. 2005. 'A Note on Ethnicity and Ethnic Groups in Iran', *Iran and the Caucasus*, Vol. 9, No. 1, pp. 37–42.

Amirahmadi, Hooshang. 1987. 'A Theory of Ethnic Collective Movements and its Application to Iran', *Ethnic and Racial Studies*, Vol. 10, No. 4, (October), pp. 363–391.

Amirahmadi, Hooshang. 1989. 'The State and Territorial Social Justice in Postrevolutionary Iran', *International Journal of Urban and Regional Research*, Vol. 13, No. 1, (March), pp. 92–120.

Amirahmadi, Hooshang. 1996. 'From Political Islam to Secular Nationalism', in *The Iranian*, online ed. (www.iranian.com), January 11. http://www.iranian.com/Jan96/Opinion/SecularNationalism.html (retrieved April 10, 2008).

Amirahmadi, Hooshang & Atash, Farhad. 1987. 'Dynamics of Provincial Development and Disparity in Iran, 1956–1984', *Third World Planning Review*, Vol. 9, No. 2, (May), pp. 156–185.

Amirahmadiyan, Bahram. 2005 'Daraje-ye towse'e-yāftegi-ye ostān-hā va hamsāzi-ye melli dar irān [The Level of Development in Provinces and National Integration in Iran]', in Qamari, D. (Ed.). 2005: *Hambastegi-ye melli dar irān [National Unity in Iran]*, pp. 145–172.

Amiri, Seyyed Reza Salehi & Samimi, Nilufar. 2007. 'Āyin-hā-ye nowruz va hambastegi-ye melli [Nowruz Traditions and National Unity]', *Farhang-e mardom-e irān*, No. 11, (Winter 1386), pp. 3–19.

Amirkhosravi, Babak. 2006. 'Derang-hā 'i darbāre-ye aqvām-e irāni va sākhtār-e siyāsi-ye matlub [Uncertainties About Iran's Ethnic Groups and the Ideal Political Structure]', *Nāme*, No. 52, Mordād 1385/July-August.

Anderson, Benedict. 1991. *Imagined Communities*, 2nd Ed. (1st Ed. 1983), London: Verso.

Ansari, Mostafa. 1974. *The History of Khuzistan, 1878–1925*, unpublished PhD dissertation, Chicago: University of Chicago.

Arjomand, Said. 1989. *The Turban for the Crown: The Islamic Revolution in Iran*, New York: Oxford University Press US.

Asatrian, Garnik. 2009. 'Prolegomena to the Study of the Kurds', *Iran and the Caucasus*, Vol. 13, No. 1, pp. 1–58.

Asgharzadeh, Alireza. 2007. *Iran and the Challenge of Diversity: Islamic Fundamentalism, Aryanist Racism, and Democratic Struggles*, New York: Palgrave Macmillan.

Ashraf, Ahmad. 1992. 'Conspiracy Theories', in *Encyclopaedia Iranica*, Vol. 6, pp. 138–147, New York: Encyclopædia Iranica Foundation.

Ashraf, Ahmad. 2004. 'Bohrān-e hoviyyat-e melli va qowmi dar irān [National and Ethnic Identity Crisis in Iran]', in Ahmadi, H. (Ed.). 2004a: *Irān*, pp. 133–170.

Ashraf, Ahmad. 2006. 'Iranian Identity', in *Encyclopædia Iranica*, Vol. 13, pp. 501–530, New York: Encyclopædia Iranica Foundation.

Atabaki, Touraj. 2000. *Azerbaijan: Ethnicity and the Struggle for Power in Iran*, London: I. B. Tauris.

Atabaki, Touraj. 2005. 'Ethnic Diversity and Territorial Integrity of Iran: Domestic Harmony and Regional Challenges', *Iranian Studies*, Vol. 38, No. 1, pp. 23–44.

Atabaki, Touraj (Ed.). 2009. Iran in the 20th Century: Historiography and Political Culture, London: I. B. Tauris.

Athanasiadis, Iason. 2005. 'Stirring the ethnic pot', Asia Times Online, www.atimes.com, April 29.

Azadi, Esma'il. 2005. 'Bar-resi-ye yek towsiye-ye mohem be nāmzad-hā-ye riyāsat-e jomhuri [On an important recommendation for the presidential elections candidates]', interview with Hamid Ahmadi in *Irān* (daily), June 9/Khordad 19, 1384.

Babai-Zarech, Ali-Mohammad. 2004. *Ommat va mellat dar andishe-ye emām khomeini (r.h.)* [*Ummah and Nation in Imam Khomeini's Thought*], Tehran: Markaz-e asnād-e enqelāb-e eslāmi.

Baharlunezhad, Abdolahad. 2006. 'Qowmiyyat va amniyyat dar irān [Ethnicity and Security in Iran]' from *Student News Network* website (www.snn.ir), May 23/Khordad 2, 1385.

Bahrami, Nejat. 2008. 'Melliyyat va qowmiyyat dar goft-o-gu bā kurosh za'im [Nationhood and ethnicity: interview with Kurosh Zaim]' from *Advār News* website (www.advarnews. us), October 27/6 Aban, 1387.

Bani-Hashemi, Mir-Qasem. 2002. 'Cheshm-andāz-e āti-ye nāsiyonālism-e qowmi dar āzarbāyjān-e irān [Future perspective on ethnic nationalism in Iranian Azerbaijan]', *Motāle'āt-e rāhbordi*, Vol. 5, No. 16, pp. 568–581.

Bani-Torof, Yusef-'Azizi. 1999. 'Dast-āvard-hā-ye jonbesh-e eslāh-talabi dar miyān-e mardom-e 'arab-e khuzestān [The accomplishments of the reformist movement among the Arab people of Khuzestan]', *'Asr-e āzādegān* daily, (Winter, nd).

Bani-Torof, Yusef-'Azizi. 2005. 'The Identity and Ancestry of the Indigenous Khuzestani (Ahwazi) Arabs of Iran: A Nation or an Ethnic Group?', speech at the Industrial University of Isfahan (transl. by Abdolreza Ameri), published on British Ahwazi Friendship Society's website, www.ahwaz.org.uk, nd.

Bani-Torof, Yusef-'Azizi. 2006. 'Tanavvo'-e qowmi; tahdid yā forsat? [Ethnic Diversity: Threat or Potential?]', *Nāme*, No. 52, (July-August/Mordād, 1385).

Baraheni, Reza. 1977. *The Crowned Cannibals*, New York: Vintage Books.

Baraheni, Reza. 2008. 'Surat-e mas'ale-ye āzarbāyjān, hall-e mas'ale-ye āzarbāyjān', *Günesh*, Vol. 5, No. 40, Tehran: University of Science and Technology, pp. 87–107. Originally published as letter by Baraheni on June 6, 2006.

Barth, Fredrik. 1961. Nomads of South Persia: the Basseri of the Khamseh confederacy (Reprinted Ed., 2011), Long Grove, IL: Waveland Press, Inc.

Bashiriyeh, Hossein. 2004. 'Ide'olozhi-ye siyāsi va hoviyat-e ejtemā'i dar irān [Political Ideology and Social Identity in Iran]', in Ahmadi H. (Ed.). 2004a: *Irān*, pp. 115–132.

Bayat, Kaveh. 2009. 'The Pahlavi School of Historiography on the Pahlavi Era', in Atabaki, T. (Ed.). 2009: *Iran in the 20th Century*, pp. 113–120.

Baztab. 2006a. 'Mas'ul-e peygiri-ye robude-shodegān-e hādese-ye teroristi-ye jāde-ye zābol ki-st?' [Who is responsible for investigating the abducted (persons taken hostage during) the terrorist incident on the Zabol route?], www.baztab.com, March 19/Esfand 28, 1384.

Beck, Lois. 2009. 'Anthropological Research in Iran', in Nadjmabadi, S.R. (Ed.). 2009: *Conceptualizing Iranian Anthropology*, pp. 157–179.

Beeman, William O. 2005. *The Great Satan vs. the Mad Mullahs: How the United States and Iran Demonize Each Other*, Connecticut: Greenwood Press.

Bigdeli, Rahmatollah. 2009. 'Karubi modāfe'-e sādeq-e hoquq-e aqvām', E'temād-e melli online (http://etemademeli.com), February 9.

Billig, Michael. 1995. Banal Nationalism, Thousand Oaks, CA: SAGE Publications Ltd.

Bonakdar, Tirdad. 2009. 'Zabān-e mādari va yek-pārchegi-ye melli va naqdi bar sāyt-e barā-ye yek irān [Mother tongue and national unity and a critique of the website "For One Iran"]', from Bāmdād Khabar online, www.bamdadkhabar.com, March 1.

Boroujerdi, Mehrzad. 1998. 'Contesting Nationalist Constructions of Iranian Identity', Critique: Critical Middle Eastern Studies, Vol. 7, No. 12, pp. 43–55.

Bosworth, C.E. 1984. 'Ajam', in Encyclopædia Iranica, Vol. 1, pp. 700–701, New York: Encyclopædia Iranica Foundation.

Bosworth, C.E. 1986. 'Arab i. Arabs and Iran in the Pre-Islamic Period', in Encyclopædia Iranica, Vol. 2, pp. 201–203, New York: Encyclopædia Iranica Foundation.

Brandon, James. 2006. 'Iran's Kurdish Threat', Terrorism Monitor, Vol. 4, No. 12, Washington, DC: The Jamestown Foundation's website (www.jamestown.org), June 15.

Brown, Cameron S. 2004. 'Wanting to Have Their Cake and Their Neighbor's Too: Azerbaijani Atttitudes Towards Karabakh and Iranian Azerbaijan', Middle East Journal, Vol. 58, No. 4, (Autumn), pp. 576–596.

Brubaker, Rogers. 2004. Ethnicity Without Groups, Cambridge, MA: Harvard University Press.

Bulookbashi, Ali A. 2009. 'The Contribution of Foreign Anthropologists to Iranology', in Nadjmabadi, S.R. (Ed.). 2009: Conceptualizing Iranian Anthropology, pp. 19–29.

Calhoun, Craig. 1997. Nationalism, Minneapolis: University of Minnesota Press.

Carvalho, Susana & Gemenne, François. (Eds.). 2009. Nations and their Histories: Constructions and Representations, New York: Palgrave-Macmillan.

Chalabi, Massoud & Janadele, Ali. 2007. 'Bar-resi-ye 'avāmel-e farhangi-ye mo'assar bar movafaqiyyat-e eqtesādi (yek motāle'e-ye moqāyese'i beyn-e qowmiyyat-hā-ye lor, 'arab va dezfuli-ye ostān-e khuzestān) [The Impact of Cultural Factors on Economic Achievement: A Comparative Study of Arab, Dezfuli and Lur Ethnicities in Khozestan Province]', Pazhuheshnāme-ye 'olum-e ensāni, Vol. 8, No. 53, (Spring), pp. 263–300.

Chehabi, Houchang. 1997. 'Ardabil Becomes a Province: Center-Periphery Relations in Iran', International Journal of Middle East Studies, Vol. 29, No. 2, pp. 235–253.

Chubin, Shahram. 1990 'Iran and the Persian Gulf States', in Menashri, D. (Ed.). 1990: The Iranian Revolution and the Muslim World, pp. 73–84.

Clark, James D. 2006. Provincial Concerns: A Political History of the Iranian Province of Azerbaijan, 1848–1906, Costa Mesa, CA: Mazda Publishers.

Daniel, E.L. 1986. 'Arab iii. Arab Settlements in Iran', in Encyclopædia Iranica, Vol. 2, pp. 210–214, New York: Encyclopædia Iranica Foundation.

Davari, Reza. 1980. Nāsiyonālizm va enqelāb-e eslāmi [Nationalism and the Islamic Revolution], Tehran: Daftar-e pazhuhesh va barnamerizi-ye farhangi.

de Planhol, Xavier. 1987. 'Azerbaijan i. Geography', in Encyclopædia Iranica, Vol. 3, pp. 205–215, New York: Encyclopædia Iranica Foundation.

Digard, Jean-Pierre. (Ed.). 1988. Le Fait Ethnique en Iran et en Afghanistan: Colloque international du Centre National de la Recherche Scientifique, Paris: Editions de Centre National de la Recherche Scientifique.

Divsalari, Majid. 2009. 'Goftāri dar bāb-e amniyyat-e melli va tahdid-hā-ye qowmi', Pegāh-e Howzeh, No. 251, Esfand 1387, pp. 7–10.

Djalili, Mohammad-Reza, Monsutti, Alessandro & Neubauer, Anna. (Eds.). 2008. Le Monde Turko-Iranien En Question, Geneve: Institut de Hautes Études.

Doane, Ashley W. Jr. 1997. 'Dominant Group Ethnic Identity in the United States: The Role of "Hidden" Ethnicity in Intergroup Relations', *The Sociological Quarterly*, Vol. 38, No. 3, (Summer), pp. 375–397.

Doerfer, G. 1989. 'Azerbaijan viii. Azeri Turkish', in *Encyclopædia Iranica*, Vol. 3, pp. 245–248, New York: Encyclopædia Iranica Foundation.

Eftekhari, Asghar. 1999. 'Zarfiyyat-e tabi'i-ye amniyyat: mowred-e motāle'āti-ye qowmiyyat dar irān [Natural Capacities of Security: Case Study on Ethnicity in Iran]', *Faslnāme-ye motāle'āt-e rāhbordi*, Vol. 2, No. 5–6, (Fall and Winter), pp. 25–62.

Elfenbein, J. 1988. 'Baluchistan iii. Baluchi Language and Literature', in *Encyclopædia Iranica*, Vol. 3, pp. 633–644, New York: Encyclopædia Iranica Foundation.

Elling, Rasmus Christian. 2012. 'Matters of Authenticity: Khomeinism, Nationalism and Ethnic Diversity in Iran', in Nabavi, N. (Ed.). 2012: *Iran*, pp. 79–100.

Elling, Rasmus Christian. Forthcoming. 'On Lines and Fences: Oil, Space and Violence in World War II Abadan', in Freitag, U. & Fuccaro, N. (Eds.). Forthcoming: *Rethinking Urban Violence*.

Entessar, Nader. 1992. *Kurdish Ethnonationalism*, Boulder: Lynne Rienner.

Entessar, Nader. 1993. 'Azeri Nationalism in the Former Soviet Union and Iran', in Young, C. (Ed.). 1993: *The Rising Tide*, pp. 116–137.

Entessar, Nader. 2010. *Kurdish Politics in the Middle East*, Lanham, Maryland: Lexington Books.

Eriksen, Thomas Hylland. 2002. *Ethnicity and Nationalism. Anthropological Perspectives*, 2nd Expanded Ed. (1st Ed. 1993), London: Pluto Press.

Eslami, Alireza. 2006. 'Qowmiyyat va eb'ād-e ān dar irān [Ethnicity and its Dimensions in Iran]', *'Olum-e siyāsi*, Vol. 9, No. 34, pp. 195–211.

Esman, Milton J. & Rabinovich, Itamar. (Eds.). 1988. *Ethnicity, Pluralism, and the State in the Middle East*, Ithaca: Cornell University Press.

Eta'at, Javad & Musavi, Seyyede Zahra. 2011. 'Rābete-ye moteqābel-e amniyyat-e nāhiye'i va towse'e-yāftegi-ye fazā-hā-ye siyāsi bā ta'kid bar sistān va baluchestān [The Relation between Regional Security and Development in Political Spaces with an Emphasis on Sistan-Baluchestan', *Faslnāme-ye zhe'opolitik*, Vol. 8, No. 1, (Spring), pp. 70–87.

Fabietti, Ugo. 2009. 'The "Discourse" of Baluchi Nationalism and its Relations to the Idea of a Baluchi "Identity" ', AAS Working Papers in Social Anthropology, available from http://hw.oeaw.ac.at/0xc1aa500d_0x002212d3.pdf, Vienna: Institut für Sozialanthropologie.

Fakouhi, Naser. 2009. 'Making and Remaking an Academic Tradition: Towards an Indigenous Anthropology in Iran', in Nadjmabadi, S.R. (Ed.). 2009: *Conceptualizing Iranian Anthropology*, pp. 87–115.

Fakouhi, Naser. 2010. *Ham-sāzi va ta'āroz dar hoviyat va qowmiyat [Iranian Identity Ethnicity (sic): Articulation and Conflict]*, Tehran: Gol-Azin.

Farrokh, Kaveh. 2005. 'Pan-Turanism takes aim at Azerbaijan: A Geopolitical Agenda', draft text (PDF) via *Rowzane* website (www.rowzanehmagazine.com), November-December.

Farrokhi, 'Abbas. 2005. 'Bar-resi-ye naqsh-e aqvām-e marz-neshin-e irāni dar amniyyat-e melli bā ta'kid bar ostān-e kermānshāh [A Survey of the Role of Iranian Border-Inhabiting Ethnic Groups in National Security, with Emphasis on the Province of Kermanshah]', *Faslnāme-ye jam'iyyat*, No. 51–52, (Spring/Summer), pp. 77–102.

Farsoun, Samih K. & Mashayekhi, Mehrdad. (Eds.). 1993. *Iran: Political Culture in the Islamic Republic*, London/New York: Routledge.

Farzanfar, Ramesh. 1992. *Ethnic Groups and the State: Azaris, Kurds and Baluch of Iran*, unpublished PhD dissertation, Massachusetts: Massachussets Institute of Technology.

Fathi, Nazila. 2008. 'Iran Says Rebels Killed 16 Soldiers', in *The New York Times* online, http://nytimes.com, December 5.

Fazeli, Nematollah. 2006. *Politics of Culture in Iran: Anthropology, Politics and Society in the Twentieth Century*, London/New York: Routledge.

Freitag, Ulrike & Fuccaro, Nelida. (Eds.). Forthcoming. *Rethinking Urban Violence in Middle Eastern Cities*.

Gellner, Ernest. 1981. *Muslim Society*, Cambridge: Cambridge University Press.

Gellner, Ernest. 1983. *Nations and Nationalism (New Perspectives on the Past)*, Ithaca, NY: Cornell University Press.

Gerdizi, Mohammad-Reza. nd.a. 'Mellat-hā, melliyyat-hā, aqaliyyat-hā-ye melli dar irān [Nations, nationalities and national minorities in Iran]' from *Bāybak* website (www.11007. baybak.com).

Gerdizi, Mohammad-Reza. nd.b. 'Irān yek vāhed-e mellat-dowlat nist [Iran is not a nation-state unit]' from *Bāybak* website (www.11007.baybak.com).

Gerdizi, Mohammad-Reza. 2007. 'Hoviyyat-talabi va barābari-khāhi: mobāreze'i 'aleyh-e nezhādparasti, ne'o-fāshism va ne'o-koloniyālism' [Seeking identity and wanting equality: resistance against racism, neo-fascism and neo-colonialism] from *TeDePe* weblog (www. tedepe.blogspot.com), September 12.

Gerecht, Reuel Marc. 1997. *Know Thine Enemy: A Spy's Journey Into Revolutionary Iran*, New York: Farrar, Straus & Giroux.

Ghahreman, Sasan. 2008. 'Hedayat interview', interview with Ensaf-'Ali Hedayat, *Gozār* online, www.gozaar.org, Issue 17, January.

Gharayaq-Zandi, Davud. 2008. *Irāniyān-e 'arab-tabār: mardom-shenāsi-ye sākhtār-e qowmi-ye a'rāb-e khuzestān* [*Iranians of Arab Origins: An Anthropology of the Ethnic Structure Among Khuzestan's Arabs*], Tehran: Nashr-e afkar.

Gheissari, Ali. (Ed.). 2009. *Contemporary Iran: Economy, Society, Politics*, Oxford: Oxford University Press.

Gieling, Saskia. 1999. *Religion and War in Revolutionary Iran*, London/New York: I. B. Tauris.

Gladney, Dru C. 1998. *Making Majorities: Constituting the Nation in Japan, Korea, China, Malaysia, Fiji, Turkey and the United States*, Stanford, CA: Standford University Press.

Glazov, Jamie. 2006. 'Symposium: Iran: To Strike or Not to Strike', roundtable summary, *Frontpage Magazine* online, www.frontpagemag.com, May 19.

Godarzi, Hossein (Ed.). 2005a. *Goftār-hā'i darbāre-ye jāme'e-shenāsi-ye hoviyyat dar irān* [*Narratives on the Sociology of Identity in Iran*], Tehran: Mo'asase-ye motale'at-e melli.

Godarzi, Hossein. 2005b. 'Towse'e-ye siyāsi va moshārekat-paziri-ye jāme'e-ye kord-e irāni [Political Development and Participation of the Kurdish Society in Iran]', in Godarzi, H. (Ed.). 2005a: *Goftār-hā'i darbāre-ye jāme'e-shenāsi-ye hoviyyat dar irān* [*Narratives on the Sociology of Identity in Iran*], pp. 103–136.

Golden, Peter. 1992. *Introduction to the History of the Turkish People: Ethnogenesis and State-Formation in Medieval and Early Modern Eurasia and Middle East*, Wiesbaden: Harrassowitz.

Gresh, Geoffrey F. 2009. 'Iranian Kurds in an Age of Globalisation', *Iran and the Caucasus*, Vol. 13, pp. 187–196.

Grillot-Susini, Francoise. 1998. 'Elam v. Elamite language', in *Encyclopædia Iranica*, Vol. 8, New York: Encyclopædia Iranica Foundation, pp. xx-xx.

Hafezniya, Mohammad-Reza & Kaviyani(rad), Morad. 2006. 'Naqsh-e hoviyyat-e qowmi dar hambastegi-ye melli (motāle'e-ye mowredi-ye qowm-e baluch) [The Role of Ethnic Identity in National Unity (Case Study on the Baluch Ethnic Group)]', *Majale-ye Pazhuheshi-ye dāneshgāh-e esfahān*, Vol. 20, No. 1, pp. 15–46.

Haghayeghi, Mehrdad. 1990. 'Agrarian Reform Problems in Post-Revolutionary Iran', *Middle Eastern Studies*, Vol. 26, No. 1, pp. 35–51.

Hanaway, William. 1993. 'Iranian Identity', *Iranian Studies*, Vol. 26, No. 1–2, (Winter-Spring), pp. 147–150.

Harris, Kevan. Forthcoming. 'A Martyrs' Welfare State and Its Contradictions: Regime Resilience and Limits Through the Lens of Social Policy in Iran', in Heydemann, S. & Leenders, R. (Eds.). Forthcoming: *Middle East Authoritarianisms: Governance, Contestation, and Regime Resilience in Syria and Iran*, pp. 61–80.

Hassan, Hussein D. 2008. 'Iran: Ethnic and Religious Minorities', CRS Report for Congress, Order Code RL34021, Washington: Congressional Research Service.

Hegland, Mary Elaine. 2004. 'Zip In and Zip Out Fieldwork', *Iranian Studies*, Vol. 37, No. 4, (December), pp. 575–583.

Helfgott, Leonard M. 1980. 'The Structural Foundations of the National Minority Problem in Revolutionary Iran', *Iranian Studies*, Vol. 13, No. 1/4, pp. 195–214.

Hersh, Seymour. 2006a. 'The Iran Plans', *The New Yorker* online, www.newyorker.com, April 17.

Hersh, Seymour. 2006b. 'The Next Act', *The New Yorker* online, www.newyorker.com, November 27.

Hersh, Seymour. 2008. 'Preparing the Battlefield', *The New Yorker* online, www.newyorker.com, July 7.

Heydemann, Steven & Leenders, Reinoud. (Ed.). Forthcoming. *Middle East Authoritarianisms: Governance, Contestation, and Regime Resilience in Syria and Iran*, Stanford, CA: Stanford University Press.

Hirschfeld, Lawrence A. 1996. *Race in the Making: Cognition, Culture and the Child's Construction of Human Kinds*, Cambridge, MA: MIT Press.

Hobsbawm, Eric. 1991. *Nations and Nationalism Since 1780: Programme, Myth, Reality*, Cambridge: Cambridge University Press.

Hobsbawm, Eric & Ranger, Terence. (Eds.). 1983. *The Invention of Tradition*, Cambridge: Cambridge University Press.

Holliday, Shabnam. 2007. 'The Politicization of Culture and Contestation of Iranian National Identity in Khatami's Iran', *Studies in Ethnicity and Nationalism*, Vol. 7, No. 1, pp. 27–45.

Hosseinbor, Mohammad Hassan. 1984. *Iran and its Nationalities: The Case of Baluch Nationalism*, PhD Dissertation, Washington, D.C: The American University.

Houleh, Maryam. 2007. 'Jundallah and Terrorism inside the Islamic Republic', in *Gozār* online, www.gozaar.org, August 1.

Hunter, Shirin T. 1992. *Iran after Khomeini*, Santa Barbara: Praeger Paperback.

Hushmand, Ehsan. 2007. 'Qowm-garā'i dar irān-e mo'āser [Ethno-Nationalism in Contemporary Iran]', interview from *For One Iran* online, www.foroneiran.com, March 11.

Hushmand, Ehsan & Kuhshekaf, Nahid. 2004. 'Ravand-e towse'e dar manāteq-e kord-neshin-e irān qabl va pas az enqelāb [The Progress of Development in Kurdish-Inhabited Areas of Iran Before and After the Revolution]', in Ahmadi, H. (Ed.). 2004a: *Irān*, pp. 441–485.

Hushmand, Ehsan & Kuhshekaf, Nahid. 2007. 'Dar-āmadi bar bāz-andishi-ye mafāhim-e qowm, qowmiyyat va aqvām-e irāni [An Introduction to Rethinking the Concepts of Ethnic Group, Ethnicity and Iranian Ethnic Groups]', *Siyāsat-e dākheli*, Vol. 1, No. 3, (Summer), pp. 211–262.

Ittig, A. 1989. 'Baktiāri tribe', in *Encyclopædia Iranica*, Vol. 3, pp. 553–560, New York: Encyclopædia Iranica Foundation.

Izadi, Rajab. 2004. 'Negāhi be yek dahe-ye chālesh bar sar-e hoviyyat-e āzarbāyjān [A Look at One Decade of Contention over the Identity of Azerbaijan]', in Ahmadi H. (Ed.). 2004a: *Irān: Hoviyyat, Melliyyat, Qowmiyyat*, pp. 355–439.

Ja'fari, Karam. 2007. *Qowmiyat-hā va qānun-e asāsi dar irān [Ethnicities and Constitution in Iran]*, Tehran: Entesharat-e Andishe-ye Now.

Jahanbakhsh, Sina. 2008a. 'Moqaddame' (Introduction), in *Günash*, Vol. 5, No. 40, Tehran: University of Science and Technology, pp. 6–7.

Jahanbakhsh, Sina. 2008b. 'Ānche gozasht' (That which happened), in *Günash*, Vol. 5, No. 40, Tehran: University of Science and Technology, pp. 8–77.

Jahani, Carina. 2005. 'State Control and its Impact on Languages in Balochistan', in Rabo, A. & Utas, B. (Eds.). 2005: *The Role of the State in West Asia*, pp. 151–163.

Jenkins, Richard. 2008. *Rethinking Ethnicity: Arguments and Explorations*, 2nd Ed. (1st Ed. 1997), London: SAGE Publications Ltd.

Johanson, Lars & Csató, Éva Ágnes. (Eds.). 1998. *The Turkic Languages*, London: Routledge.

Juergensmeyer, Mark. 1993. *New Cold War? Religious Nationalism Confronts the Secular State*, Berkeley: University of California Press.

Kamrava, Mehran & Dorraj, Manochehr. (Eds.). 2008. *Iran Today: An Encyclopaedia of Life in the Islamic Republic*, Vol. 1, Westport, CT: Greenwood Publishing Group.

Kashani, Manuchehr Aryanpour. 2007. *Farhang-e bozorg-e yek-jeldi-ye pishrow-e āryānpur, fārsi-engilisi* [The Aryanpur Progressive Persian-English Dictionary, One Volume, Concise], Tehran: Nashr-e elektroniki va ettelā'-resāni-ye jahān-e rāyāne.

Kashani-Sabet, Firoozeh. 1999. *Frontier Fictions: Shaping the Iranian Nation, 1804–1946*, New Jersey: Princeton University Press.

Kaufman, Eric P. (Ed.). 2004. *Rethinking Ethnicity: Majority Groups and Dominant Minorities*, London: Routledge.

Kaussler, Bernd. 2007. 'Iran Moves Against PJAK in Northern Iraq', *Terrorism Focus*, Vol. 4, No. 29, www.jamestown.org, September 18.

Kaviyan, Setare & Hosseini, Ruzbeh. 2008. 'Separatists discuss future of Iran', *Marz-e porgohar* online, www.marzeporgohar.org, published October 3, 2008.

Kaviyanirad, Morad. 2007. 'Nāhiye-garā'i-ye siyāsi dar irān: motāle'e-ye mowredi-ye baluchestān [Political Regionalism in Iran: A Case Study on Baluchistan]', *Faslnāme-ye motāle'āt-e rāhbordi*, Vol. 10, No. 1, pp. 89–121.

Kazemi, Farhad. 1988. 'Ethnicity and the Iranian Peasantry', in Esman, M. & Rabinovich, I. (Eds.). 1988: *Ethnicity, Pluralism, and the State*, pp. 201–214.

Keddie, Nikki. 1962. 'Religion and Irreligion in Early Iranian Nationalism', *Comparative Studies in Society and History*, Vol. 4, No. 3, (April), pp. 265–295.

Keddie, Nikki. 1995. *Iran and the Muslim World: Resistance and Revolution*, New York: New York University Press.

Keddie, Nikki. 2006. *Modern Iran: Roots and Results of the Revolution*, Updated Ed. (1st Ed. 1981), New Haven: Yale University Press.

Keddie, Nikki & Matthee, Rudolph P. (Eds.). 2002. *Iran and the Surrounding World: Interactions in Culture and Cultural Politics*, Seattle: University of Washington Press.

Kermanshahi, Kaveh Qasemi. 2008. 'Az esālat tā heqārat: naqdi bar mosāhebe-ye kurosh za'im taht-e 'onvān-e "melliyyat va qowmiyyat" [From Authenticity to Scorn: a Critique of the Interview with Kurosh Zaim Entitled "Nationhood and Ethnicity"]' from *Asr-e Now* webiste (www.asre-nou.net), December 5/Azer 15, 1387.

Khaz'al, Faisal. 2008. 'Arabistan: Fact or Fiction?', paper from SANA (State of Arabistan National Association), US. Available at www.stateofarabistan.org.

Khiabany, Gholam. 2008. 'The Iranian Press, State and Civil Society', in Semati, M. (Ed.). 2008: *Media, Culture and Society in Iran*, pp. 17–36.

Kia, Mehrdad. 1998. 'Persian Nationalism and the Campaign for Language Purification', *Middle Eastern Studies*, Vol. 34, No. 2, (April), pp. 9–36.

Kian, Azadeh & Riaux, Gilles. 2009. 'Crafting Iranian Nationalism: Intersectionality of Aryanism, Westernism and Islamism', in Carvalho, S. & Gemenne, F. (Eds.). 2009: *Nations and their Histories*, pp. 189–203.

Koohi-Kamali, Farideh. 2003. *The Political Development of the Kurds in Iran: Pastoral Nationalism*, New York: Palgrave Macmillan.

Kurzman, Charles. 2005. 'Weaving Iran into the Tree of Nations', *International Journal of Middle Eastern Studies*, Vol. 37, No. 2, pp. 137–166.

Lahsaeizadeh, A., Moghadas, A.A. & Taghavi Nassab, S.M. 2009. 'Bar-resi-ye 'avāmel-e dākheli-ye mo'asar bar hoviyyat-e qowmi va hoviyyat-e melli dar miyān-e a'rāb-e shahrestān-e ahvāz [The Study of Internal Factors Affecting Ethnic and National Identities Among Arab People of Ahwaz]', *Jāme'e-shenāsi-ye kārbordi*, Vol. 33, No. 1, (Spring 1388), pp. 45–70.

L'Estrange, Fawcett Louise. 2009. *Iran and the Cold War: The Azerbaijan Crisis of 1946*, Cambridge: Cambridge University Press.

Limbert, John. 1968. 'The Origins and Appearance of the Kurds in Pre-Islamic Iran', *Iranian Studies*, Vol. 1, No. 2, pp. 41–51.

Lowther, William & Freeman, Colin. 2007. 'US funds terror groups to sow chaos in Iran', *The Telegraph* online, www.telegraph.co.uk, February 25.

Madih, 'Abbas-'Ali. 2007. 'The Kurds of Khorasan', *Iran and the Caucasus*, Vol. 11, No. 1, pp. 11–31.

Mahmudi, Jalil & Sa'idi, Naser. 2002. *Showq-e yek khiz-e boland: nakhostin ettehādiye-hā-ye kārgari dar irān* [The Thrill of a Great Uprising: the First Labour Unions in Iran], Tehran: Nashr-e Qatre.

Malbrunot, Georges. 2012. 'L'Iran défie l'Amérique', *Le Figaro* online, www.lefigaro.fr, January 9.

Malesevic, Sinisa. 2006a. *Identity as Ideology: Understanding Ethnicity and Nationalism*, New York: Palgrave-Macmillan.

Malesevic, Sinisa. 2006b. 'Book Review: Rogers Brubaker, Ethnicity Without Groups', *Nations and Nationalism*, Vol. 12, No. 4, pp. 699–715.

Malesevic, Sinisa. 2011a. 'Ethnicity in Time and Space: A Conceptual Analysis', *Critical Sociology*, Vol. 37, No. 1, pp. 67–82.

Malesevic, Sinisa. 2011b. 'The Chimera of National Identity', *Nations and Nationalism*, Vol. 17, No. 2, pp. 272–290.

Mann, Brian. 2010. 'The Khuzistani Arab Movement, 1941–1946: A Case of Nationalism?' paper presented at the *Rethinking Iranian Nationalism* Conference, Austin, TX.

Maqsudi, Mojtaba. 2001. 'Qowmiyyat-hā va hoviyyat-e farhangi-ye irān [Ethnicities and Iran's Cultural Identity]', *Nāme-ye pazhuhesh*, No. 22–23, (Fall & Winter), pp. 209–232.

Maqsudi, Mojtaba. 2003. *Qowmiyyat-hā va naqsh-e ānān dar tahavvolāt-e siyāsi-ye saltanat-e mohammad-rezā pahlavi* [*Ethnicities and their Role in the Political Developments Under Mohammad-Reza Pahlavi's Monarchy*], Tehran: Markaz-e asnad-e enqelab-e eslami.

Maqsudi, Mojtaba. 2006. 'Moshārekat-e entekhābāti-ye aqvām dar irān; bar-resi-ye mowredi: entekhābāt-e riyāsat-e jomhuri' [Electory Participation of Ethnic Groups in Iran; Case Study: Presidential Elections]', *Faslnāme-ye motāle'āt-e melli*, Vol. 7, No. 4, pp. 83–108.

Marashi, Afshin. 2008. *Nationalizing Iran. Culture, Power, & The State, 1870–1940*, Seattle: University of Washington Press.

Marx, Anthony W. 2005. *Faith in Nation: Exclusionary Origins of Nationalism*, New York: Oxford University Press.

Mashayekhi, Mehrdad. 1993. 'The Politics of Nationalism', in Farsoun, S.K. & Mashayekhi, M. (Eds.). 1993: *Iran*, pp. 56–79.

Matin-asgari, Afshin. 1995. 'Reviewed work(s): Iran as Imagined Nation: The Construction of National Identity by Mostafa Vaziri', *Iranian Studies*, Vol. 28, No. 3/4, pp. 260–263.

May, Stephen. 2008. *Language and Minority Rights: Ethnicity, Nationalism and the Politics of Language*, London: Routledge.

McDowall, David. 2004. *A Modern History of the Kurds*, 3rd Ed. (1st Ed. 1996), London/New York: I. B. Tauris.

Mehran, Golnar. 2002. 'The Presentation of "Self" and "Other" in Postrevolutionary Iranian School Textbooks', in Keddie, N.R. & Mathee, R.P. (Eds.). 2002: *Iran and the Surrounding World*, pp. 232–253.

Menashri, David. 1988. 'Khomeini's Policy Toward Ethnic and Religious Minorities', in Esman, M. & Rabinovich, I. (Eds.). 1988: *Ethnicity, Pluralism, and the State*, pp. 201–214.

Menashri, David (Ed.). 1990. *The Iranian Revolution and the Muslim World*, Boulder, CO: Westview Press.

Menashri, David. 2001. *Post-Revolutionary Politics in Iran: Religion, Society and Power*, London/Portland: Frank Cass Publishers.

Meskoub, Shahrokh. 2008. *Hoviyyat-e irāni va zabān-e fārsi* [*Iranian Identity and the Persian Language*], 4th Ed. (1st Ed. 1999), Tehran: Farzān.

Mihelj, Sabina. 2007. ' "Faith in Nation Comes in Different Guises": Modernist Versions of Religious Nationalism', *Nations and Nationalism*, Vol. 2, No. 2, pp. 265–284.

Mir-Mohammadi, Davud (Ed.). 2004. *Goftār-hā'i darbāre-ye hoviyyat-e melli dar irān* [*Narratives on National Identity in Iran*], Tehran: Mo'asase-ye motāle'āt-e melli.

Moaddel, Mansoor. 2005. *Islamic Modernism, Nationalism, and Fundamentalism: Episode and Discourse*, Chicago: University of Chicago Press.

Mo'azzampur, Esma'il. 2004. *Naqd va bar-resi-ye nāsioynālism-e tajaddod-khāh dar 'asr-e rezā shāh* [*Critique and Evaluation of Modernist Nationalism in the Age of Reza Shah*], Tehran: Markaz-e asnād-e enqelāb-e eslāmi.

Moin, Baqer. 1999. *Khomeini: Life of the Ayatollah*, London: IB Tauris.

Mojab, Shahrzad & Hassanpour, Amir. 1995. 'The Politics of Nationality and Ethnic Diversity', in Rahnema, S. & Behdad, S. (Eds.). 1995: *Iran after the Revolution*, pp. 229–250.

Moradbeigi, Hossein. 2004. *Tārikh-e zende: Kordestān, chap va nāsiyonālism* [*Living History: Kurdistan, the Left and Nationalism*], Stockholm: Nasim.

Morshedizad, Ali. 2001. *Rowshanfekrān-e āzari va hoviyyat-e melli va qowmi* [*Azeri Intellectuals and National and Ethnic Identity*], Tehran: Nashr-e Markaz.

Motallebi, Masud. 2008. 'Joghrāfiyā-ye siyāsi-ye aqvām-e irāni [The Political Geography of Iran's Ethnic Groups]', in *Zamāne*, online version (www.zamaneh.info), No. 70, nd.

Musavi, Mir-Hossein. 2009. 'Bayāniye-ye mir-hosein musavi dar mowred-e aqvām-e irāni', May 17.

Nabavi, Negin (Ed.). 2012. *Iran: From Theocracy to the Green Movement*, New York: Palgrave-Macmillan.

Nabavi, Seyyed Abd-ol-Amir. 2004. Khuzestān va chālesh-hā-ye qowm-garāyāne [*Khuzestan and Ethnicist Conflicts*], in Ahmadi, H. (Ed.). 2004a: *Irān*, pp. 487–530.

Nadjmabadi, Shahnaz (Ed.). 2009. *Conceptualizing Iranian Anthropology. Past and Present Perspectives*, New York/Oxford: Berghahn Books.

Nassaj, Hamid. 2009. 'Jahāni-shodan va hoviyat-e aqvām-e irāni. Bā ta'kid bar mo'alefe-hā-ye zabān va ādāb va rosum [Globalization and the Identity of Iranian Ethnic Groups: With an Emphasis on the Language and Traditions Factors]', *Pazhuhesh-e siyāsat-e nazari*, (Summer and Spring), No. 5, pp. 129–156.

Natali, Denise. 2005. *The Kurds and the State: Evolving National Identity in Iraq, Turkey and Iran*, Syracuse: Syracuse University Press.

Nateq, Naseh. 1980. *Zabān-e āzarbāyjān va vahdat-e melli-ye irān* [*The Language of Azerbaijan and Iran's National Unity*], Tehran: Enteshārāt-e bonyād-e mowqufāt-e doktor mahmud afshār.

Navah, 'Abd-ol-Reza & Taqavi-Nasab, Mojtaba. 2006. 'Qowm-e 'arab; vā-garā'i yā ham-garā'i [The Arab Ethnic Group: Reaction or Cooperation]', *Faslnāme-ye dāneshgāh-e āzād-e eslāmi vāhed-e shushtar*, Vol. 1, No. 2, pp. 19–48.

Nazmi-Afshar, Alireza Amir. 2005. 'South Azerbaijan and Iranian Turks', April 19, report, Washington, DC: the Center for Strategic International Studies.

Nissman, David. 1987. *The Soviet Union and Iranian Azerbaijan: The Use of Nationalism for Political Penetration*, Boulder, CO: Westview Press.

Nurbakhsh, Yunes. 2008. 'Farhang va qowmiyat: modeli barā-ye ertebātāt-e farhangi dar irān [Culture and Ethnicity: A Model for Cultural Communication in Iran]', *Tahqiqāt-e farhangi*, Vol. 1, No. 4, pp. 67–78.

Oberling, Pierre. 1999. 'Fārs vii. Ethnography', in *Encyclpædia Iranica*, Vol. 9, pp. 360–362, New York: Encyclopædia Iranica Foundation.

Oberling, Pierre & Hourcade, Bernard. 1986. 'Arab iv. Arab Tribes of Iran', in *Encyclopædia Iranica*, Vol. 2, pp. 215–220, New York: Encyclopædia Iranica Foundation.

Olson, Robert. 2002. 'The "Azeri" Question and Turkey-Iran Relations, 2000–2002', *Nationalism and Ethnic Politics*, Vol. 8, No. 4, pp. 61–85.

Oppel, Richard A. Jr. 2007. 'Kurdish militants' other front: Iran', *The New York Times* online, www.nytimes.com, October 22.

Pak, Mohammad-Reza Khobruye. 1998. *Naqdi bar federālism [A critique of federalism]*, Tehran: Mo'asase-ye Nashr-e Pazhuhesh-e Shirazeh.

Pak, Mohammad-Reza Khobruye. 2004. 'Nokhbegān-e mahali, jahāni-sāzi va ro'yā-ye federālism [Local Elites, Globalization and the Dream of Federalism]', in Ahmadi, H. (Ed.). 2004a: *Irān*, pp. 171–188.

Pak, Mohammad-Reza Khobruye. 2007a. 'Sokhanrāni pirāmun-e qowm va qowmiyyat, mowqe'iyyat-e kolli-ye aqvām dar irān, pishine-ye tārikhi-ye keshvar-dāri dar irān [A Speech on Ethnic Groups and Ethnicity, the General Situation of Ethnic Groups in Iran, the History of Administering a Country in Iran]' from *Talāsh* online, www.talash-online. com, March 27.

Pak, Mohammad-Reza Khobruye. 2007b. 'Hefz-e yegānegi-ye melli va chandgunegi-ye qowmi [The Preservation of National Unity and Ethnic Diversity]' from *Talāsh* online, www. talash-online.com, July 31.

Pak, Mohammad-Reza Khobruye. 2009. 'Dar irān, qowmi be nām-e qowm-e irāni vojud nadārad' [In Iran, there is no ethnic group called the Iranian ethnic group], from *Talāsh* online, www.talash-online.com, May 29.

Parsi, Rouzbeh. 2009. *In Search of Caravans Lost: Iranian Intellectuals and Nationalist Discourse in the Interwar Years*, Lund: Department of History, Lund University.

Parsi, Trita. 2008. *Treacherous Alliance: The Secret Dealings of Israel, Iran and the United States*, New Haven: Yale University Press.

Paul, Ludwig. 1999. ' "Iranian Nation" and Iranian-Islamic Revolutionary Ideology', *Die Welt des Islams*, Vol. 39, No. 2, pp. 183–217.

Paul, Ludwig. 2008. 'Kurdish Language i. History of the Kurdish Language', in *Encyclopædia Iranica*, Online Ed. (www.iranica.com), December 15.

Paul, Ludwig. 2010. 'Iranian Language Reform in the Twentieth Century: Did the First Farhangestān (1935–40) Succeed?' *Journal of Persianate Studies*, Vol. 3, pp. 78–103.

Payedar, Said. 2008. 'Rāh-e rahā'i az kābus va do-gānegi / Naqdi bar mosāhebe-ye mohandes za'im' [Ways to escape nightmare and schizophrenia / A critique of the interview with Engineer Zaim] from *Advār News* website (www.advarnews.us), November 6 / Aban 16, 1387.

Perry, John. 2009. 'Tajik i. The Ethnonym: Origins and Application', in *Encyclopædia Iranica*, Online Ed. (www.iranica.com), July 20.

Perry, Mark. 2012. 'False Flag', *Foreign Policy* online, www.foreignpolicy.com, January 13.

Peters, Ralph. 2006. 'Blood Borders: How a better Middle East would look', in *Armed Forces Journal*, Online Ed. (www.armedforcesjournal.com), June.

Piran, Parviz. 2000. *Poverty Alleviation in Sistan & Baluchestan. The Case of Shirabad*, Tehran: United Nations Development Programme in the Islamic Republic of Iran.

Price, Massoume. 2005. *Iran's Diverse Peoples: A Reference Sourcebook*, Santa Barbara: ABC Clio.

Purjavadi, Nasrollah. 1992. 'Ta'dod-e aqvām va vahdat-e mellat [Plurality of Ethnic Groups and the Unity of the Nation]', *Nashr-e dānesh*, No. 4, May-August/Khordad-Tir, 1371.

Purkazem, Hajj Kazem. 2006. *Jāme'e-shenāsi-ye qabāyel-e 'arab-e khuzestān. Tahqiqi pirāmun-e ādāb va rosum va farhang-e jāme'e* [*The Sociology of the Tribes of Khuzestan's Arabs. A Study in Traditions, Customs and Culture*], Tehran: Nashr-e Ame.

Qamari, Dariyush (Ed.). 2005. *Hambastegi-ye melli dar irān* [*National Unity in Iran*], Tehran: Entesharat-e Tamaddon-e Irani.

Qamari, Mohammad-Reza. 2006. 'Naqsh-e zabān dar ta'min-e amniyyat-e melli [The Role of Language in Safeguarding National Security]', *Faslnāme-ye dānesh-e entezāmi*, Vol. 8, No. 4, pp. 94–107.

Qayem, 'Abdolnabi. 2005. 'Negāhi jāme'e-shenākhti be zendegi va farhang-e mardom-e 'arab-e khuzestān [A Sociological View on the Life and Culture of the Arab People of Khuzestan]', in Godarzi, H. (Ed.). 2005a: *Goftār-hā'i darbāre-ye jāme'e-shenāsi-ye hoviyyat dar irān* [*Narratives on the Sociology of Identity in Iran*], pp. 59–76.

Rabo, Annika & Utas, Bo (Eds.). 2005. *The Role of States in West Asia*, Istanbul: Swedish Research Institute.

Rabihe, Khaled 'Abbasi. (nd.): 'E'terāz-e nemāyande-ye khafājiye (dasht-e āzādegān) be mosādere-ye zamin-hā-ye bumiyān-e 'arab-e khuzestān' from *Azadegy* (website), www.azadegy.de, no date.

Rahimirad, Mohammad-Reza. 2006. 'Mas'ale'i be nām-e qowmiyyat-hā; goftogu-ye majid tavallā'i, kurosh za'im va 'abbās 'abdi [An Issue Called Ethnicities: Interview with Majid Tavalla'i, Kurosh Za'im and Abbas Abdi]', *Name*, No. 48, *Farvardin 1385*.

Rahmani, Arash. 2008. ' 'Asabāniyyat-e qowm-garāyān az mosāhebe-ye mohandes za'im/pāsokhi be naqd-hā-ye montasher-shode pirāmun-e goftogu-ye kurosh za'im bā advār news [The ethnicists' anger over an interview with Engineer Zaim/An answer to the published criticisms of Kurosh Zaim's interview with Advar News]' from *Advār News* website (www.advarnews.us), November 8/Aban 18, 1387.

Rahnema, Saeed & Behdad, Sohrab. (Eds.). 1995. Iran after the Revolution: Crisis of an Islamic State, London/New York: I. B. Tauris.

Ra'is-Tusi, Reza. 2006. *Sarzamin-e sukhte: diplomāsi-ye britāniyā dar sistān* [*Burned Soil: Britain's Diplomacy in Sistan*], Tehran: Gām-e Now.

Ram, Haggai. 2009. *Iranophobia: The Logic of an Iranian Obsession*, Palo Alto: Stanford University Press.

Ramezanzadeh, Abdollah. 1996. *Internal and International Dynamics of Ethnic Conflict: the Case of Iran*, Doctoral Thesis, Leuven: Katholieke Universiteit.

Ravasani, Shapour. 2004. 'Ta'āmol-e farhang va hoviyyat-e melli [Thoughts on culture and national identity]', interview in Mir-Mohammadi, D. (Ed.). 2004: *Goftār-hā'i darbāre-ye hoviyyat-e melli dar irān*, pp. 109–149.

Razmi, Moshollah. 2000. *Āzarbāyjān va jonbesh-e tarafdārān-e shari'atmadāri dar sāl-e 1357* [Azerbaijan and Shari'atmadari's Supporters' Movement in 1978–9], Stockholm: Teribun.

Reza, Enayatollah. 2006. *Āzarbāyjān va arrān*, 3rd Ed., Tehran: Nashr-e hezār kermān.

Reza'i, Mohammad & Kazemi, 'Abbas. 2008. 'Bāznamā'i-ye aqaliyyat-hā-ye qowmi dar seriyāl-hā-ye televizyoni', *Tahqiqāt-e farhangi*, Vol. 1, No. 4, pp. 78–91.

Rezakhani, Khodadad. 2003. 'Fārs-garā'i va bohrān-e qowmi dar irān: negāhi be pishine-ye tārikh-negāri-ye irāni', unpublished paper.

Riaux, Gilles. 2008. 'The Formative Years of Azerbaijani Nationalism in Post-Revolutionary Iran', *Central Asian Survey*, Vol. 27, No. 1, pp. 45–58.

Ross, Brian & Isham, Christopher. 2007. 'The Secret War Against Iran', ABC News Investigative Unit, www.abcnews.go.com, April 3.

Saad, Joya Blondel. 1996. *The Image of Arabs in Modern Persian Literature*, Lanham: University Press of America.

Sabbaghpur, Ali-Asghar. 2002. 'Jahāni-shodan, hākemiyat-e melli va tanavvo'-e qowmi dar irān [Globalization, National Sovereignty and Ethnic Diversity in Iran]', *Motāle'āt-e melli*, Vol. 3, No. 11, pp. 143–161.

Sadr (ol-Ashrafi), Zia'. 1998. *Kesrat-e qowmi va hoviyyat-e melli-ye irāniyān* [Ethnic Diversity and the National Identity of Iranians], Tehran: Andishe-ye now.

Salehi-Amiri, Seyyed Reza. 2006. *Modiriyyat-e monāze'āt-e qowmi dar irān: naqd va bar-rasi-ye olgu-hā-ye mowjud va erā'e-ye olgu-ye matlub* [*Ethnic Conflict Management in Iran: Critique and Analysis of Existing Models and Presentation of Ideal Model*], Tehran: Majma'-e tashkhis-e maslahat-e nezam, Markaz-e tahqiqat-e esteratezhik.

Samii, A. William. 2000. 'The Nation and Its Minorities: Ethnicity, Unity and State Policy in Iran', *Comparative Studies of South Asia, Africa and the Middle East*, Vol. 20, No. 1–2, pp. 128–142.

Samii, A. William. 2005. 'Iran: Ethnic Politics Out of Bounds', RFE/RL Website, www.rferl. org, March 31, 2005.

Sanasarian, Eliz. 2000. *Religious Minorities in Iran*, Cambridge Middle East Studies, Cambridge: Cambridge University Press.

Sarajzade, Seyyed Hosein & Adhami, Jamal. 2008. 'Bar-rasi-ye tafāvot-hā-ye qowmiyati-ye dāneshjuyān az nazar-e fa'āliyat dar kānun-hā-ye farhangi-ye dāneshgāh-hā', *Faslnāme-ye tahqiqāt-e farhangi*, Vol. 1, No. 2, pp. 135–157.

Savalanli, Aslan. 2008. 'Ta'moli bar goftogu-ye advār news bā kurosh za'im dar mowred-e melliyyat va qowmiyyat dar irān [Reflection on Advar News' interview with Kurosh Zaim about nationality and ethnicity in Iran]' from *Dirānish* website (www.diranish.org).

Saveli, Solmaz. 2008. 'Bar-rasi-ye mavāze'-e goruh-hā-ye siyāsi-ye markaz-garā [An Examination of the Views of the Centralistic Political Groups]', *Günash*, Vol. 5, No. 40, pp. 124–145.

Semati, Mehdi. (Ed.). 2008. *Media, Culture and Society in Iran: Living with Globalization and the Islamic State*, Oxon/New York: Routledge.

Seyyed-Emami, Kavus. 2004. 'Naqsh-e zabān va adabiyyāt-e fārsi dar shekl-giri-ye hoviyyat-e melli' [The role of Persian language and literature in the formation of national identity], interview in Mir-Mohammadi, D. (Ed.). 2004: *Goftār-hā'i darbāre-ye hoviyyat-e melli dar irān*, pp. 161–170.

Seyyed-Emami, Kavus. 2008. 'Edrāk-e goruh-hā-ye qowmi az tasāvir-e resāne'i-ye khod [Ethnic Groups' Perception of their Representations in Media]', *Tahqiqāt-e farhangi*, Vol. 1, No. 4, pp. 78–119.

Seyyed-Sa'idi, Farzane. 2005. 'Jenāh-hā-ye dākheli barā-ye kasb-e ārā '-e bishtar be bahs-e qowmiyyat va tazād-hā dāmen zadeand [Domestic factions are abusing the discussion about ethnicity and difference to gain more votes]', interview with Hamid Ahmadi from *Sinā* News Agency via *Gooya* website (http://news.gooya.com), April 19/Farvardin 30, 1384.

Shabani, Maryam. 2006. 'Moruri bar 28 sāl-e qowm-garā'i dar irān [A Review of 28 Years of Ethno-Nationalism in Iran]', *Nāme*, No. 52, (July-August/Mordād 1385).

Shaffer, Brenda. 2002. *Borders and Brethren: Iran and the Challenge of Azerbaijani Identity*, Cambridge, MA: The MIT Press.

Shahbazi, Mohammad. 2009. 'Past Experiences and Future Perspectives of an Indigeneous Anthropologist on Anthropological Work in Iran', in Nadjmabadi, S.R. (Ed.). 2009: *Conceptualizing Iranian Anthropology*, pp. 143–156.

Shahidi, Hossein. 2007. *Journalism in Iran: From mission to profession*, Oxon/New York: Routledge.

Shahshahani, Soheila. 1986. 'History of Anthropology in Iran', *Iranian Studies*, Vol. 19, pp. 65–87.

Shahshahani, Soheila. 2009. 'Iranian Anthropologists are Women', in Nadjmabadi, S.R. (Ed.). 2009: *Conceptualizing Iranian Anthropology*, pp. 116–132.

Shatzmiller, Maya. (Ed.). 2005. *Nationalism and Minority Identities in Islamic Societies*, Montreal: McGill-Queen's University Press.

Shaykhi, Shahaboddin. 2010. 'Bar-resi-ye jonbesh-e sabz va vaz'iyyat-e aqvām-e irāni [An Analysis of the Green Movement and the Condition of Iranian Ethnic Groups]' from *Gozaar* website (http://gozaar.org), July 13.

Sheikhavandi, Davar. 2005. 'Osture-ye nowruz: namād-e hambastegi-ye melli-ye aqvām-e irāni [The Nowruz Mythos: Symbol of Iranian Ethnic Groups' National Unity]', in Qamari, D. (Ed.). 2005: *Hambastegi-ye melli dar irān*, pp. 61–70.

Shoup, John A. 2011. *Ethnic Groups of Africa and the Middle East: an Encyclopedia*, Santa Barbara, CA: ABC-CLIO.

Slavin, Barbara. 2007. *Bitter Friends, Bosom Enemies: Iran, the US and the Twisted Path to Confrontation*, New York: St. Martin's Press.

Smith, Anthony D. 2003. *Chosen Peoples: Sacred Sources of National Identity*, Oxford: Oxford University Press.

Smith, Anthony D. 2009. *Ethno-Symbolism and Nationalism: A Cultural Approach*, London & New York: Routledge.

Soghdi, Amineh. 2010. 'Baluch Celebrate Rebel's Arrest', in *Institute for War and Peace Reporting*, http://iwpr.net, March 10.

Soucek, Svat. 1984. 'Arabistan or Khuzistan', *Iranian Studies*, Vol. 17, No. 2–3, (Spring-Summer), pp. 195–213.

Spooner, Brian. 1985. 'Anthropology', *Encyclopaedia Iranica*, Vol. 2, No. 1–2, pp. 107–116.

Spooner, Brian. 1988. 'Baluchistan i. Geography, History and Ethnography', in *Encyclopædia Iranica*, Vol. 3, New York: Encyclopædia Iranica Foundation.

Spooner, Brian. 1998. 'Ethnography', *Encyclopædia Iranica*, Vol. 4, No. 1, pp. 9–28.

Stokes, Jamie (Ed.). 2009. *Encyclopedia of the Peoples of Africa and the Middle East*, New York: Facts on File.

Strunk, William Theodore. 1977. *The Reign of Shaykh Khaz'al Ibn Jābir and the Suppression of the Principality of 'Arabistān: A Study in British Imperialism in Southwestern Iran, 1897–1925*, unpublished PhD dissertation, Indianapolis: Indiana University.

Sultan-Qurraie, Hadi. 2008. 'Baluchis and Baluchistan', in Kamrava, M. & Dorraj, M. (Eds.). 2008: *Iran Today*, pp. 63–65.

Swietochowski, Tadeusz. 1995. *Russia and Azerbaijan: A Borderland in Transition*, New York: Columbia University Press.

Tabrizi, Boyuk. 2009. 'Cherā nemitavānam be zabān-e mādari'am dars bekhānam? [Why can't I study in my mother tongue?]' from *Akhbār-e ruz* website (www.akhbar-rooz.com), February 21/Esfand 2, 1387.

Tabrizli, Okhtay. 2008. 'Negāhi be ruydād-hā-ye khordād-māh-e 1385-e āzarbāyjān (1) [A Look at the Events in May 2006 in Azerbaijan, Part One]', *Günash*, Vol. 5, No. 40, pp. 156–164.

Tapper, Richard. (Ed.). 1983. *The Conflict of State and Tribe in Iran and Afghanistan*, New York: St. Martin's Press.

Tapper, Richard. 1988. 'Ethnicity, Order and Meaning in the Anthropology of Iran and Afghanistan', in Digard, J-P. (Ed.). 1988: *Le Fait Ethnique en Iran et en Afghanistan*, pp. 21–34.

Tapper, Richard. 1997. *Frontier Nomads of Iran: A Political and Social History of the Shahsevan*, Cambridge: Cambridge University Press.

Tapper, Richard. 1998. 'What is this Thing Called "Ethnography"?' *Iranian Studies*, Vol. 31, No. 3/4, pp. 389–398.

Tapper, Richard. 2008a. 'Who are the Kuchi? Nomad Self-identities in Afghanistan', *JRAI. Journal of the Royal Anthropological Institute*, Vol. 14, pp. 97–116.

Tapper, Richard. 2008b. 'Local-Level Constructions of "Turk" and "Persian" ', in Djalili, M-R., Monsutti, A. & Neubauer, A. (Eds.). 2008: *Le Monde Turco-Iranien*, pp. 69–80.

Tapper, Richard. 2009. 'Personal Reflections on Anthropology of and in Iran', in Nadjmabadi, S.R. (Ed.). 2009: *Conceptualizing Iranian Anthropology*, pp. 225–241.

Tavakoli-Targhi, Mohamad. 1994. 'Review: Iran as Imagined Nation: The Construction of National Identity by Mostafa Vaziri', *International Journal of Middle Eastern Studies*, Vol. 26, No. 2, (May), pp. 316–318.

Tavakoli-Targhi, Mohamad. 2001. *Refashioning Iran: Orientalism, Occidentalism and Historiography*, New York: Palgrave.

Tohidi, Nayereh. 2009. 'Ethnicity and Religious Minority Politics in Iran', Gheissari, A. (Ed.). *Contemporary Iran*, pp. 299–323.

Toyserkani, Yahya Fowzi. 2006. *Emām khomeini va hovviyyat-e melli* [*Imam Khomeini and National Identity*], Tehran: Markaz-e asnād-e enqelāb-e eslāmi.

Vahabzadeh, Peyman. 2011. 'Secularism and the Militant Left: Political Misconception or Cultural Issues?' *Comparative Studies of South Asia, Africa and the Middle East*, Vol. 31, No. 1, pp. 85–93.

Vali, Abbas. 2011. *Kurds and the State in Iran: The Making of Kurdish Identity*, London: I. B. Tauris.

Van Bruinessen, Martin. 1983. 'Kurdish Tribes and the State of Iran: The Case of Simko's Revolt', Tapper, R. (Ed.). 1983: *The Conflict of State and Tribe*, pp. 364–400.

Van Bruinessen, Martin. 1991. *Agha, Shaikh and Khan: Social and Political Structures of Kurdistan*, London: Zed Books.

van der Veer, Peter. 1994. *Religious Nationalism: Hindus and Muslims in India*, Berkeley: University of California Press.

Varjavand, Parviz. 2000. 'Nāme-ye varjāvand be khātami [Varjavand's letter to Khatami]', dated October 3, replicated on www.azdemokrasi.wordpress.com.

Vatanka, Alex & Aman, Fatemeh. 2006. 'The Making of an Insurgency in Iran's Balochistan province', *Jane's*, May 19.

Vaziri, Mostafa. 1994. *Iran as Imagined Nation*, New York: Marlowe & Co.

Windfuhr, Gernot (Ed.). 2009. *The Iranian Languages*, London/New York: Routledge.

Yar-Shater, Ehsan. 1993. 'Persian Identity in Historical Perspective', *Iranian Studies*, Vol. 26, No. 1/2, (Winter-Spring), pp. 141–142.

Yildiz, Kerim & Taysi, Tanyel B. 2007. *The Kurds in Iran: The Past, Present and Future*, London/Ann Arbor, MA: Pluto Press.

Young, C. (Ed.). 1993. *The Rising Tide of Cultural Pluralism*, Madison: University of Wisconsin Press.

Yusefi, Ali. 2005. 'Ravābet-e beyn-e qowmi va ta'sir-e ān bar hoviyyat-e aqvām dar irān [Inter-Ethnic Relations and their Impact on the Identity of Ethnic Groups in Iran]', in Qamari, D. (Ed.). 2005: *Hambastegi-ye melli dar irān*, pp. 186–209.

Zambelis, Chris. 2006. 'Violence and Rebellion in Iranian Balochistan', *Terrorism Monitor*, Vol. 4, No. 13, June 29.

Zambelis, Chris. 2008. 'Insurrection in Iranian Balochistan', *Terrorism Monitor*, Vol. 6, No. 1, January.

Zambelis, Chris. 2011. 'The Factors Behind Rebellion in Iranian Kurdistan', *CTC Sentinel*, www.ctc.usma.edu, March 1.

Zia-Ebrahimi, Reza. 2011a. The Emergence of Iranian Nationalism: Modernity and the Politics of Dislocation 1860–1940, DPhil thesis (to be published under a different title in 2013), Oxford: University of Oxford.

Zia-Ebrahmi, Reza. 2011b. 'Self-Orientalization and Dislocation: The Uses and Abuses of the "Aryan" Discourse in Iran', *Iranian Studies*, Vol. 44, No. 4, pp. 445–472.

Zubaida, Sami. 2004. 'Islam and Nationalism: Continuities and Contradictions', *Nations and Nationalism*, Vol. 10, No. 4, pp. 407–420.

MEDIA ARTICLES (NO AUTHOR)

Advar (News Website). 2008. 'Sodur-e ahkām-e sangin barā-ye fa'ālān-e qowmi-ye āzarbāyjān [Heavy sentences for ethnic activists in Azerbaijan]', www.advarnews.us, June 10/Khordad 21, 1387.

AdvarNews. 2009. 'Bayāniye-ye mehdi karubi dar mowred-e hoquq-e aqvām va aqaliyat-hā-ye mazhabi [Mehdi Karubi's statement regarding the rights of ethnic groups and religious minorities]', http://advarnews.biz, May 9.

AFP (Online). 2008. 'Iran says Pakistan hands over four rebels', www.afp.com, June 14.

Aftab (News Website). 2005. 'Qatl-e yek ma'mur dar mahābād [The killing of an officer in Mahabad]', www.aftabnews.ir, July 18/27 Tir, 1384.

Aftab. 2006a. 'Modir-mas'ul-e ruznāme-ye irān: do nowbat 'ozr-khāhi kardim [The editor-in-chief of Irān: "We have apologized twice"]', www.aftabnews.ir, May 18/Ordibehesht 28, 1385.

Aftab. 2006b. 'Goft-o-gu bā nemāyandegān darbāre-ye havādes-e āzarbāyjān [Interview with MPs on the events in Azerbaijan]', www.aftabnews.ir, June 3/Khordad 13, 1385.

Aftab. 2007. 'Nā-amni bā dekhālat-e āshkār-e 3 keshvar, ettelā'āt-e jadid az hamle be otobus-e sepāh [Destabilization with the obvious interference of three countries; new information about the attack on (the Revolutionary) Guard's bus]', www.aftabnews.ir, February 17/Bahman 28, 1385.

Akhbar-e Rooz. 2011. 'Ākharin gozāresh-hā az nā-ārāmi dar ahvāz', www.akhbar-rooz.com, April 16.

Asr-e Iran. 2010. 'Firuzābādi: ezhārāt-e mashā 'i jorm 'aleyh-e amniyyat-e melli ast [Firuzabadi: "Masha'i's statements constitute a crime against national security"]', www.asriran.com, August 10, 2010.

Azadtribun (Website). 2004. '80 darsad-e kudakān-e dasht-e āzādegān az su'-e taghziye ranj mi-barand [80% of the children in Dasht-e Azadegan is suffering from malnutrition]', www.azadtribun.net, nd.

Baztab (News Website). 2005a. 'Dah-hā koshte va majruh dar dargiri-hā-ye qowmi dar ahvāz [Tens killed and injured in ethnic clashes in Ahvaz]', www.baztab.ir, April 16/27 Farvardin, 1384.

Baztab. 2005b. ' "Al-jazire": az māh-e 'asal bā eslāh-talabān tā bolandgu-ye ekhtesāsi-ye tajziye-talabān [Al-Jazeera: From honeymoon with reformists to special loudspeaker for separatists]', www.baztab.ir, April 18/29 Farvardin, 1384.

Baztab. 2005c. 'Ākharin gozāresh-hā az nā-ārāmi dar ahvāz [Latest report on the unrest in Ahvaz]', www.baztab.ir, April 16/27 Farvardin, 1384.

Baztab. 2005d. 'Kālbodshekāfi-ye nā-ārāmi dar khuzestān [Autopsy of unrest in Khuzestan]', www.baztab.ir, April 24/4 Ordibehesht, 1384.

Baztab. 2005e. 'Qatl-e mashkuk barā-ye gostaresh-e bohrān dar oshnaviye [A suspicious murder aimed at deepening crisis in Oshnaviye]', www.baztab.ir, July 26/4 Mordād, 1384.

Baztab. 2005f. 'Dargiri-ye khunin bā pezhāk dar ertefā'āt-e pirānshahr [Bloody clashes with PJAK in the heights of Piranshahr]', www.baztab.ir, July 27/5 Mordād, 1384.

Baztab. 2005g. 'Oriyān kardan-e mardom, ākharin shive-ye tahrik 'aleyh-e jomhuri-ye eslāmi [To strip people naked: the latest tactic of provocation against the Islamic Republic]', www.baztab.ir, July 28/6 Mordād, 1384.

Baztab. 2005h. 'Posht-e parde-ye taharokāt-e akhir-e goruh-e tajziye-talab dar shomāl-e gharbi-ye irān [Behind the scenes of recent actions by separatists in Northwestern Iran]', www.baztab.ir, July 28/6 Mordād, 1384.

Baztab. 2005i. 'Nā-ārāmi, in bār dar saqqez [Unrest, this time in Saqqez]', www.baztab.ir, August 3/12 Mordād, 1384.

Baztab. 2006b. 'Nā-ārāmi-hā 'aleyh-e kārikātur be orumiye keshide shod [Unrest over caricature spreads to Orumiye]', www.baztab.com, May 23/2 Khordad, 1385.

Baztab. 2006c. 'Nā-gofte-hā-ye nā-ārāmi-hā-ye ruz-e gozashte dar tabriz [Untold stories about yesterday's unrest in Tabriz]', www.baztab.com, May 23/2 Khordad, 1385.

Baztab. 2007. 'Vorud-e showrā-ye amniyyat be bombgozāri-hā-ye zāhedān, be naf'-e irān yā āmrikā?! [The entry of the Security Council into (the case of) the Zahedan bombings: In the interest of Iran or the US?]', www.baztab.com, February 17/Bahman 28, 1385.

BBC Persian (News Website). 2005a. 'Bar-khord bā kord-hā-ye irāni ke riyāsat-e jomhuri-ye tālebāni-rā jashn gereftand [Confrontation with Iranian Kurds who celeberated Talibani's presidency]', www.bbc.co.uk/persian, April 7.

BBC Persian. 2005b. 'Ettehām-e naqsh dāshtan-e beritāniyā dar nā-ārāmi-hā-ye akhir-e khuzestān [Britain accused of having a role in recent unrest in Khuzestan]', www.bbc.co.uk/persian, April 25.

BBC Persian. 2005c. 'Jashn-e kord-hā-ye irāni be khoshunat keshide shod [Iranian Kurds' celebrations turns into violence]', www.bbc.co.uk/persian, June 15.

BBC Persian. 2005d. 'Nā-ārāmi-hā dar mahābād edāme dārad [Unrest continues in Mahabad]', www.bbc.co.uk/persian, July 17.

BBC Persian. 2005e. 'Vezārat-e keshvar darbāre-ye khoshunat-hā-ye mahābād tahqiq mikonad [Interior Ministry is investigating Mahabad violence]', www.bbc.co.uk/persian, July 19.

BBC Persian. 2006a. 'Mohājemān-e mosallah dar jāde-ye zāhedān dast-e kam 21 nafar-rā koshtand [Armed attackers have killed at least 21 persons on the Zahedan road]', www.bbc.co.uk/persian, March 17.

BBC Persian. 2006b. 'Enteshār-e joz'iyāti tāze az hamle-ye mosallahāne dar jāde-ye zābol-zāhedān [Publication of new details on the armed attack on the Zabol-Zahedan road]', www.bbc.co.uk/persian, March 18.

BBC Persian. 2006c. 'Edāme-ye nā-amni dar sistān va baluchestān va tadābir-e tāze dar irān [Continuing insecurity in Sistan-Baluchestan and new measures in Iran]', www.bbc.co.uk/persian, April 9.

BBC Persian. 2006d. 'Dalāyel-e nā-ārāmi dar tabriz: rishe-hā-ye qowmi yā en'ekās-e nā-rezā'i-ye 'omumi dar keshvar [Reasons behind the Tabriz unrest: ethnic roots or a reflection of public discontent in the country?]', www.bbc.co.uk/persian, May 23.

BBC Persian. 2007. 'Enfejār-e otobus dar zāhedān hejdah koshte dād [Bus bombing in Zahedan leaves 17 dead]', www.bbc.co.uk/persian, February 14.

DW-World (Deutsche Welle's Persian Website, Sedā-ye ālmān). 2007. 'Mowj-e feshār bar fa'ālān-e madani-ye kordestān [A wave of repression against civil society activists of Kurdistan]', www.dw-world.de/persian, July 21.

Entekhab News. 2006a. 'Farmānde-ye nājā: zarbe-ye mohlaki be terorist-hā-ye fāje'e-ye dārzin vāred kardim [Commander of NAJA: "We have dealt a fatal blow to the terrorists behind the Darzin catastrophe"]', www.entekhab.ir, May 17/Ordibehesht 27, 1385.

Entekhab News. 2006b. 'Basij be komak-e niru-ye entezāmi shetāft [The Basij hurried to help the Disciplinary Forces]', www.entekhab.ir, May 17/Ordibehesht 27, 1385.

Entekhab News. 2006c. 'Hokumat dar moqābel-e khun, vahshigari va dadmaneshi kutāh nemiāyad [The state will never give into blood, savagery and beastly behavior]', www.entekhab.ir, May 18/Ordibehesht 28, 1385.

Entekhab (News Website). 2006d. 'Qātelān-e jāde-ye kermān-bam dar yeki az ghār-hā dar mohāsere-ye niru-hā-ye entezāmi hastand [The murderers of the Kerman-Bam road are surrounded by Disciplinary Forces in a cave]', www.entekhab.ir, May 19/Ordibehesht 29, 1385.

Entekhab. 2006e. 'Vazir-e keshvar: dowlat bā tamām-e tavān barā-ye pāyān dādan be ghā'ele-ye terorist-hā talāsh khāhad kard [Interior Minister: "The government will strive with all its ability to end the evil of terrorists"]', www.entekhab.ir, May 19/Ordibehesht 29, 1385.

Entekhab. 2006f. 'Dastgir nakardan-e " 'abdolmālek" be ma'nā-ye tavān-e khās-e vey nist [That 'Abdolmalek has not been arrested doesn't reflect any special ability of his]', www.entekhab.ir, May 20/Ordibehesht 30, 1385.

Entekhab. 2006g. 'Ra'isi: bedun-e eghmāz bā nā-amn-konandegān-e jāme'e bar-khord mikonim [Ra'isi: "We will confront those who destabilize society without toleration"]', www.entekhab.ir, May 20/Ordibehesht 30, 1385.

Entekhab. 2006h. 'Dastgiri-ye sarkarde-ye 'āmelān-e jenāyat-e jāde-ye bam [The arrest of the leader of the culprits behind the crime on the Bam road]', www.entekhab.ir, May 20/Ordibehesht 30, 1385.

Entekhab. 2006i. 'Towhin-e yek ruznāme be āzari-zabān-hā peygiri mishavad [A daily's insult against Azeri-speakers is being investigated]', www.entekhab.ir, May 20/Ordibehesht 30, 1385.

Entekhab. 2007. 'Nemāyande-ye zāhedān: āqāyān-e mas'ul! agar nemitavānid amniyyat-rā bar-qarār konid mardom-rā mosallah konid [Zahedan MP: "Gentlemen in charge! If you cannot bring about security then arm the people"]', www.entekhab.ir, February 17/Bahman 28, 1385.

Esteqamat (news website). 2010. 'Matn-e kāmel-e sokhanrāni-ye mashā'i dar ekhtetāmiye-ye hamāyesh-e irāniyān [The Complete Text of Masha'i's Speech at the Opening of the Iranians' Congregation]', www.esteghamat.ir, August 16, 2010.

EurasiaNet (website). 2008. 'Iran: US Government Planning Azeri-Language Broadcasts to Iran', www.eurasianet.org, March 9.

Farda (Radio, Website). 2006. 'Hamzamān bā tazāhorāt-e khoshunat-āmiz dar tabriz, anjoman-e eslāmi-ye dāneshjuyān-e dāneshgāh-e zanjān jomhuri-ye eslāmi-rā bāni-ye "tafraqe-afkani beyn-e aqvām" khānd [Simultaneously with the violent demonstrations in Tabriz, Zanjan University's ISA called the Islamic Republic for "creating division amongst ethnic groups"]', www.radiofarda.com via www.jebhemelli.org, May 23/Khordād 2, 1385.

Farhang-e ashti (Daily, Online Version). 2006a. 'Rāhpeymā'i-ye mardom-e tabriz dar e'terāz be āshub-hā-ye akhir [The people of Tabriz's rally against recent riots]', www.ashtidaily.com, May 25/Khordad 4, 1385.

Farhang-e ashti. 2006b. 'Hāshemi rafsanjāni: havādes-e akhir-e āzarbāyjān neshāne-ye za'f-e tadbir ast [Hashemi Rafsanjani: "Recent events in Azerbaijan are the result of weak policy"]', www.ashtidaily.com, May 25/Khordad 4, 1385.

Fars (News Agency, Online). 2005a. 'Bar-resi-ye masā'el-e akhir-e ostān-e khuzestān dar jalase-ye shamkhāni va mo'tamedān-e 'arab-e khuzestān [Investigation of Recent Issues in Khuzestan Province in Shamkhani's Meeting with Arab Notables of Khuzestan]', www. farsnews.com, April 19/Farvardin 30.

Fars. 2005b. "Āmel-e asli-ye havādes-e khuzestān dastgir shode ast [The original perpetrator behind the Khuzestan events has been apprehended]', www.farsnews.com, May 5/Ordibehesht 15, 1384.

Fars. 2006a. 'Ashrār-e mosallah 22 tan az mas'ulān va mardom-e sistān va baluchestān-rā koshte va goruhi-rā be gerowgān gereftand [Armed rebels have killed 22 officials and civilians of Sistan-Baluchestan (Province) and taken a group as hostages]', www.farsnews. com, March 17/Esfand 26, 1384.

Fars. 2006b. 'Ashrār-e mosallah ehtemālan 'ede'i az mardom-rā ham be gerowgān gerefte-and [The armed rebels probably also took a number of (civilian) people hostage]', www. farsnews.com, March 17/Esfand 26, 1384.

Fars. 2006c. 'Hanuz radd-pā'i az 'āmelān-e hadese-ye teroristi-ye dishab dar zāhedān be dast nayāmade ast [There is still no trace of the perpetrators of last night's terrorist incident in Zahedan]', www.farsnews.com, March 17/Esfand 26, 1384.

Fars. 2006d. 'Mohem-tarin angize-ye terorist-hā dar hādese-ye zābol tafraqe beyn-e shi'e va sonni ast [The most important motive for the terrorists in the Zabol incident is to sow discord between Shi'ites and Sunnis]', www.farsnews.com, March 18/Esfand 27, 1384.

Fars. 2006e. 'Vazir-e keshvar: bā ārāyesh-e jadidi dar sistān va baluchestān zāher mi-shavim [Interior Minister: "We will become present with a new structure in Sistan and Baluchestan"]', www.farsnews.com, March 18/Esfand 27, 1384.

Fars. 2006f. 'Kārvān-hā-ye mavād-e mokhader be rāhati az marz-hā-ye sistān mi-gozarad [Caravans of illegal substances easily cross Sistan's borders]', www.farsnews.com, March 18/Esfand 27, 1384.

Fars. 2006g. 'Vazir-e keshvar: te'dādi az 'avāmel-e jenāyat-e bam dastgir va koshte shodand [Minister of Interior: "A number of the perpetrators of the crime at Bam have been arrested and killed"]', www.farsnews.com, May 14/Ordibehesht 24, 1385.

Fars. 2006h. 'Towte'e-ye doshman barā-ye ijād-e ekhtelāfāt-e qowmi shekast khorde [The enemy's conspiracy to create ethnic discontent has suffered defeat]', www.farsnews.com, May 28/Khordad 7, 1385.

Fars. 2007a. 'Jebhe-ye mottahed-e kord dar chārchub-e tamāmiyyat-e arzi-ye keshvar fa'āliyyat mikonad [The United Kurdish Front works within the framework of the country's territorial integrity]', www.farsnews.com, January 4/Day 14, 1385.

Fars. 2007b. 'Ahmadinezhād dar jam'-e mardom-e omidiye: vahdat-e irān nā-gosastani ast [Ahmadinejad before a Gathering of the People of Omidiye: "Iran's Unity is Unshakable"]', www.farsnews.com, January 4, 2007.

Fars. 2007c. '11 nafar dar enfejār-e sobh-e emruz-e zāhedān be shahādat residand [11 persons were martyred by the Zahedan bombing this morning]', www.farsnews.com, February 14/Bahman 25, 1385.

Fars. 2007d. 'Joz'iyāt-e tāze az havādes-e emshab-e zāhedān [New details about tonight's events in Zahedan]', www.farsnews.com, February 16/Bahman 27, 1385.

Fars. 2007e. 'Tasvir-e mohemmāt-e āmrikā'i-ye 'avāmel-e havādes-e teroristi-ye zāhedān [Picture of the American ammunition belonging to the culprits behind the Zahedan terrorist events]', www.farsnews.com, February 17/Bahman 28, 1385.

Fars. 2008. 'Bāzdāsht-e 3 tim-e teroristi dar sistān va baluchestān [The arrest of three terrorist groups in Sistan-Baluchistan]', www.farsnews.com, June 27/Tir 7, 1387.

Fars. 2009a. 'Hozur-e qowmiyyat-hā-ye mokhtalef-e orumiye dar masir-e esteqbāl az ra'is-jomhur [The presence of various ethnic groups of Orumiye in the welcome ceremonies for the president]', www.farsnews.com, March 4, 2009.

Fars. 2009b. 'Tajammo'-e jam'i az sākenān-e shahrak-e jushkārān-e shahr-e zāhedān dar moqābel-e majles [Demonstration of a group of inhabitants from Jushkaran District of Zahedan in front of Parliament]', *Fārs News* via http://news.gooya.com, April 7/Farvardin 18, 1388.

Fars. 2011. 'Artesh va sepāh barā-ye nābudi-ye kāmel-e pezhāk hamkāri mikonand [The Army and the (Revolutionary) Guard is working together for the complete annihilation of PJAK]', *Fārs* News Agency, Shahrivar 20, 1390/September 11, 2011.

Gooya (News Website). 2005. 'Dar nāme'i ke ruz-e 22-e farvardin tavassot-e mohammad-'ali abtahi dar veblāgash takzib shod, che neveshte bud? [What was in the letter that Mohammad-'Ali Abtahi rejected on his weblog on *Farvardin* 22?]', http://news.gooya.com, April 16/27 Farvardin, 1384.

Gooya. 2006. 'Ettelā'iye-ye gozāreshgarān-e bedun-e marz darbāre-ye dastgiri-ye do ruznāme-negār dar ostān-hā-ye ardabil va āzarbāyjān-e sharqi [Reporters Without Borders' communique about the arrest of two journalists in the provinces of Ardabil and Eastern Azerbaijan]', http://news.gooya.com, May 27/Khordad 6, 1385.

Gooya. 2008a. 'Bayāniye-ye bish az 700 tan az talāshgarān-e dāneshju'i, siyāsi, ejtemā 'i, farhangi va dāneshgāhiyān dar poshtibāni az āzādi-ye dāneshjuyān-e hoviyyat-talab-e āzarbāyjān [Communique by more than 700 student, political, social, cultural and university activists in support of the release of identity-seeking students from Azerbaijan]', http://news.gooya.com, August 16/Mordād 27, 1387.

Gooya. 2008b. 'Ettelā'iye-ye gozāreshgarān-e bedun-e marz darbāre-ye bāzdāsht-e chahār ruznāme-negār-e āzari dar irān [Reporters Without Borders' Communiqué about the arrest of four Azeri journalists in Iran]', http://news.gooya.com, August 31/Shahrivar 27, 1387.

Ham-mihan (Daily, Online). 2009. 'Irāni-tarin irāni-hā kord-hā hastand [The most Iranian of Iranians are the Kurds]', http://hammihannews.com, nd.

Hamshahri (Daily, Online). 2005a. 'Nā-ārāmi dar ahvāz foru neshast [The unrest in Ahvaz has calmed down]', www.hamshahrionline.ir, April 17/Farvardin 28, 1384.

Hamshahri (Daily, Online). 2005b. 'Bar-resi-ye eb'ād-e nā-ārāmi-hā-ye akhir-e khuzestān [Analysis of dimensions of the recent unrest in Khuzestan]', www.hamshahrionline.ir, April 18/Farvardin 29, 1384.

Hamshahri (Daily, Online). 2005c. 'Yunesi: estrātezhi-ye bar-andāzi-ye narm-e āmrikā bā sho'ār-e demokrāsi hamrāh ast [Yunesi: "The US strategy of soft (regime) overthrow is accompanied by the slogan of democracy"]', www.hamshahrionline.ir, April 19/Farvardin 30, 1384.

HRANA (Human Rights Activists News Agency). 2009. 'Tadāvom-e yuresh-e be manāzel va bāzdāsht-e mo'allemān dar baluchestān [Continued raids on houses and arrests of teachers in Baluchistan]', HRANA via http://news.gooya.com, August 14/Mordād 23, 1388.

ILNA (Iranian Labour News Agency). 2005a. 'Vazir-e ettelā'āt: 'avāmel-e tahrik-e havādes-e ahvāz nesh'at-gerefte az goruh-hā va 'avāmel-e televeziyoni-ye bar-andāz ast [Information Minister: "The instigators of the Ahvaz incidents are rooted in groups and TV agents (aimed at) overthrow(ing the Islamic Republic)"]', www.ilna.ir, April 18/Farvardin 29, 1384.

ILNA (Iranian Labour News Agency). 2005b. 'Dādsetān-e koll-e keshvar: resāne-hā-ye abzār-dast-e engelis be havādes-e akhir-e khuzestān dāmen zadand [The national public prosecutor: "Media instrumentally used by the British have abused the recent incidents in Khuzestan"]', www.ilna.ir, April 21/Ordibehesht 1, 1384.

ILNA (Iranian Labour News Agency). 2006. 'E'terāz-e dāneshjuyān-e āzari-zabān be kārikātur-e ruznāme-ye irān dāneshgāh-e zanjān-rā be ta'tili keshānd [Azeri-speaking students' protest over the *Iran* daily caricature has forced Zanjan University to close down]', www.ilna.ir, May 20/Ordibehesht 30, 1385.

ILNA (Iranian Labour News Agency). 2007a. 'E'terāfāt-e chahār nafar az 'avāmel-e enfejār-e emruz dar zāhedān emshab az simā-ye ostān pakhsh mishavad [The confessions of four culprits behind today's explosion in Zahedan will be broadcast tonight on provincial TV]', www.ilna.ir, February 14/Bahman 25, 1385.

ILNA (Iranian Labour News Agency). 2007b. '15 nafar be ettehām-e towzi'-e shabnāme-hā-ye gheyr-e qānuni dar ostān-e āzarbāyjān-e sharqi bāzdāsht shodand [15 persons accused of distributing illegal pamphlets in East Azerbaijan Province have been arrested]', www.ilna. ir, May 22/Khordad 1, 1386.

ILNA. 2009. 'Karubi: Bāyad sath-e moshārekat-e hame-ye aqvām va mazāheb rā dar hākemiyat afzāyesh dād', www.ilna.ir, February 18.

Iran (Daily, Online). 2005a. 'Bā kontrol-e dargiri-hā-ye māhshahr owzā'-e tamāmi-ye shahr-hā-ye ostān-e khuzestān taht-e kontrol va 'ādi ast [Having established control over confrontations in Mahshahr, all cities in Khuzestan province are under control and the situation is normal]', www.iran-newspaper.com, April 19/Farvardin 30, 1384.

Iran. 2005b. 'Yek hafte-ye nā-ārāmi pāyān yāft [One week of unrest came to an end]', www. iran-newspaper.com, April 23/Ordibehesht 3, 1384.

Iran. 2005c. 'Hey'ati az vezārat-e keshvar emruz be mahābād mi-ravad [A committee from the Ministry of Interior is going to Mahabad today]', www.iran-newspaper.com, July 19/28 Tir, 1384.

Iran. 2005d. 'Nemāyande-ye mardom-e mahābād khabar dād [Mahabad MP has made an announcement]', www.iran-newspaper.com, July 26/4 Mordād, 1384.

Iran. 2005e. 'Gozāresh-e yek maqām-e siyāsi-amniyyati darbāre-ye vaqāye'-e oshnaviye [A political-security authority's report on events in Oshnaviye]', www.iran-newspaper.com, July 27/5 Mordād, 1384.

Iran. 2005f. 'Chahār personel-e niru-ye entezāmi dar havādes-e oshnaviye shahid shodand [Four members of NAJA have been martyred during the Oshanviye events]', www.iran-newspaper.com, July 28/6 Mordād, 1384.

Iran. 2005g. 'Ezhārāt-e mas'ulān-e amniyyati-ye sanandaj pirāmun-e vaqāye'-e doshanbe shab [Sanandaj security officials' statements on the events of Monday night]', www. iran-newspaper.com, August 3/12 Mordād, 1384.

Iran. 2005h. 'Bar-resi-ye eb'ād-e havādes-e mahābād dar komisiyon-e amniyyat-e melli [Investigation into (various) dimensions of the Mahabad events in the National Security Commission]', www.iran-newspaper.com, August 4/13 Mordād, 1384.

Iran. 2005i. 'Gozāresh-e mas'ulān-e kordestān az havādes-e saqqez [Kurdistan officials' report on events in Saqqez]', www.iran-newspaper.com, August 7/16 Mordād, 1384.

Iran. 2005j. 'Talāsh-e tashakkol-hā va chehre-hā-ye siyāsi barā-ye hall-e nā-ārāmi-hā-ye kordestān [Political organizations and figures' attempt to find a solution to the Kurdistan unrest]', www.iran-newspaper.com, August 17/26 Mordād, 1384.

Iran. 2005k. 'Gozāresh-e mas'ulān-e mahali az parvande-ye havādes-e manāteq-e kord-neshin [Local officials' report on the case of unrest in Kurdish-populated areas]', www. iran-newspaper.com, August 18/27 Mordād, 1384.

Iran. 2005s. 'Hokm-e zendān barā-ye sherkat-konandegān dar yek tahasson [Prison sentence for participants in a protest gathering]', www.iran-newspaper.com, August 11/20 Mordād, 1384.

Iran. 2006a. 'Bāz-khāni-ye parvande-ye vaqāye'-e teroristi-ye zāhedān dar goft-o-gu-ye "irān" bā ostāndār-e sistān va baluchestān/ta'qib-e yek goruh-e mājarā-ju dar marz-hā-ye sharqi

[Revisiting the case of the Zahedan terrorist incident in *Irān*'s interview with the Governor-General of Sistan-Baluchestan/Pursuit of a provocative group on the eastern borders]', www.iran-newspaper.com, May 4/Ordibehesht 14, 1385.

Iran. 2006b. 'Che konim ke susk-hā, suskemān nakonand? [What shall we do to prevent the cockroaches from turning us into cockroaches?]', cartoon and text, Iran Daily (Friday appendix) via wikipedia.org, May 19/Ordibehesht 30, 1385.

Iran-e emruz (Online Magazine). 2005. 'Mehdi karubi: in entekhābāt siyāh-tarin parvande-ye khātami ast [Mehdi Karubi: "This election is the darkest chapter of Khatami's case"]', www.iran-emrooz.net, June 22/Tir 1, 1384.

IRANEWS (News Services). 2006. 'Ra'is-e herāsat-e helāl-e ahmar-e keshvar va chand tan az niru-hā-ye sepāh dar jam'-e 7 gerowgān-e irāni dar sistān va baluchestān [The security head of the country's (branch of) Red Crescent and a number of Revolutionary Guards among the 7 Iranian hostages in Sistan-Baluchestan]', www.iranews.biz, March 23/Farvardin 3, 1385.

IRIN (Online). 2005. 'Interview with Human Rights Special Rapporteur on Adequate Housing, Miloon Kothari', www.irinnews.org, August 9.

IRNA (Islamic Republic News Agency). 2005a. 'Enteshār-e yek nāme-ye ja'li mansub be abtahi, nā-ārāmi-hā'i dar barkhi manāteq-e 'arab-neshin-e ahvāz dar pey dāsht [The publication of a fake letter attributed to Abtahi concluded in some unrest in certain Arab-populated areas of Ahvaz]', www.irna.ir, April 16/Farvardin 27, 1384.

IRNA (Islamic Republic News Agency). 2005b. 'Nemāyande-ye ahvāz az "takzib-e dir-hengām-e yek nāme-ye maj'ul" gelāye kard [Ahvaz MP complains "late rejection of fake letter"]', www.irna.ir, April 17/28 Farvardin, 1384.

IRNA (Islamic Republic News Agency). 2005c. 'Vazir-e keshvar: 'avāmel-e borun-marzi dar eghteshāshāt-e khuzestān dakhil bude ast [Interior Minister: "Foreign agents were involved in the Khuzestan unrest"]', www.irna.ir, April 17/28 Farvardin, 1384.

IRNA (Islamic Republic News Agency). 2005d. 'Mardom-e mahābād az vaqāye'-e akhir-e in shahr ezhār-e ta'assof mikonand [The people of Mahabad expresses regret over recent events in this city]', www.irna.ir, July 18/27 Tir, 1384.

IRNA (Islamic Republic News Agency). 2006a. 'Jā-neshin-e nājā: harakat-e ashrār dar jāde-ye zābol-zāhedān harakati siyasi-amniyyati ast [The successor to (the chief of) NAJA: "The actions of rebels on the Zabol-Zahedan road (were) political and security-related acts"]', www.irna.ir, March 18/Esfand 27, 1384.

IRNA (Islamic Republic News Agency). 2006b. 'Farmānde-ye niru-ye entezāmi: jenāyat-e sistān va enfejār-hā-ye khuzestān rishe-ye khāreji dārand [Commander of the Disciplinary Forces: "The crimes in Sistan and the explosions in Khuzestan have foreign roots"]', www.irna.ir, March 26/Farvardin 6, 1385.

IRNA (Islamic Republic News Agency). 2006c. 'Nemāyande-ye tabriz: qaziye-ye ruznāme-ye "irān" pāyān yāfte tallaqi mishavad [Tabriz MP: "The case of *Irān* daily is considered over"]', www.irna.ir, May 23/Khordād 2, 1385.

IRNA (Islamic Republic News Agency). 2007. 'Sedā-ye enfejār-e yek bomb dar zāhedān shenide shod [The sound of a bomb explosion has been heard in Zahedan]', February 16/Bahman 27, 1385.

ISCA (Iran Student Correspondents Association). 2005. 'Ansār-e hezbollāh-e dezful: bā āshubgarān barkhord-e qāte' shavad [Ansar-e Hezbollah of Dezful: Rioters must be confronted harshly]', www.iscanews.ir, April 18/Farvardin 29, 1384.

ISNA (Iranian Students News Agency). 2005a. 'Dādsetān-e ahvāz: kār-e tashkil-e parvande barā-ye dastgir-shodegān-e havādes-e akhir-e ahvāz az sobh-e emruz āghāz shod [Ahvaz public prosecutor: "The creation of cases against arrestees from the recent events in Ahvaz has begun today"]', www.isna.ir, April 17/Farvardin 28, 1384.

ISNA. 2005b. 'Hoshdār-e karrubi nesbat be fa'āl shodan-e dast-hā'i barā-ye tahdid-e yekpārchegi va vahdat-e melli-ye irān [Karrubi's warning about the activation of agents threatening Iran's national unity and solidarity]', www.isna.ir, April 18/29 Farvardin, 1384.

ISNA. 2005c. 'Dorri-najaf-ābādi bā eshāre be havādes-e ahvāz: 'anāser-e asli dastgir shodeand [In reference to recent events in Ahvaz, Dorri-Najafabadi: "The original perpetrators have been arrested"]', www.isna.ir, April 21/Ordibehesht 1, 1384.

ISNA. 2005d. 'Farmāndār-e mahābād bā eshāre be havādes-e akhir-e in shahr: hey'ati az vezārat-e keshvar, qovve-ye qazā'iye va niru-ye entezāmi e'zām shodeand [Mahabad Governor, referring to recent events in this city: "A committee from Ministry of Interior, the Judiciary and NAJA has been dispatched"]', www.isna.ir, July 19/Tir 28, 1384.

ISNA. 2006a. 'Goruhak-hā'i nazir-e zarqāvi ke mortakeb-e jenāyat-e sistān shodand, qābel-e gozasht nistand [Small groups under Zarqawi, who have perpetrated the crime in Sistan, are not forgiveable]', www.isna.ir, March 18/Esfand 27, 1384.

ISNA. 2006b. 'Ashrār-e mosallah 12 tan az hamvatanān-rā dar jāde-ye bam-kermān qatl-e 'ām kardand/hoviyyat-e ashrār hanuz shenāsā'i nashode ast [Armed rebels have massacred 12 compatriots on the Bam-Kerman road/The identity of the rebels is not yet clear]', www.isna.ir, May 14/Ordibehesht 24, 1385.

ISNA. 2006c. 'Eqdām-e teroristi-ye kermān va vākonesh-e nemāyandegān [The terrorist act in Kerman and the reactions of MPs]', www.isna.ir, May 14/Ordibehesht 24, 1385.

ISNA. 2006d. 'Gozāreshi az eqdām-e jenāyatkārāne-ye ashrār dar mehvar-e bam-kermān [A report from the criminal acts of rebels on the Bam-Kerman highway]', www.isna.ir, May 14/Ordibehesht 24, 1385.

ISNA. 2006e. 'Vazir-e kesvar bā e'lām-e khabar-e be dām oftādan-e te'dādi az 'avāmel-e hādese-ye teroristi-ye jom'e shab: ba'id midānam terorist-hā betavānand az marz khārej beshavand [Interior Minister, announcing that a number of Friday night's terrorist attack's perpetrators have fallen into a trap: "I think it's impossible for the terrorists to cross the border"]', www.isna.ir, May 14/Ordibehesht 24, 1385.

ISNA. 2006f. 'Bālgard-hā-ye polisi be donbāl-e makhfigāh-e ashrār-e hādese-ye bam-kermān [Police helicopters chasing the base of the rebels (who perpetrated) the attack on Bam-Kerman (road)]', www.isna.ir., May 14/Ordibehesht 24, 1385.

ISNA. 2006g. 'Tajammo'-e jam'i az dāneshjuyān-e dāneshgāh-hā-ye tabriz va orumiye be enteshār-e matlabi dar yek ruznāme [Demonstration by a number of students from Tabriz and Orumiye universities against the publication of an issue in a daily]', www.isna.ir, May 16/Ordibehesht 26, 1385.

ISNA. 2006h. 'Ruznāme-ye irān towqif shod [Irān daily closed]', www.isna.ir, May 23/Khordād 2, 1385.

ISNA. 2006i. 'Dādsetān-e tabriz: 54 nafar dar nā-ārāmi-hā-ye ruz-e gozashte dastgir shodand [The Tabriz Public Prosecutor: "54 persons were arrested during yesterday's unrest"]', www.isna.ir, May 23/Khordād 2, 1385.

ISNA. 2006j. 'Ra'is-e qovve-ye qazā'iye: 'anāser-e ziyadi az dastgirshodegān-e taharokāt-e akhir az 'avāmel-e khāreji va goruhak-hā budand [Chief of Judiciary: "Many of those arrested in recent unrest are foreign agents and from small (political) groups"]', www.isna.ir, May 29/Khordād 8, 1385.

ISNA. 2006k. 'Vazir-e keshvar: dastgirshodegān-e vaqāye'-e akhir dar ekhtiyār-e marja'-e qazā'iye qarār gerefteand [Interior Minister: "Those arrested in recent events are placed under the custody of judiciary authorities"]', www.isna.ir, May 29/Khordād 8, 1385.

ISNA. 2006l. 'Dar pey-e shahādat-e 8 ma'mur-e entezāmi dar ertefā'āt-e bam; yek mas'ul dar ostāndāri-ye kermān: ashrār-e jenāyatkār ertebāti bā "rigi" nadārand; eqdāmāt-e amniyyati barā-ye dastgiri-ye ashrār āghāz shod [After the martyring of 8 Disciplinary (Forces) offi-cers in the heights of Bam; one official in Kerman Governorate: "The criminal rebels do not have any connection with Rigi; security operations for apprehending the rebels have begun"]', www.isna.ir, August 13/Mordād 22, 1385.

ISNA. 2006m. 'Farmānde-ye nājā ta'kid kard: āghāz-e tard-e atbā'-e gheyr-e mojāz dar sistān bā ensedād-e marz-hā [NAJA Commander emphasized: "With the consolidation of bor-ders, the program for expulsion of illegal immigrants from Sistan has begun"]', www.isna.ir, September 5/Bahman 14, 1385.

ISNA. 2007. 'Mahkumiyyat-e hamle-ye teroristi dar zāhedān [Condemnation of the terrorist attack in Zahedan]', www.isna.ir, February 14/Bahman 25, 1385.

Jahan News (news website). 2008. 'Mashā'i: dowre-ye eslāmgarā'i be pāyān reside ast [Masha'i: "The era of Islamism has reached its end"]', www.jahannews.com, August 20, 2008.

Jomhuri-ye eslami (Daily, Online). 2005a. 'Edāme-ye dargiri dar ahvāz va māhshahr [Contin-uing unrest in Ahvaz and Mahshahr]', www.jomhourieslami.com, April 19/30 Farvardin, 1384.

Jomhuri-ye eslami. 2005b. 'Eghteshāsh va dargiri dar mahābād dar sālgard-e teror-e qāsemlu [Unrest and fighting in Mahabad on the anniversary of Qasemlu's assassination]', www.jomhurieslami.com, July 14/23 Tir, 1384.

Kayhan (Daily, Online). 2005a. 'Bar khalāf-e mājarā-ye kordestān sokhangu-ye dowlat in bār be tahrik-e qowmiyyat-hā enteqād kard [In contrast to the Kurdistan affair, the government spokesman criticized the provokation of ethnic groups this time]', www.Kayhannews.ir, April 17/Farvardin 28, 1384.

Kayhan. 2005b. 'Vazir-e keshvar: 'avāmel-e borun-marzi dar hādese-ye ahvāz dekhālat dāshtand [Interior Minister: Foreign agents were involved in the Ahvaz incident]', www.Kayhannews.ir, April 18/Farvardin 29, 1384.

Kayhan. 2005c. 'Be khāter-e sheytanat dar mājarā-ye nā-ārāmi-ye ahvāz fa'āliyat-e shabake-ye al-jazire dar irān be hālat-e ta'liq dar āmad [Due to mischieviousness in the Ahvaz unrest, Al-Jazeera TV network's activities in Iran have been suspended]', www.kayhannews.ir, April 19/Farvardin 30, 1384.

Kayhan. 2005d. 'Naqsh-hā-ye doshmanān barā-ye janjāl-āfarini dar āstāne-ye entekhābāt [Enemies' plots to create uproar on the eve of elections]', www.Kayhannews.ir, April 19/Farvardin 30, 1384.

Kayhan. 2005e. 'Be khāter-e sheytanat dar mājarā-ye nā-ārāmi-ye ahvāz fa'āliyat-e shabake-ye al-jazire dar irān be hālat-e ta'liq dar āmad [Due to their mischieviousness in the Ahvaz unrest, Al-Jazeera TV network's activities in Iran have been suspended]', www.Kayhannews.ir, April 19/Farvardin 30, 1384.

Kayhan. 2005f. 'Dast-e bigānegān dar havādes-e khuzestān efshā shod [The hands of for-eigners exposed in the Khuzestan events]', www.Kayhannews.ir, April 21/Ordibehesht 1, 1384.

Kayhan. 2005g. 'Tajalli-ye hambastegi-ye melli dar rāhpeymā'i-ye bā-shokuh-e mardom-e ahvāz [Manifestation of national solidarity in the Ahvaz people's magnificent parade]', www.Kayhannews.ir, April 23/3 Ordibehesht, 1384.

Kayhan. 2005h. 'Naqsh-e engelis dar havādes-e khuzestān [Britain's role in the Khuzestan events]', www.Kayhannews.ir, April 25/Ordibehesht 5, 1384.

Kayhan. 2006a. 'Hadaf dar hādese-ye baluchestān [The aim with the Baluchestan incident]', www.Kayhannews.ir, March 18/Esfand 27, 1384.

Kayhan. 2006b. 'E'terāz be yek kārikātur dar chand shahr be khoshunat keshide shod [Protests against a caricature has turned violent in several towns]', www.Kayhannews.ir, May 23/Khordād 2, 1385.

Kayhan. 2006c. 'Forsat-talabān, e'terāz-e mardom-e tabriz-rā be tashannoj keshāndand [Opportunists turned the Tabrizi people's protests into turmoil]', www.Kayhannews.ir, May 24/Khordād 3, 1385.

Kayhan. 2006d. 'Hāshemi rafsanjāni: makhdush kardan-e hambastegi-ye melli khiyānat ast [Hashemi Rafsanjani: "To tamper with national solidarity is treason"]', www.Kayhannews. ir, May 25/Khordād 4, 1385.

Kayhan. 2006e. 'Maleki: āzari-zabān-hā hargez bahāne be dast-e forsat-talabān nemidahand [Maleki: "Azeri-speakers will never give a chance to the opportunists"]', www.Kayhannews. ir, May 25/Khordād 5, 1385.

Kayhan. 2006f. 'Ra'is-e majles dar pāsokh be ezhārāt-e tahrik-āmiz-e a'lami: mellat-e irān dar sāye-ye eslām bā ham motahhed hastand [The Parliament Chairman in response to A'lami's provocative statements: "The Iranian nation is united in the shade of Islam"]', www.Kayhannews.ir, May 25/Khordād 5, 1385.

Kayhan. 2007. 'Dastgiri-ye 'avāmel-e dovvomin bombgozāri dar zāhedān [The arrest of the culprits behind the second bombing in Zahedan]', www.Kayhannews.ir, February 17/Bahman 28, 1385.

Khandaniha (News Website). 2009. 'Jodā'i-talab-e holandi dar dādgāh-e irāni be 30 sāl zendān mahkum shod [A Dutch separatist (sic) sentenced 30 years in jail by Iranian court]', www. khandaniha.eu, February 24/'Esfand 6, 1387.

Kurdistan Media (News Website). 2007. 'Dastgiri va zarb-o-shatm-e peyrowān-e maktab-e qor'ān (shāgardān-e ahmad moftizāde) dar māh-e ramazān [Arrest and beating of Followers of the Qoran School (disciples of Ahmad Moftizade) in the month of Ramadan]', Kurdistan Media via http://news.gooya.com, October 9/Mehr 17, 1386.

Mehr (News Agency). 2005a. 'Modākhele va sheytanat-e āshkār-e shabake-ye al-jazire dar masāyel-e dākheli-ye irān [The obvious intervention and mischievousness of Al-Jazeera network in Iran's internal affairs]', www.mehrnews.com, April 17/Farvardin 28, 1384.

Mehr. 2005b. 'Moruri bar yek hādese [Concerning an incident]', www.mehrnews.com, April 19/Farvardin 30, 1384.

Mehr. 2005c. 'Nashriyāt va shabake-hā-ye televizyoni-ye bigāne sa'y dar taghyir-e esālat-e 'arabi-ye mardom-e mantaqe dārand [Foreign magazines and TV networks are trying to change the Arabic origins of the region's people]', www.mehrnews.com, April 20/Farvardin 31, 1384.

Mehr. 2005d. 'Mā qorbāniyān-e va'de-hā-ye farāmush-shode-ye dowlat hastim [We are victims of the government's forgotten promises]', www.mehrnews.com, May 24/3 Khordād, 1384.

Mehr. 2005e. 'Mazhab-e shi'e 'āmel-e asli-ye peyvand-e qowmiyyat-hā dar khuzestān [The Shi'ite creed is the real factor that unites ethnic groups in Khuzestan]', www.mehrnews. com, May 24/3 Khordād, 1384.

Mehr. 2005f. 'Agar be moshkelāt-e ma'ishati-ye khuzestān residegi shavad, hezārān nāme-ye ja'li ham nemitavānad bā'es-e tahrik o eghteshāsh shavad [If Khuzestan's livelihood problems are dealt with, a thousand fake letters could not provoke or cause unrest]', www. mehrnews.com, May 29/8 Khordād, 1384.

Mehr. 2005g. 'Irān ya'ni khuzestān; khuzestān ya'ni irān [Iran is Khuzestan, Khuzestan is Iran]', www.mehrnews.com, May 30/9 Khordād, 1384.

Mehr. 2005h. 'Taharokāt-e posht-e parde-ye servis-hā-ye ettelā'āti va resāne-hā-ye bigāne dar havādes-e ahvāz [Foreign intelligence agencies and media's provocations behind the scene of the Ahvaz events]', www.mehrnews.com, June 7/17 Khordād, 1384.

Mehr. 2007. 'Vezārat-e ettelā'āt: se sarbāz-e niru-ye entezāmi az changāl-e ashrār-e mosallah āzād shodand [Ministry of Information: "Three soliders from the Disciplinary Forces have been freed from the claws of armed rebels"]', www.mehrnews.com, March 27/Farvardin 7, 1385.

MEW (Middle East Wire, Online). 2005a. 'Agency says British security forces trained masterminds of unrest' (based on ISNA report from August 10), www.mideastwire.com, August 12.

MEW. 2005b. 'British "sabotage" group in southern Iraq acting against Iran' (based on *Fārs* report from September 27), www.mideastwire.com, September 28.

Miras (News Agency). 2006. 'Darj-e matlab-e towhināmiz be āzari-zabān-hā towte'e-ye doshman ast [The publication of an item offending Azeri-speakers is the enemy's conspiracy]', www.chn.ir via http://news.gooya.com, May 21/Ordibehesht 31, 1385.

Mizan. 2008a. 'Marg-e fa'āl-e nāpadide-shode-ye āzarbāyjān dar bāzdāshtgāh-e vezārat-e ettelā'āt-e tabriz [The death of a disappeared activist from Azerbaijan in the Information Ministry detention center in Tabriz]', www.mizannews.com, June 13/Khordād 23, 1387.

Mizan. 2008b. 'Fa'āl-e kord be yāzdah sāl zendān mahkum shod [Kurdish activists sentenced to 11 years in jail]', www.mizannews.com, June 24/Tir 3, 1387.

Mukrian (News Agency). 2007a. 'Shesh māh habs barā-ye peymān ne'mati, dāneshju-ye sanandaji [Six months of jail for Peyman Ne'mati, a Sanandaji student]', www.mukriannews.blogfa.com, May 21/Ordibehesht 31, 1386.

Mukrian. 2007b. 'Do sāl habs barā-ye mohammad ārām nosratpur, shahrvand-e sanandaji va 'ozv-e sābeq-e tim-e melli-ye kuhnavardi [Two years of prison for Mohammad Aram Nosratpur, citizen of Sanandaj and former member of the National Mountaineering Team]', www.mukriannews.blogfa.com, May 22/Khordād 1, 1386.

Mukrian. 2007c. '4 sāl habs barā-ye shahrām ansāri, shahrvand-e saqqez be dalil-e hamkāri bā opuzisiyun [4 years of prison for Shahram Ansari, citizen of Saqqez, for cooperation with the opposition]', www.mukriannews.blogfa.com, June 13/Khordād 23, 1386.

Mukrian. 2007d. 'Dādgāhi-ye āsu sāleh 'ozv-e hey'at-e tahririye-ye hafte-nāme-ye didegāh [Court case for Asu Saleh, member of the editorial team on the weekly Didegāh]', www.mukriannews.blogfa.com, June 24/Tir 3, 1386.

Mukrian. 2007e. '6 sāl habs barā-ye 'abdollāh hoseini, shahrvand-e ahl-e khoy [6 years of prison for 'Abdollah Hoseini, citizen of Khoy]', www.mukriannews.blogfa.com, June 26/Tir 5, 1386.

Mukrian. 2007f. '4 sāl habs barā-ye zāhed qāderi, shahrvand-e bukāni [4 years of prison for Zahed Qaderi, citizen of Bukan]', www.mukriannews.blogfa.com, July 9/Tir 18, 1386.

Mukrian. 2007g. '8 sāl habs barā-ye mohammad-sāleh kuykhāshire, shahrvand-e bukāni [8 years of prison for Mohammad-Saleh Kuykhashire, citizen of Bukan]', www.mukriannews.blogfa.com, July 12/Tir 21, 1386.

Mukrian. 2007h. 'Ta'tili-ye bāzār dar mahābād va saqqez [Closing of the bazaar in Mahabad and Saqqez]', www.mukriannews.blogfa.com, July 13/Tir 22, 1386.

Mukrian. 2007i. '15 sāl habs barā-ye khalil mostafā rajab, zendāni-ye kord [15 years of prison for Khalil Mostafa Rajab, Kurdish prisoner]', www.mukriannews.blogfa.com, July 18/Tir 27, 1386.

Mukrian. 2007j. 'Mahkumiyyat-e mojaddad-e semko qāderpur, zendāni-ye bukāni [Resentencing of Semko Qaderpur, Bukani prisoner]', www.mukriannews.blogfa.com, September 4/Shahrivar 13, 1386.

Mukrian. 2007k. 'Tab'id-e mas'ud kordpur ruznāme-negār va dabir-e bā-sābeqe-ye āmuzesh va parvaresh dar kordestān [Exile of Mas'ud Kordpur, journalist and experienced high school teacher from Kordestan [Province's Department for] Education and Cultivation]', www.mukriannews.blogfa.com, February 11/Bahman 22, 1386.

Mukrian. 2008. 'E'terāz be nā-padid shodan-e māmustā ayyub ganji dar sanandaj [Protests against the disappearnce of Mamusta Ayyub Ganji in Sanandaj]', *Mukrian News* via http://news.gooya.com, February 3/Bahman 14, 1386.

National Front. 2004. 'Jenāb āqā-ye mortezā hāji [(Addressed to) Mr. Morteza Haji' via Mediya Net, mediya.net, nd.

National Front. 2009. 'Bayāniye-ye e'terāzi-ye fa'ālān-e farhangi [A protesting communiqué by cultural activists]' via Pan Iranist, pan-iranist.net, nd.

Parsine (News Website). 2008. 'Hame chiz darbāre-ye esfandiyār rahim-mashā'i [Everything about Esfandiyar Rahim-Masha'i]', www.parsine.com, May 31/Khordad 11, 1387.

Parsine. 2010. 'Pāsokh-e daftar-e ahmad khātami be rahim-mashā'i [Ahmad Khatami's office's reply to Rahim-Masha'i]', www.parsine.com, August 7.

QalamNews (Online). 2009. 'Mir-hosein musavi dar mahābād: negāh-e amniyati nesbat be qowmiyat-hā bāyad kenār begozārim [Mir-Hosein Musavi in Mahabad: We must put aside the security view on ethnicities]', via Gooya, http://news.gooya.com, May 28.

RFE/RL (Radio Free Europe/Radio Liberty). 2005. 'Urban holiday celebrations get political', from *Iran Report,* vol. 8, no. 13, www.rferl.org, March 30.

Resalat (Daily, Online). 2007. 'Dekhālat-e bigānegān! [Foreign intervention!]', www.resalat-news.com, February 19/Bahman 30, 1385.

Rooz Online English. 2006. 'Interview with the Commander of Jondollah and his Hostage', www.roozonline.com/english, May 18.

Rooz Online Persian. 2006. 'Āzarbāyjān dar eltehāb [Azerbaijan agitated]', www.rooz.com, May 24/Khordād 3, 1385.

Rooz (Online). 2008. 'Avval be zendān mi-ferestand, ba'd ta'ajjob mi-konand [First they send to prison, then they are surprised]', www.roozonline.com, December 8/Azar 18, 1387.

SahamNews. 2009. "Abbas 'abdi dar hamāyesh-e qowmiyat-hā va entekhābāt: mote'assefāne emruz modiriyat-e qowmiyat-hā dar dast-e nahād-e ettelā'āti ast ['Abbas 'Abdi in the "Ethnicities and Elections" conference: "Unfortunately, management of ethnicities today is in the hands of the security establishment"]', via Gooya, http://news.gooya.com, May 15.

Shahrvand (Online Magazine). 2005. 'Marg-e "shwāne" va nā-ārāmi-hā-ye mahābād: seyr-e vaqāye' va pishzamine-hā [The death of "Shwane" and the Mahabad unrest: on the events and the background]', www.shahrvand.com via http://news.gooya.com, July 22/31 Tir, 1384.

Shahrvand. 2007. 'Dar keshvar-e kasir-ol-melle'i chun irān, az tamarkoz be demokrāsi nemi-tavān resid [In a multi-national country such as Iran, one cannot reach democracy through centralization]', www.shahrvand.com, May 17 / 27 Ordibehesht, 1386.

Shams-e Tabriz (News Website). 2006. 'Gozāresh [Report]', *Shams-e tabriz* via www.jebhemelli.org, May 23/Khordād 2, 1385.

SharNews. (News Website). 2007a. 'E'terāz-e gostarde-ye mardom-e saqqez be qat' shodan-e gāz-e shahri [The widespread protest of the people of Saqqez against the cut in the town's gas supply]', www.sharnews.com, January 3/Dey 13, 1385.

SharNews. 2007b. 'Nāme-ye sar-goshāde-ye nemāyande-ye mardom-e saqqez va bāne dar majles be ra'is-e jomhur dar ertebāt bā qat' shodan-e gāz [Open letter from the Saqqez and Bane MP to the President regarding the cutting off of gas]', www.sharnews.com, January 4/Dey 14, 1385.

Sharq (Daily, Online). 2005a. 'Ahvāz ārām ast [Ahvaz is calm]', www.sharghnewspaper.com, April 17/Farvardin 28, 1384.

Sharq. 2005b. 'Nāme-ye ja'li va ettehām-e mokhālefān-e eslāhāt [The fake letter and accusations by the opposition to reform]', www.sharghnewspaper.com, April 20/Farvardin 31, 1384.

Shomal News (Online). 2009. 'Esfandiyār rahim-mashā'i kist? [Who is Esfandiyar Rahim-Masha'i?]', www.shomalnews.com, May 22/Khordad 1, 1388.

Sobh-e sadeq (Online). 2009. 'Basij va maʿmuriyyat-e moqābele bā tahdid-e narm [Mobilizing and guarding against "soft threats"]', in *Sobh-e sadeq*, www.sobhesadegh.ir, February 16, 2009.

SunniOnline (The Official Website of Sunni Community in Iran). 2010. 'Baluch & Sunnis of Iran acquitted from Wahhabism, separatism and sectarianism', www.sunionline.us, June 22.

Tabnak. 2010. 'Rahbar-e enqelāb: "qowmiyyat" dar masāʾel-e donyā-ye eslām bozorgtarin ʿāmel-e tafraqe ast [The Leader of the Revolution: "Ethnicity is the biggest agent of disunity in the world of Islam"]', www.tabnak.ir, March 15.

Tabriz News (Website). 2006. 'Tajammoʿ-e hezārān tan az mardom-e tabriz dar eʿterāz be chāp-e kārikāturi dar ruznāme-ye dowlati-ye irān [The demonstation of thousands of Tabriz inhabitants in protest against the publication of a caricature in the state-run daily *Irān*]', www.tabriznews.com, May 23/Khordād 2, 1385.

Washington Times. 2003. 'Pentagon officials meet with regime foe', www.washingtontimes.com, June 3.

Zamaneh Online. 2011. 'Kurdistan officials say Wahabis [sic] responsible for recent attacks', www.radiozamaneh.com/english, April 23.

ONLINE RESOURCES, COMMUNIQUÉS, ARCHIVAL MATERIAL AND OFFICIAL REPORTS

AKU (Amir Kabir University Newsletter). 2007. 'Sodur-e ahkām-e habs barā-ye chand tan az faʿālin-e hoviyyat-talab-e āzarbāyjān [Arrest orders issued for several identity-seeking activists in Azerbaijan]', AKU via http://news.gooya.com, December 13/Azar 22, 1385.

AKU (Amir Kabir University Newsletter). 2008. 'Shekanje-ye do faʿāl-e bāzdāshti dar ardabil barā-ye gereftan-e eʿterāf [Torture of two detained activists in Ardabil in order to extract confession]', AKU via http://news.gooya.com, February 14/Bahman 26, 1387.

Amnesty International. 2006a. 'Iran: Need for restraint as anniversary of unrest in Khuzestan approaches', www.amnesty.org, posted April 13.

Amnesty International. 2006b. 'Arbitrary Arrest/Incommunicado Detention/ Torture and Ill-treatmen; Mostafa Evezpoor (M), Member of the Azeri Turkish Minority Community', www.amnesty.org, May 5.

Amnesty International. 2006c. 'Defending Minority Rights: The Ahwazi Arabs' from www.amnesty.org, posted May 17.

Amnesty International. 2007. 'Iran: Human rights abuses against the Baluchi minority' from www.amnesty.org, posted September 17.

Amnesty International. 2008. 'Iran: Human rights abuses against the Kurdish minority' from www.amnesty.org, posted 2008 (nd).

Amnesty International. 2011. 'We are Ordered to Crush You: Expanding Repression of Dissent in Iran', www.amnesty.org, February 28.

BAFS (British-Ahwazi Friendship Society). 2007. 'Human Rights and the Ahwazi Arabs', PDF available at www.hic-mena.org.

Baloch Front. 2006. 'Eʿterāz be bombārān-e rustā-hā va koshtār-e mardom-e bi-gonāh tavassot-e artesh va sepāh-e pāsdārān dar baluchestān [Protest against the Army and the Revolutionary Guards' bombing of villages and killing of innocent people in Baluchestan]', www.balochfront.org via http://news.gooya.com, May 19/Ordibehesht 29, 1385.

BHRW (Balochistan Human Rights Watch). 2008. 'Life of several young Balochis, recently arrested in Iran, seriously in danger', www.bhrw.blogspot.com, June 18.

CHRA (Coalition of Human Rights Activists). 2008. 'Ta'viq-e mojaddad-e dādgāh-e residegi be ettehāmāt-e hedāyat ghazāli va sabbāh nasri [Renewed postponement of the court hearing of Hedayat Ghazali and Sabbah Nasri]', CHRA via http://gooya.news.com, August 12/Mordād 22, 1387.

CHRR (Committee for Human Rights Reporters). 2008. 'Bāzdāsht-e 18 nafar-e fa'āl-e madani-ye āzarbāyjān dar yek marāsem-e eftāri [The arrest of 18 civil society activists from Azarbaijan during a Ramadan ceremoni]', CHRR via http://news.gooya.com, September 11/Shahrivar 21, 1387.

CIA. 2007 & 2011. 'World Factbook: Iran', https://www.cia.gov/library/publications/the-world-factbook/geos/ir.html.

CPPE (Center for Political Prisoners of Iran in Exile). 2005. 'Mahābād hamchanān moteshan-nej va nā-ārām ast [Mahabad continues to be agitated and in unrest]', CPPE via http://news.gooya.com, July 16/Tir 25, 1384.

FIDH (International Federation for Human Rights). 2010. 'The Hidden Side of Iran: Discrimination against ethnic and religious minorities', report available at www.fidh.org, October.

GAMOH (Southern Azerbaijan National Awakening Movement). 2010. 'Southern Azerbaijan', UNPO Representation, June.

Gooya (News Website). 2006a. 'Bayāniye-ye 175 tan az ruznāmenegārān darbāre-ye vaqāye'-e akhir-e tabriz va dastgiri-ye ruznāmenegārān [Statement from 175 journalists on recent events in Tabriz and the arrest of journalists]', www.gooya.com, May 26/Khordad 5, 1385.

Gooya. 2006b. 'Ettelā'iye-ye gozāreshgarān-e bedun-e marz darbāre-ye dastgiri-ye do ruznāme-negār dar ostān-hā-ye ardabil va āzarbāyjān-e sharqi [Reporters Without Borders' communique about the arrest of two journalists in the provinces of Ardabil and Eastern Azerbaijan]', http://news.gooya.com, May 27/Khordad 6, 1385.

Gooya (News Website). 2008a. 'Bayāniye-ye bish az 700 tan az talāshgarān-e dāneshju'i, siyāsi, ejtemā'i, farhangi va dāneshgāhiyān dar poshtibāni az āzādi-ye dāneshjuyān-e hoviyyat-talab-e āzarbāyjān [Communique by more than 700 student, political, social, cultural and university activists in support of the release of identity-seeking students from Azerbaijan]', http://news.gooya.com, August 16/Mordād 27, 1387.

Gooya (News Website). 2008b. 'Ettelā'iye-ye gozāreshgarān-e bedun-e marz darbāre-ye bāzdāsht-e chahār ruznāme-negār-e āzari dar irān [Reporters Without Borders' Communiqué about the arrest of four Azeri journalists in Iran]', http://news.gooya.com, August 31/Shahrivar 27, 1387.

HRANA (Human Rights Activists News Agency). 2009. 'Tadāvom-e yuresh-e be manāzel va bāzdāsht-e mo'allemān dar baluchestān [Continued raids on houses and arrests of teachers in Baluchistan]', HRANA via http://news.gooya.com, August 14/Mordād 23, 1388.

HRW. 1997. 'Iran. Religious and Ethnic Minorities: Discrimination in Law and Practice' from www.hrw.org, Vol. 8, No. 7, September (accessed February 20, 2010).

HRW. 2005. 'Iran: Reports of Ethnic Violence Suppressed', www.hrw.org, posted May 11.

HRW. 2007. 'Iran: End Executions After Unfair Trials', www.hrw.org, posted February 15.

HRW. 2009. *Iran: Freedom of Expression and Association in the Kurdish Regions*, report, New York: Human Rights Watch.

HRW. 2011. 'Iran: Investigate Reported Killings of Demonstrators', www.hrw.org, April 29.

HRW. 2012. 'Iran: Arrest Sweeps Target Arab Minority', www.hrw.org, February 7.

IAS (Immigration Advice Service, UK). 2005. 'IAS Research Analysis: Iran: Kurds, Security, Unrest, Demonstrations' from the IAS Research and Information Unit, www.iasuk.org, October.

IHRDC (International Human Rights Documentation Center). 2012. 'On the Margins: Arrest, Imprisonment and Execution of Kurdish Activists in Iran Today', released April 11, 2012. http://www.iranhrdc.org.

ISA-Amir Kabir (Islamic Student Association, Amir Kabir University Chapter). 2005. 'Bayāniye-ye anjoman-e eslāmi-ye dāneshgāh-e amir kabir dar e'terāz be qatl-e yeki az fa'ālin-e kord dar mahābād [ISA of Amir Kabir University's statement in protest against the killing of one of the Kurdish activists in Mahabad]', ISA via http://news.gooya.com, July 21/30 Tir, 1384.

ISA-Zanjan (Islamic Student Association, Zanjan University Chapter). 2006. 'Mowj-e jadid-e e'terāzāt dar dāneshgāh-e zanjān be khāter-e matlab-e montasher-shode dar ruznāme-ye "irān" [A new wave of protests in Zanjan University over a published item in *Irān* daily]', ISA via http//news.gooya.com, May 17/Ordibehesht 27, 1385.

ISC (Iran's Statistical Center, Ministry of Interior). 2006. *Natāyej-e kolli-ye sar-shomāri-ye 'omumi, nofus va maskan* [General Results of the Public Census, Population and Dwelling], report available at www.amar.org.ir.

Khamene'i (The Office for Protecting and Publishing His Excellency Grand Ayatollah Khamene'i's Works). 1991. 'Sokhanrāni dar didār bā mas'ulān va kārgozārān-e nezām-e jomhuri-ye eslāmi-ye irān [Speech during meeting with officials and managers of the Order of the Islamic Republic of Iran]', www.khamenei.ir, February 13.

Khamene'i. 2006. 'Bayānāt-e rahbar-e mo'azzam-e enqelāb-e eslāmi dar didār-e kārgozārān-e sāzmān-e hajj va ziyārat [Statements by the Exalted Leader of the Islamic Revolution during meeting with managers of the Hajj and Pilgrimage Organization]', www.khamenei. ir, November 22.

Khamene'i. 2009. 'Bayānāt dar didār-e ostādān va dāneshjuyān-e kordestān [Statements during meeting with professors and students of Kurdistan]', www.khamenei.ir, May 17.

LCMM (Land Mine and Cluster Munition Monitor). 2010. 'Iran', www.the-monitor.org, accessed July 5.

Library of Congress. 2008. 'Country Profile: Iran', Federal Research Division, May. Available at http://lcweb2.loc.gov/frd/cs/profiles/Iran.pdf.

Mosharekat (Islamic Iran Participation Front). 2008. 'Bayāniye-ye jebhe-ye moshārekat darbāre-ye tazayyo'-e hoquq-e shahrvandi-ye aqaliyat-hā-ye qowmi va mazhabi [The Participation Front's communiqué regarding the repression of ethnic and religious minorities' civil rights]', via Gooya, http://gooya.com, November 5.

National Archives (Kew, UK) FO973/40, FCO 8/3394, FCO 8/3574, FCO 8/3575.

National Front (Leadership Assembly of the National Front of Iran). 2004. Open Letter to Morteza Haji, Minister of Education. Dated February 9. Available at: www.melliun.org/jebhe/edu2.htm.

Pasdaran (The Revolutionary Guard). nd. *Kordestañ: Emperiyalîzm va goruh-hā-ye vā-baste* [Kurdistan: Imperialism and Connected Groups], report, Tehran: Daftar-e siyasi-ye sepah-e pasdaran-e enqelab-e eslami.

President (Website of the Presidency of the Islamic Republic of Iran). 2005. 'Ahmadinezhād bar haqq-e irān dar dāshtan-e charkhe-ye sukht-e haste'i ta'kid kard [Ahmadinejad emphasized Iran's right to have a nuclear fuel cycle]', www.president.ir, September 28.

President. 2006. 'Kordestān sarzamin-e qahremāni va sar-afrāzi ast [Kurdistan is the homeland of heroism and bravery']', www.president.ir, November 15.

President. 2007. 'Doktor ahmadinezhād dar ejlās-e vozarā-ye khāreje-ye jonbesh-e 'adam-e ta'ahhod [Dr. Ahmadinejad in the meeting of foreign ministers from the Non-Aligned Movement]', www.president.ir, September 3.

President. 2009a. 'Labās-e torkaman, labās-e gheyrat, shojā'at va jāvedānegi ast [The Turkmen dress is the dress of pride, courage and immortality]', www.president.ir, June 3, 2009.

President. 2009b. Doktor ahmadinezhād dar didār-e nokhbegān va farhikhtegān-e ostān-e āzarbāyjān-e sharqi [Dr. Ahmadinejad in meeting with elites and notables of Eastern Azerbaijan Province]', www.president.ir, November 20, 2009.

President. 2010a. 'Mo'āven-e avval-e ra'is-jomhur dar irānshahr [First Vice-President in Iranshahr]', www.president.ir, 1 Shahrivar 1389/August 23.

President. 2010b. Ra'is-jomhur dar hamāyesh-e melli-ye "jang-e narm" [The President in the National Conference on "Soft War"]', www.president.ir. October 25.

President. 2011a. 'Sokhanrāni dar marāsem-e ruz-e 22-e bahman [Speech during the 22nd of Bahman Ceremonies]', www.president.ir, February 11, 2011.

President. 2011b. 'Sokhanrāni dar didār bā montakhabin-e ostān-e bushehr [Speech during meeting with electees in Bushehr Province]', www.president.ir, February 17, 2011.

President. 2011c. 'Ra'is-jomhur dar didār-e a'zā-ye bist-o-chahāromin konferāns-e beyn-ol-melali-ye vahdat-e eslāmi [President in meeting with members of the 24th International Conference on Islamic Unity]', www.president.ir, February 20, 2011.

President. 2011d. 'Doktor ahmadinezhād dar jam'-e montakhabin-e lorestān' [Dr. Ahmadinejad in an assembly of electees in Luristan]', www.president.ir, March 3, 2011.

RAHANA (CHRR's English Edition Website). 2010. 'The Week in Kurdistan', www.rhairan.biz, May 14.

RSF (Reporters Without Borders, Persian). 2007. 'Haftenāme-ye 'ayyārān be dastur-e dādsetāni-ye sistan-baluchestān towqif shod [The Weekly Ayyārān has been suspended on Sistan-Baluchistan's public prosecutor's order]', www.rsf-persan.org, May 21/Ordibehesht 31, 1386.

RSF. 2011. 'Reporters Without Borders condemn "crackdown" on Iran's Arab community', www.rsf.org, April 23.

SAHR (South Azerbaijan Human Rights). 2005. 'Urgent appeal: Condemn the Massacre of Indigenous Ahwazi Arabs in Iran', www.iri-crimes.de, posted April (nd.).

SCHRR (Students Committee of Human Rights Reporters). 2007. 'Se tan az fa'ālin-e jonbesh-e dāneshju'i-ye āzarbāyjān dastgir shodand [Three activists from Azerbaijan's student movement have been arrested]', via Gooya, http://news.gooya.com, February 15/Bahman 26, 1385.

SCCR (Supreme Council for Cultural Revolution). 2010. 'Osul-e siyāsat-e farhangi-ye jomhuri-ye eslāmi [The Principles of Cultural Policy in the Islamic Republic]', accessed November 22, 2010.

Sistan va Baluchestan (Provincial Administration). 2009. Sālnāme-ye āmāri-ye ostān-e sistān va baluchestān 1388 [Statistical Yearbook of Sistan-Baluchistan Province, 2009], report, Zahedan: www.sbportal.ir.

UNCHR (United Nations Commission on Human Rights). 2005. 'Iran: UN Commission on Human Rights Special Rapporteur on adequate housing' via Reliefweb, www.reliefweb.int, July 31.

UNDP. 1999. 'Human Development Report of the Islamic Republic of Iran, 1999', report, http://hdr.undp.org.

UNPO (Unrepresented Nations and Peoples Organization's Website). 2005. 'Iran's "Bloody Friday" Massacre in City of Ahwaz', statement from British-Ahwazi Friendship Organization via UNPO, www.unpo.org/content/view/2346/236, April 17.

INDEX

media
international, 59, 65, 68, 71, 75, 77, 81
minority, 11, 49, 52, 59, 60, 65–6, 68, 70, 73, 74, 97, 176–7, 185, 195, 197
social, 65, 195, 198
state, 59, 60, 65, 73, 100, 101, 102, 196, 216n74
MEK, *see Mojāhedin-e khalq* (MEK)
Menashri, David, 92
Meskoub, Shahrokh, 126, 165
migration, 21
militarization, 4, 54, 58, 63, 73, 101, 108, 184, 193
minority (concept), 6
religious versus ethnic, 18–19
minority rights, 5, 25, 28, 43, 50–3, 59, 60, 62, 74, 97, 98, 129, 138, 147, 148, 150, 155, 158, 162, 163, 173, 176, 184, 186, 187, 188, 189, 191
see also constitution; language rights; state discrimination
Mo'azzampur, Esma'il, 94, 95
Moftizade, Ahmad, 47
Mohammerah, *see* Khorramshahr (Mohammerah)
Mojāhedin-e khalq (MEK), 47, 62, 74, 109
Mosaddeq, Mohammad, 86, 89, 105, 173
Motahhari, Morteza, 86, 98
mother tongue, 1, 19, 20, 162, 174, 175, 194, 197
*mowlavi*s, 41, 49, 74, 193
MUP, *see* Muslim Unity Party (MUP)
Musavi, Mir-Hosein, 96, 186, 187, 188, 191, 193
Muslim conquest, 37, 39
Muslim Unity Party (MUP), 49

Nadjmabadi, Shahnaz, 196
Nagorno-Karabakh War, 63, 64, 66
naming, 70, 127, 154–5
Nateq, Naseh, 127
National Front, The (*Jebhe-ye melli*), 89, 135, 140, 147, 148, 149, 150, 155, 201
national identity, 2, 5, 7, 8, 19, 25, 26, 27, 57, 91, 92, 95, 98–9, 100, 120, 140, 141, 145, 149, 163, 164, 197, 205
Kurdish (*kordāyeti*), 33, 48
see also Iranian-ness
nationalism, 4, 5, 7, 9–10, 12–13, 45, 134–5
as concept, 7
Islamist, *see* Islamo-nationalism
religious (*melli-mazhabi*), 60, 89
secular, 60, 86, 89, 123
state, 59, 60, 85, 88–90, 91–2, 115, 123
see also ethnicism; ethno-nationalism; Islamo-nationalism; nationalist (*melli-garā*); Persian-centrism
nationalist (*melli-garā*), definition of, 4, 9–10
nationality (*melliyyat*), 17, 49, 51, 53, 83, 98, 100, 121, 123, 138, 146, 167, 171, 172, 173, 176, 178, 199, 201
National Studies Institute, The, 136
national unity, 59, 61, 115

nationhood (concept), 7, 88, 120, 121, 122, 123, 124, 138, 145, 156, 171, 200
nation (*mellat*), 7, 9, 27, 115, 121, 136–7, 140, 141, 161
nation-state congruence, 119
nativism, 26
neo-conservatives (US), 62
nomadism, 33, 39
Nowruz, 74
nuclear issue, 113

Obama, Barack, 185
Öcalan, Abdullah, 69
oil industry, 37, 38, 50, 70, 105
Order, The (*nezām*), 84, 102, 112–14
Orientalism, 25, 26
Orumiye, 30, 77
Other, 1, 4
see also "Internal Other"; *Self*
Ottoman Empire, 30, 34

Pahlavis, 31, 34–5, 38, 45
Pakistan, 38, 40, 41, 49, 73, 74, 75, 77, 104, 108, 185, 192
pan-Arabism, 50
pan-Iranism, 122
pan-Turkism, 31, 64, 66, 78, 92, 104, 111, 128, 129, 145, 154, 178, 194
Parsi, Rouzbeh, 124, 155
Party for Kurdistan's Free Life, *see* PJAK (Party for Kurdistan's Free Life)
perennialism, *see* "ancientism"
Persepolis, 101
Persia, 25
Persian-centrism, 4, 5, 15, 23–4, 27, 31, 43, 44, 61, 64, 65, 70, 73, 83, 94, 97, 150–5, 157, 161, 163, 166, 169, 170, 177, 179, 180, 182, 183, 196, 197, 199, 205
Persian Gulf, 36, 108
Persianization, 29, 31, 40–1, 52, 64, 94, 162
"Persian nationalism," 28
Persians, 1, 18, 19, 22–6, 43, 71, 92, 97, 144, 150, 151, 162, 170, 171, 172, 174, 199
as ancient term, 25
conflation with "Iranians," 23–4
as *fārs*, 1, 24, 25, 44, 57, 94–5
questioning the existence of, 24–5
Pishevari, Ja'far, 31
PJAK (Party for Kurdistan's Free Life), 68, 69, 80, 106, 109, 110, 111, 185
PKK (Kurdistan's Workers' Party), 69
poverty, *see* socio-economic issues
protests, *see* ethnic unrest; Green Movement (2009)
provincial framework, 21, 31, 40, 51, 53, 57
see also centralization; regional disparity; regionalism
Provincial and Regional Councils, 173, 198

Purjavadi, Nasrollah, 141
Purpirar, Naser, 182

Qajars, 37, 40
Qalat, khanate of, 40
Qamari, Mohammad-Reza, 154
Qara-Qoyunlu, 30
Qasemlu, Abdolrahman, 47, 68
Qashqa'i language, 20
Qashqa'is, 20, 24, 30, 42
Qazi Mohammad, 35
qowm, see ethnic group (*qowm*)
qowmiyat, see ethnicity

race, 22, 130
racism, 92, 93
    see also "Aryan" (racialized concept); race
Rafsanjani, Ayatollah Hashemi, 55, 58, 59, 88, 89,
    96, 101, 111, 114, 115
Ramezanzadeh, Abdollah, 60, 68, 96–7, 99, 143, 151
reformism, 4, 58, 59–60, 67, 68, 69, 70, 73, 76, 79,
    80, 81, 85, 89, 91, 96, 97, 98, 99, 100, 101,
    115, 118, 133, 135, 136, 149, 169, 178, 180,
    186, 187, 188, 189, 191, 193, 195, 197, 201,
    203, 204
refugees, 21
regional disparity, 54, 55–6
regional identity, 21
regionalism, 21, 58, 72
relative deprivation, 46, 56, 79, 204
    see also socio-economic issues
religion
    as factor in ethnicity, 18–19, 42
    see also Islamism; religious minorities; Shiism;
        Sunnis
religious minorities, 3, 18–19, 51, 95
    see also Armenians; Assyrians; Jews; Sunnis;
        Zoroastrians (or Zarathustrians)
relocations, 73
Republic of Mahabad, 35
revisionism, 182
Revolutionary Guard (*sepāh-e pāsdārān*), 47, 48, 49,
    50, 66, 73, 76, 78, 90, 106, 112, 192, 193
Reza'i, Mohsen, 186
Rezakhani, Khodadad, 25
Reza Shah, 25, 29, 30, 34, 40, 43, 94, 96, 97, 123,
    127, 128, 129, 130, 145, 155, 161, 171, 173
Rigi, Abdolmalek, 74, 77, 110
Roshdiyyeh, Haji Mirza Hasan, 30
Russia, 22, 29, 32, 34, 40
    see also Soviet Union

sabotage, 75
"Sacred Defense" (*defā'-e moqaddas*), 112
    see also Iran-Iraq War (1980–8)
Sa'edi, Gholam-Hossein, 166–7
Safavids, 30, 34, 37, 40, 85, 114, 147, 152, 182

Salafists, 39, 192
Salehi-Amiri, Seyyed Reza, 96
Sanandaj, 32, 34
Saqqez, 32
Sasanian Empire, 29, 37, 39
Saudi-Arabia, 71
sectarianism, 19, 74, 108–9, 192–3
    see also Sunnis; Shiism, Shiite exceptionalism
secularism, 90
    see also nationalism; secularist
secularist, 10, 30, 86, 95, 135, 148, 155, 164, 165,
    179, 180
"security view," 147, 154, 197
"selective ethno-symbolism," 156
Self, 4
Semitic (linguistic concept), 19
Semnan, 24, 36
Semnanis, 21
separatism, 37–8, 41, 48, 53, 61, 62, 64, 66, 71
Seyyed-Emami, Kavus, 144
Shah Isma'il, 85
Shāhnāme, 25, 34, 39, 89, 124, 126, 141, 142, 143,
    170, 174, 183, 200
Shahriyar, Mohammad-Hosein, 178
Shahsevan, 25, 30, 42
Shakak, Esma'il Aqa, *see* Simko
Shamkhani, 'Ali, 76
Shari'ati, 'Ali, 86
Shari'atmadari, Ayatollah Mohammad-Kazem, 49
Sheikh Khaz'al, 37–8
Shiism, 30, 33–4
    Shiite exceptionalism, 27, 45–6, 49, 51, 122
Shiraz, 24
Shirvan, *see* Azerbaijan, Republic of (ROA)
Shushtaris, 21
Simko, 34
Sistan-Baluchistan, 38, 78
    see also Baluchistan
Sistanis, 39
Smith, Anthony D., 116
smuggling, 35, 54, 55, 72, 73, 76, 107, 110, 190, 193
Social Democrat Party (Kurdistan), 34
socialism, 31, 34, 35, 41
social sciences (in Iran), 120, 131–4
socio-economic issues, 54–6, 67, 70, 72, 73, 114,
    190, 213n87, 213n88
    see also smuggling
solidarity, 201
Soviet Union, 31, 35, 41, 59, 63, 98, 145, 146, 163
Stalin, Josef, 29, 32
state-building, 42
state discrimination, 21, 36, 38, 45, 51, 52, 53, 54,
    59, 65, 67–8, 70–1, 72
state repression, 52, 54, 67–8, 70, 72, 75–9, 150,
    184–6
    religious, 19
stereotypes, 64–5